BELTON M. FLEISHER

Professor of Economics
Ohio State University

LABOR ECONOMICS
theory and evidence

Prentice-Hall, Inc., Englewood Cliffs, New Jersey

to Elizabeth

13-517441-4

Library of Congress Catalog Card Number: 74-102907

Current printing (last digit):

10 9 8 7 6 5 4 3 2 1

Printed in the United States of America

PRENTICE-HALL INTERNATIONAL, Inc., London
PRENTICE-HALL OF AUSTRALIA, Pty. Ltd., Sydney
PRENTICE-HALL OF CANADA, Ltd., Toronto
PRENTICE-HALL OF INDIA, (Private) Ltd., New Delhi
PRENTICE-HALL OF JAPAN, Inc., Tokyo

preface

I wrote this book because I believe that it is fruitful to develop a central theoretical framework for dealing with the subject matter of labor economics and to apply the hypotheses derived from the theory to a wide variety of topics. I believe this for two reasons: (1) the economic theory of competition[1] and appropriate modifications of the theory which include the implications of monopoly situations (e.g. when dealing with the subject of labor unions) are potentially able to provide a framework for understanding a wide variety of important topics in labor economics; (2) the only way we shall ever progress beyond a most crude perception of the way labor markets function is by developing a central or unifying theoretical framework and applying it to the subject matter of labor economics.

---

[1] I shall avoid using the term "perfect" competition so as not to confuse the discussion with an irrelevant issue—namely, whether the theory of "perfect" competition requires the assumptions of perfect information and foresight (i.e., zero cost of information) and of zero cost of adjustment to a changing environment. Clearly the theory of competition, as contrasted to the theories of monopoly, oligopoly, and monopolistic competition does not depend on a particular assumption about information or adjustment costs and can be used to develop interesting and potentially useful hypotheses about the real world when information and adjustment require scarce resources.

I feel very strongly that the approach used here is consistent with the goal of promoting responsible and informed citizenship through a liberal education. Today's citizen needs to understand not only the simply described characteristics of the economic environment, but also the basic features of the scientific method applied to understanding human behavior. Our government is increasingly using the advice of social scientists to design programs to increase social welfare, and citizens therefore ought to understand the methods and criteria used in formulating the ideas that suggest which policy actions will induce particular changes in the social environment. In this way, citizens can decide on more relevant grounds whether they approve of alternative programs for reaching desired goals and at the same time they can develop a fuller appreciation of the importance of the goals themselves.

how this book is different from other labor texts

I have attempted to treat several topics that have been emphasized in recent contributions to the theoretical analysis of labor economics and some of their applications. Thus, the text includes discussions of investment in human beings and implications of a capital theoretic approach to the demand and supply of labor including applications of the concepts that acquiring information and adjusting to a changing environment use scarce resources. The analytical backbone of the text is neoclassical economic theory, brought up to date by including the adaptations of the traditional discussions required by our recognition of the capital theoretic approach, and by a much more explicit and detailed discussion of unemployment and the level of money wage rates than has been associated with traditional theoretical labor economics in the past.

However, most professional readers will recognize that the major difference between this book and others is that I have maintained a strong position throughout that the economic theory discussed is useful in helping to advance our understanding of real world behavior. I have emphasized what I believe to be true—that competitive economic theory brought up to date is not only useful but necessary to understand the behavior of labor and labor markets.

In discussing how this book differs from other labor economics texts, I should emphasize that this is not a monograph, but rather a summary and exposition of the work of others. I have consciously avoided the pitfall of attempting investigations on my own, since the results of any new research would be of uncertain usefulness.

the basic ideas of this book

I hope to set forth here a brief outline of what I believe to be the central theme of the theory of labor economics and its applications. As implied above, "the" theory referred to is the theory of competition, or competitive theory, adapted to suit a variety of situations and occasionally modified to incorporate elements of monopoly and monopsony. The reason for adhering to competitive theory *and its adaptations and modifications* is pragmatic. The practical reason for wanting to develop a theory is ultimately to be able to predict the results of our actions and of events beyond our control. A theory is developed as a basis for prediction because we do not fully understand the interrelationships among the events we observe, and we strive to achieve understanding in order to control our environment and to protect ourselves from misfortunes. The degree of understanding we are able to achieve is reflected in our ability to predict behavior by using our theory of behavior. Since we have limited opportunities and resources to enable us to decide which among alternative theories of labor economics is the most useful in each situation where prediction is required, we are forced to search for a relatively general theoretical framework which is applicable to a wide variety of situations. Among its alternatives, I believe the theory of competition offers those who search for a useful framework of prediction an adaptable and efficient tool and that it is the most valuable theory available to us.

The distinguishing characteristics of the theory of competition are the basic postulates that households seek to maximize their utility, that firms seek to maximize their profits, and that both households and firms view all prices as parameters—i.e. they are "price takers." Elements of monopoly and/or monopsony can be incorporated in the theory by dropping the price-taking postulate when and where it is appropriate to do so. Note that the theory of competition as defined here does not necessarily incorporate the postulates that adjustment to a changing environment is costless and that acquiring information about the environment requires no resources. The appeal of noncompetitive theories of behavior which are often based on assumptions different than profit and utility maximization, frequently is due to the unnecessary belief that a theory cannot be competitive if it is to deal with situations where knowledge is not "perfect" and/or adjustment does not take place instantaneously. Once information and adjustment are themselves viewed as subject to economic analysis because they require scarce resources, the usefulness of competitive theory in helping us to understand behavior is significantly broadened.

Analyzing the logical interconnections of a theory such as the theory of competition requires considerable effort and attention. Nevertheless, the more difficult task is to decide, when hypotheses derived from the theory are confronted with the data of actual behavior, whether to accept the theory as a useful predictive instrument or to reject it in favor of another. Much of this book deals with just this task, and it is in dealing with it that the most controversial issues are raised. The main reason for the possibility of controversy is that while in deriving hypotheses to be confronted with data we can conveniently assume all but a few related variables to be unchanging (i.e., we assume *ceteris paribus*), in the confrontation we are forced to ignore or to *guess* about the behavior of these "other" variables, which theoretically influence the variables whose performance we wish to predict, and whose values may or may not behave in accordance with our guesswork. We may dignify these guesses by calling them *maintained hypotheses*, but we cannot evade the issue that controlled experiments in economics, in the sense that they are sometimes possible in, say, physics or chemistry. are virtually an impossibility. Therefore, economists are forced into using their "judgment" about many conditions which influence whether or not a theory seems to be a useful predictive instrument, and in matters of judgment, economists of good will are often known to disagree.

Since we are seldom in a position to know whether hypotheses *maintained* (but not confirmed) while a given hypothesis is confronted with the data could themselves be confirmed if we had data bearing on them, we are generally in the uncomfortable position of not knowing, when the data appear to refute the hypothesis being tested, whether the underlying *theory* is false or whether a *maintained hypothesis* is false. A simple example of this problem arises in trying to deal with the effect of minimum wage legislation on the quantity of labor demanded. The underlying theory of competition leads to the hypothesis (*cet. par.*) that effective minimum wage legislation will reduce the quantity of labor demanded because the demand for labor is negatively related to the wage rate. In testing this hypothesis we are generally forced by inadequate information to *maintain* the hypothesis, for instance, that labor-saving devices would not have been introduced in the production process in any event. Similarly, confirmation of a theory is subject to the difficulty induced by lack of sufficient information to perform adequately controlled experiments. This difficulty has made a substantial contribution to the lengthy controversy over the importance of the "realism" of assumptions (which are simply maintained hypotheses to which we assign a fundamental role and which characterize a theory in a way that the other maintained hypotheses do not) in deciding whether to accept or reject a theory of behavior in economics or other disciplines.

Thus, all the hypotheses derived from the theory of competition, its adaptations, and its modifications, are dealt with in the context of explicitly stated and implicit maintained hypotheses which are not often subjected to possible confirmation or refutation. This is true not only in this text, but in all the literature on which the text is based. The hypotheses tested, then, are implied by the underlying theory only when the maintained hypotheses are true. When the underlying theory is the theory of competition, the hypotheses derived from it are referred to as "competitive hypotheses," and the material in this text seldom if ever goes beyond the stage of examining such hypotheses in the light of available data. Thus, readers may often feel uncomfortable, in that data which appear to confirm a competitive hypothesis will often be consistent with hypotheses derived from a noncompetitive theory of behavior, because a competitive hypothesis is often consistent with more than one underlying theory, depending on the hypotheses that have been maintained in deriving it.

An hypothesis that is almost always maintained when deriving hypotheses to test from the theory of competition is that the data to be examined correspond to *equilibrium values* of the underlying theoretical relationships (such as demand curves or supply curves). An example of how this maintained hypothesis is used, in conjunction with others, is found in Chapter 13, where the additional hypotheses are maintained that over time, changes in the demand for labor among industries are not correlated with changes in the quality of labor employed and that instances in which industries employ labor of such skills that cannot be acquired through training are few and unimportant. The purpose of these maintained hypotheses is to derive the competitive hypothesis that average hourly earnings of workers in different industries do not, in the long run, tend to increase most where the demand for labor increases the most. This competitive hypothesis, of course, corresponds to the familiar proposition that competition tends to eliminate the effect on the structure of wage rates of changes in the industrial demand for labor. Since we have derived the proposition from the theory of competition on the assumption that the maintained hypotheses are true, we are forced to realize that, since we do not test the maintained hypotheses, consistency between the tested competitive hypothesis and the data (which is the case with this hypothesis in Chapter 13) may not provide strong confirmation of the theory of competition. For instance, suppose it just happens that there is a negative correlation between changes in the demand for labor among industries and changes in the average skill level of the workers, or that our observed wage rates are not equilibrium values; then we might have observed little or no correlation between changes in the demand for labor and changes in wage rates even if the underlying theory of competition were false. Whether we think that this is likely to have been the case will influence our judgment about the degree to which the theory of competition is confirmed when the competitive hypothesis is confirmed. Readers will no doubt think of implicitly maintained hypotheses which are not elucidated here or in the text which, if they were contrary to fact, would negate a confirmation of the theory of competition based on confirmation of the competitive hypothesis in question.

I ask readers who strongly doubt the usefulness of the theory of competition to consider their alternative predictive instruments and to contemplate the proposition that if the theory of competition, its modifications, and its adaptations are rejected, one is left with a hodge-podge of often-conflicting hypotheses and theories each of which may fit some of the data some of the time, but among which it is almost impossible to choose whenever a new constellation of events seems to have occurred.

I also ask such readers to consider carefully what they believe to be the most persuasive evidence against using the theory of competition as a predictive tool. I suspect that if one were to conduct an opinion poll of economists, one would find that the two most important reasons given for rejecting competitive theory are: (1) a disbelief that free markets can be expected to bring about reasonable agreement between the number of people who want to work and the number of jobs—such a disbelief stems largely from the experiences of the Great Depression; and (2) a deep-seated distrust of the postulate that households or household members aim to maximize their utility—hence severe doubt is created about the welfare implications of competitive equilibrium. To deal with the second point first, I should emphasize that one can find the theory of competition a useful predictive device—one that is capable of use in support of economic policy—even if one does not derive welfare implications from the theory in the sense of Pareto-optimality. For instance, if one believes that increasing the minimum wage will result in an increase in unemployment (open or hidden), one may use this belief to help develop a policy position regarding minimum wage legislation even if one attaches no importance to the possibility that competitive forces may promote equality between relative prices and marginal rates of substitution among market goods and leisure. Granted, disbelief in the basic postulates of a theory cannot be expected to leave one's belief in the theory's predictive power unaffected; nevertheless, it seems prudent to judge the usefulness of a theory on the basis of its predictive power relative to its alternatives, even if one does not believe that the theory is "true" in some other sense. Furthermore I should not want to be understood to claim that it is a straightforward proposition to infer from a consistency between observed data and a competitive hypothesis, or a number of such hypotheses, that the postulates of the theory of competition are thereby confirmed. Not only is there a difficulty created by our lack of knowledge about whether maintained hypotheses could be confirmed, but there is also the difficulty that many of the hypotheses we deal with, such as those which treat the shapes of demand and supply curves, can be derived from theories which *do not* postulate utility maximization and/or price-taking behavior. (An excellent example of how some common economic hypotheses may be derived from more than one "psychological" postulate is found in an article by Gary S. Becker, "Irrational Behavior and Economic Theory," *Journal of Political Economy*, V. LXX [February, 1962].)

To deal with the first point raised—that free markets do not provide a satisfactory solution to the problem of unemployment—I believe that the severe unemployment of the Great Depression was due mainly to what would now be considered inept handling of a garden variety recession by the monetary and fiscal authorities, and that its severity cannot be simply attributed to a failure of the market mechanism. Furthermore, the discussion in Chapters 14 and 15 attempts to show that some (difficult-to-specify) amount of unemployment is consistent with the theory of competition when information and adjustment costs are positive. Thus, I feel that the best way to gain a fuller understanding of the nature of unemployment and of policies to deal with it is through the theory of competition adapted to the ideas of costly information and adjustment to a changing environment, modified where necessary to incorporate elements of discretionary control over prices by buyers and sellers, and including a development of its macroeconomic implications adequate to allow inferences regarding appropriate monetary and fiscal policies.

acknowledgements

My greatest debt is to the numerous scholars whose attempts to relate economic theory to the real world have resulted in the articles, dissertations, monographs, and books that provide the basis for most of this text. Secondly, I have benefitted greatly from the comments of the four reviewers engaged by the publisher. W. Lee Hansen has read the entire manuscript and provided detailed comments on every part; his criticisms have enabled me to improve a great deal of the content, presentation and exposition of the text. The entire text was read also by Stuart Altman, whose comments on the overall design and scope have been helpful and encouraging. Burton A. Weisbrod and Eugene L. Loren have also provided useful comments on various chapters. In addition, several students at The Ohio State University have read all or part of the manuscript and have aided me greatly in improving the book. These students are Karl Egge, Thrainn Eggertsson, and Jack Purdum. Parts of the book have also benefitted from presentation to our Labor Economics Workshop and from the comments of various of my colleagues.

My research assistants, Thomas Kniesner and George Kaitsa, have combed the book for inaccuracies and inconsistencies; they found many, and, hopefully, few remain.

The manuscript was typed by Mrs. Kandy Bell and by Mrs. Alice Egge, and I owe them both a debt of gratitude for their painstaking efforts to produce something presentable from my scribbles and scrawls.

contents

PART I

the supply of labor: theory and evidence

introduction to labor economics

LABOR ECONOMICS AS A SCIENCE

This is an introduction to the way economists think about labor. By contrast, we might concern ourselves with how employers think about labor, or with how they ought to think about it. Another possibility would be to discuss labor problems from the point of view of employees and other members of the labor force. Each of these approaches has merits, and they are not mutually exclusive. The emphasis of this book, however, is on labor economics as a science.

Economists engage in the scientific study of the allocation of scarce resources among alternative uses. Labor, or labor power, is an extremely important resource. It is so important that there have been attempts to found economics on the proposition that labor is the source of all value. While it has turned out to be more useful to consider the production of commodities as dependent upon a variety of resources in addition to labor, such questions as the pricing and allocation of labor are still among the most important in economics.

Economists are social scientists, and this a book about the science of labor economics. Let us spend a little time exploring the implications of the phrase "the science of labor economics" for the content of this book. The emphasis is on the word "science," which is taken to mean a systematic study leading to the discovery of regular patterns of behavior. But what events lead to such discoveries, and how can we tell a discovery when we see one? The events leading to discoveries and the criteria for evaluating them are much the same as in other sciences. For example, let us consider the science of aeronautics. Aeronautical engineers have rather good ideas about what combinations of metals, design, and power will cause an airplane to fly. By means of analysis, engineers can plan an airplane in advance, and be fairly confident of most of its aeronautical characteristics. When a new design has passed through the final stage of production, its designers have hypothesized that it will fly. The hypothesis is tested by a pilot (usually a highly paid pilot, which suggests that the hypotheses of aeronautical engineers are not always true), and if the plane flies, we say the hypothesis is confirmed by observed phenomena, or by "the facts," and if it crashes, we say it is disconfirmed. Of course, before we finally decide to accept the hypothesis as useful for predicting the behavior of the airplane, many test flights are necessary. If the first flight is a failure, a minor modification of design may result in a substantial improvement in the predictive value of the hypothesis that the airplane will fly. On the other hand, even the best-tested airplanes sometimes crash because of factors over which the designers did not have adequate control. Thus, even a widely accepted hypothesis, such as "Under certain conditions, a Piper Cub can fly," will occasionally be contrary to observed phenomena. We accept the hypothesis that Piper Cubs are airworthy, even though it does not predict perfectly, because it is the best available hypothesis about Piper Cubs.

Scientific studies in many fields have led to the formulation of hypotheses whose predictions of observable behavior are accepted with widely varying degrees of certainty. Most of our hypotheses about airplanes probably fall somewhere in the middle of the certainty scale. Near the most certain extreme of the scale is the hypothesis that if a lead ball is dropped from a roof, it will fall to the ground; near the most uncertain extreme lie the attempts of geologists to predict earthquakes and of meteorologists to forecast the weather. In some branches of economics, behavior patterns are rather accurately predicted by existing hypotheses (for example, the hypothesis that the long-run marginal propensity to consume in the United States is .9), while in others, we have only begun to develop an orderly framework for observing behavior (a good example of unreliable hypotheses pertains to our ability to predict the turning points of business cycles).

How are hypotheses developed? Of course, there is no surefire "recipe" for developing useful hypotheses about economic or any other kind of behavior. Nevertheless, on the basis of experience, two ingredients appear to be necessary. One is intuition—the ability to apprehend what is relevant and interesting. Some people might substitute for the word "intuition" the phrase "the ability to ask the right questions." The second ingredient is the ability to develop an orderly or logical framework or theory, rationalizing what has been seen and suggesting additional phenomena that will be observed if the theory is a useful one. The implications of a theory about observable phenomena are hypotheses, and the two most important ingredients in formulating useful theories and hypotheses are relevance and logic.[1]

This book explores some of the important hypotheses that economists have developed about labor. Not all of them have been thoroughly tested; many of them have hardly been tested at all. Nevertheless, they represent an index of the degree of knowledge we possess about labor and labor markets. As you may have guessed while reading the preceding paragraphs, we shall explore aspects of economic theory that are important for developing hypotheses about labor; the important hypotheses will be developed and explained, and, where possible, we shall relate the hypotheses to data of the real world in order to see how they stand up when tested.

Some readers may object that labor, being a human resource, is not properly subjected to logical, quantitative analysis as is appropriate, say, for the investigation of the markets for money, agricultural goods, and other commodities. This objection has an element of truth: the analysis of labor is complicated because it is a human resource; individuals do not always act as if they were maximizing an easily ascertainable index of utility or happiness; labor markets sometimes adjust relatively slowly to changing circumstances; convention as well as short-run profit-maximizing calculations often appears to be an important determinant of employers' labor force decisions. But the objection implies that a good labor market theory is difficult to develop, not that one is undesirable. Because a subject is complex does not mean that theory is irrelevant; if anything, theory becomes even more crucial as organized thinking becomes more difficult. Insights, intuition, and institutional knowledge of the "real world" are indispensable ingredients in developing relevant theory, but they are not substitutes for it. Labor economics has developed as a field of investigation because a great deal of special knowledge is necessary to develop useful hypotheses about labor markets; it would be wrong to say that it has developed because a scientific approach to the study of labor is not a useful one.

---

[1] By relevance we refer to the quality of useful theories and hypotheses—that they deal with events in which people are interested, for one reason or another. By logic, we refer to the quality of internal consistency—that the predictions of a theory or hypothesis follow by rigorous deduction from initial postulates or assumptions.

LABOR AS A FACTOR OF PRODUCTION

Labor is important because it is an essential ingredient in the production of nearly every commodity. Usually we think of productive resources as different kinds of raw material, such as soil, water, or iron ore. Of course, most productive factors are seldom used in their pure states. By the time they enter productive processes they have usually gone through several stages of production or refinement. Soil is graded, fertilized, and contoured; ore has to be discovered, mined, and transported; water must be purified and piped. Labor, by contrast, is a very highly refined resource, and it appears in many varieties. Very few persons enter the labor force before the age of sixteen; by that time, we have all been fed, clothed, educated, doctored, tested, and sometimes psychoanalyzed, repaired, and moved, so that even the most basic labor power is the result of an intricate production process.

Nevertheless, as a first approximation let us imagine that there are basic factors which go into the production of commodities, which commodities eventually are consumed in the various sectors of the economy. By doing this, we can develop a framework for viewing the economic system which helps illustrate graphically some of the basic questions the subject of labor economics is designed to answer. Such a graphic illustration is contained in Figure 1-1, which is a simple *input-output table*. It consists of six numbered or lettered rows and six columns. Each number represents an industry, such

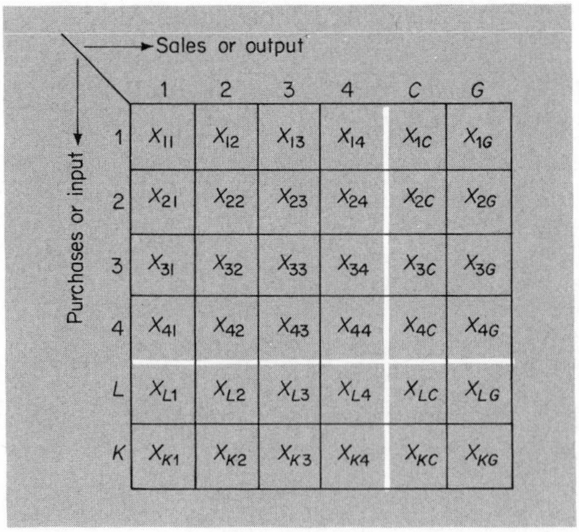

FIG. 1-1

Input-Output Table

NOTE: X_{ij} = Sales of industry i to industry j; thus X_{12} represents the *output* of industry 1 sold to industry 2; X_{1C} represents the output of industry 1 sold to households; X_{L1} represents purchases of labor by industry 1. [i = a row, j = a column.]

as agriculture, steel, or automobiles, which combines factors of production and semifinished commodities in the production of further commodities. The rows lettered L and K represent factors of production, such as labor and capital. The columns labeled C and G represent the sectors of the economy which purchase the goods and services produced by industries one through four and some of the factor services yielded by L and K. The sectors C and G represent two divisions of the economy, a household and a government sector (we assume for simplicity there is no investment or foreign trade).

Each row of the input-output table represents the sales or output of an industry or factor; each column represents input. Thus, going across row 1 from left to right, we observe the amount of industry 1's output used by itself in further production, the amount used by industries 2 through 4, and the amount of 1's output which is finally sold to households as consumption or to the government. Similarly, going down column 1, we observe the input of industry 1 into itself, of industries 2 through 4 into industry 1, and inputs of basic factors L and K. It may seem strange to you that the basic factors are also purchased by households and government, but such purchases merely reflect the use of labor as domestic service in households and as stenographic and other services in the government; and the use of capital services by households in the form of houses, automobiles, refrigerators, etc., and in government in the form of buildings, typewriters, airplanes, and the like.

By definition, the output of each industry is equal to its inputs. Thus, the sum of the entries in columns 1 through 4 equals the sum of the entries in each of the corresponding rows. It follows that the sum of the columns C and G must equal the sum of the rows L and K. This is in accordance with our usual procedures of accounting; all inputs are accounted for. It would be very simple to construct your own input-output table, inserting numbers such that the output of each industry equals its input, and thus convince yourself that the sum of columns C and G must equal the sum of rows L and K. In terms of national income accounting, the sum of C and G represents "final sales" and equals gross national product. The sum of L and K represents all the payments to factors of production, and it also equals gross national product, sometimes called gross national income.[2]

The purpose of the input-output table is to provide a conceptual framework for viewing the role of labor as a factor of production. The factors are used in combination as inputs in the productive processes which will eventually turn out final goods and services. The input-output table in Figure 1-1 is very simple. More accurately, we could show labor and other

---

[2] We are ignoring such complications as indirect business taxes and capital consumption allowances which cause GNP, as usually measured, to diverge from net national product and/or national income.

factors themselves being transformed in the productive process. Thus, we might have several entries for each factor, such as L_1, L_2, L_3, with L_1 (e.g., eighth-grade graduates) being employed directly in some of the industries but also entering into the production of L_2 (e.g., high school graduates), and so on.

LABOR AS THE HUMAN RESOURCE

The input-output table is a useful device for portraying part of the structure of the economy—showing how productive factors, industries, and final output are related. However, it does not demonstrate how the economy functions to allocate labor among alternative uses. This is an important problem, because labor is a scarce resource. That is, if labor's price were zero, more would be demanded than supplied. Economics is the science of the allocation of scarce resources, and we might ask, Why does the allocation of labor command special treatment? This question has already been partially answered: labor markets function somewhat differently than most others. One of the reasons for this deserves special attention. While labor, like all other productive factors, is ultimately a part of the household sector (if we may include government as ultimately part of the household sector), it is the only factor which is physically inseparable from human beings. Thus, nonpecuniary matters are much more important in decisions about the allocation of labor than of almost anything else. For instance, if you owned a truck rental service, you wouldn't care very much whether the trucks were driven in hot or cold climates, in smoky or clean air, in the rain or in the sun, except insofar as these conditions affected their productivity. Certainly you wouldn't care as much as if your were making a decision about the conditions under which *you* would work. You don't have to live or work where your money (nonhuman assets) does; however, you do have to be in the place where you perform labor services.

One of the most important aspects of the physical inseparability of labor power and human beings is that our social mores have led us to outlaw certain kinds of contracts between sellers and buyers of labor which are perfectly legitimate between sellers and buyers of almost anything else. One cannot, for example, sell or buy the labor of one person indefinitely. Slavery is against the law. This has important implications for labor market processes which take place over long periods of time, such as education and training. In subsequent chapters we shall explore a theory of human capital that has grown to accommodate the special nature of labor market processes that take place through time.

LABOR AS A SOURCE OF INCOME

While all the factors of production are directly or indirectly owned by persons who constitute part of the household sector, labor is the most widely owned factor. Household sales of labor constitute about 70 per cent of the sales of all factors of production; that is, the share of wages, salaries, and the wage component of entrepreneurial income constitute about 70 per cent of the national income. In your elementary economics course, you undoubtedly were introduced to a "circular flow" diagram, such as that in Figure 1-2.

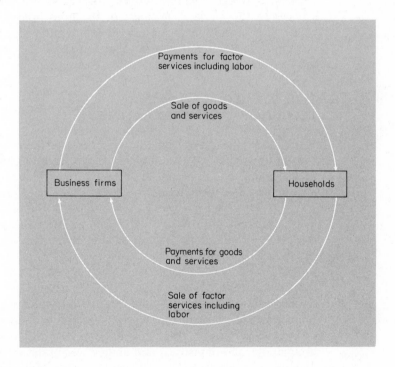

FIG. 1-2
Circular Flow of Payments and Purchases

This emphasizes the importance of thinking of labor as a source of income, as well as a factor of production. Part of what determines the allocation of labor among alternative uses is decisions by households regarding the expenditure of the income from the sale of labor and other factors.

In addition, households determine their income (given wage rates and unemployment conditions) by deciding how much labor to sell. Thus income determines, and is determined by, the allocation of labor among alternative uses, including the alternative of productive and "unproductive," or leisurely, employment within the household sector.

At the bottom of the circular flow diagram, we see the household sector, which sells factors of production, including labor, to the business sector. The business sector is shown at the top of the diagram. The business sector pays the household sector for the right to employ the factors. Sales of factors by the household sector to the business sector determine both the amount of employment and its direction. Each sale of labor is made not only with respect to a specific amount of work, but with respect to the characteristics of the employer, occupation, and industry in which the worker will be employed. Business firms can compete among themselves to obtain the services of workers and to induce workers to offer more or less of their services to the market; members of the household sector make decisions about where to sell their services, how much to sell, and at the same time, determine their command over the output of the business sector. These relationships are at the heart of labor economics.

THE WORLD OF LABOR:
BEHAVIOR TO BE EXPLAINED

What kinds of behavior do the hypotheses of labor economics attempt to explain or predict? While emphasis varies according to individual interests, the following questions are important to labor economists, judging by the amount of time spent trying to answer them.

(1) What determines the price of labor? The price of labor is what we conventionally call a wage rate or salary, and sometimes it is included in profits. We shall adopt the convenient convention of referring to the price of labor as the wage rate, no matter how the form of payment may be described in everyday usage. We are interested in the wage rates paid to individual sellers of labor and how they are determined. We are interested in the relationship among the wage rates paid to different sellers; this is sometimes called the structure of wage rates, and we may analyze the structure among wage rates of different amounts; among wage rates in different occupations and industries; and among wage rates in different geographical regions. The general level of wage rates is important: it is related to economic welfare and to the price level, and these have serious implications for social welfare, international trade, and the level of economic activity.

(2) What determines the allocation of labor among alternative uses? This question is intimately related to the preceding one, of course, and they must be answered simultaneously. We are interested in the allocation of labor among occupations, industries, and regions, and also between the household sector (including school) and the business sector.

(3) How rapidly do the prices and allocation of labor change in response to changes in their determinants? Do adjustments take place so that bargains may always be struck between households and businesses, or does unemployment imply that households often cannot sell as much labor as they like while vacancies imply that firms cannot buy as much labor as they want? While the answers to some of these questions lie partly outside the scope of this text, we cannot avoid attempting to answer them, because the answers have crucial implications for the operations of labor markets, as well as for social and economic welfare.

(4) What are the roles of labor unions and labor legislation in the economy, and what is their influence on the answers to questions (1) through (3)? Largely because labor and people are inseparable, unique problems of legislation and social organizations have arisen. What are their implications for the ability of the economic system to achieve an efficient allocation of resources and desirable levels of social and economic welfare?

In the remainder of this book, we shall explore how the framework suggested in sections I through IV leads us to answers for the questions posed in Section V.

APPENDIX TO CHAPTER ONE

Measurement in Labor Economics

This appendix is meant to provide information useful for following the discussion throughout the remainder of the text—especially in those chapters where we attempt to demonstrate the relevance of economic theory to the understanding of actual economic behavior. It is by no means an exhaustive survey of sources of data and quantitative methods used in labor economics. Rather, it is illustrative, and attempts to provide a minimum background in measuring and using labor market variables to enable students to appreciate some of the obvious and some of the subtle aspects of labor market (and other) behavior.[3]

---

[3] In deciding whether to include much of this discussion here or elsewhere in the book, I felt it would be best to put most of the methodological considerations in one place for easy reference. This has the disadvantage that some of the terms used in this appendix are best understood after reading other parts of the book. Thus, I have not hesitated to repeat much of the material in one form or another at relevant places throughout the text. These repetitions are intended to remind readers that they may wish to refer back to this appendix occasionally for reference.

SOURCES AND
INTERPRETATION OF DATA

In the following chapters we shall discuss some important aspects of the economics of labor markets. In the discussion, such terms as wage rates, quantity of labor, employment, and unemployment represent crucial variables. In order to show how the theory of labor markets helps us to understand real world phenomena we must investigate the way in which many of the important labor market variables can be measured. At first it may seem unnecessary to discuss the measurement problem. Everyone knows what a wage rate is, or what labor is—or does one?

There are many sources for the data used in the study of labor markets. However, all of the sources fall into one of two important categories; one category consists of answers to questions asked of household members, and the other consists of anwers to questions asked of business firms. In the first category are data sources such as the decennial population census of the United States, the *Current Population Surveys* conducted monthly by the U.S. Census Bureau, and many surveys conducted by nongovernment research organizations. In the second category are data sources such as the *Employment and Earnings* surveys of the Department of Labor and the *Census of Manufactures* of the Census Bureau.

These data sources differ in the kinds of information they provide. Household surveys provide answers to questions about whether household members were working, looking for work, attending school, etc., during the survey week (i.e., the calendar week prior to the date of the survey). Using answers to such questions, we can estimate the size of the labor force (all persons 16 years of age and over who were working or looking for work during the survey week), the number of unemployed persons (all persons 16 years of age and over who were not working and who were judged by their answers to questions to be seeking work), and the number of persons not in the labor force (the remainder). Household surveys are also used to gather information about earnings and other income of family members, hours worked, family size, and other information important for studying labor force behavior.

Data gathered from firms also provide information about wage rates, and this information is readily obtainable from the firms' financial records. On the one hand, wage data gathered from firms are likely to be more accurate than those gathered from household surveys, because such hard-to-remember items as withholding taxes, social security payments, fringe benefits, insurance premiums, and the like are recorded there. On the other hand, if one wishes to relate wage rates or earnings to the personal and family characteristics of persons receiving them, it is almost impossible to do this on the basis of the records of firms alone. Very few studies of labor force behavior have been able to make use of a combination of firm and household surveys in order to combine the best features of both kinds of information sources, since the two kinds of surveys are almost always conducted independently. In addition, data gathered from firms provide information about the volume of labor turnover (quits and layoffs), the combinations of labor of different degrees of skill used in production and nonproduction activities, and so on.

It is beyond our scope and purpose to evaluate critically the many data sources used in labor market investigations; nevertheless, it is useful and interesting to point out the weaknesses of some very important labor force measures. This we do in the next few paragraphs. By "weaknesses" we mean essentially deviations from the ideal of the measurements of labor force variables available to us in the various data sources. The ideal measurements must be inferred from the content of the theory or hypothesis that one wishes to use as a framework for analyzing the data, and such inference and the subsequent relating of the ideal to the actual data are two of the most difficult and interesting features of empirical work in all branches of economics. They are essential parts of what we call *econometrics*.

measuring the quantity of labor

When we begin our study of the theory of labor markets, one of the most important aspects of the discussion will be to specify a quantity of labor and the units in which labor is measured. Often we shall specify "manpower-hours" as units—i.e., uniform units of work of constant quality. Although at times we shall speak as if we could more or less easily measure homogeneous manpower-hours of labor, in fact such measurement is never easy. In the following paragraphs we consider a few of the problems of measuring the quantity of labor in the context of measuring the total size of the labor force.

One often sees and hears references to the size of the labor force, but just what does such a measure mean? Most people would agree that the "labor force" should measure the amount of labor resources in the economy, much as other measures provide information about the amount of coal in inventories or in unmined reserves, iron in ore deposits, and so on. A moment's thought will indicate, however, that even for such readily identifiable resources as coal, a figure representing available resources does not necessarily reflect the quantity of coal remaining to be used. It is common knowledge that our known coal reserves have grown over the years. This is not because the geological rate of formation of coal is outpacing our use of coal; it is because we have continually devoted resources to searching for new deposits. Furthermore, the quantity of coal reserves is meaningful only with respect to given standards of the profitability of mining coal of given quality. It may be relevant to exclude from a measure of coal resources known deposits which (at present) are too costly to mine or are particularly low in quality. Similarly, measurement of the economy's labor resources is meaningful only in reference to a carefully framed set of rules.

Measuring the Volume of Employed Labor. The strengths and weaknesses of measures of the size of the labor force can best be understood in the context of the economic theory of the labor market. Figure 1-A1 represents

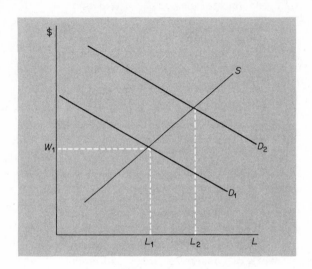

FIG. I-AI
Labor Demand, Supply, and Employment

an extremely simple but useful theory. It shows the supply and demand for labor in the economy; the quantity of labor of uniform quality in hours per period of time (manpower-hours per time period) is measured on the horizontal axis, and "the" wage rate for labor of uniform quality is measured on the vertical axis. Later on, we shall see why the demand curve has a negative slope, and we shall also see that the supply curve may not be upward sloping; but Figure 1-A1 as it stands is sufficient to demonstrate some important problems of measuring the quantity of labor resources. In its simplest form, the theory implies that the wage rate and the level of employment are determined at the intersection of the supply and demand curves (L_1 and L_2 correspond to such points of intersection); the employment level so determined is an "equilibrium" value.

In a very important sense, the current official measure of the labor force in the United States corresponds to an equilibrium value of employment such as L_1 or L_2 in Figure 1-A1; this is because the most important component of the official measure of the labor force is the number of people who are actually working. An important problem of measuring labor resources by a magnitude such as L_1 or L_2 is that it depends upon the *demand* for labor as well as the supply. (We temporarily ignore some other important problems: (1) that L_1 or L_2 measures the number of *people* employed rather than the total *hours* of employment; (2) whether the unemployed as well as the employed are a part of the labor resources of the economy; and (3) that it is difficult to measure the quality of heterogeneous workers.) There would be no problem if the supply curve of labor were vertical (completely inelastic and insensitive to demand); but in general it is not, and thus the volume of employment does not in general tell us how much labor could be drawn upon in the case of, say, a war or other national emergency; neither does it tell us how many persons might be put to work if the demand for labor in private industry were to grow.

Employment data for the United States are gathered from household surveys as follows: The total number classified as employed are all persons aged 16 years and over who answer survey questions in such a way as to indicate that they were working or had a job from which they were temporarily absent during the survey week. Table 1-A1 shows the actual questions asked monthly of a sample of the United States population, whose answers are subsequently adjusted according to statistical procedures to yield an estimate of the number that would have been obtained if everyone in the United States had been interviewed. (Not every person about whom answers are obtained is interviewed personally; often questions about several family members are answered by only one respondent.) Persons classified as "employed" are those who answer to question 1 that they were "working" most of the prior week, Yes to question 2 that they worked at all during the prior week, or who were classified as "with a job but not at work"; this last category includes those who answered Yes to question 3 and who were absent for reasons 1 through 4 in question 3a.

At first a simple way out of the problem that measured employment depends on demand conditions might seem to be to measure the *total population*, rather than L_1 or L_2. But then, should we count the ill, the very young, the aged, and those in school? We probably should not; in fact we should probably adopt some criterion for measuring labor resources that would exclude certain segments of the population on grounds of our social values or of the economic efficiency of trying to put those of very low productivity to work. In fact, we might find no better measure of "potential" or "maximum" labor force than to observe the employment behavior of the economy during periods of high labor demand. We cannot avoid evaluating the population's labor force potential according to some more or less arbitrary criteria, and the volume of employment under conditions of strong demand may provide as readily available and efficient a measure as any other.

Table I-AI

CURRENT LABOR FORCE STATUS QUESTIONNAIRE

I. CURRENT LABOR FORCE STATUS

1. What were you doing most of LAST WEEK —

{ Working

{ Looking for work

or something else?

- 1 ☐ WK – Working – *SKIP to 2a*
- 2 ☐ J – With a job but not at work
- 3 ☐ LK – Looking for work
- 4 ☐ R – Retired
- 5 ☐ S – Going to school
- 6 ☐ U – Unable to work – *SKIP to 5*
- 7 ☐ OT – Other – *Specify*

2c. Do you USUALLY work 35 hours or more a week at this job?

- 1 ☐ Yes – What is the reason you worked less than 35 hours LAST WEEK?
- 2 ☐ No – What is the reason you USUALLY work less than 35 hours a week?

(Mark the appropriate reason)

- 01 ☐ Slack work
- 02 ☐ Material shortage
- 03 ☐ Plant or machine repair
- 04 ☐ New job started during week
- 05 ☐ Job terminated during week
- 06 ☐ Could find only part-time work
- 07 ☐ Holiday (legal or religious)
- 08 ☐ Labor dispute
- 09 ☐ Bad weather
- 10 ☐ Own illness
- 11 ☐ On vacation
- 12 ☐ Too busy with housework, school, personal business, etc.
- 13 ☐ Did not want full-time work
- 14 ☐ Full-time work week under 35 hours
- 15 ☐ Other reason – *Specify*

(If entry in 2c, SKIP to 6 and enter job worked at last week.)

FORM LGT-111 (3-10-67)

2. Did you do any work at all LAST WEEK, not counting work around the house?

(Note: If farm or business operator in household, ask about unpaid work.)

1 ☐ Yes   x ☐ No – *SKIP to 3*

2a. How many hours did you work LAST WEEK at all jobs? _____

2b. INTERVIEWER CHECK ITEM

- 1 ☐ 49 or more – *SKIP to 6*
- 2 ☐ 1 – 34 – *ASK 2c*
- 3 ☐ 35 – 48 – *ASK 2d*

2d. Did you lose any time or take any time off LAST WEEK for any reason such as illness, holiday, or slack work?

- 1 ☐ Yes – How many hours did you take off? _____
- 2 ☐ No

(Correct 2a if last time not already deducted; if 2a reduced below 35, fill 2c, otherwise SKIP to 6.)

2e. Did you work any overtime or at more than one job LAST WEEK?

- 1 ☐ Yes – How many extra hours did you work? _____
- 2 ☐ No

(Correct 2a if extra hours not already included and SKIP to 6.)

Notes

(If "J" in 1, SKIP to 3a.)

3. Did you have a job (or business) from which you were temporarily absent or on layoff LAST WEEK?

1 ☐ Yes   x ☐ No – *SKIP to 4*

3a. Why were you absent from work LAST WEEK?

- 1 ☐ Own illness
- 2 ☐ On vacation
- 3 ☐ Bad weather
- 4 ☐ Labor dispute
- 5 ☐ New job to begin within 30 days – *ASK 4c2*
- 6 ☐ Temporary layoff (Under 30 days)
- 7 ☐ Indefinite layoff (30 days or more or no definite recall date) } *ASK 4c3*
- 8 ☐ Other – *Specify*

3b. Are you getting wages or salary for any of the time off LAST WEEK?

- 1 ☐ Yes
- 2 ☐ No
- 3 ☐ Self-employed

3c. Do you usually work 35 hours or more a week at this job?

- 1 ☐ Yes   2 ☐ No

(SKIP to 6 and enter job held last week.)

Page 2

Measuring Employment in Hours. Let us now consider the problem of measuring the employed labor force in terms of manpower-hours, concentrating on the problems associated with hours, and still temporarily ignoring

I. CURRENT LABOR FORCE STATUS – Continued	
(If "LK" in 1, SKIP to 4a.) **4.** Have you been looking for work during the past 4 weeks? 1 ☐ Yes x ☐ No – *SKIP to 5*	**5.** When did you last work at a regular full-time or part-time job or business? 1 ☐ June 15, 1966 or later – *Specify month and ASK 6.* Month _____ 2 ☐ Before June 15, 1966 and "Unable" in both item 1 and item 68R on REFERENCE PAGE – *SKIP to 41a, page 15* x ☐ All other – *SKIP to 19a, page 8*
4a. What have you been doing in the last 4 weeks to find work? *(Mark all methods used; do not read list.)* Checked with – 1 ☐ State employment agency 2 ☐ Private employment agency 3 ☐ Employer directly 4 ☐ Friends or relatives 5 ☐ Placed or answered ads 6 ☐ Nothing – *SKIP to 5* 7 ☐ Other – *Specify – e.g., MDTA, union or professional register, etc.* _____	
	6. DESCRIPTION OF JOB OR BUSINESS
	6a. For whom did you work? *(Name of company, business, organization or other employer)* _____ _____
	6b. In what city and State is . . . . located? City _____ State _____
4b. Why did you start looking for work? Was it because you lost or quit a job at that time *(Pause)* or was there some other reason? 1 ☐ Lost job 4 ☐ Wanted temporary work 2 ☐ Quit job 5 ☐ Other – *Specify in notes* 3 ☐ Health improved	**6c.** What kind of business or industry is this? *(For example, TV and radio manufacturer, retail shoe store, State Labor Department, farm.)* **Census Use Only** _____ _____
4c. 1) How many weeks have you been looking for work? 2) How many weeks ago did you start looking for work? 3) How many weeks ago were you laid off? Number of weeks _____	
	6d. Were you – 1 ☐ P – An employee of PRIVATE company, business, or individual for wages, salary, or commission? 2 ☐ G – A GOVERNMENT employee (Federal, State, county, or local)? 3 ☐ O – Self-employed in OWN business, professional practice, or farm? *(If not a farm)* Is this business incorporated? 1 ☐ Yes 2 ☐ No 4 ☐ WP – Working WITHOUT PAY in family business or farm?
4d. Have you been looking for full-time or part-time work? 1 ☐ Full-time work 2 ☐ Part-time work	

4e. Is there any reason why you could not take a job LAST WEEK?
 	
1 ☐ Yes   2 ☐ Already has a job
6 ☐ No   3 ☐ Temporary illness
    4 ☐ Going to school
    5 ☐ Other – *Specify*	

4f. When did you last work at a regular full-time or part-time job or business? 1 ☐ June 15, 1966 or later – *SKIP to 6* 2 ☐ Before June 15, 1966 – *SKIP to 19a, page 8* 3 ☐ Never worked – *SKIP to 41a, page 15*	**6e.** What kind of work were you doing? *(For example, electrical engineer, stock clerk, typist, farmer.)* **Census Use Only** _____ _____

Page 3

256–776 O–67—2

those associated with variations in labor quality and the measurement of the unemployed. In measuring labor resources in terms of total hours, it is again useful to resort to a simple theory of the labor market. According to economic theory, the number of hours spent in the labor force depends on labor supply and demand, and the number of hours persons choose to spend may respond either positively or negatively to demand changes. If we adopt a market criterion for measuring labor force hours as we do for measuring the employment component of the labor force, then hours actually worked measures hours in the labor force. But does hours actually worked reflect the hours of work people desire to sell? The answer depends on one's view of how the economy functions. Surely we all know persons who take over-time work whenever they can get it and others who wish their workweek were shorter. Regarding persons such as these, the market criterion (i.e., hours actually worked) of labor force hours is probably not an accurate measure of labor resources. However, there is no simple solution to the hours prob-lem, and the market criterion seems to present the fewest problems.

But, given the market criterion, how do we find out how many hours persons work? In many cases, we may resort to questioning employers. This is actually done by the government, and one of the principal sources of data on hours worked is provided by the answers to monthly questionnaires sent to employers of a large number of the economy's workers. Monthly surveys of the population also provide information about hours of work, in the answers given by people who worked or by their relatives. Apart from the statistical problems of sampling, which are of a rather technical nature and probably introduce few serious errors into our presently available measures of labor hours, rather important errors may arise simply because of our inability to find out from respondents exactly what their behavior has been, even in the recent past. The problems are serious enough when it is necessary to ask an employee who is paid by the hour how many hours he worked in the previous week; the respondent may have worked overtime hours that he has forgotten, or he may neglect to report a temporarily shortened workweek. Even worse, interviewers may be forced to ask crucial questions of one family member about the labor force behavior of all persons living with him. Still worse, the self-employed and many salaried workers probably cannot accurately define when they are working and when they are not. Questions 2a through 2e in Table 1-A1 show the painstaking procedure used by interviewers to find out how many hours were worked during the survey week. Notice that it is virtually impossible to discern from the answers whether anyone who worked 35 hours or more was working more or less than he desired to. It is possible, however, to get some idea of whether respondents who worked less than 35 hours did so voluntarily. Presumably, the ideal measure of manpower-hours would reflect the hours workers voluntarily would work under given labor market conditions; both actual hours worked and desired hours are subject to measurement error, the latter more so than the former.

Measuring Labor Quality.   The problem of measuring labor *quality* is so serious that at present there is no generally accepted measure of the labor force which allows for quality variation. Economic theory suggests ways in which labor quality might be accounted for, because if we adopt the view that "labor is what labor does," then labor force members ought to be weighted by their marginal productivities (see Chapter 6) in order to arrive at aggregate labor force measures. If we knew everyone's marginal product in value terms, we could apply a productivity-based index to each labor force member in order to arrive at a measure of the labor force which reflected variations in quality (as it affects output) as well as in the number of workers and hours worked. Lacking such information, we may at least try to account for the variation in labor quality which is associated with conditions generally thought to affect productivity and which may be more or less easily measured.

One such condition is the education of the labor force. If we observe a simple measure of labor force hours declining but the average educational level of workers rising, we have reason to suspect that labor resources are declining less rapidly than the simple hours figure indicates. Other readily observable correlates of labor quality are age and sex; perhaps slightly more difficult to observe is health. Thus, if we observe that since 1900, the proportion of the population in the labor force has remained roughly constant (which happens to be true), while hours worked per week have declined, education has risen, more women relative to men are working, a higher proportion of youth are in school, and a higher proportion of the elderly are retired (although a higher proportion of the population is elderly), may we conclude that the labor force would have risen or fallen if the population had remained the same size? At present there is no generally accepted answer to this question, although there may be a presumption that it would have risen, the principal impetus having been given by the increase in educational attainment.

The Unemployed Component of the Labor Force.   We have so far assumed that the labor force might be measured, albeit imprecisely, by counting the number of people at work. However, there are always persons who have lost their jobs and who are not able to find work, even though they would accept jobs at going wage rates; those who have quit their jobs but who have not found new work; and those who are just entering the labor force but who have yet to find work. These people constitute the unemployed, and the unemployed are by official definition a part of the labor force. All of the problems discussed so far pertain to measuring the unemployed labor force as well as the employed labor force, but the problems associated with inferring from the answers of nonworking respondents whether the respondents are unemployed or are not in the labor force merit special attention.

Consider first a simple definition of unemployment suggested by economic theory. In Figure 1-A2 we see a diagrammatic description of a labor market in which the wage rate is higher than the level that would equate demand and supply. Consequently, L_1 units of labor are demanded and $L_2 > L_1$ supplied. $L_2 - L_1$ represents an excess supply of labor (there could just

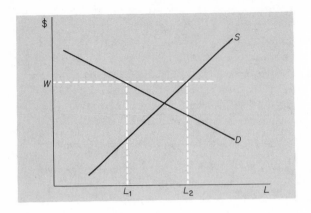

FIG. I-A2
*Labor Demand, Supply, Employ-
ment, and Unemployment*

as well be an excess demand if the wage were less than equilibrium). Thus, at the "going wage," W, $L_2 - L_1$ persons (or other units of labor, such as manpower-hours) are "unemployed." This is a theoretical definition of unemployment, but how do we discover the amount of unemployment in fact?

Such a theoretical definition of unemployment is probably much too simple, as we shall see in Chapters 14 and 15. It always associates the un-employed with an excess *supply* of labor, whereas in fact, labor markets do not operate so smoothly that if supply and demand were reasonably in bal-ance, no one would be looking for work and no jobs would remain unfilled. In the real world information and adjustment to change are costly, so there are always some job vacancies and some workers seeking employment. We shall not concern ourselves here with the difficult question of what level of unemployment is associated with *no* excess demand or supply of labor; rather, we shall confine ourselves to the problem that is immediately relevant for measuring the size of the labor force. How do we know when someone who is not working should be counted as a worker for the purposes of measuring the total labor force? The answer is related to the theoretical definition of unemployment: a worker is unemployed if he would accept a job at the going wage rate (i.e., W in Figure 1-A2). Defining the labor force to include unemployed workers can now be seen to yield a problem: it is clear in Figure 1-A2 that if the wage rate were lower, *or* if the demand curve were moved to the right, *or* if the supply curve were moved to the left, unemployment would be lower and the size of the labor force would be larger or smaller. As we shall see, any of these events could be induced by an appropriate expenditure of resources and/or adjustment of expectations about future price and wage levels. Thus, our measures of the size of the labor force and of unemployment depend upon the extent to which searchers for work and for workers, and expectations about wages and prices, have helped determine labor supply, demand, and wage rates. A further difficulty in identifying the unemployed is to find out who would accept jobs at the going wage rate.

To begin with, we (and nonworking respondents themselves) generally have a very imperfect idea what the going wage is for individual respondents. Since the unemployed are, by definition, not at work, the best we can do is to rely on information provided by previous occupations and wage rates earned, educational level, age, sex, region or residence, and so on in order to establish a going wage rate for an individual. In fact, our official measures of unemployment do not explicitly consider the wage rate aspect of unemployment; the problems associated with identification of the correct going wage rate for each worker are almost insurmountable, given the need for nationwide estimates of unemployment, our present techniques for collecting and evaluating information, and the costs involved. Rather, we rely on answers to questions designed to find out whether respondents are *actively seeking work*. Thus, the unemployed are those who answered question 1 of Table 1-A1 that they were looking for work last week and who did not do any work (a No answer to question 2), who answered question 3 No and question 4 Yes, or who answered question 3 Yes and question 3a with answers 5, 6, or 7. Persons who answered question 1 that they were "looking for work" must *also* answer question 4 affirmatively and question 4a with something definite (as opposed to possible answer no. 6) in order to be counted as unemployed. In all cases, a person must be currently available for work to be counted as unemployed.[4]

The concept of looking for work corresponds to a common sense definition of unemployment. However, there are aspects of our usual measurements which do not match precisely the theoretical concept of willingness to accept a job at the going wage. The difficulty is to identify under what circumstances a person would accept a job. Consider a coal miner who is laid off work due to mechanization and who cannot find another job as a coal miner. Suppose he has been earning $4.50 per hour, but because of his age, previous training, and so on, the best job he can find now will pay only $2.50; or perhaps the job would necessitate his moving away from his old home. Now, if the miner does not realize this—after all, a decline in one's market worth is not easy to accept or easy to discover in a short period of time—he may turn down or not look for jobs that pay less than, say, $4.00 per hour. In fact, if and when he discovers that he can find work only at $2.50, he may choose to retire from the labor force if he is an older worker— or he may decide to do the best he can with part-time work and/or relief. Thus, while the miner would probably be classified as unemployed, there

---

[4] U.S. Department of Labor, Bureau of Labor Statistics, *Employment and Earnings*, Vol. 13, No. 8 (February, 1967), pp. 5 and 6.

would be good theoretical reason for classifying him as out of the labor force instead, since if the miner had full information he probably would stop looking for work and would not take a job if he were offered one.

The implication for our measurement of the labor force is clear: to the extent that persons have an incorrect perception of their going wage rates and would change their behavior if they had full information, we probably do not estimate unemployment and the size of the labor force correctly. (This is not to say that persons such as the hypothetical coal miner should not be classified as unemployed for purposes of determining the allocation of unemployment compensation, aid to depressed areas, and so on, but rather that in using unemployment data to help measure the size of the labor force, it would be wise to consider the differences between actual and theoretically desirable measures of unemployment.) Furthermore, when unemployed workers do stop looking for work and are thus counted as out of the labor force, we should recognize that they might be productive workers and labor force members if they had information about jobs unknown to them, perhaps in other regions of the country. Thus, in order to obtain a theoretically correct measure of the labor force, adequate recognition must be given to the influence on our available measures of the costliness of obtaining correct information about alternative jobs and their wage rates as well as the private and social costs of moving workers to jobs and jobs to workers.

the interpretation of wage
rate data

Formally, a wage rate is represented by the slope of a budget constraint showing the rate of transformation of workers' hours into purchasing power over market goods (see Chapter 2). That is, it is the value of market goods which can be purchased for an hour's work. The wage rate is an important element in economic theory both because it represents an inducement for workers to sell hours and because it represents the cost to business firms of buying hours. However, many aspects of the inducement to work and of the cost of hiring labor are not represented by the wage rates that are recorded in the various sources of wage data.

Fringe Benefits and Costs.   Most readers already are aware that a substantial proportion of today's jobs involve not only an hourly rate of pay but also payments into private pension funds, health plans, social security, unemployment insurance schemes, and the like. To what extent do these wage supplements represent additional inducements to workers and additional costs to employers?

From the employer's point of view, a dollar contributed to federal Old-Age and Survivors Insurance, a pension fund, or a health insurance program is a cost of production, just the same as a dollar of wage payments.

Thus, in measuring the relationship between wage rates and production patterns, all the costs associated with hiring labor should be measured, not just the nominal wage rate. When measures of the cost of fringe benefits are not available, the question arises, To what extent is the analysis of labor markets affected? This question can only be answered in the context of a particular study; however, in general it is probably true that the amount of fringe benefits is positively related to nominal wage rates. Thus, the principal effect would be to understate real wage costs more or less consistently by a fraction. The effect of this error on most studies is probably relatively unimportant. Table 1-A2 and Figure 1-A3 suggest the relationship between

Table 1-A2

ANNUAL WAGE SUPPLEMENTS
BY MAJOR INDUSTRY

Industry	(1) (2) Supplement Earnings (in dollars)		(3)	(3a)
Agriculture, Forestry, and Fisheries	55	1816	0.3	2.0
Mining	688	6030	1.6	13.8
Contract Construction	464	5890	2.3	5.7
Manufacturing	613	5715	0.9	8.6
Wholesale and Retail Trade	278	4661	0.6	4.4
Finance, Insurance and Real Estate	606	5163	2.6	9.3
Transportation	582	6328	2.0	8.3
Communications and Public Utilities	768	6130	2.0	12.7
Services	196	3887	0.4	3.0
Government and Government Enterprises	438	5009	3.5	8.2

(1) Average annual supplements to wages and salaries per full-time employee in 1962.
   Source: *Historical Statistics of the United States, Continuation to 1962 and Revisions,* D 708–719.

(2) Average annual earnings per full-time employee (1962).
   Source: Same as (1) Series D 696–707.

(3) Wage supplements as a percentage of wages and salaries (1929).
   Source: H. G. Lewis, *Unionism and Relative Wages in the United States* (Chicago: University of Chicago Press, 1963), pp. 236–37.

(3a) Wage supplements as a percentage of salaries (1958).
   Source: Same as (3).

wage rates and wage supplements, or fringe benefits, and also between the size of wage rates and the proportion of supplements in total wages. The former relationship appears to be more consistent than the latter.

If we know their exact amount, wage supplements may be added directly to wage and salary payments to determine the total cost of labor to employers. (However, it is at times important to distinguish between

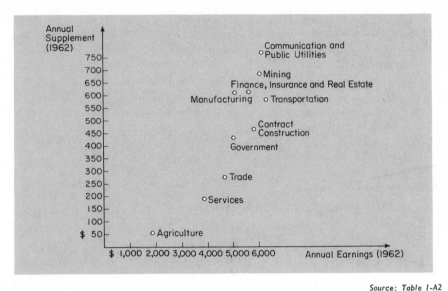

Source: Table 1-A2

FIG. 1-A3
Annual Wage Supplements and Earnings

supplemental benefits which depend on the number of hours worked and those which do not, as they will affect employer and employee behavior in different ways.) To what extent may we similarly evaluate the total payment to workers? Consider a case in which workers voluntarily agree to have employers contribute part of their wages to a fund, such as social insurance, health insurance, or the like. They might do this because of certain economies of scale in such financial arrangements. These contributions might then be recorded as wage supplements. Such supplements to wages should no more be considered reductions in the inducement to work than the "deduction" due to purchases of food, clothing, or other commodities. That is, the workers receive something in return for the withheld supplements which they presumably value at least as highly as any alternative uses to which they might have put the wages not received in the form of cash. However, such plans usually mean that each person must behave in a manner essentially similar to his co-workers. Social security payments, for example, differ among workers only as wages differ; there is no room for adjustment of the amount paid according to personal wishes. To the extent that workers are bound by institutional arrangements to contribute more of their gross wages than they would prefer to supplemental programs, the value of the supplemental benefits received must be less than the amount paid in. (However, to the extent that more is paid in than would be paid voluntarily, private expenditures of a similar nature may be curtailed; this would mitigate the difference between the value of benefits received and costs. For instance, as a result of social security payments, some workers may reduce the amount of life insurance they buy.) If the value of supplemental benefits is less than the amount paid, then net "real" wages should not include the discrepancy. Indeed, observed wage rates should be reduced by the amount of employees' contributions to such programs as social security, if it is thought that the benefits received are viewed as zero by workers.

The Time Period. So far we have spoken of the wage rate almost as if it were given to each person for all time. However, later on we shall learn that time plays an important role in many labor market decisions. Consequently, time plays an important role in the measurement of labor market phenomena. For instance, we shall analyze the response of labor supply to wage rates by means of "income" and "substitution" effects (see pp. 46–51) Income is a tricky concept; its value depends on the period of time over which it is measured. To the extent that a change in the wage rate affects income, it must persist for a certain period of time. Thus, it is necessary to specify whether we are measuring a wage rate which is more or less permanent (i e., normal) or one which reflects transitory phenomena.

Suppose, for instance, we wanted to estimate the income and substitution effects for the families of farm workers and that in areas where farm wage rates are *persistently* relatively high, we expected to observe fewer wives and children of farm workers in the labor force than elsewhere. But, since harvests vary from year to year and from place to place, we should also expect to find that hourly wage rates are unusually high where crops are unusually good, and vice versa. If the relatively high wages are a transitory phenomenon, we should not expect to observe much labor force withdrawal of women and children, and men may work even more than usual, since it pays to supply labor when the wage rate is highest. That is, a change in the wage rate that is expected to be temporary cannot have a significant effect on a family's view of its normal level of income. Therefore, the substitution effect will be extremely important in determining the labor supply response to transitory changes in wage rates, even though the income effect may dominate when wage rate changes are expected to be permanent.

Of course, the extent to which one must be careful to distinguish between long-term normal wages and transitory deviations depends upon the variability of labor market conditions. If one wished to study the labor force behavior of the families of bank tellers, much less care would need to be taken than in the case of farm workers.

Another problem in measuring wage rates that is due to the role of time in economic behavior arises from the importance of certain kinds of on-the-job training. The analysis of on-the-job training is part of the theory of human capital discussed in Chapter 4. In addition to formal and informal training programs, it is reasonable to suppose that much on-the-job training takes the form of learning-by-doing. Whatever form on-the-job training takes, it is expected to have the effect of raising future productivity and—usually—earnings; thus, workers in general may be expected to be willing to pay for it. That workers are willing to pay for on-the-job training is suggested by the relatively low wage rates of apprentices, physicians in residency, and the like. That is, payment is affected in many cases by accepting a wage lower than productivity in order to compensate employers for providing training. Whatever the nature of the training process, invest-ment affects typical age-earnings profiles of many kinds of workers.

Consider the age-earnings profiles of college graduates in 1960, as shown in Table 1-A3 and Figure 1-A4. Earnings several years after leaving

Table 1-A3

AGE–INCOME PROFILE U.S. MALES 14 AND OVER
BY YEARS OF EDUCATION (MEDIAN INCOMES)

Age	(Elementary) 8 years	(4 years HS) 12 years	4 years College
14–15	$ 575	$1,719	
16–17	630	750	
18–19	1,155	1,057	
20–21	1,914	2,442	$1,751
22–24	2,712	3,496	2,852
25–29	3,683	4,745	5,477
30–34	4,293	5,452	7,365
35–44	4,541	5,848	8,669
45–54	4,609	5,806	8,949
55–64	4,278	5,413	8,345
65–74	2,095	2,969	5,236
75–	1,312	1,727	3,017

Source: 1960 Census Subject Reports: *Educational Attainment*, Table 6.

college are not much higher than earnings of high school graduates of similar ages. However, the earnings shown in Figure 1-A4 do not reflect the value of on-the-job training typically acquired by college graduates upon entering the labor force. The amount of training acquired has been estimated to be substantial, and certainly greater than that acquired by high school graduates. That is, the earnings figures reflect the willingness of workers to accept lower initial wages in return for training and other experiences which are expected to induce higher earning power later on in life; the low reported earnings in earlier years therefore understate *real* earnings because the value of much of the training being acquired is not included. It has been estimated that over an average worker's lifetime, the rate of return to college education

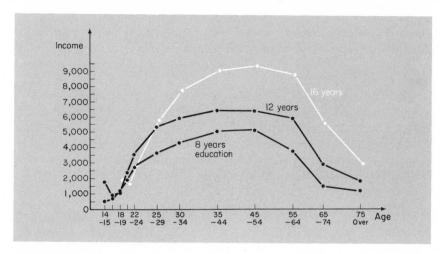

FIG. I-A4
Age-Income Profile by Education

and subsequent on-the-job training is in the neighborhood of 10–15 per cent. The payoffs on these investments are reflected in recorded earnings only later in life. Thus, the age-earnings profile of college graduates is typically steeper than that of high school or grammar school graduates and lies above them throughout much, but not all, of a typical working life.

The point here is not to develop a theory of on-the-job training but rather to indicate that the relationship between the wage rate and, say, hours worked per week, or any other variable, may be seriously obscured by faulty measurement of the wage rate. If the payment "in kind" which reflects payment for being in a job which allows some kind of training or learning to take place is ignored, the measured wage rate will reflect only money earnings; this will result in an underestimate of the real wage rate, and the underestimation may be very large for persons with a great deal of education.

Workers Not Paid by the Hour. In many cases, it is necessary to convert observed payments for labor services to a time basis comparable with a standard measure adopted for purposes of studying labor force behavior. For instance, if the hourly wage rate is the standard measure, the payments made to workers paid by the week, month, or year must be converted to an hourly basis. This is a straightforward procedure if the hours worked per week, month, or year are well defined. However, errors of measurement in estimating hours worked will induce related errors in the calculation of hourly wages. These errors can have an important effect on estimated behavioral relationships. For instance, an overestimate of hours worked will induce an underestimate of the wage rate; in estimating the substitution effect in labor supply behavior, this measurement error imparts a bias toward zero, if the true substitution effect is positive as suggested by economic theory.

The problem is probably very serious in studying the behavior of professional workers and the self-employed. Here it is not only difficult to measure hourly wage rates, but it is not clear that the *marginal* contribution to income of an hour's extra work is anywhere near equal to *average* hourly earnings. At this point it is probably best only to point out this problem without suggesting possible solutions.

USING ECONOMIC DATA

It is important to apply the kind of information described in Section I and used in much of the remainder of this book in such a way that it sheds light on the economic hypotheses to which the information is related. That is to say, economic theory not only suggests what kinds of economic data it may be useful to examine but also has implications for the way in which the data should be analyzed.

exact theories and inexact behavior

A very important step in using economic theories and hypotheses to help understand real world behavior is to make the transition in one's thinking from the *exact* nature of most theories and hypotheses to the *inexact* nature of actual human behavior. Everyone is first introduced to the study of economic theory by means of studying exact relationships such as demand and supply curves—we shall develop such relationships for labor markets in subsequent chapters of this book. Thus, whenever relationships like demand and supply curves are developed theoretically, explicit statements are made regarding which variables are thought to change either independently or in response to other variables (such as price and quantity), and which variables, *although they influence the behavior of the dependent variable under investigation*, are assumed to be constant for purposes of theoretical analysis. Thus, we often see statements such as, *ceteris paribus* (other things equal or unchanging), the amount of labor demanded is a negative function of the wage rate. In making such a statement, the theorist does not fail to recognize that changing knowledge of productive techniques, changing prices of other productive factors, deviations of firms from profit-maximizing behavior, the existence of disequilibrium situations, and so on, may indeed also influence behavior in reality. However, he recognizes that under conditions of unchanging values of these other variables which influence the behavior of labor demand, he can deduce a negative relationship between wage rates and the quantity demanded. Such a deduced relationship is *exact* because uniques values of the quantity of labor demanded are implied for each wage rate. There are often no implications deduced about deviations from the theoretical relationship.

We can provide here only a brief sketch of ways in which exact economic theory is made useful for the empirical investigation of inexact behavior; the detailed study of such problems is taken up in econometrics, and there is an increasing tendency for even undergraduate economics majors to be required to take one or more courses in elementary statistical analysis in which some of the simple econometric problems are discussed. The ensuing discussion is meant to supplement what most students, hopefully, will have learned in such courses, and to provide for the uninitiated enough of an outline so that they can follow the discussion in this text without too much difficulty. We shall use here, as a starting point, part of the discussion found in Chapters 6 through 8, where the theory of the demand for labor and some elementary tests of the theory are developed.

One of the clearest implications of the theory of labor demand developed in Chapters 6 and 7 is that the amount of labor demanded by a firm or industry is a negative function of the wage rate or wage rates of the labor employed. The relationships deduced are exact, but it is often observed that it is difficult to predict the responses of individual employers or industries to particular changes in wage rates. Thus, critics of the hypothesized downward-sloping labor demand curve often dwell on the observation that observed behavior is inexact. One often hears the expression that "the labor demand curve should be drawn with the broad side of the chalk," meaning that the theoretical implication of a negatively sloped demand relationship is perhaps useful for understanding the effects of very large changes in labor supply and/or wage rates, but not small changes.

However, in testing the hypothesis of downward-sloping labor demand, it is essential to translate into a concept usable in statistical analysis the *ceteris paribus* assumption used in deducing the theoretical relationship. The inexact relationships which are observed between the quantities of labor demanded and wage rates arise because, in fact, many variables other than wage rates actually influence demand behavior and are not constant in real world situations. Statistical analysis has been developed to handle this kind of problem. The important point to recognize is the following: If we observe a relationship between two variables, such as wage rate and quantity of labor demanded, we are justified in inferring that, *on the average*, we are observing the real world counterpart of the hypothetical labor demand curve *if the other variables which affect demand behavior, but which are not accounted for in our observations, are uncorrelated with wage rates.* This condition is usually stated that the variables affecting the behavior being studied (demand in this case), which are *not* observed, are *randomly* related to the observed variable(s) influencing the behavior under consideration. Thus, the notion that "the demand curve ought to be drawn with the broad side of the chalk" can be reinterpreted in terms of conventional statistical inference—that we expect to observe a number of labor demand observations at each different wage rate, the *averages* of which demand observations are the real world counterparts of the points on a theoretical demand curve.

There are many ways in which the effects of "left out" random variables may be taken into consideration when inexact human behavior is being investigated with hypotheses developed from exact economic theory. However, they all involve the use of some kind of averaging. The usefulness of averages is that even though many variables not considered or observed may influence the behavior in which we are interested, if such omitted variables are indeed randomly related to the independent variables whose influences on behavior we hope to measure, and if we observe a large enough number of events, the influences of the omitted variables will cancel each other. This is a simple statement of an application of the "law of large numbers." One of its most common applications is in the business world, where insurance companies can quite accurately predict death rates as a simple function of age for large groups of people. Another example is the ability of banks to meet their daily demands even though they never have enough cash in their vaults to pay all their creditors at once.

Simply *assuming* that variables which influence the behavior being investigated are indeed randomly related to the independent variables whose influence is being measured does not itself eliminate the problem of inferring something about exact theoretical relationships from the observation of inexact behavior. The assumption must also be consistent with reality; often we don't know whether the maintained hypothesis of the randomness of omitted variables is true, and we are therefore subject to the possibility of serious error. The possible error is of the following kind. Suppose in our labor demand study, we think we observe a situation in which wage rates are determined at levels such as W_1, W_2, and W_3 in Figure 1-A5 and in which the firms or industries observed can hire all the labor they desire at those wage rates, the wage rate depending, say, on the date or place of observation. That is, the different wage rates occur at different places or points in time, but at each place or date the labor supply curve is infinitely elastic. We believe also that the labor demand *function* is the same everywhere or unchanged throughout the period of our study and is the same for each firm or industry; in addition to wage rates, other variables uncorrelated with wage rates determine the amount of labor demanded. Thus, at each wage rate we observe different quantities of labor demanded, and these quantities are denoted by the x's in Figure 1-A5. Each x represents an observation of the quantity of labor demanded by one of the firms or industries in the sample under one

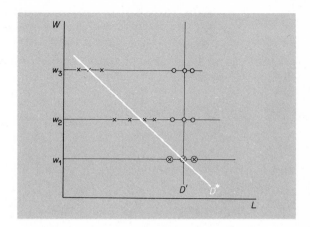

FIG. 1-A5
Illustration of the Omitted Variable Problem

of the various wage rate conditions. After striking an average of the observed quantities of labor at each wage rate, we can connect the average quantities demanded by a line such as D^*, and that line represents the real world counterpart, or estimate, of the hypothetical labor demand curve.

One of the most commonly used statistical procedures for estimating relationships such as D^* is called *regression analysis*.[5] Regression analysis is a method of finding a line such as D^* which passes through the mean of all the labor quantities observed, at the same time minimizing the sum of the squared deviations of each labor quantity (in the quantity dimension) from the resulting estimate of D^*. Statistical theory shows that such an estimate has desirable qualities under a wide variety of circumstances. (Regression equation estimates will not necessarily be the same as estimates resulting from passing a line through the mean quantity corresponding to *each* wage rate observed; but this is unimportant for the meaning of the present discussion.) Now, suppose that we were incorrect in assuming that the omitted variables which influence labor demand were uncorrelated with wage rates. Imagine, for instance, that for reasons we did not take into consideration, firms were unable to hire all the labor they desired at wage rates W_2 and W_3 because legal restrictions were placed on the number of workers who could be employed in the firms or industries studied. Indeed, we may suppose that the firms would have liked to have amounts of labor represented by the *o*'s in Figure 1-A5; thus, the *x*'s, except at wage W_1, would not represent points on the true demand curve at all. We have left out a variable, legal restrictions on the quantity of labor employed (which would equal the difference between the

---

[5] For a simple treatment of regression analysis, see, for example, M. Ezekiel and K. A. Fox, *Methods of Correlation and Regression Analysis*, 3rd ed. (New York: John Wiley & Sons, Inc.), 1959.

respective x's and o's at each wage rate), which was correlated with the wage rates observed (obviously the restriction would have been positively correlated with W, being zero at W_1). The true demand curve could have been estimated if we had taken the legal restrictions into consideration and passed the estimated line through the o's in Figure 1-A5, yielding the labor demand curve

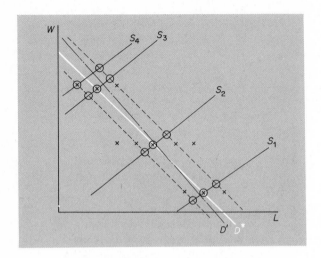

FIG. 1-A6
Illustration of the Identification Problem

D' which happens to have zero elasticity. In statistical terms, we say, then, that D^* is a *biased* estimate of the true demand curve D', if the assumption about the lack of correlation between the omitted variables and the independent variables included in the analysis is untrue. The nature of the bias depends, of course, on the influences of the omitted variables on the behavior being studied *and* on their correlation with the *included* independent variables.

Another, related, source of biased estimates is shown in Figure 1-A6. In this example, the *false* assumption is that each observation represents the intersection of a demand curve with one or another *infinitely elastic* supply curve. Thus the scatter of observed labor quantities is determined not only by the slope of the underlying demand curve, but by the slopes of the supply curves as well. Notice what this does to our estimated demand curve: the reason that the observed quantities of labor may take on different values at the same wage rate is thought to be that omitted variables cause the demand curve to shift to the right and left in a manner uncorrelated with wage rates. These shifts, or deviations, from the demand curve we hope to estimate produce deviations of the observed quantities of labor from the hypothesized (*cet. par.*) demand curve. If our assumptions about omitted variables were correct, we would obtain observations corresponding to, say, the x's in

Figure 1-A6 and we would obtain D^* as an unbiased estimate of labor demand. (Note that the x's lie along infinitely elastic supply curves like those of Figure 1-A5.) However, if we have left out relevant information about the degree of inelasticity of the supply curves, then the wage rate observations will correspond to observed labor quantities represented by the o's in Figure 1-A5. Notice what this does to observations along the lowest and highest supply curves. Regression analysis, in minimizing the sum of the squared deviations of quantity demanded from the estimated demand curve, will pull the estimated curve clockwise from D^*, yielding a curve like D'. This is because the averaging process involved in estimating the regression line will result in an average quantity, corresponding to the highest wage rate, that is "too great" and, corresponding to the lowest wage rate, that is "too small." The errors induced by leaving out information about the supply curves' inelasticity are correlated with the wage rate observations. On your own, you can construct an example where the shifts in the demand curve are so large that the resulting scatter of observations resembles a supply curve more closely than a demand curve. Failure to consider the inelasticity of the supply curves moves the estimated demand curve in the direction of the supply curves—possibly even changing the sign of the estimated slope from negative to positive. This aspect of bias is called the *identification problem*, because if it exists we cannot properly identify a regression line estimated through the scatter of observations either as a demand curve or as a supply curve.

Although it is possible that our assumptions, or maintained hypotheses, about the processes which generated the data used in empirical investigation are subject to error, we must not be so afraid of making mistakes that we avoid the use of economic theory in trying to understand real world behavior. Without a theory to guide us, we would also make mistakes—presumably bigger ones than when theory is used to help interpret observed behavior; indeed the purpose of a theory is to help us watch out for mistakes in inferring relationships from observed behavior from which "common sense" alone cannot protect us. Of course, we should also watch for less subtle kinds of errors. Thus, the more we know about how underlying processes have generated the data we observe (e.g., knowledge of how a questionnaire is administered), the more likely we are to take relevant information into account and to obtain relatively unbiased estimates of hypothetical economic relationships.

Bivariate and Multivariate Relationships. The estimating of relationships such as those shown in Figure 1-A5 can be accomplished in several ways, but the most common method referred to in this text is regression analysis. In this section, we outline briefly how regression estimates are presented and interpreted. An estimated regression relationship such as discussed in the preceding section represents the equation of straight line such that the quantity of labor demanded (or whatever the dependent variable might be) is expressed as a linear function of the wage rate (or whatever the independent variable might be); e.g., $L = a + bW$, where L is the quantity of labor demanded, a is a constant (the quantity demanded when the wage rate is zero), and b is the slope of the demand curve (a negative number in this case). Whenever we feel that more than one variable influences behavior, and we wish to consider their influences simultaneously, the estimated relationship will contain two or more independent variables, and it represents, not a straight line, but a plane or hyperplane. Regression estimation has the following property: when a multivariate relationship (one containing two or more independent variables) is estimated, the estimation procedure is such that the slope coefficients (the coefficients of the independent variables) are estimates of the effects of their respective independent variables on the behavior of the dependent variable, *holding constant* the values of all the other independent variables. Thus, if we estimate family consumption expenditures as a function of family income and the interest rate, the coefficient of the income variable measures the influence of income on expenditures, at given interest rates, and the coefficient of the interest variable measures the influence of the interest rate, at given levels of family income. Only the number of observations in a set of data limit the number of independent variables whose influence on behavior can be estimated simultaneously. Of course, considerations of economic theory will suggest the most important variables to include in estimated relationships, and in general it is true that the greater the number of variables whose influences are estimated, the more difficult it becomes to relate all the variables to the processes which theoretically are thought to have generated the observed data.

Nonlinear Relationships.   Even though the basic estimation procedure in the kind of regression analysis we have discussed here (which is the only kind used throughout this text) yields a *linear* estimated relationship between dependent and independent variables, underlying *nonlinear* estimated relationships can often be approximated by transforming either the dependent or independent variables, or both.

A very common transformation, for instance, is appropriate when one believes that the hypothetical relationship whose real world counterpart is to be estimated is one of constant *elasticity*, i.e., when one believes that proportional changes in the dependent variable are a constant multiple of proportional changes in the independent variables. (Note that the linear relationship mentioned above—$L = a + bW$—does *not* represent a constant elasticity relationship, except under the special circumstances that $a = 0$; for such a relationship to be economically meaningful, b would have to be positive.) A common and useful relationship assuming constant elasticities is the Cobb-Douglas-type[6] production function

$$Q = aL^\alpha K^\beta \tag{1}$$

where Q represents the quantity produced of some good, L and K represent inputs of labor and capital, respectively, and a, α, and β are parameters of the relationship. Note that the elasticity of production with respect to either input is constant and equal to the exponent of the input in the production function. Thus the elasticity of output with respect to labor inputs $\left(\text{defined as } \dfrac{\partial Q}{\partial L}\dfrac{L}{Q}\right)$ is

$$\frac{\partial Q}{\partial L}\frac{L}{Q} = \frac{\alpha a L^{\alpha-1} K^\beta L}{aL^\alpha K^\beta} = \alpha \tag{2}$$

In order to estimate (1) with linear regression procedures, the production function is used in its logarithmic transformation, namely,

$$\log Q = \log a + \alpha \log L + \beta \log K \tag{3}$$

That is, the production function (1) is linear in its logarithmic transformation and is thus susceptible of linear regression analysis. Other common transformation involves taking the logarithm of one side of a relationship only (note that taking the natural log of the dependent variable yields a constant "rate of growth" relationship), expressing some or all of the independent variables in higher powers, and so on.

Another very useful kind of transformation of the data so that difficult-to-approximate relationships can be estimated with linear estimation procedures is the so-called "dummy variable" technique. An outstanding example of the usefulness of this technique is found in Table 13-5, where the relationships between earnings and various independent variables, including education, are estimated. There is a great deal of evidence that the effect of education on earnings is nonlinear, the effect of a given amount of additional schooling changing as the level of education rises; thus, the variable "number of years of schooling" is divided into eight categories; 0–4 years, 5–7 years, 8 years, 9–11 years, 12 years, 13–15 years, 16 years, and 17+ years. Each of these categories becomes a variable of the following kind: every observation will fall into one and only one of the schooling categories; the variable representing the category into which an observation falls takes

---

[6] The Cobb-Douglas production function is referred to elsewhere in the text. Strictly speaking, and for historical reasons, the Cobb-Douglas function is one identical to that in (1), except that $\alpha + \beta \equiv 1$. In this text we shall not in general constrain ourselves to referring to a functional relationship such as (1) by the name Cobb-Douglas only if $\alpha + \beta \equiv 1$.

on the value of 1 for that observation, and all the other variables representing education categories take on the value of 0 for that observation. 1 and 0 are the only values a dummy variable can assume. Any combination of dummy variables and continuous variables can be used in a regression equation. The interpretation of the estimated coefficients of the dummy variables is that the coefficient represents (in this example) the *addition* to total earnings attributable *on the average* to a particular education category. For important reasons which we shall not discuss here, one category of a set of dummy variables which by definition exhausts the sample must be excluded from the estimation procedure. In the example of Table 13-5, the category 12 years was excluded. Thus, all the other variables' coefficients take on values with respect to 12 years. If years of schooling were the only set of variables used in Table 13-5, we could find the estimated earnings of any observed individual as the sum of the constant term and the coefficient of the variable representing the inidividual's educational category (probably if education were the only variable, the constant term would not turn out to be negative as it is in Table 13-5).

Other Statistics of Regression Relationships. By and large, economic theories and hypotheses are expressed in terms to which the slope coefficients of regression relationships are relevant. However, other estimated statistics of regression relationships are important in trying to decide whether a theory or hypothesis is helpful in understanding real world events. Three of these statistics are the R^2 statistic, the standard error of a regression coefficient, and the t-ratio of a regression coefficient.

For any relationship, either bivariate, such as the relationship shown in Figures 1-A5 and 1-A6, or multivariate, it is important to know whether the estimated relationship between the dependent and independent variable(s) is a reliable estimate of an underlying hypothetical economic relationship. One test of whether an estimate is reliable is the extent to which the variation of the dependent variable (the amount of labor demanded in Figure 1-A5) is "accounted for" by the variation of the independent variable(s) (the wage rate in Figure 1-A5). In the simple bivariate case of Figure 1-A5, the concept of the degree to which variation of the independent variable accounts for variation of the dependent variable can be viewed as the degree to which the x's are dispersed in the vertical dimension (wage rate) as compared to the horizontal dimension (quantity of labor). R^2 essentially measures the degree to which the latter dispersion is related to the former. As one can see, the x's might be so widespread horizontally that one would be hardput to identify any difference in the average location of the x's at wage rate W_1 from their average location at W_3. In such a case, the variation in the wage rate would account for very little variation in the quantity of labor demanded, and R^2 would be close to 0. R^2 may by definition take on values from 0 to 1.

The value is defined to be a measure of the fraction of the variation in the dependent variable accounted for by variation of the independent variable(s). If all the observations lay precisely on an estimated relationship (e.g., if the x's of Figure 1-A1 all lay on D^*), the R^2 statistic would equal 1. The square root of R^2, r, is called the correlation coefficient.

Economic theory has very little to say about the value of R^2; that is, both low and high values are consistent with economic theory as usually stated. However, statistical theory implies that, depending on the number of observations, the value of R^2 may be "significant" or "insignificant." The reason for concern about statistical significance is that the regression estimation procedure will almost always yield some kind of relationship among a set of variables; however, it is important to have some knowledge about whether such a relationship is likely to have resulted merely from a chance constellation of observations or whether it is likely that subsequent estimates would yield similar results.

We also are interested in the probability that particular values of the estimated slope coefficient (regression coefficients) of a regression rather closely approximate the relationships of an underlying hypothetical process. Some insight into this question is provided by the standard errors of the regression coefficients, or the ratios of the regression coefficients to their individual standard errors, which are called t-ratios. T-ratios shed light on whether estimated values of the regression coefficients are statistically significant. If the ratios are low, then we cannot be sure whether the regression coefficient estimates are merely chance occurrences or whether they do indeed approximate some "true" underlying relationship which generated the observed data. (However, high t-ratios do not by themselves tell us much about how strongly an hypothesis is confirmed.) Standard errors are related in their meaning to R^2, and also provide a measure of the degree to which the variation of the independent variable(s) accounts for variation of the dependent variables.

It is very important to note that it is possible for an estimated regression relationship to be statistically significant but economically untenable or insignificant. That is, statistically significant relationships may contradict information derived from other investigations which we may hold with great certainty; or statistically significant relationships may imply "small" or negligible effects of one variable on another. As an example, suppose we gathered data about consumption and income in the United States which showed total consumption expenditures to increase by 20 per cent whenever family incomes rose by 100 per cent. Since there is reliable evidence already available that the long-run response of consumption to income is much greater than that implied by an elasticity of .2, we would under almost no circumstances accept the estimate, even though statistically significant, as a good estimate of the long-run relationship between consumption and income.

We would, rather, try to find out whether we mismeasured our variables, collected the data in such a way as to provide an inconclusive test of the hypothesis being investigated, and so on. Suppose, as another example, we wished to measure the effect of the corporate income tax on the amount of equity capital made available to corporations. Imagine that we have carefully formulated our hypotheses and collected data relevant to them, and that our estimates imply with a higher degree of statistical significance that a 100 per cent increase in the corporate income tax rate will reduce the amount of equity capital available to corporations by 5 per cent. Such a relationship would probably be unimportant from the point of view of economic policy and could be described as economically insignificant, even though well established by empirical investigation.

It is equally important to recognize that statistical insignificance does not necessarily imply that a theory or hypothesis is incorrect but rather that the results of a particular investigation are probably not to be strongly relied upon as a good estimate of an underlying relationship. Furthermore, it should be reemphasized that a high degree of statistical significance as measured, say, by R^2 or standard error of regression coefficients has almost no implication for whether the theory being tested is indeed correct. Economic theory usually has little to say about how much of the observed variation of a particular dependent variable is due to the effects of the hypothetical relationship being studied. Of course, economists believe that economic relationships are "important" in helping determine certain kinds of observed behavior; however, importance is only vaguely related to statistical significance and/or fraction of variation attributable to independent variables included in theoretical relationships.

The major point to remember is that there is no way to evaluate the statistical results of an empirical investigation without reference to an economic theory which explains how the variables are thought to be related and the kinds of estimates that are acceptable evidence bearing on the theory. This means that there is much room for judgment and experience in interpreting the results of empirical investigations, and reasonable and competent economists can and do often disagree on whether a given theory or hypothesis has been confirmed or rejected or whether it is useful in helping to understand the real world. This is something to bear in mind in reading the remainder of this book. Most of the material bearing on the empirical relevance of the economic theory of the labor market is interpreted by the author as he sees it. Other economists may well have wished to use the results of different empirical investigations, to interpret the results reported in this book differently, and/or to have developed different implications of economic theory as being more relevant to the real world. These are matters of judgment; the important thing for the student is not so much to read and believe as to read and understand.

2

the theory of labor supply: family members in the short run

We begin our study of the theory of labor markets by considering the labor supplied by family members in the short run. For purposes of labor supply analysis, the short run is taken to mean a period of time in which decisions are made about whether to sell labor services and how much to sell; this period of time is shorter than the period in which decisions are formed involving education, occupational choice, migration, etc.[1]

In the analysis of labor supply, the family plays a role similar to that of the firm in the theory of the demand for labor. That is, we consider the family (or unrelated individual) as the basic decision-making unit. Of course, we are concerned here with only a particular kind of labor: that performed in the market for pay (including self-employment). There are other kinds of labor, such as housework, child care, and "do-it-yourself" projects in the home. However, these nonmarket activities are not included

---

[1] This concept of the short run is similar to that used in the standard theory of the firm, where the short run is a period of time in which some inputs (usually plant and equipment) are not variable. We define the short run here in terms of whether conditions affecting the *quality*, *skill*, *location*, etc., of labor are adjusted. In the short run they are not.

under the rubric of work or labor for our purposes; rather they constitute the complement of work, which it is convenient to call "leisure." We are concerned with the determinants of family members' decision to sell their labor power in the market.

We assume that individual family members make their labor force decisions in consideration of the decisions made by other family members; thus labor supply decisions are the result of simultaneous processes which work toward achieving a maximum of satisfaction for the family, given its limited resources. That is, the husband may consider his wife's wage rate, the nonlabor income of the family (i.e., income due to rent, dividends, interest, capital gains or, in general, the family's income from *nonhuman* assets, as well as payments from public and private welfare agencies), his expected duties in the home, and the attitudes of the community, his wife and his children in deciding when, where, and how much to work in the labor force. We may think of the wife, children, and other family members as behaving similarly. While it is important to emphasize that each family member's labor market decision is reached via a simultaneous process in which all family members' decisions are made, to incorporate all the important variables in a first approach to the theory of labor supply would make the analysis unnecessarily complicated. Therefore, we shall analyze the behavior of a representative family member, which we shall assume to be a function of his income, wage rate, and tastes, keeping in mind that the influence of these variables will depend in part on the values of other factors we are not considering explicitly—such as the wage rates, incomes, health, and tastes of other family members. Subsequently, we may introduce these other variables where necessary to relate our analysis to actual behavior.

THE UTILITY FUNCTION

As we shall later treat the firm as a decision-making unit that aims to maximize profits, we now discuss the family as a decision-making unit which aims to maximize its utility, or satisfaction. We postulate a relationship between basic commodities and utility such that the family members are better off with more, rather than fewer, commodities. The relationship between commodity inputs and utility is called a *utility function*.

In the analysis of labor supply, it is useful to divide commodities into two mutually exclusive and exhaustive groups—goods and time (or "leisure"). We assume for simplicity that all goods are produced by firms in the market and must be paid for in money. Money income may be received from the ownership of physical and financial assets (income in the form of rent, dividends, interest, and the like) or from human assets (which are "rented" as work in return for wages and salaries).

The postulated relationship between commodity inputs and utility—the

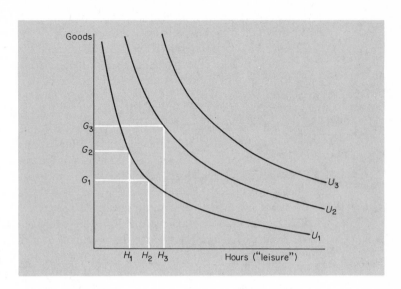

FIG. 2-1
A Family Member's Utility Function

utility function—is represented graphically in Figure 2-1, which shows the utility function of a typical family member. We measure the consumption of the two basic commodities—time and goods—on the horizontal and vertical axes respectively. Time is measured as a flow of hours per unit of time, such as hours per week or per year. Goods are measured in terms of dollars per unit of time. Moving outward along either axis represents increasing consumption: for example, moving to the right along the time axis represents more hours *not sold* in the market place, that is, more consumption of hours in the form of "leisure".

The utility function consists of a family of negatively sloped, convex lines called *indifferent curves*, such as U_1, U_2, and U_3 in Figure 2-1. Each indifference curve represents a constant level of utility, or satisfaction, with the curves lying further from the origin representing higher levels of utility. Along each indifference curve, the different combinations of consumption of hours and goods all yield the same satisfaction; that is, the consumer is "indifferent" between the consumption of commodity combinations denoted by any two points along a particular curve. Thus we might have named the indifference curves, *iso-utility* curves. The meaning of the statement that the consumer, or family member, is indifferent to consuming any of the alternative combinations of commodities along a given indifference curve is illustrated in Figure 2-1. The consumption of commodity combination G_1 and H_2 is defined to yield satisfaction equal to the consumption of the combination G_2 and H_1; however, consuming a combination of G_3 and H_3 yields more satisfaction than either of the first two combinations.

The most important characteristics of the indifference curves are their slope and their shape. Their *negative slope* implies that it is possible to hold the level of utility constant while substituting hours for goods in consumption; thus the negative slope implies the condition of *substitutability* in consumption between hours and goods. A term often applied to the slope of an indifference curve is the *marginal rate of substitution (MRS)* between the two commodities; the term *marginal* denotes the rate at which a *small* amount of hours can be substituted for a *small* amount of goods, holding utility constant. The *convex shape* of the indifference curves implies *imperfect substitutability* between hours and goods. If hours and goods were perfect substitutes, then the *MRS* would be the same, no matter what combination of hours and goods was being consumed; the indifference curves would thus be straight lines. The principle of imperfect substitutability implies that although family members can be kept at a constant level of utility by causing them to trade time for goods, and vice versa, the greater the proportion of time consumed to goods consumed, the greater the marginal (additional) amount of hours required to compensate for giving up a marginal amount of goods. Clearly, this relationship works in the opposite direction too: the greater the proportion of goods consumed to hours consumed, the greater the marginal amount of goods required to compensate a family member for giving up a marginal amount of hours.

It is important to be careful in discussing the measurement of the utility levels denoted by the numbers attached to the indifference curves. Note that each indifference curve in Figure 2-1 is numbered, with the numbers increasing as we move outward from the origin toward the northeast, implying higher levels of satisfaction as consumption increases. However, the numbers attached to the indifference curves are not unique; we may use any set of numbers which fulfills the condition that as we move toward the northeast, the numbers get larger. We are indifferent as to whether we measure successively higher utility levels as 1, 2, 3; 1.1, 1.2, 1.3; 100, 200, 300, and so on. The reason for this is that we wish to avoid the implication that the amount of satisfaction achieved by a consumer in one family can be compared with, or added to, the amount achieved by a consumer in another. Therefore, we are willing only to *rank* the indifference curves. More precisely, we adopt an *ordinal* rather than a *cardinal* utility index. This means that we measure utility similarly to the way we measure the events at a horse race—"1st," "2nd," etc., with the *ordering* of the events being the only important characteristic of the measurement. This does not in any way limit our ability to describe labor supply decisions as arising from the utility-maximizing behavior of family members. (We do imply, however, that family units act as if they have a method of comparing and adding the satisfactions achieved by family members; thus, it is meaningful to talk about a utility function for the entire family.)

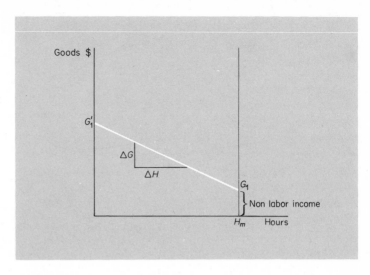

FIG. 2-2
The Budget Constraint

CONSUMPTION OPPORTUNITIES:
THE BUDGET CONSTRAINT

Obviously, if utility increases with the consumption of commodities, a utility-maximizing family member would proceed indefinitely far to the north east of his utility map—consuming an infinite amount of goods and hours. On the other hand, there are *constraints* which prohibit family members from consuming infinite quantities of commodities. We first must recognize that time is in fact strictly limited to twenty-four hours per day: this is a basic constraint. Secondly, we assume family members are able to sell their time as labor services in a competitive market; thus, the amount they wish to sell has little or no influence on the price at which they may sell it. The rate of exchange between goods measured in dollars and time measured in hours is the *wage rate* (measured in dollars per hour).

The constraint preventing family members from consuming an infinite quantity of goods and hours is the result of a limited number of hours, limited income from sources other than that of selling hours in the labor market ("nonlabor income"), and the wage rate, or the rate of exchange between hours sold and dollars' worth of goods. These limitations on consumption are summarized in the *budget constraint*. The budget constraint summarizes the family members' *consumption opportunities*.

Figure 2-2 shows the budget constraint of a typical family member. In Figure 2-2, as in Figure 2-1, goods are measured along the vertical axis in terms of dollars, and hours consumed (not worked or sold) are measured along the horizontal axis. There is an additional line, parallel to the vertical axis, and intersecting point H_m, the total number of hours there are in a period of time (e.g., twenty four hours per day); this line limits the relevant area of the graph to consumption of hours not in excess of H_m. The budget constraint intersects the line through H_m at a point G_1; G_1 denotes how many dollars' worth of goods can be consumed if no hours are sold in the labor market. The distance $H_m G_1$ is nonlabor income; nonlabor income represents dollars that arise from the ownership of nonhuman assets or from gifts and payments from friends, relatives, or the government. If the budget constraint passed through point H_m, the family member would have no nonlabor income; hence if he sold no hours in the labor market—if he did no work—he would have no command over goods other than this allocation of total family consumption. The constraint passes from some point such as G_1 to one such as G_1', on the goods axis. G_1' is the amount of goods the family member could buy (earn) if he sold all of his available hours in the market—if he worked constantly. (We ignore here the effect of lack of proper sleep, food, and recreation on the ability to sell hours; we may assume for convenience that H_m excludes the number of hours necessary to maintain productivity.)

The budget constraint is linear between G_1 and G_1', denoting that the rate of exchange between hours and goods, i.e., the wage rate, is independent of the number of hours the family member wishes to sell. This is implied by the assumption that the labor market is competitive. The linearity of the budget constraint implies that its slope, $\Delta G/\Delta H$ (the wage rate), is constant for all levels of consumption and is determined by conditions other than the family member's decision to consume hours and goods.

UTILITY MAXIMIZATION—THE DETERMINATION OF HOURS OF WORK

We have assumed that the family member attempts to maximize his utility. We now proceed to find out what utility maximization implies, given the utility function and the budget constraint. In order to see how the family member maximizes his utility, given the budget constraint, start at G_1' in Figure 2-3a and proceed toward G_1 until the highest indifference curve is reached. This will be at point P, where we see that the family member maximizes utility by consuming H_0 hours and G_0 goods such that his budget constraint is tangent to an indifference curve. It follows from the assumed shape of the budget constraint and the indifference curves that there is one, and only one, point such as P for each family member; a possible exception is a "corner solution," when an indifference curve is never tangent to the budget constraint within the area bounded by the two axes and the line passing through H_m. In such a case, the family member would either work all the time or not at all. The two possible corner solutions are shown in Figure 2-3b.

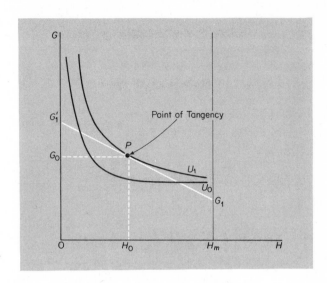

FIG. 2-3a
Utility Maximation—Tangency Solution

Let us examine more closely the proposition that the point of tangency between an indifference curve and the budget constraint represents the maximum utility obtainable, given the wage rate, income, and hours available. Suppose the family member decided to consume a combination of goods and hours corresponding to point Q in Figure 2-3c, which does not represent a point of tangency between $G'_1 G_1$ and an indifference curve. The indifference curve passing through Q is U_0, representing a *lower* level of utility or satisfaction than U_1, the curve which passes through P. It is clear that at Q the family member's consumption possibilities are such that by giving up some goods and consuming more hours, he can increase his level of utility. This

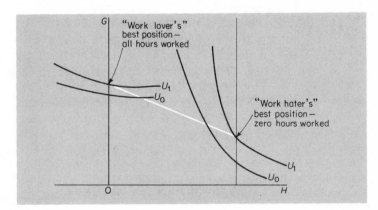

FIG. 2-3b
Utility Maximation— Corner Solution

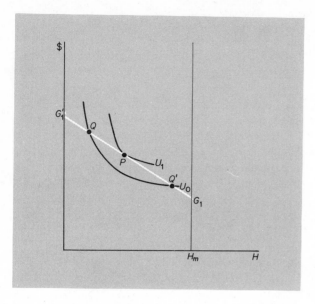

FIG. 2-3c
Further Illustration of Utility Maximization

will be true until the consumption combination represented by point P is obtained. Obviously, the same argument would apply if the initial point chosen were Q', where "too many" hours and "too few" goods would be consumed.

Formally, we can express the condition of utility maximization as follows. Recall that the slope of the budget constraint, $\Delta G/\Delta H$, represents the rate of exchange between goods and hours, or the price of hours (P_H) in terms of goods (i.e., it is the wage rate). Thus, along a budget constraint

$$\Delta G/\Delta H = P_H/P_G \tag{1}$$

where P_G is the price of goods in dollars. (If expression (1) seems strange, it will not if you recognize that the price of hours in dollars *is* the number of dollars' worth of goods for which an hour can be exchanged; the price of a dollar's worth of goods in dollars is one dollar. Thus, $P_G = 1$.) The slope of the indifference curves, on the other hand, can be discussed in terms of Figure 2-3d. Consider points P, Q, and M, which are sufficiently close together so that we may think of "the" slope of U_1 at P and ignore the change in the slope between P and M. Along U_1, the ratio $\Delta G/\Delta H$ is the slope of U_1, which we already know to be the *MRS* between hours and goods. Consider the following, however; subtracting ΔG from consumption at P without adding ΔH will lower utility from U_1 to U_0, and adding ΔH to consumption at Q will increase utility by an equal amount. Thus, we may think of *MRS* as the ratio of the *marginal inputs* into a given change in utility of the two commodities, G and H. We use the term *marginal* because we are talking about the effects on satisfaction or utility of very small changes

44

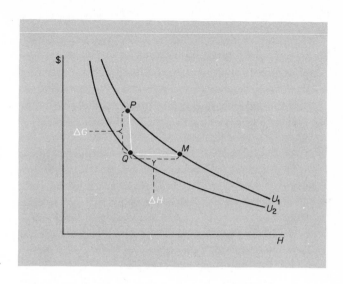

FIG. 2-3d
Further Illustration of Utility Maximation

in the consumption of the two commodities. Obviously, the larger the ratio $\Delta G/\Delta H$, the more goods must be added to consumption relative to hours in order to increase utility by a given small amount; thus, even though we do not allow ourselves to quantify the difference between utility levels U_1 and U_0, we nevertheless can make the statement that the additional utility derived from consuming a small additional amount of G *relative* to the additional utility derived from consuming a small additional amount of H is inversely proportional to the MRS, $\Delta G/\Delta H$, along an indifference curve. We name the relative marginal contribution to utility of G and H, the ratio of the marginal utilities of G and H. Symbolically, this ratio is MU_G/MU_H. Therefore, by definition,

$$MRS = \Delta G/\Delta H = MU_H/MU_G \tag{2}$$

Thus, the tangency condition of utility maximization can be expressed symbolically as follows. Tangency occurs when the slope of the budget constraint is equal to the slope of an indifference curve having a point in common with the budget constraint. At this point,

$$\Delta G/\Delta H_{\text{budget constraint}} = \Delta G/\Delta H_{\text{indifference curve}} \tag{3}$$

From our previous discussion and equations (1) and (2), we know that (3) is the equivalent of

$$P_H/P_G = MU_H/MU_G \tag{4}$$

That is, when utility is maximized, the relative price ratio of the commodities is equal to the ratio of their marginal utilities; the price of hours in terms of goods (the wage rate) is equal to the marginal utility of leisure relative to that of market goods. The converse is also true as long as the indifference curves

45

and budget constraint have the slope and shape described in Figures 2-1 through 2-3.

THE AMOUNT OF LABOR SUPPLIED

Now that we have established the condition of utility maximization, we may proceed to discuss the determinants of the amount of labor supplied by the family member. We shall derive the supply curve of labor with respect to the wage rate; the labor supply curve of the family member answers the question, How many labor hours per period of time will the family member supply at various wage rates, or equivalently, how many hours will the family member sell in the labor market?

Let us reexamine Figure 2-3a. The point of tangency, P, between the budget constraint and an indifference curve shows how many hours and goods will be consumed. We measure hours consumed by the length of the line segment OH_0 and hours *sold* or *supplied* by its complement, $H_m - H_0$. That is, hours of labor supplied by the family member is simply the difference between the number of hours available and the number consumed, or not sold.

In order to investigate the effect of changes in the wage rate on labor supplied, it is instructive first to examine the influence of changes in nonlabor income, with wage rates unchanged. Differences in nonlabor income are respresented by a family of parallel budget constraints. Each parallel budget constraint intersects the vertical line through H_m at a different point, which represents a different level of nonlabor income. The parallel budget constraints (which are similar to the firm's family of iso-expenditure lines described in Chapter 6) are shown in Figure 2-4. We may imagine that we

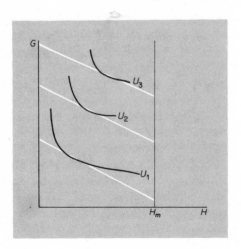

FIG. 2-4

The Effect of Income Change on Hours Worked

are performing the experiment of observing the family member's behavior while giving him different amounts of nonlabor income and holding his wage rate constant. As Figure 2-4 is drawn, successively higher levels of nonlabor income raise the family members' point of utility maximization higher and higher. The points of tangency lie roughly on a line extending toward the northeast, which implies that as the level of utility rises, with wage rates unchanged, the consumption of *both* hours and goods will increase.

We assume that the consumption of both hours and goods increases as utility rises, but there is nothing in economic theory compelling us to do so. Nevertheless the assumption of a forward-sloping utility-consumption path for the family member has intuitive appeal. One can imagine cases in which either goods or hours were an "inferior commodity." If goods were an inferior commodity, the utility-consumption path would slope toward the southeast, and if hours were inferior, toward the northwest. However, with broad commodity groups, the assumption of a northeasterly sloping utility-consumption path does not overtax one's sense of relevance. We may summarize this assumption with the phrase, "Both goods and hours are 'normal' commodities; their income elasticities of demand are positive."[2]

In order to continue our investigation of the effect of a change in the wage rate on hours worked, let us redraw the indifference curve map and budget constraint in Figures 2-5a and 2-5b. A change in the wage rate is shown by a change in the slope of the budget constraint. We now wish to examine the effect of a change in the wage rate *with nonlabor income unchanged*, so we *rotate* a budget constraint about a single point on the vertical line going through H_m. As the budget constraint is rotated clockwise, the wage rate increases. Figures 2-5a and 2-5b show two budget constraints, each depicting a different wage rate, but the same nonlabor income. The wage rate is lower along the constraint $H_m G'_2$ than along $H_m G'_3$. We see that the point of utility maximization is P along $H_m G'_2$ and Q along $H_m G'_3$. Note

---

[2] In elementary economics, most readers will have learned that "normal" goods are those whose income elasticities of demand are positive, while here we define normality in terms of a positive relationship between utility and consumption, holding constant relative prices. The reason for not using the criterion of income elasticity here is fairly obvious; we do not want to confuse the exposition with too many terms containing the word "income." On the one hand, the conceptual experiment represented in Figure 2-4 involves changing the level of *nonlabor* income; on the other hand, *actual* income received is measured by the ordinate of a point of tangency between a budget constraint and an indifference curve. Still another definition of income is the intercept of a budget constraint with the goods axis. This is the amount that would be received if all available hours were worked; this measure of income is sometimes called "full income," and it most closely corresponds to the income concept used in the standard discussion of the income elasticity of demand. Clearly, whenever the full income elasticity of demand for hours is positive, the relationship between utility and hours (holding $\Delta G/\Delta H$ constant) will also be positive, and the converse also holds.

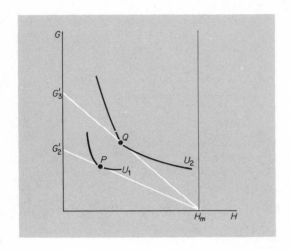

FIG. 2-5a
Reduced Labor Supply with Increased Wage Rate

that Q may lie either to the right or to the left of P. We cannot predict from economic theory whether an increase in the wage rate will result in a larger or a smaller amount of labor being supplied by the family member! The case of a reduced amount being supplied is shown in Figure 2-5a, while the case of a increased amount is shown in Figure 2-5b.

What lies behind the ambiguity concerning the effect of a change in the wage rate on the change in the amount of labor supplied by a family member? We can see more clearly if we redraw Figures 2-5a and 2-5b in Figure 2-6. Note that by increasing the wage rate, the family member is moved to a higher indifference curve; that is, when the wage rate increases, workers are better off. In Figure 2-6, we note that indifference curve U_2, the highest achievable after the budget constraint rotates from H_mG_2' to

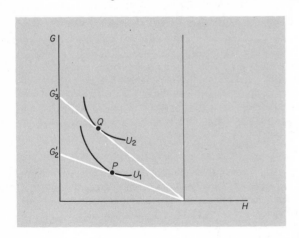

FIG. 2-5b
Increased Labor Supply with a Rise in the Wage Rate

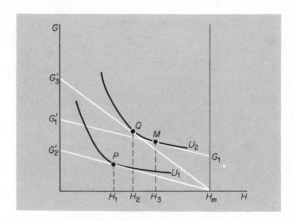

FIG. 2-6
The Substitution and Income Effects

$H_m G_3'$, lies above U_1, the previously highest attainable indifference curve. (We assume that Q lies to the northeast of P.) Now, we could also increase the family member's welfare to U_2 without increasing the wage rate by giving him an additional amount of nonlabor income that would be just enough to compensate him for not having his wage increased. In other words, imagine placing the family member on budget constraint $G_1 G_1'$, which is parallel to $H_m G_2'$, but tangent to indifference curve U_2. The distance along the line through H_m, $G_1 - H_m$ represents just enough nonlabor income to compensate the family member for not receiving an increase in his wage rate; note that since $G_1 G_1'$ is parallel to $H_m G_2'$, the wage rates along the two constraints are the same.

But what would be the difference in behavior if the budget constraint were $G_1 G_1'$ rather than $H_m G_2'$ or $H_m G_3$? We see that along $H_m G_3'$, $H_m - H_2$ hours are worked and H_2 hours consumed, whereas along $G_1 G_1'$, only $H_m - H_3$ hours would be worked, while H_3 hours would be consumed. The implication is that if we were to raise the family member to U_2 by increasing his nonlabor income rather than his wage rate, he would not have as great an incentive to work as if his wage rate had been increased. In other words, keeping the family member on the *same* indifference curve (U_2), but changing his budget constraint, will change his hours of work in the same direction that his wage rate is changed. Theoretically this *must* happen because of the negative slope of the indifference curve. The difference in the number of hours worked along U_2 at the two different wage rates, $H_2 - H_3$, is called the *substitution* effect of a change in the budget constraint from $H_m G_2$ to $H_m G_3$. Alternatively, we could lower the wage rate from $H_m G_3'$ to $H_m G_2'$ and measure the substitution effect on U_1. (For small changes in the budget constraint, there is a negligible difference in these two ways of measuring the substitution effect.)

When the family member is moved from U_1 to U_2 by means of a change in his nonlabor income only, his comsumption of hours rises from H_1 to H_3, and his hours worked falls by $H_3 - H_1$. This is called the *income effect* of the initial change in the budget constraint.

To summarize, the initial change in the budget constraint from $H_m G_2'$ to $H_m G_3'$ causes the family member to change his consumption of hours from H_1 to H_2. We note that the change from H_1 to H_2 can be broken down into two components: (1) $H_2 - H_3$, the change that is due to the change in the wage rate, holding the level of utility constant, called the substitution effect; (2) $H_3 - H_1$, the change that is due to the change in the level of utility, holding the wage rate constant, called the income effect. Thus, the gross effect on consumption of hours of a change in the wage rate is $(H_2 - H_3) + (H_3 - H_1) = H_2 - H_1$. Since we have assumed that hours are a normal commodity, the income effect is to raise hours consumed, and reduce hours worked, when the wage rate rises. On the other hand, the substitution effect *always* causes hours worked to rise so long as the indifference curves are negatively sloped. It can now be seen that the income and substitution effects have oppposite impact on hours worked when hours are a normal commodity. Thus, economic theory implies that hours worked may either rise or fall as the result of an increase in the wage rate, and the issue may only be resolved by empirical investigation.

What, then, does the family member's labor supply curve look like? It is difficult to say. However, many economists agree, and empirical evidence is not inconsistent with their concept, that the labor supply curve of family members looks something like that in Figure 2-7. Over a low range of wage rates, the substitution effect dominates the income effect, and the supply curve slopes upward with respect to the wage rate. Beyond this, the income effect dominates, and the labor supply curve is "backward bending," implying

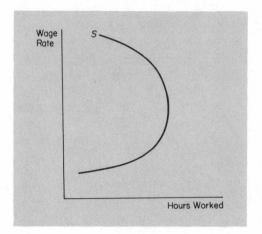

FIG. 2-7

The Labor Supply Curve of a Family Member with Respect to the Wage Rate Over a Long Time

that family members work less as a result of increases in the wage rate.

Note that when the labor supply curve is negatively sloped with respect to the wage rate, there is no implication that as wage rates increase, earned income declines. Whether earned income rises or falls with respect to wage rate increases depends on the elasticity of the supply curve; if the elasticity of the labor supply curve is algebraically greater than −1, then income rises as the wage rate rises. (Note that a supply curve with an elasticity of −1 throughout would have the form of a rectangular hyperbola.)

Another point to remember when using the theory of labor supply to help understand real world behavior is that we have been treating the income effects of changes in nonlabor income and of changes in wage rates as though they were commensurable. They are, in theory, if wage rate changes are thought to be of long duration, or permanent. To help understand this point, consider the following example: if a worker is offered the opportunity of working overtime hours for a few weeks, the effect on his normal income is relatively small. Even though his weekly income may rise considerably, the increase has to be treated in the context of his normal income in the absence of overtime work (and in the context of whatever nonlabor income may accrue to him). Thus, the income effect of a wage rate change that is expected to be temporary—i.e., what economists often call a transitory change in the wage rate—is theoretically much smaller than the income effect of a permanent or persistent wage rate change. On the other hand, the effect of such a change in the wage rate on the price of market goods relative to hours is independent of whether the change in the wage rate is of permanent or transistory nature. Thus, for transitory wage rate changes, the substitution effect is much more likely to dominate the income effect than it is for permanent changes. An example of the application of this point is that if we accept the existence of a backward-bending labor supply curve as the principal explanation of the long-term decline in hours of work per week (this is discussed in Chapter 3), we may be troubled by the fact that over short periods of time (such as the period of a business cycle) workers tend to work longer when unemployment is low, and wage rates including overtime premiums are high, than at other times. The difference between the effects of permanent and transitory wage rate changes should help in accounting for this phenomenon.

AN ALTERNATIVE APPROACH

An alternative approach to exploring the influence of changes in the wage rate on the number of hours sold in the labor market by the family member is perhaps intuitively more appealing. This approach recognizes that in fact "hours" are never consumed by themselves, nor are goods. Hours are not enjoyable without goods, and all goods require time to consume. Thus, we may think of consumption decisions being made among alternative commodities, some of which require more time to consume than others. All commodities have a goods component, and time must be sold (if nonlabor income is not available) to buy goods. Thus, the family member's labor hours supplied are determined simultaneously with consumption.[3]

For instance, eating caviar is a type of consumption which requires a relatively low input of time. So do certain forms of recreation, which we usually think of as leisure, such as nightclubbing, skiing, and polo. On the other hand, sleeping requires a relatively low input of market goods, in the form of wear and tear on bed, blankets, sheets, and sometimes pajamas,

Table 2-1

HIGH TIME GOODS AND LOW TIME GOODS COMPARED

Wage Rate	Price in Dollars Low Time	High Time	Maximum Consumption Low Time	High Time	Relative Prices Low Time ÷ High Time
$ .60	1.01	1.60	59	38	.63
1.20	1.02	2.20	118	55	.45
2.40	1.04	3.40	230	71	.31

and a relatively high input of time. For convenience in illustrating this alternative approach we divide all commodities into two groups; one requiring a high input of time per dollar of goods, and the other requiring a low input.

To make our two groups distinctively different, let us suppose that the group of "low-time" (high-goods component) commodities require, on the average, one minute of time per dollar of market goods; let the "high-time" commodities require one hour of time per one dollar of market goods. Now it is apparent that the full cost of consuming one unit of either kind of commodity includes not only the dollar cost of its goods component, but also the cost of the time involved, since if the time weren't spent in consumption, it could be sold for dollars.

Table 2-1 provides us with information which we can use to construct a budget constraint using the alternative approach. We see in the first row that if the wage rate is $.60 per hour, then consuming one unit of low-time goods costs $1 plus $.01, while consuming one unit of the high-time good costs $1 plus $.60. Thus the relative price of low-time goods in terms of high-time goods is $101/160 \simeq .63$.

This is perhaps seen more clearly if we find the maximum possible consumption of low-time and high-time commodities. Assume that the

---

[3] This approach to the theory of labor supply has been developed by Gary S. Becker. See, for instance, "A Theory of the Allocation of Time," *Economic Journal* (September, 1965), LXXV, 493–517.

family member has available to consume, or sell, 100 hours per week. Thus, if his wage rate is $.60 per hour, he could earn $60 by selling (i.e., working) all 100 hours. In any event, all the hours that are not worked will be spent in consumption, and the total dollar value of all available hours is $60. Maximum consumption of low-time commodities is achievable by consuming only low-time commodities and no high-time commodities. In order to find out how many low-time commodities could be consumed if no high-time commodities were consumed, we divide the cost per unit into $60, which yields $60/$1.01 ≅ 59. Thus, if only low-time commodities were consumed, 99

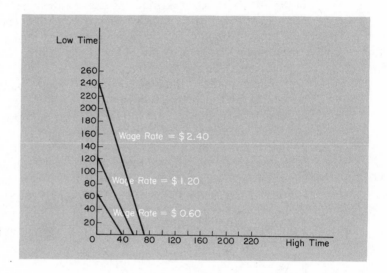

FIG. 2-8
The Budget Constraint for Low- and High-Time Goods

hours would be sold for $59. The $59 would be used to purchase 59 units of low-time goods, which would be combined with the remaining 59 minutes (approximately) in consumption of low-time commodities. Thus all hours are accounted for and the number of hours of work supplied has been established. Similarly, the maximum number of high-time commodities that could be consumed if no low-time commodities were consumed would be $60/$1.60 ≅ 38: 62 hours would be sold in the labor market for $38, and the remaining 38 hours would be spent in consuming high-time goods. Thus, determining the consumption of low-time and high-time commodities simultaneously determines labor supplied.

In Figure 2-8 we measure units of the low-time commodity on the vertical axis and units of the high-time commodity on the horizontal axis. The budget constraint intersects the vertical axis at 59, the maximum consumption of low-time commodities, and it intersects the horizontal axis at 38, the maximum consumption of high-time commodities. Since we have assumed a competitive situation, the rate of exchange between the two commodities is independent of the amount consumed. Thus the budget constraint is linear, with a slope of $59/38 \cong 1.55$, implying that the relative price of low-time commodities in terms of high-time is $1/1.55 \cong .63$.

In Table 2-1 and Figure 2-8 we see the effect of raising the wage rate to $1.20 and then to $2.40 per hour. The price of high-time commodities rises relative to low-time commodities, moving the budget constraint upward and in a clockwise direction. Note that in the analysis of sections I through IV an increase in the wage rate moved the budget constraint in a rotating fashion about a fixed point which represented maximum hours and nonlabor income. In the alternative approach of this section, the maximum possible consumption of both high-time and low-time commodities increases when the wage rate rises. However, low-time commodities become relatively cheaper *because* they require a relatively low input of time, which is becoming more expensive as the wage rate reaches higher levels.

Rising nonlabor income (*cet. par.*) would be shown by a parallel movement of the budget constraint toward the northeast. Obviously, an increase in nonlabor income will increase the consumption of both high-time and low-time consumption, if they are "normal" goods, and will thus increase hours consumed and reduce hours supplied to the labor market. An increase in the wage rate, holding utility constant, will cause a shift toward the consumption of low-time goods and thereby increase labor supply. The total effect of an increase in the wage rate includes a probably negative income effect on hours worked and a positive substitution effect, and the sign of the sum is indeterminate, just as in the first approach, where hours and goods are viewed as separate commodities.

LABOR SUPPLY OF ALL
FAMILY MEMBERS

We should discuss briefly the complications introduced by considering the response of all family members to changes in the wage rate. In the two-dimensional diagrams we have been forced to work with, we have had to ignore the effect of an increased wage rate of one family member upon the amount of labor supplied by others. In fact, these "cross effects" may be very important, especially for so-called "supplementary" earners, such as wives and children. The diagrams through Figure 2-7 probably best describe the labor supply behavior of the husband, or principal earner, or the total supply of all family members taken together.

For some family members, however, the labor supply curve may be upward sloping over a considerable range. For instance, if there is an increase in the wage rate of the wife, this increases the income of the family, probably causing the labor supplied by the family taken together to decrease (i.e., there is an income effect). However, the wife's hours are now more valuable in the market than previously, and it may pay the family, especially if it prefers to keep its children in school or not to have the husband work overtime, to reduce the labor supplied by family members other than the wife. Thus the response of the wife to an increase in her wage rate may well be to increase labor hours supplied over rather a wide range of wage rate increases while other family members may reduce their hours supplied to the labor market as a result.

LABOR SUPPLY IN THE LONG RUN

In this chapter we have considered the labor supply behavior of family members as a function of the wage rate and nonlabor income in the short run. The essential distinction between the long run and the short run from the point of view of labor supply is that we have taken as given those factors over which family members have control that in part determine the wage rates they are offered and the quantity and quality of labor hours that are available. Thus, we have ignored labor supply decisions that involve health, education, apprenticeship and on-the-job training, migration, family size, and so on. These involve long-run commitments and are made with respect to expected long-run values of wages and incomes as well as non-financial considerations. They will be touched upon in Chapter 4, where the theory of human capital is introduced.

3

evidence
bearing on the theory
of labor supply

INTRODUCTION

The short-run theory of the labor supply presented in Chapter 2 is one of the most widely tested and applied parts of the economic theory of labor markets. The discussion does not refer to decisions made about the accumulation of human capital—education, training, etc.—which is treated further on in this book; rather, the term refers to decisions made about when and how much to work, given the quality of labor. Of course, decisions about when and how much to work cannot be separated completely from decisions about the accumulation of human capital, because choosing the time of initial entry into the labor force is connected with decisions about education and training (both formal and on-the-job); similarly, the number of hours worked per day or per week may also depend on decisions about enrolling in education and training courses. Nevertheless, since it generally pays to acquire education and training early in the careers of workers, rather than later on, most decisions about hours of work, withdrawal from the labor force, and retirement are made subsequently to earlier decisions about education and training. This is not to say that such decisions are not influenced by the actual amounts of human capital accumulated; they probably are.

The principal means of investigating labor supply responses to wage and income levels is to examine the behavior of individuals or groups of individuals who differ in their wage rates and incomes. Such differences can be observed either over time or among individuals or groups at a moment of time. Both kinds of observation are subject to the problem that a major correlate of wage rate and income differences is differences in the amount of education and other forms of human capital. Thus, it is an open question whether we can legitimately claim to be testing a *short-run* theory of labor supply, the response of the amount worked to wage and income changes, when the amount of human capital per person is also variable. In some of the studies reported, attempts have been made to estimate the effects of wage rates and incomes holding education (but not explicitly other forms of human capital) constant; in others, this has not been done. Therefore, the reader should bear in mind that the estimated effects of wage rates and incomes on the amount of labor supplied must be interpreted with caution as evidence bearing on the short-run theory of labor supply responses to *permanent* wage and income levels. (The importance of measuring permanent changes in wage rates is discussed on pp. 23–24 of the appendix to Chapter 1 and p. 51 of Chapter 2.)

The theory of the supply of labor—especially as it bears on hours of work—was discussed in Chapter 2. There it was asserted that the principal problems to be dealt with are the income and substitution effects of wage changes on labor supply, the effect of nonlabor income on labor supply, and the allocation of market work among family members.

In addition, there is a time dimension to labor supply that was not discussed in Chapter 2. That is, workers can decide to supply more or less hours per day, more or less weeks per year, and more or less years during their lives. Economic theory has something to say about the division of the amount of desired work, or labor supplied to the market, among these dimensions. In his classic article "Hours of Work and Hours of Leisure,"[1] H. Gregg Lewis points out that while the simplest basic assumptions of economic theory imply nothing more than the possibility of a "backward-bending" supply curve of labor in one or all dimensions of labor supply, a slightly more complicated, but plausible, set of asumptions yields implications regarding the timing of leisure and working hours. Thus, assuming that workers do respond to rising wage and income levels by increasing their demand for leisure time, they can be expected to prefer some of the increased leisure to be in the form of "on-the-job" leisure such as coffee breaks and

---

[1] *Proceedings of the Industrial Relations Research Association*, December, 1956, pp. 196–206.

longer lunch hours, because such leisure makes work more pleasant; further-more, employers may find that up to a certain point "on-the-job" leisure improves productivity. On the other hand, certain kinds of leisure-time activities (such as weekend vacations) require continuous hours of leisure; hence workers can be expected to want some of their increased leisure to be in the form of consecutive hours, days, or weeks away from work. If we assume that tastes for leisure do not change with age, in the sense that, *cet. par.*, a uniform distribution of leisure over one's life would be preferred to other distributions, it is nevertheless reasonable to expect people to take much of their leisure in the form of years retired from the labor force during the last years of life because old age usually implies falling productivity and earning power. (This is discussed further in Section III.) Thus, the *cost* of leisure is generally less during the later years of life than during the earlier years. It is also reasonable to expect years of schooling to be bunched to-gether before entering the labor force, because (as will be clearer after the discussion of investment in human capital in Chapter 4), the value of the increased earnings due to education is generally greatest when the number of years a worker can benefit from the training received is greatest. Clearly, this implies that education has the most impact on total earnings when it occurs earlier rather than later in life, *cet. par.*

In this chapter, we treat only two of the dimensions in which the amount of time people supply to the labor market can be measured: (1) hours worked per week, particularly as the behavior of the length of the workweek is relevant to the evaluation of the income and substitution effects of changes in wage rate over time and differences among groups at a moment of time; and (2) the labor force participation rate, which is relevant to the timing of labor force participation in the life cycle and to the allocation of work and leisure among family members. Just how it is relevant is treated more thoroughly in Section III of this chapter. In Section II we discuss hours of work, treating mainly hours worked by individuals in different occupations at a moment in time and changes in hours of work over the past seventy years in the United States. The evidence available suggests that in response to rising wage rates, labor force members tend to work fewer hours per week. In Section III we discuss the determinants of the fraction of the population who are found to be in the labor force (i.e., the labor force participation rate). By focusing attention on the labor force participation rates of three of the age-sex groups whose participation has changed markedly over the years—male youth, elderly males, and married women—we gain insight into some determinants of the timing of work in the life cycle and the allocation of work and leisure among family members. The available evidence suggests that the economic theory discussed in Chapter 2 provides a useful framework for analyzing these questions.

HOURS

determinants of average weekly
hours by occupation: 1950

The Type of Data and Variables Employed and Their Relationship to the Theory of Labor Supply. One way of examining the relationship between average weekly hours and the wage rate is to look at data on individuals or some grouping thereof at a moment of time. Such a study of adult male workers was made by T. Aldrich Finegan from data in the *U.S. Census of Population: 1950* and other sources.[2] The data are for 323 Census occupations.[3]

One might raise the question, To what extent is it reasonable to suppose that mean hours worked by occupational groups represents an approximation of the equilibrium choices of hour by individuals responding to their opportunities (i.e., real wage rates), given their other economic circumstances, tastes, and attitudes? After all, is it not likely that these data merely represent weekly hours largely imposed on workers by employer preferences, technological constraints, and wage and hours legislation?

In fact, it is not at all obvious that such factors are likely to dominate worker preferences in determining average weekly hours of work. To be sure, employer preferences and technological constraints may be important in some occupations, and it would certainly be inefficient for employers to have work forces composed of personnel who at any moment of time work different numbers of hours per week at their own discretion and who change the number of hours worked at will. However, for the purpose of analyzing how the actual numbers of hours worked per week have been determined, we should think of employers as expressing their demands for labor in terms of total labor hours, not in terms of hours per week per employee (an exception is that employers are not likely to ignore the extra hiring and training costs per hour of labor when the average workweek declines; we assume, however, that such considerations are not important enough to warrant

---

[2] "Hours of Work in the United States: A Cross-Sectional Analysis," *Journal of Political Economy*, October, 1962, pp. 452–70.

[3] The following occupations were excluded from the sample: (1) apprentice occupations (since they contain mainly youths); (2) farm and housekeeping occupations (since unreported income in kind may be important in these groups); (3) occupations with less than 5,000 male wage-and-salary workers for whom hours worked during the Census week were reported (presumably because these data were thought to be unreliable due to the small sample—only $3\frac{1}{3}$ per cent of the Census returns were sampled); (4) occupations in which the median number of school years completed by male workers was 16 years or more; and (5) occupations in which the median age of wage-and-salary workers was less than 26 years. *Ibid.*, p. 458, fn. 21 and p. 460, fn. 23.

dropping the assumption that the demand of employers for hours per week per employee is infinitely elastic). Theoretically, it is possible that employer preferences and technological considerations dominate the behavior of average weekly hours. However, if such dominance were to determine the overall relationship between weekly hours and hourly wage rates, then the number of workers in occupations whose hours are determined by employers' preference or technological requirements (or legal restrictions) would have to be large relative to the number of workers with access to the same jobs who would have preferred such hours of work in any event. That is to say, it is not at all obvious that because we can think of occupations where there is little opportunity to adjust employees' weekly hours of work that the workers found in such occupations have therefore been *coerced* into working the number of hours required. Presumably they were not forced into accepting jobs in such occupations and they had knowledge of the length of the work-week before doing so. Thus it would seem that employers would find it easier to hire workers who prefer the required length of the workweek than workers who object to it.

Even if there were an important number of cases where workers do not achieve their desired number of weekly hours of work, it would not auto-matically follow that the overall relationship between hourly wage rates and weekly hours of work does not reflect worker preferences. We must realize that in dealing with data of economic behavior, we seek to measure *average* relationships, knowing full well that individual observations will often deviate from the average. The question thus becomes whether or not failure to consider employer preferences and technological considerations will lead us to infer an incorrect average relationship between wage rates and workers' desired weekly hours of work. That is, will our measured relation-ship be a biased estimate of a supply curve? In the language of the appendix to Chapter 1, for the most part we are forced by lack of information to *omit* from our investigation information pertaining to technological or other constraints on weekly hours. Whether this *omitted variable* is correlated with our principal independent variable—hourly wage rates—is crucial in deter-mining whether or not the estimated relationship between weekly hours of work and wage rates is a biased estimate of a supply curve. In the absence of information to the contrary, we assume that the omitted information is not correlated with wage rates and that we therefore do not obtain a biased estimate of the supply of hours per week on that account.

What about the effects of unions on hours? Are such effects likely to bias the inferences we draw from the occupational data? Relatively little is known about the combined effects of the distribution of union membership and the effects of unionism on relative wage rates among occupations. However, what knowledge we have suggests that there has been little or no effect of unionism on the occupational wage dispersion. (Some evidence on this is presented in Chapter 13.) Thus, even though it is likely that unions often raise the relative wage rates of union members and have a negative effect on average hours, it is unlikely that these forces induce a bias in the observed relationship between wage rates and average hours worked by occupational groups. We conclude this because there is no evidence that the effect of unions on wage rates is significantly correlated with wage rate levels among occupations, and the effects of unions on hours are probably randomly distributed among the occupational groups.

At this point, before going on to examine some of the results of Finegan's study, it should prove worthwhile to review the discussion in the appendix to Chapter 1 of the use of regression analysis in applying economic theory to real world data. There we pointed out that in formulating a theory in such a way as to make it usable in empirical investigation, it is necessary to postulate that independent variables whose effects on the behavior being studied are *not* (for lack of information) estimated simultaneously with the effects of the included independent variables are not significantly correlated with them. If they are correlated, then the effects attributed to the included variables may be properly attributable—at least in part—to the excluded variables. The estimated effects of the included variables would be *biased* if the excluded independent variables were not random and if they truly influenced the dependent variables. In the preceding paragraphs, we have essentially been arguing that excluded variables such as employers' preferences, technological factors influencing hours, the effects of unions, and implicitly, nonpecuniary benefits of particular occupation, as well as such factors as nonlabor income and workers' attitudes toward work (other than as they are influenced by wage rates), are either unimportant determinants of hours worked or are uncorrelated with the included independent variables.[4] Thus, we are subject to the possible error that our maintained hypotheses about the omitted variables are false. If the empirical results fail to confirm our expectations (that hours are negatively related to the wage rate), we cannot know for sure whether it is because the *true* relationship is nonnegative or because our maintained hypotheses are false. The same is true if the results confirm our expectations. Thus there is always

---

[4] One of the most important excluded variables is nonlabor income, and it is in fact unlikely to be uncorrelated with variables that are included in Finegan's study, such as education and wage rates. However, to the extent education is correlated with nonlabor income, it *may* act as a proxy for the excluded variable, and the estimated effect of wage rates *may* therefore be relatively unbiased. However, this is a highly speculative statement, and further information would be required before one could reasonably assert that education acts as an effective proxy variable for nonlabor income, thus helping to assure an unbiased estimate of the effect of wage rates. One thing one would wish to know, for instance, is whether nonlabor income is more highly correlated with education or with wage rates. For education to act as a proxy for nonlabor income, it should be more highly correlated with the excluded variable than is the wage rate variable.

reason to want to confirm one's belief that the results of an investigation are reliable by checking the validity of the maintained hypotheses. For instance, further investigation of the degree to which technological and other forces hinder the adjustment of weekly hours of work is clearly called for.

Some Results of Finegan's Study. The results of part of Finegan's study are shown in Table 3-1. The regression coefficients " · · · indicate that in 1950 a work week shorter by one hour was associated · · · with (1) higher hourly earnings of about $0.12, (2) a lower marriage ratio of about six percentage points, (3) less schooling of about one year, (4) about fifteen fewer years of age, (5) a higher Negro-employment ratio of about eighteen percentage points, and (6) a higher female-employment ratio of about forty-three percentage points."[5]

The estimated negative net relationship between hours and earnings is consistent with the results of many other studies. In fact, the consistency is remarkable; the elasticity of the supply of hours, at mean hours and

Table 3-1

RESULTS OF MULTIPLE REGRESSION OF AVERAGE WEEKLY HOURS[1] ON HOURLY EARNINGS AND OTHER VARIABLES, 1950

E[1]	M[1]	S[1]	A[1]	N[1]	F[1]
−.085	+.173	+1.041	+.066	−.056	−.023
(.0056)	(.023)	(.10)	(.034)	(.020)	(.0081)

(1) Definitions of Variables: H (dependent variable) = mean hours worked by male wage-and-salary workers during Census Week, 1950 (in hours); E = Median hourly wage-and-salary income in 1949 of male wage-and-salary workers in experienced civilian labor force during Census Week, 1950 (in cents); M = fraction of male workers married with wife present (in percentage points); S = median number of years of school completed by male workers (in years); A = median age of male wage-and-salary workers (in years); N = ratio of employed Negro males to all employed males (in percentage points); F = ratio of female workers to all workers (in percentage points). F was included to help hold constant any tendency of female workers to be employed in occupations where average weekly hours tend to be low because of female preferences; insofar as it would be difficult to employ female and male employees doing similar or complementary work for different lengths of time per week, such occupations would likely attract males who, *cet. par.*, prefer relatively low weekly hours.

Figures in first row are regression coefficients; constant term = 29.8 hours per week; $R^2 = .54$.

Figures in parentheses (second row) are standard errors.

Source: T. Aldrich Finegan, "Hours of Work in the United States: A Cross-Sectional Analysis," *Journal of Political Economy,* October, 1962, pp. 452–70.

---

[5] Finegan, *op. cit.,* p. 460. Readers who are puzzled by Finegan's inclusion of such variables as (2) through (6) are encouraged to think about how these variables may reflect the influences of forces other than wage rates which affect hours of work. Their inclusion is an attempt to achieve a relatively unbiased estimate of the effect of wage rates on hours of work as well as simultaneously to obtain an idea of the influences of the forces the variables are thought to represent. These forces are discussed briefly on pp. 454–55.

earnings, based on the results shown in Table 3-1, is —.31 (i.e., a 1 per cent rise in wage rates causes a .31 per cent decline in average weekly hours).[6] This is very close to the elasticity of the relationship between the full-time workweek in the United States during the period 1890 to 1950 estimated in a well-known study by Clarence Long (see column 4, Table 3-3).[7]

The estimated effects of some of the other variables also have interesting interpretations. (1) The coefficient of the marriage rate suggests that married men work longer hours on the average than nonmarried men. This is consistent with the result of other studies.[8] It suggests the hypothesis that the desire to attain a relatively high standard of living as measured by total purchasing power over goods and services is stronger among married men than among others. (2) The level of schooling is also generally positively associated with average hours and other measures of labor supply. The association suggests the hypothesis that highly educated people have access to more pleasant jobs than others; consequently, differences in money wage rates between persons of low and high education understate the differences in real wage rates, when nonpecuniary aspects of jobs are taken into consideration. Since the nonpecuniary aspects of a job cannot be "spent" outside the place of work, they tend to increase hours worked for the highly educated. Such nonpecuniary factors of jobs would probably include more interesting kinds of work, more pleasant working surroundings, possibly more contact with desirable working companions, and so on. Another possible explanation of the positive association between educational level and hours of work is that differences among people in basic attitudes toward market work and/or market goods induce higher educational attainment *and* more hours worked. At this stage we are not in a position to decide which of the two omitted variables—nonpecuniary benefits of jobs or attitudes—is

---

[6] In linear relationships such as those discussed here, the elasticity is not constant over the range of possible values of the variables since the elasticity is the product of the slope of the regression line $\left(\frac{dy}{dx}\right)$ and the reciprocal ratio of values of the dependent and independent variable $\left(\frac{x}{y}\right)$. For simplicity, we usually summarize the elasticity in such relationships by presenting its value calculated at the means of the dependent and independent variables. (Recall that *by definition* the regression line passes through the mean values of the dependent and independent variables.) Thus the elasticities described above are $\frac{dy}{dx}\frac{\bar{x}}{\bar{y}}$ where the bars denote mean values.

[7] *The Labor Force Under Changing Income and Employment*, National Bureau of Economic Research (Princeton, N.J.: Princeton University Press, 1958), p. 272. This study is referred to by Finegan, *op. cit.*, p. 460.

[8] For instance, William G. Bowen and T. A. Finegan, "Labor Force Participation and Unemployment," in Arthur M. Ross, ed., *Employment Policy and the Labor Market* (Berkeley and Los Angeles. University of California Press, 1965), pp. 115–61.

reflected by education.[9] (3) This and other studies show that Negroes work fewer hours than others,[10] even after other factors influencing hours of work are held constant. Finegan hypothesizes that an important reason for this is that since Negroes are discriminated against in many markets where money is spent on goods and services, there is less tendency for Negroes than for others to give up leisure hours in return for purchasing power over market goods. In a sense, discrimination against Negroes when they spend money for housing, restaurant services, travel, etc., acts as a tax on wages which reduces, at the margin, the attractiveness of trading leisure hours for market goods.

The results of Finegan's study are consistent with the idea that when wage rates increase, a positive income effect on the consumption of hours dominates a negative substitution effect—leading to a reduction in hours worked per week. However, as is often the case, additional questions are raised in the attempt to isolate the influence of wage rates on hours of work from the influence of other variables. Thus, in an attempt to hold constant the influences of forces other than wage rates which are thought to affect weekly hours worked, variables not often dealt with explicitly in the economic theory pertaining to hours of work have been incorporated in the analysis of the data. These variables include marital status, educational attainment, age, race, and the sex-mix of employment. While each of these additional variables has a plausible relationship to hours of work and may indeed influence hours in a manner related to the hypotheses suggested in the preceding paragraph, we are not on firm ground if we believe that the hypotheses that are suggested by our observations have also been confirmed by them. On the other hand, consistency of the apparent effects of variables such as race, education, age, and marital status in the Finegan study reported here with the effects of these variables reported in related studies does increase our confidence that these variables do represent underlying forces influencing hours of work. Furthermore, the similarity between the estimated influence of wage rates on hours of work in the Finegan study and evidence based on changes in wage rates and hours over time (discussed in more detail in the next section) also lends support to our belief that we have been able to observe a real world counterpart to the theoretical relationship between wage rates and hours of work.

---

[9] In section I it was pointed out that the *exclusion* of human capital variables from studies of the relationship between labor supply and wage rates might lead to biased estimates of the short-run response of labor supply to permanent wage rate changes. The estimated effect of education—an important component of human capital—in Table 3-1 suggests that the bias may be toward zero. This is because wage rates and education are positively correlated and their estimated effects on hours of work are opposite in sign.

[10] For instance, see the data described in Figure 3-1 and Table 3-2 of this chapter.

average hours by rate of pay: U.S. male wage and salary workers in 1965

In June, 1965, a representative sample of 5,000 males, aged 45–49, was made the subject of an intensive investigation of labor force behavior. Questionnaires were administered by the U.S. Census Bureau to be used in research conducted by a group at Ohio State University. Using the information contained in the questionnaire, one can relate hours worked during the week prior to the survey to the hourly rate of pay of the respondents. These data are shown separately for white and nonwhite respondents in Table 3-2

Table 3-2

AVERAGE WEEKLY HOURS OF U.S. MALES AGED 45–59, 1965

Whites		Nonwhites	
Rate of Pay	Hours Worked Last Week	Rate of Pay	Hours Worked Last Week
Under $1.25	51.9	Under $1.25	49.8
1.25–1.49	46.9	1.25–1.49	45.2
1.50–1.99	48.2	1.50–1.99	47.2
2.00–2.49	45.6	2.00–2.49	45.3
2.50–2.99	44.8	2.50–2.99	44.4
3.00–3.49	44.1	3.00–3.49	43.9
3.50–3.99	44.1	3.50–3.99	44.0
4.00–4.99	43.0	4.00–4.99	42.9
5.00–5.99	40.3	5.00–5.99	40.2
6.00 and over	42.2	6.00 and over	42.0

and Figure 3-1. The relationship is remarkably close, in that the observations representing average hours worked for respondents in various wage rate classes lie very close to least-squares regression lines fitted to the data; thus the estimated coefficients are statistically significant by generally accepted criteria.

The regression result for whites is

$$Y = 49.8 - 1.6X$$

where Y represents weekly hours of work and X the hourly rate of pay in dollars. (The regression was performed on the data as shown in Table 3-2, using the means of the rate of pay and omitting the two extreme wage categories.) For nonwhites, the regression result is

$$Y = 48.3 - 1.3X$$

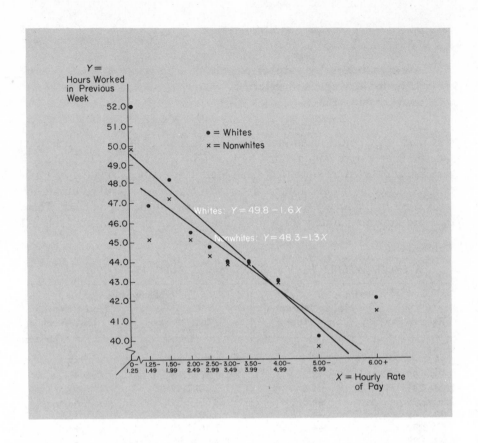

FIG. 3-I
Weekly Hours and Hourly Rate of Pay

The regression coefficients imply that a reduction of one hour in the work-week is associated with an increase in the rate of pay of $.63 for whites and of $.77 for nonwhites. These imply elasticities of hours worked with respect to the hourly wage rate of $-.11$ for whites and $-.09$ for nonwhites. These elasticity estimates are substantially smaller than those obtained by Finegan in his research cited earlier in this section. The reasons may lie in the use of only one independent variable in the example cited in this paragraph and possibly in the use of the age group 45–59, rather than the wide spectrum of ages represented in Finegan's sample. (Recall that the likely bias induced by excluding education from the regression is toward zero.) Nevertheless, the crude results of the Ohio State investigation bear out the already well-established relationship between average hours and wage rates found in other studies. In the Ohio State sample, nonwhites in every wage rate class averaged fewer hours per week than whites; this is consistent with Finegan's findings. Note that the regression line fit to the data for nonwhites does rise above that for whites at high wage rates, even though the average hours worked by nonwhites at high wage rates remain below those of whites. This may be due to the effects of approximating a nonlinear relationship with an estimated linear relationship.

average weekly hours for the economy and in selected industries: 1900–65

Perhaps the most dramatic change to have taken place in labor supply during this century has been the decline in average weekly hours worked. The response of workers to rising wage rates and income levels has taken the form of a decline in the length of the average workday and in the number of days worked per week. Table 3-3 shows average weekly hours in three important and representative industries—manufacturing, building trades, and retail trade.[11] It also shows the economy-wide figures gathered by Clarence D. Long for the years 1890–1950. The hours figure presented by Long and reported in Column (4) of Table 3-3 implies an average per decade reduction in the workweek of 4.2 hours or at the average geometric rate of slightly less than 8 per cent per decade.

Because the industry series are not comparable over the entire period covered—1890–1960—we are forced to examine the decline in hours in columns (1), (2) and (3) during subperiods. Between 1890 and 1920, average weekly hours in manufacturing declined by 8.7, or 14.0 per cent overall; in the building trades by 7.5 per week, or 14.6 per cent. Both of these figures are considerably less than the overall average decline reported by Long—13 hours. One of the reasons for this discrepancy is probably that there was a movement of workers out of high-hours industries into low-hours industries, which would make the overall average number of weekly hours worked decline more than the average, holding industry mix constant.[12]

Between 1920 and 1940, average weekly hours in manufacturing fell by 9.3, or 19.6 per cent, and Long's overall average figure by 10 hours, or 19 per cent. However, this almost certainly overstates the supply response of rising wage and incomes, because in 1940 the effects of high unemployment of the Great Depression were still influencing average hours; thus the 1940 figure is no doubt cyclically low. Furthermore, the late 1930's and early 1940's was a period of unprecedented growth of union strength in manufacturing. Such growth probably accelerated the decline in average hours

---

[11] In 1960, these industries accounted for the following proportions of production workers in nonagricultural industries of the United States: manufacturing, 31 per cent; building trades as represented by contract construction, 5.3 per cent; retail trade, 15.5 per cent. *Statistical Abstract of the United States*, 1967, pp. 227–28.

[12] Long, *op. cit.* p. 271.

Table 3-3

AVERAGE WEEKLY HOURS IN MANUFACTURING AND SELECTED NON-MANUFACTURING INDUSTRIES, 1890–1965

	(1) Manufacturing		(2) Building Trades and Building Construction			(3) Retail Trade		(4) Hours in Standard Workweek
	a	b	a	b	c	a	b	
1890	62.2		51.3					66
1895	62.3		50.3					
1896	62.1							
1897	61.9							
1898	62.2							
1899	62.1							
1900	62.1		48.3					62
1905	61.1		46.1					
1910	59.8		45.2					57
1915	58.2		44.8					
1920	53.5	47.4	43.8					53
1925	52.2	44.5	43.9					
1930		42.1						52
1935		36.6		30.1		41.8		
1940		38.1		33.1		42.5		43
1945		43.4		39.0		40.3		
1946		40.4		38.1		40.7		
1950		40.5		36.3		40.5		41
1955		40.7		36.2		39.0		
1959		40.3		35.8		38.1		
1960		39.7			35.4		38.5	
1961		39.8						
1962		40.4						
1963		40.4						
1964		40.7						
1965		41.2			36.1		36.6	

Source: *Historical Statistics of the United States, Colonial Times to 1957 and Continuation to 1962.* 1961–65 data are from U.S. Department of Labor, "Employment and Earnings for States and Areas," BLS Bulletin No. 1370-4, pp. LXII, LXIII, and various issues of the *Monthly Labor Review*, Table C-1.

Col. (1a) Series D 593 (data from employer payrolls).
(1b) Series D 627 (production workers). This series has a downward bias induced by oversampling of large firms.

through 1945 or 1946. The principal means through which union growth accelerated the trend toward shorter hours was by increasing wages in manufacturing relative to other industries; this probably caused desired hours to decline more rapidly than they would have otherwise and possibly necessitated some rationing of hours among union members. (This point is treated in Chapter 11; see especially Figure 11-1.)

Still another factor which is apt to have influenced the course of average weekly hours in the late 1930's was the Fair Labor Standards Act[13] (federal wage and hours legislation), which went into effect in 1938. This act requires the payment of overtime premiums for work in excess of 40 hours per week in covered industries. (Manufacturing was one of the industries most severely affected by the legislation. Retail trade was not covered until much later.) To the extent that this raised the price of overtime hours to employers above preexisting levels, the legislation probably induced a decline in the demand by employers for hours per worker in excess of 40 per week.

Between 1945 and 1959, average weekly hours in building construction fell by 3.2 per week, or 8.2 per cent; in retail trade, by 2.2, or 5.5 per cent; and in manufacturing by 3.1, or 7.1 per cent. In manufacturing, however, almost all of the decline (3.0 hours) took place between 1945 and 1946. Thus, if we consider 1946 to be the first year after the war, it would appear that the decline in weekly hours of work in manufacturing was far less than in either building construction or retail trade during the fifteen years or so after World War II. It is evident that the high number of weekly hours worked in manufacturing in 1945 reflected the abnormally long workweek during World War II, which was due to the extremely tight labor market that existed during the period. (The overall unemployment rate averaged under 2 per cent of the labor force in 1945; the workweek in building construction and in retail trade never rose as high as it did in manufacturing during the war.)[14]

One suspects that in 1945 the influence of the Fair Labor Standards Act and possibly the influence of union wage gains were still exerting a great deal

---

[13] FLSA was not the first effective legislation aimed at controlling hours of work. Various states passed laws governing hours of work, especially for women and children, and some of these laws were in effect in the 1930's.

[14] See the sources noted in Table 3-3.

(2a) Series D 598 (union hours).
(2b) Series D 670 (building construction), (production workers).
(2c) Contract Construction (general building construction).
(3a) Series D 676 (production workers).
(3b) This series, from the *Monthly Labor Review*, is apparently not strictly comparable with that in Column (3a) (production workers).
(4)   Clarence D. Long, *The Labor Force Under Changing Income and Employment*, National Bureau of Economic Research (Princeton, N.J.: Princeton University Press, 1958), p. 272.

of pressure on manufacturing employers to keep average weekly hours per worker from exceeding the number (generally 40) over which overtime premiums had to be paid. Thus, as soon as labor market conditions eased, employers in manufacturing reduced their employees' weekly hours to 40 or less whenever possible.

The explanation of why average weekly hours in manufacturing tended to fall less rapidly than in building construction or in retail trade during the postwar period and less rapidly than in manufacturing during the period 1920–40 is probably consistent with the explanation (unionism and maximum hours legislation) of the quite rapid decline of weekly hours in manufacturing during 1920–40. After World War II, the growth of union strength in manufacturing leveled off relative to the two other representative industries we have been examining;[15] this diminished the growth of a force tending to accelerate the decline in hours of work in manufacturing relative to the other industries. Furthermore, while the Fair Labor Standards Act had probably accelerated the decline of hours worked in manufacturing by reducing employers' *demands* for "overtime" hours, this effect was only gradually absorbed by the continuing reduction of hours *supplied* as wage rates and incomes rose during the war and after.[16] Thus, continuing reductions of weekly hours supplied in manufacturing would not have been reflected in postwar data of actual hours worked until the number of weekly hours workers desired to put in matched, on the average, the number of weekly hours employers wanted to hire. It is extremely difficult to say whether weekly hours worked in manufacturing have reflected a downward trend in weekly hours supplied at any time since World War II. At no time since the abrupt decline in weekly hours between 1945 and 1946 has there been a marked tendency for hours worked to decline. Between 1960 and 1965, average weekly hours worked actually rose; this probably reflects the increasingly tight labor market of the first half of the 1960's that was caused by the growing severity of the conflict in Viet Nam, among other things. (See Table 15-3.) Thus, it is difficult to conclude, on the basis of the evidence in manufacturing industries, whether the long-run tendency toward a decline in the number of weekly hours employees desire to work has continued during the postwar period.

---

[15] While unionization of construction workers was nearly as high just before World War II as in 1953 and 1960 (about 48 per cent of the production workers were union members in 1939), the percentage of production workers in manufacturing who were union members more than doubled (from about 23 per cent to about 52 per cent) during the same period, with much of the growth taking place before 1953. Unionism probably contributed little to the decline in weekly hours worked in retail trade, since even during the period after the war until 1960, unionism probably amounted to only about 10 per cent of production workers in the industry. H. G. Lewis, *Unionism and Relative Wage Rates in the United States* (Chicago: University of Chicago Press, 1962), p. 250.

[16] On this point see H. Gregg Lewis, "Hours of Work and Hours of Leisure," *Proceedings of the Industrial Relations Research Association*, December, 1956.

In building construction, the downward tendency in average weekly hours that reappeared after the end of World War II was also arrested by the upswing in economic activity of the early 1960's. However, the length of the average workweek in retail trade continued to decline. Unfortunately, however, we cannot infer a great deal regarding overall tendencies of the supply of weekly hours from the behavior of retail trade in the first half of the 1960's, since the Fair Labor Standards Act was extended to retail trade for the first time during this period, and this undoubtedly had a negative impact on the length of the workweek.[17]

An interesting question to ask is, To what extent do the differences in the reductions of the average workweek in manufacturing, building construction, and retail trade since the war correspond to differences in increases in average wage rates in these industries? Would we not expect to observe, over a period as long as fifteen or twenty years, the average workweek declining most where wage rates have increased the most, if we are correct in assigning the major cause of the length of the workweek to workers' supply decisions? As the data of Table 3-4 show, no matter whether we take as our base year 1945 (when the effects of wartime wage controls still influenced the wage figures) or 1947, and whether we examine the change in wage rates through 1959 or through 1965, wage rates increased more rapidly in building construction than in either manufacturing or retail trade (the latter two industries having experienced roughly equal wage rate growth—particularly if the growth is measured from 1947 rather than 1945). Thus, if we confine ourselves to the period after 1945 and prior to 1960 or so, after which we have the confounding influences of the extension of the Fair Labor Standards Act to retail trade and the influence of hours worked of the Viet Nam situation, the relationship between the reductions of the workweek and the growth of wage rates in the three industries appears to be not grossly inconsistent with the hypothesis that we have observed a supply response of hours of work. That is, the length of the workweek declined most in building construction, where the average wage rate rose the most.

Thus, over the period 1890–1965, the average workweek declined substantially, but evidently not steadily, and there were periods during which it increased. The decline in the average workweek consisted of a mixture of a reduction in hours worked in individual industries and a shift in the industrial composition of the labor force toward industries in which the workweek has traditionally been lower than in the rest of the economy—the declining importance of agricultural employment being the most noteworthy example. The explanation of the decline in weekly hours of work as a supply response

---

[17] On this issue, see William J. Shkurti and Belton M. Fleisher, "Employment and Wage Rates in Retail Trade Subsequent to the 1961 Amendments of the Fair Labor Standards Act," *Southern Economic Journal*, July, 1968.

Table 3-4

AVERAGE HOURLY EARNINGS FOR PRODUCTION WORKERS, 1945–1965

	(1) Manufacturing	(2) Building Construction	(3) Retail Trade
1945	$1.02	$1.38	$.78
1947	1.24	1.68	1.01
1959	2.22	3.22	1.76
1960	2.29	2.93*	1.62
1965	2.61	3.55*	1.82
1959 ÷ 1945	2.18	2.33	2.26
1959 ÷ 1947	1.79	1.92	1.74
1965 ÷ 1960	1.14	1.21	1.12

* These figures are not from the same source for the years 1960 and 1965 as for years prior to 1960 and are not strictly comparable between the two periods.

Source: Historical Statistics of the United States, Colonial Times to 1957 and Continuation to 1962. 1965 figures for manufacturing, and 1960 and 1965 figures for building construction and retail trade, are from various issues of the *Monthly Labor Review*, Table C-1.

Col. (1) Series D 626

Col. (2) Series D 669

Col. (3) Series D 675

to rising wage and income levels possesses intuitive appeal for many economists; those who would ascribe the major role to unionism and to federal legislation can probably find evidence that these were forces reducing hours, at least in manufacturing, during the late 1930's and the 1940's. However, during the period prior to the 1930's weekly hours declined, and although legislative and union pressures were not absent, they could not have been powerful influences, judging by the number of workers that could have been directly affected. Furthermore, even during the period subsequent to the late 1930's, hours of work declined in areas of the economy (e.g., retail trade) which have been little affected by unionism and to which federal maximum hours regulations did not apply (e.g., retail trade before 1961).

It is unfortunate that we cannot obtain sufficient information to duplicate the type of study conducted by Finegan with time series data. However, the consistency between the estimated relationship of wage rates and average weekly hours in Finegan's cross-sectional study, on the one hand, and the simple relationship over time between these variables implied by Long's study (Long's data on hours are reported in column 4 of Table 3-3), on the other, suggest that there is something more than a mere chance occurrence in the relationships we have observed between wage rates and hours of work. A similar relationship appears also in the Ohio State study discussed briefly in this section. The data we have examined on hours of work and wage rates appear to be consistent with the theory of labor supply presented in Chapter 2, in which the additional assumption is made that hours of leisure are a "normal" good and the income effect outweighs the substitution effect, thus inducing a backward-bending supply curve of labor. In the next section we explore the question whether evidence on another dimension of labor supply—labor force participation—also displays this relationship.

LABOR FORCE PARTICIPATION[18]

The concept of labor force participation deals with labor supply in a categorical sense; that is, in discussing labor force participation we treat the question of whether an individual offers any hours at all to the labor market. By official definition, any individual who responds to questions such as those discussed in the appendix to Chapter 1 (see pp. 14–15), indicating that he was employed or unemployed during the survey week, is considered to participate in the labor force, whether he worked one hour or sixty hours, whether he was unemployed or employed. The proportion of a group who participate in the labor force at any moment of time is the labor force participation *rate*.

In this section we are going to discuss the labor force participation rates of parts of the population which have exhibited very interesting behavior over the past few decades, because their labor force participation has changed so remarkably. These groups are men aged 65 and over, men aged 14–19, and married women living with their husbands. As we pointed out in the introduction to this chapter, one of the interesting aspects of labor supply is likely to be the clustering of years in the labor force in the life cycle. As a rule, we do not expect years in the labor force to be uniformly distributed over the typical individual's life, but rather to reflect the opportunity costs of leisure time (recall that by leisure we refer to any time not sold to the market, regardless of whether an individual uses that time for recreation, work in the home, to improve his future earning power, or whatever), which are especially high during the early years when most young people attend school, and reflect productivity in the market, which tends to decline as people grow older. By the second observation, that we should expect the clustering of time spent in the labor market to be related to the behavior of productivity in the market

---

[18] I am indebted to Aba Schwartz for helpful comments on this section.

over the life of a typical individual, we make use of the fact that as people grow older, their health typically deteriorates and all or part of the education and training they have acquired in earlier years tends to become obsolete. Thus, earning power tends to level off and even decline in the later years; furthermore, deteriorating health probably makes work less pleasant on the average. Even individuals whose earning power in money terms does not actually decline as they grow older probably experience increasing difficulty in obtaining the job assignments they wish, find themselves with less influence in their places of work, and so on. Such occurrences would make work less pleasant. Consequently, it tends to be relatively cheaper to take leisure during the later years of life than at other times. Before the reader objects violently that clearly the main reason people don't "retire" until they are relatively old is that they can't afford to do so earlier, let him consider that family arrangements whereby the old work and the young-to-middle aged members enjoy leisure activities are conceptually possible and that, as we shall show further on, the (negative) *effect* of income on labor force participation appears to be unusually large for older men. Another interesting aspect of labor supply is how families' offers of labor hours are distributed among the family members. It is the timing of work in the life cycle and its allocation among family members that we focus on in treating the labor force participation rates of older and younger men and of married women.

In analyzing the labor force participation of *individuals*, we clearly cannot make use of a continuous scale of measurement in an ordinary sense, since any individual can only be either in the labor force or out of the labor force. However, we can conceive of the *probability* that any individual will be a member of the labor force at a particular moment of time. To help grasp the idea of what is implied by such a probability concept, imagine being able to select an individual at random from the population and to place him in a given set of circumstances (i.e., same family type, wage rate, income, etc.) a large number (e.g., 100) of times. Since we realize that the economic behavior of individuals is inexact in the sense that many variables besides those we are able to specify on the basis of economic theory and the hypotheses derived therefrom impinge on such behavior, we should expect that, even specifying and holding constant a set of circumstances thought to affect the labor force participation of this individual, other variables which we do not specify and thus which may vary from observation to observation will also affect whether or not he is in the labor force at any particular time. Thus, some of the times we observe this individual, he will be in the labor force and other times he will not. The fraction of the times he is in the labor force in the conceptual experiment specified above is the *probability* that he will be in the labor force any of the times we observe him. Of course, we cannot perform the experiment described here, but an approximation of such an experiment is to observe a group of individuals whose circumstances in respect of those conditions which are thought to affect labor force participation are roughly the same (and whose behavior patterns in respect to nonspecified conditions are mutually independent). Thus, each *individual* in the group is a counterpart of each one of the large number of *times* we conceptually observe the *same* individual in the experiment described above, and the labor force participation *rate* of a group is thus analogous to the *probability* that an individual member of the group can be expected to participate in the labor force at any moment of time. If, then, we wish to discover how the probability of labor force participation varies with respect to variables hypothetically thought to affect this aspect of labor supply, we may do so by measuring the values of such variables among groups of people for which the values differ and relate these values to the respective labor force participation rates. Thus, questions about the changing sex composition of the labor force can be thought of in the context of the changing *probability* that women in given circumstances (e.g., married, living with their husbands) will participate in the labor force or in terms of the changing *labor force participation rate* of such women. Similarly, we can treat the changing age composition of the labor force as a question pertaining to changes in the clustering of working time in the life cycle and the corresponding changes in the probabilities that persons of given ages will participate in the labor force.

To emphasize and clarify the preceding discussion, consider that for a group of similar individuals, the labor force participation rate reflects the fraction of a typical individual's time he can be expected to be a labor force member. Since practically any data we have available defines labor force participation with respect to a *survey week*, we are clearly speaking here of the *fraction of weeks* in a person's life during which he will be in the labor force. Thus, when we say something like, "The labor force participation rate of men aged 65 and over has declined from 50 per cent to 30 per cent," we are saying something equivalent to, "A man aged 65 or over, selected at random, will spend a fraction of his weeks in the labor force that is 20 percentage points fewer than it used to be." Clearly, not all men aged 65 years or over are the same, particularly with respect to health, which is especially important in determining labor force participation in this age group, or with respect to retirement income, which is also very important. Thus, we would attempt to explain the change imagined in the labor force participation of men aged 65 and over as having resulted from changes in these variables, among others. When we had done so, we would no doubt find that men taking on certain values of these explanatory variables (e.g., good health and low retirement income) would be in the labor force a high fraction of weeks (perhaps all of them), while others would not be in the labor force at all. Nevertheless, even for given values of the variables, we would observe some variation in labor force participation; by dividing the men aged 65 years of age or over into groups according to the values of the variables we found to affect their labor force participation, however, we would then be able to relate more closely the *labor force participation rate* to the fraction of weeks a man selected at random from any of the groups would in fact be a labor force member.

The decennial censuses of the United States population provide information about the number of people in the labor force as far back as 1890. While the precise definition of a member of the labor force has changed over the years, the series shown in Table 3-5 yield reasonably reliable information

Table 3-5

LABOR FORCE PARTICIPATION RATES, 1890–1960 (Per Cent)

Year	Total Labor Force (Age 14 and Over)	Males 14–19	Males 65 and Over	Women Married, Spouse Present
1890 (June)	52.	50.	68.	04.5
1900 (June)	54.	62.	63.	—
1920 (Jan.)	54.	52.	56.	—
1930 (April)	53.	40.	54.	—
1940 (April)	53.	35.	42.	15.
1950 (April)	54.	40.	41.	22.
1960 (April)	55.	38.	31.	31.

Sources: 1890–1950: *Historical Statistics of the United States, Colonial Times to 1957 and Continuation to 1962*, Series D3, D14, D19, and D34.

1960: *U.S. Census of Population: 1960, Detailed Characteristics: United States Summary*, DP(1)-1D, p. 501.

about major trends in labor force participation over the last seventy years or so.

The apparently stable portion of the population which participates in the labor force masks dramatic changes that have taken place in labor force composition. Columns (2), (3), and (4) of Table 3-5 show the labor force participation rates for those segments of the population whose labor force attachment has changed the most over the years. The changes are: (1) a moderately large (about 25 per cent) decline in the participation rate of male youth in the labor force; (2) a substantial decline (over 50 per cent) in the participation rate of elderly men in the labor force; and (3) an increase of over 500 per cent in the labor force participation rate of married women living with their husbands. These changes imply a more equal sharing of market work among family members; in fact, the proportion of each of these "fringe" groups in the labor force in 1960 was nearly the same, the changes that have taken place since 1890 having brought the rates closer and closer together over the years.

In the next few pages, we explore a few of the historical changes in labor force participation in some detail. The most satisfactory explanation of changing labor force participation has been developed for married women living with their husbands, and we shall examine this explanation rather closely. First, however, we shall outline some of the factors which have probably been important causes of the declining participation rates of male youth and of males aged 65 and over.

males aged 14–19

One of the principal uses of the time of male (and female) youth, alternative to labor force participation, has been school attendance. Between

Table 3-6

SCHOOL ENROLLMENT BY AGE, 1910–1960
(PER CENT OF POPULATION IN EACH
AGE GROUP ENROLLED IN SCHOOL)

	Age 14–17	Age 18–19
1910	58.9	18.7
1920	61.6	17.8
1930	73.1	25.4
1940	79.3	28.9
1950	83.7	32.3
1960	87.5	41.7

Sources: 1910–50: *Historical Statistics of the United States, Colonial Times to 1957 and Continuation to 1962*, p. 214.

1960: *Statistical Abstract of the United States, 1965*, p. 109 (simple averages of fractions enrolled by single years of age).

1920 and 1960, labor force participation of males aged 14–19 fell by 14 percentage points, while school attendance rose by 26 percentage points for 14–17-year-olds and by 24 percentage points for 18–19-year-olds. (The school attendance figures are for males and females combined, but such information as is available for school attendance by sex strongly suggests that over the past seventy years or so, the proportions of male and female youth 18 years of age and under attending school have been nearly equal. See Table 3-6 for the school enrollment figures.)

It is, of course, impossible to infer from the simple relationship between rising school attendance and declining labor force participation that the former has caused the latter, or vice versa. (Furthermore, the data presented provide no separate information about the behavior of *part-time* workers who attend school.) However, some of the considerations discussed in subsequent chapters suggest the causation runs mainly from increased school attendance to declining labor force participation (see Chapter 4 and Chapter 13). As economic growth takes place, rising incomes facilitate greater investment in human capital, a crucial component of which is school attendance. Further adding to incentives to increase school attendance is a tendency for the rate of return to investment in human capital to rise as economic progress takes place (see, in particular, pp. 220–21). Thus, investment in human capital is complementary to the other kinds of investment which cause economic growth, and this investment, reflected partly in rising school attendance, has probably been an important cause of the declining labor force participation of male youth.[19]

Despite the probability that the principal causal relationship has run from rising school attendance to declining labor force participation, there almost certainly have been causal forces working in the opposite direction. These forces have to do with various institutional barriers which separate youthful workers from access to many jobs; they include minimum wage laws, restrictions on entry into certain unions and apprenticeship programs, and laws which limit the kind and extent of work that may be performed by young people. Further evidence that factors which make it difficult for youths to find work also encourage school attendance is found in studies which show a positive relationship between the unemployment rate and school attendance. Such a relationship appears to hold both over time[20] and among places at a moment of time.[21] Another force has probably been an overall decline in the demand for labor in industries such as agriculture, where restrictions against youthful workers have always been weak. While it is difficult to assess the overall or relative importance of barriers to jobs in inducing school attendance, such restrictions no doubt have exerted some influence on the negative relationship between school attendance and labor force participation over time. The increasing importance over time of factors which mitigate against the employment of youthful workers would reduce the alternative costs of school attendance and thus would tend to increase the rate of return to education and the incentives to attend school.

---

[19] Needless to say, changes in school attendance laws have worked in the direction of increasing school attendance at the expense of labor force participation. However, one needs to know what underlying changes have caused such laws to be passed and to be readily obeyed. The laws themselves cannot be considered a basic cause of changes in school attendance.

[20] Beverly Duncan, "Dropouts and the Unemployed," *Journal of Political Economy*, (April, 1965), LXXIII, 121–34.

[21] Robert M. Fearn, "Labor Force and School Participation of Teenagers" (unpublished Ph.D. dissertation, University of Chicago, 1968).

males aged 65 and over

The participation of elderly males in the labor force has dropped more or less continually, but not by uniform amounts, over the decades since 1890. The decline from 1950 to 1960 was 10 percentage points, the biggest ten-year reduction observable in the Census data during a period of reasonably full employment. Between 1890 and 1930, the average decline was 4.7 percentage points per decade, and between 1930 and 1950, 6.5 percentage points per decade.

While it is probably true that increased social security benefits and increasing coverage of workers by social security programs have contributed to the acceleration of the decline in labor force participation of elderly males in recent decades, one cannot rely on this explanation to account for much of the decline up to 1940. In 1940, only about 25 per cent of the male labor force aged 65 and over were eligible for OASDI benefits (although a larger percentage was eligible for either OASDI or old-age assistance); thus, about 10 per cent of all males aged 65 and over were eligible.[22] Even more relevant, the benefits actually paid were small. The average primary benefit paid in 1941 was only $23 per month, an amount few persons could live on without help.[23]

What factors, then, were important in causing the decline in labor force participation of elderly males up to 1940? The explanation which has the most intuitive appeal is that the trend toward early retirement was a predictable response to rising per capita income levels. There is some evidence, in fact, that the labor force participation of elderly males is quite sensitive to changes in per capita income levels—more sensitive than that of other age-sex groups. Regarding this, it is instructive to compare the labor force behavior of older males with that of married women. In a study aimed mainly at discovering the relationship between labor force participation and unemployment, William G. Bowen and T. A. Finegan[24] estimated the relationship between labor participation and various economic and social variables for several age-sex groups in major United States cities for the years 1960, 1950, and 1940. As a part of the study, Bowen and Finegan estimated the relationships (holding several other variables including unemployment constant) between labor force participation and earnings and nonlabor income for males 65 years old and over and for married women living with

---

[22] U.S. Department of Health, Education, and Welfare, *Social Security Bulletin, Annual Statistical Supplement*, 1965, p. 41; *Historical Statistics of the United States*, p. 71.

[23] Edna C. Wentworth, "Income of Old-Age and Survivors Insurance Beneficiaries, 1941 and 1949," *Social Security Bulletin*, May, 1950; referred to in Clarence Long, *The Labor Force Under Changing Income and Employment* (Princeton: Princeton University Press, 1958), p. 163.

[24] "Labor Force Participation and Unemployment," in Ross, *op. cit.*, pp. 115–61.

Table 3-7

THE RESPONSE OF LABOR FORCE PARTICIPATION
RATES (IN PER CENT) TO FULL-TIME EARNINGS
AND TO NONLABOR INCOME

	1960	1950	1940
	Males 65 Years and Over		
Earnings	−0.04	+0.64	+0.44[n]
($100/year)	(0.53)	(2.78)	(1.07)
Other Income	−1.81[n]	−2.33[n]	−0.35[n]
	(4.33)	(4.16)	(3.63)
	Married Women with Husband Present		
Female Earnings	+0.37	+1.05	+1.47
($100/year)	(3.04)	(4.71)	(3.05)
Other Income	−1.27[n]	−1.09[n]	−0.15[n]
	(0.29)	(3.02)	(2.05)

Numbers in parentheses are t-ratios; n signifies that a coefficient is not entirely comparable with those for other years due to an important difference in the definition of the variable.

Definitions of Variables:

Earnings: 1960 and 1950—median income in preceding year of all males who worked 50 to 52 weeks; 1940—median wage-or-salary income in 1939 of all males in the labor force who received at least $100 of such income.

Other Income: 1960—mean income from nonemployment sources in 1959 per recipient of any kind of income; 1950—median income in 1949 of all persons aged 14 and older with income from nonemployment sources only; 1940—percentage of all families who received some income in 1939.

Female Earnings: 1960 and 1950—median income in preceding year of all females who worked 50 to 52 weeks that year; 1940—estimated median wage-or-salary income received in 1939 by all females in experienced civilian labor force who worked 12 months and earned at least $100 of such income.

Source: William G. Bowen and T. A. Finegan, "Labor Force Participation and Unemployment" in Arthur M. Ross (ed.), Employment Policy and the Labor Market (Berkeley and Los Angeles: University of California Press, 1965), pp. 131 and 136.

their husbands. These estimates are shown in Table 3-7. They suggest that the labor force participation of elderly males responds strongly and negatively to the presence of income from nonlabor sources. By comparison, the labor force participation of married women does not appear to respond as strongly, although the response is in the same direction. Furthermore, while the estimated response of married women to the income of full-time workers, which is a proxy for full-time earnings, appears to be positive, statistically significant, and perhaps large, that of elderly males varies in sign and tends to be statistically insignificant.

What light do these estimates shed on the hypothesis that the declining labor force participation of elderly males, at least through 1940, was primarily a response to rising income levels? It is probably not unrealistic to assume that over the years the nonlabor income of the families containing elderly males and the families containing married women (which would often, of course, be the same families) have risen by roughly the same amount.[25] If this is true, then the Bowen-Finegan estimates shown in Table 3-7 imply a substantial reduction in the labor force participation of elderly men relative to that of married women (which is what is actually observed), on account of changes in nonlabor income over time. Furthermore, given the relatively large positive response of married women to earnings, the earnings of elderly males would have had to rise by substantially more than those of married women if the effect of earnings, possibly increasing the participation of men, were to have offset the effect of rising income from nonlabor sources. There is very little information regarding the behavior over time of the earnings of elderly males compared to those of married women; the most reasonable estimate seems to be that the earnings of women have risen more, not less, than those of elderly men.[26] Thus the effect of nonlabor income and of earnings has probably been to increase the participation of women relative to elderly males.

The Bowen-Finegan estimates also imply an absolute reduction in the labor force participation of elderly males that is rather close to the actual behavior of participation rates over time. For instance, if we assume that the change from 1889 to 1939 in the nonlabor income to which elderly males respond increased by one-half the amount of the change in the full-time

---

[25] This is a difficult point. To the extent that rising levels of economic welfare and increased social security for elderly persons have facilitated the disintegration of family units containing two or more generations of adults, the apparent rise in incomes of the elderly may be diminished because of the change in the units over which income is measured. (That this phenomenon actually influenced the inequality of income during the 1950's was emphasized by Margaret G. Reid in the results of unpublished research delivered to a seminar at Ohio State University in 1967.) In order to observe the true changes in the nonlabor income of the elderly over time, the effect on observed income of changes in the level of family integration would have to be accounted for.

[26] Clarence Long (*op. cit.*, p. 356) presents data implying a more or less continuous rise in the wages of females relative to males from 1889 to 1949. Long also notes (p. 179) that "... the amount of formal education possessed by elderly men has been rising more slowly than that of men and women below middle age ..." This would be some evidence that the wages of married women have risen relative to those of older men. If they have not, employers in any event would perhaps have desired to substitute younger females for older male workers if changes in their relative educational attainment were not offset by opposite changes in relative wage rates. Long thinks that such a demand change may have been one of the important causes of the historical shift in the labor force composition in favor of married women and away from older men.

earnings of all males (in 1949 prices),[27] the estimated response, using the 1950 males' coefficient in Table 3-7, is a decline in labor force participation between 1890 and 1940 of 22 percentage points; the actual decline was 26 percentage points. Thus the hypothesis that the observed decline in the labor force participation of elderly males, at least through 1949, is essentially a response to rising income levels seems to fare rather well when confronted with the data.

Four qualifications are in order, however. The first is that the variables used as the basis for the estimates in Table 3-7 are often only tenuously related to the theoretical variables they are supposed to represent. For instance, "other income" in 1940 is represented in each city observed by the percentage of all families which received some income in 1939. The second qualification is that even the best measurements of "other income" available in the Census data *include* income from social security and other sources which require that the recipient not work (very much) as a condition of payment. This introduces an obvious negative bias in the estimation procedure. The bias may not be very large, however, since none of the "other income" measures used in the study are for elderly males only; they all refer to the entire age distribution. The third qualification is that we may be observing, in part, not the response of elderly workers to rising income levels, but rather their response to declining demand for elderly workers relative to younger workers—especially younger women. This would have been the case, perhaps, if the rising level of education of younger male and female workers relative to that of older males (see footnote 26) was not offset sufficiently by declining relative wage rates for older workers. An insufficient decline might have been the result of a "social minimum" wage[28] preventing employers from offering older workers less than some amount deemed to be the minimum socially acceptable wage rate. This alternative is a difficult hypothesis to test, and we merely set it forth without attempting to assess its possible importance relative to the hypothesis that we have observed principally a supply response to rising income levels. The fourth qualification is that we have not considered the possible role of the requirement in an increasing number of jobs that workers retire at age 65. However, compulsory retirement does not imply compulsory withdrawal from the labor force, although it is clear that workers who might have remained on their jobs beyond the age of compulsory retirement will often find no alternatives to their customary work more desirable than withdrawing from the labor force. The more important point is that, as in the case of compulsory school attendance laws

---

[27] This is probably not too unrealistic an assumption, since the share of labor income in national income is roughly twice the share of nonlabor income. (See Table 12-1.) The source of the data is originally Long, *op. cit.*, modified and reported in Jacob Mincer, "Labor Force Participation of Married Women," in *Aspects of Labor Economics*, (Princeton, N.J.: Princeton University Press, 1962), p. 93.

[28] The concept of the social minimum wage is introduced in Chapter 13, p. 224.

(see footnote 19), one questions the validity of attributing a basic causal role to changes in retirement regulations themselves. Rather, one is led to suspect that such policies reflect an increased willingness of employees to withdraw from the labor force in the older years and, in the face of an increasing number of workers who actually reach age 65, the necessity of employers to adopt workable procedures to protect themselves from the difficulties of having to treat on an individual basis the cases of workers whose usefulness has declined due to age. Thus, on the employers' side, adopting compulsory retirement regulations may go along with conditions outlined in the third qualification discussed above.

Since 1940, the effects of rising incomes on retirement have probably been substantially reinforced by the rising level and coverage of various social security programs (particularly what is now OASDHI). These programs not only raise potential nonlabor income levels for workers who may leave the labor force, but they implicitly lower real wage rates to the extent that social security benefits are lowered if monthly earnings surpass certain levels.[29] Between 1940 and 1950, the sharp decline in unemployment overwhelmed other factors tending to reduce the labor force participation of elderly males. Between 1950 and 1960, however, the dominant factors were probably rising levels of income and social security benefits.

married women living with their husbands

The most striking change in labor force participation has been that of married women living with their husbands. The increase that has taken place over the years seemed paradoxical to many scholars at one time, because it has occurred in the presence of rising income and wage levels which appear to have resulted in declines in the labor force participation of other age-sex groups; furthermore, among families at a moment in time, the labor force participation rate of married women living with their husbands is lower, the higher the income received by husbands. This relationship is shown as it existed in 1960 in Table 3-8; it stands out most clearly when women 20–40 years old are studied separately, since the low-income groups among all wives tend also to have a large proportion of the elderly, who have low labor force participation. The data in Table 3-8 also show that there is an important relationship between labor force participation and the presence of children under 6 years of age.

A major breakthrough in understanding the determinants of the labor

---

[29] A discussion of the influence of social security programs on the labor force participation of the elderly is contained in Jacob Mincer, "Labor Force Participation and Unemployment: A Review of Recent Evidence," in R. A. and M. S. Gordon, eds., *Prosperity and Unemployment* (New York: John Wiley & Sons, Inc., 1966), pp. 91–98.

Table 3-8

LABOR FORCE PARTICIPATION RATES OF MARRIED WOMEN, HUSBAND
PRESENT, MARCH, 1960, BY PRESENCE AND AGE OF CHILDREN
AND INCOME OF HUSBAND IN 1959 (Per Cent)

Income of Husband	All Wives 14 Years Old and Older	Wives 20–44 Years Old			
		Total	No Children Under 18 Years	Children 6 to 17 Years Old Only	Children Under 6 Years
Total	30	32	59	40	19
Under $2,000	30	41	54	53	29
$2,000–$2,999	32	37	64	48	24
$3,000–$4,999	36	37	63	49	22
$5,000–$6,999	30	29	60	38	17
$7,000–$9,999	25	21	51	32	9
$10,000 and Over	16	15	a	19	8

[a] The number of observations is less than the minimum required for sampling
reliability.

Source: Glen G. Cain, Married Women in the Labor Force (Chicago: University of
Chicago Press, 1966), p. 3.

force participation of married women occurred when Jacob Mincer attempted
to reconcile the apparent contradiction: the labor force participation of
married women has risen sharply over time in the presence of rising incomes,
while at a moment in time the labor force participation of married women is
lower, the greater the income of husbands.[30] Essentially, Mincer found that
for married women, the *substitution* effect of rising wage rates has probably
been very large relative to the *income* effect of rising wages and rising levels
of family income.[31] Thus, while for men, the income effect seems to have
predominated—inducing a secular decline in the length of the workweek and
a decline in participation rates, we observe a rise in participation rates for
married women. (Recall that in Table 3-7 the participation response of
married women to earnings is positive and significant, while that of older

---

[30] Mincer, "Labor Force Participation of Married Women."

[31] One possible reason that the substitution effect for married women has been large
relative to the income effect is that we observe here, more than for men or for youth, a
substitution of women's work in the market for work in the home—i.e., a substitution
between *kinds* of work rather than between work and leisure. A second possible explanation
is that the married women are substituting their work for market work of their children,
either immediately if the children are old enough to attend high school or college, or in the
future if the family plans to keep their children in high school through graduation and/or
send them to college.   •

males is uncertain—perhaps zero.) Following Mincer's study, Glen Cain[32] explored the determinants of the labor force participation of married women in great depth.

Cain's study confirmed the essential features of Mincer's findings, and some representative results of his study are shown in Table 3-9. The effects of

Table 3-9

REGRESSION RESULTS: LABOR FORCE PARTICIPATION RATE IN 1950 OF MARRIED WOMEN, HUSBAND PRESENT (Per Cent)

(For Standard Metropolitan Areas in the North with Populations 250,000 and Over)

	y	w	e	u	c'	R^2
Regression Coefficient	−.84	1.48	.95	−.56	−.53	.56
Elasticity at Means	−1.31	1.49				
Standard Error	(.31)	(.35)	(.45)	(.26)	(.16)	
Regression Coefficient	−.30	1.29				
Elasticity at Means	−.47	1.26				
Standard Error	(.29)	(.31)				.38

Definitions of Variables:

y: Median income (in hundreds of dollars) in 1949 of male family heads, wife present.

w: Median income (in hundreds of dollars) in 1949 of females who worked 50 to 52 weeks.

e: Median years of schooling completed by females aged 25 years and older·

c': Per cent of husband-wife families with one or more children under 6 years of age.

u: Male employment rate (in per cent).

Source: Glen G. Cain, *Married Women in the Labor Force* (Chicago: University of Chicago Press, 1966), p. 23.

wage rates and nonlabor income on labor force participation are reflected in the coefficients of the income of wives who worked 50–52 weeks in 1949 and of husbands' incomes, respectively. Holding, constant the income of women who worked 50–52 weeks (a proxy for wives' wage rates), the effect of changes in husbands' incomes is assumed to reflect the effect of differences in the

---

[32] *Married Women in the Labor Force* (Chicago: University of Chicago Press, 1966), p. 139.

income available to families if the wives do not work.[33] Such differences hypothetically affect the labor supplied by wives much the same as differences in nonlabor income in the analysis of Chapter 2. If we examine the regression reported in Table 3-9 which contains only the variables representing wives' and husbands' incomes (lower portion of table), we find that the estimated "income effect" of an increase in husbands' incomes (holding constant wives' incomes in 1949 prices) is to reduce the labor force participation of wives by the amount of the regression coefficient of husbands' incomes—.3 percentage points. The estimated effect of a $100 increase in the incomes of women who worked 50–52 weeks, holding husbands' incomes constant, is to raise the labor force participation rate of married women by about 1.3 percentage points. This estimated effect of a change in wage rates includes *both* an income and a substitution effect, since we are holding constant a proxy for *nonlabor* income.

The regression results shown in the top portion of Table 3-9 represent an attempt to estimate the influence of additional variables which hypothetically influence the labor force participation of married women. If the influence of such variables is not estimated simultaneously with that of income and earning power, then the estimated effects of incomes and earning power are likely to reflect other influences as well, because the variables affecting labor force participation are rather highly intercorrelated. The additional variables are the median years of schooling completed by females aged 25 years and older, the unemployment rate of males, and the fraction of husband-wife families with at least one child under 6 years of age. The regression coefficients of these variables suggest the following: (1) Education is presumed to represent much the same kind of phenomenon as that represented by education in Finegan's study of hours of work (see pp. 62–64): namely, highly educated people are assumed to be employed in jobs with relatively high nonpecuniary benefits; other things being equal, such benefits are hypothesized to raise the amount of labor supplied. The coefficient of education—

---

[33] This assumption implies that we may ignore the effects of any tendency for husbands to substitute work in the home or leisure for their own market work when wives work more in response to higher wage rates; thus, observed differences in husbands' incomes are assumed to reflect a major component of differences in the income available to the family other than wives' earnings. To the extent substitution occurs, however, it is an additional factor reducing husbands' labor supplied and, hence, income when wives' wage rates are high; in such circumstances the income effect of increases in wives' wages tends to reduce the total amount of labor supplied to the market by the family, but the tendency to substitute wives' for husbands' work tends further to raise the labor supplied by women and reduce that supplied by husbands. To the extent we cannot control for such substitution and it is important, the coefficient of husbands' income is probably a biased estimate of the income effect on the labor force participation of married women. The analysis of this possible bias is complex, however, and it would be difficult to state its likely size or sign.

.95—implies that an increase by one year in the median level of schooling of females aged 25 years and over increases labor force participation by .95 percentage points. This is consistent with the hypothesis and with the positive effect of education on hours worked per week which Finegan found in his study of United States males.

(2) The coefficient of the male unemployment rate sheds light on the important issue of whether increases in the level of excess supply of labor induce, on balance, net increases or decreases in the size of the labor force. The male unemployment rate is supposed to represent the general state of demand for labor, which varies from city to city because areas are affected differently by the economy's occasional fluctuations in the general level of business activity and by the rises and declines of different industries. Of course, differences in labor supply conditions among areas may affect the unemployment rate; it is probably true, however, that labor supply differences affecting unemployment rates among cities are unimportant compared to differences in demand conditions.

The question which the effect of unemployment on labor force participation of married women sheds light on is, "When labor demand falls, causing some workers to lose their jobs and making it more difficult for anyone to find work, what is the effect on the amount of labor supplied?" An increase in unemployment has a direct effect on family income: it reduces the income of the family temporarily below its normal level. In order to maintain consumption at a level consistent with normal income, families experiencing unemployment may resort to drawing on their savings, they may resort to borrowing if their credit is good, and/or family members (specifically, wives in the study represented in Table 3-9) who typically do not hold jobs may attempt to find them. Such attempts to find jobs by family members who are usually not in the labor force is sometimes called "the added worker effect" of unemployment. There is not much doubt that, *given* overall labor market conditions, i.e., given the difficulty of finding a suitable job, temporary labor force participation of wives is more common in families where the husband is unemployed than in other husband-wife families. However, increases in the level of unemployment not only result in a reduction below normal of certain families' incomes, but they also result in increases in the difficulty of finding work. This increase in difficulty is hypothesized to influence the amount of labor supplied in the same way as the substitution effect of a wage rate reduction; i.e., an increase in the difficulty of finding work at any wage rate reduces the attractiveness of seeking employment. The impact of the increased difficulty of finding work is hypothesized to have a "discouraged worker" effect, reducing the likelihood of a person's being in the labor force. Therefore, in cities with relatively high unemployment rates, the added worker effect operates to force more wives than usual into the labor force, while the discouraged worker effect works in the opposite direction—inducing some wives who would like jobs to give up the search and no longer be counted as labor force participants.

The regression coefficient of unemployment in Table 3-9 is —.56, implying that the discouraged worker effect outweighs the added worker effect for wives living with their husbands. A 1 percentage point rise in the unemployment rate is associated on the average with a .56 percentage point decline in the participation rate. The dominance of the discouraged worker effect over the added worker effect is borne out in other studies of the labor force behavior of married women, and it is also probably typical of the behavior of other components of the labor force, especially other fringe, or marginal, labor force groups, such as youth and the elderly; there is considerable disagreement, however, regarding the *amount* by which the discouraged worker effect outweighs the income effect and the overall importance of the effect of unemployment on labor force participation.[34]

(3) It is almost unnecessary to discuss the expected effect of the presence of young children on the labor force participation of married women. It is intuitively appealing that the effect of the desire to care personally for such children outweighs on the average the effect of the need for additional income to pay for clothing, doctors' bills, etc. Indeed, to the extent that family planning is practiced, wives can plan their labor force activity to complement the periods of time when they expect to need extra income to support their children but at the same time desire to be home to rear their pre-school-age offspring. The coefficient of the variable representing the fraction of families with children under 6 years of age is negative, as hypothesized, implying that a 1 percentage point increase in the fraction of such families is associated on the average with a .53 percentage point reduction in the labor force participation rate of married women.

How well do the results of cross-sectional studies resolve the apparent contradiction between the behavior of the labor force participation of married women over time and among families at a moment in time? Data for variables other than husband's and wives' income or earning are not readily available for years prior to 1940; and therefore we rely on the results of regressions such as the second one shown in Table 3-9 to see whether the estimated effects of variables affecting labor force participation among cities can help explain the rise in the labor force participation of married women over time. If we apply the regression coefficients of husbands' and wives' incomes in Table 3-9 to the changes in these variables that occurred between 1889 and 1949 (the source of these data is given in footnote 32), we infer a 15 percentage point increase in the labor force participation of married women between the years 1890 and 1950. The actual increase was 17 percentage points—remarkably close to the predicted change. Thus, cross-sectional

---

[34] See, for instance, Jacob Mincer, "Labor Force Participation and Unemployment."

studies of the kind reported in Table 3-9 appear to be capable of isolating crucial variables explaining the labor force participation of married women.

Alternative Hypotheses. Are there alternative hypotheses capable of explaining the long-term increase in the labor force participation of married women? If there are such hypotheses, are they inconsistent with the explanation set forth in the preceding section? It is possible to develop alternative explanations; for instance, a long-run change in attitudes toward the role of women in the family, in the labor force, and in society in general may have increased the labor supply of women, independent of movements in incomes and wage rates. Also, increasing productivity in the home based on the introduction of labor saving devices and appliances might have pushed women into the labor force.

There is little doubt that opinions about the propriety of women entering the labor force have changed over the years in the same direction as women's labor force participation. However, it would be difficult to discern whether such changes in opinions played a causal role or whether they responded to independent changes in economic conditions. One suspects but cannot prove that during World War II, and perhaps during World War I, increases in the number of women in the labor force due to increases in the number of jobs and reduced availability of civilian men brought about concomitant changes in attitudes toward women in the labor force, which changes might have taken longer to come about under other circumstances. However, if a change in attitudes toward working wives has been the crucial force underlying the rise in the labor force participation of married women, it is difficult to explain why there has been no long-run tendency for wage rates of women to fall relative to men (assuming men and women are not perfect substitutes in the labor force); indeed, there has been an increase in the relative wage of women in manufacturing.[35] Between 1940 and 1960, the increase in the labor force participation of married women was greater than during any comparable previous period, but at the same time the absolute increase in the full-time earnings of females was greater than that of males.[36] It is probably true, then, that attitudes toward married women in the labor force have changed largely in response to increases in labor force participation of married women, although at times, particularly after the two World Wars, changes in attitudes may have had a causal role to play. Gradual changes in attitudes may also have accelerated the responses of married women to increased earning power.

In regard to evaluating the second explanation suggested—that the introduction of laborsaving devices and appliances in the home has increased

[35] Long, *op. cit.*, p. 356.

[36] Jacob Mincer, "Labor Force Participation of Married Women," p. 93.

the supply of women to the labor force—many of the same difficulties arise as in evaluating the role of changing attitudes. Principally, how can we tell whether the introduction of laborsaving devices was a cause or effect of rising labor force participation of married women? Parenthetically, it should be pointed out that the introduction of laborsaving appliances in the home constitutes only a small part of the various laborsaving activities that have helped supplement the labor of housewives in performing household duties. Some other activities are: (1) the purchase of ready-made clothing and other goods that were formerly produced in the home; (2) the purchase of laundry and other services outside the home; (3) the purchase of prepared foods. Such activities do help explain how household production has been carried on despite the rising labor force participation rate of married women,[37] but they do not in themselves provide evidence that laborsaving activities have *caused* the observed rise in labor force participation. The hypothesis that the growth of laborsaving activities in the home caused the rise in labor force participation runs foul of the observation mentioned above in discussion of the influence of attitudes—the relative wage of women has not declined secularly; indeed the absolute real wage rate of women rose more than that of men during the period 1940–60, when the labor force participation of married women was increasing faster than during any previous decade.

To summarize, the alternative hypotheses do not appear to be powerful contenders as explanations of the long-term increase in the labor force participation of married women. While it is probably true that changes in attitudes and the introduction of laborsaving activities in the home have facilitated and perhaps accelerated the labor force response of married women to rising wage rates, they probably have not had important causal role to play.

conclusion

We have completed our first chapter dealing with evidence bearing on the economic theory of labor. In this chapter we have dealt with two dimensions of labor supply, hours worked per week and labor force participation. The theory that was developed in Chapter 2 proves helpful in understanding some interesting aspects of supply behavior. For instance, we found that there is a similarity between the relationship of the length of the workweek to wage rates at a moment of time and that over several decades. We found that cross-sectional analysis of labor force participation rates is useful in helping to understand the behavior over time of this dimension of labor supply. The framework that helps us to understand why the labor force participation rate of male youth has dropped substantially over roughly the

---

[37] Long, *op. cit.*, pp. 123–32.

past half century meshes with the set of ideas that helps explain changes in the labor force participation of married women and of older men, and the explanation of changes in labor force participation in general apears to be consistent with the explanation of changes in hours of work. These consistencies among the explanations of the behavior of various aspects of labor supply are intellectually satisfying and lend credibility to the theory from which they are derived. Nevertheless, much remains to be done, even in the few areas we have discussed here. For instance, we have not developed a logically tight explanation of why the labor force participation response of married women to changes in their wage rates should reflect a substitution effect that is much more pronounced than for other labor force groups (although we have some intuitively appealing reasons for believing that this is what we observe); consequently, our *explanation* of the marked positive response of married women's labor force participation to wage rates is weaker than we would like it to be. Another area where further thought and information should prove useful is the behavior of the length of the workweek in manufacturing. Can we expect it to continue to fall, as hours of work has done over the years, or does the increase in hours of work since the early 1960's reflect an underlying trend much more basic than an increased demand for labor due to the Viet Nam situation? Many other questions have been raised by our analysis. Among them are questions of interpreting the influence of variables such as education and maritial status, which were included in the analysis of labor supply behavior at various points, and for which we have intuitively appealing explanations. Often these explanations are consistent with those of the observed influence of such variables in a number of studies. But the relationship of these variables to an underlying theory of labor supply has not been very clearly demonstrated. Time, space, and the state of our knowledge preclude exploring these interesting problems at this point; hopefully, however, readers will feel themselves better able to interpret labor supply behavior as a result of the development of the theory of labor supply in Chapter 2 and its application to some of the evidence bearing on it in Chapter 3. In the next two chapters, the theory of labor supply is extended to the long run, and short- and long-run labor supply are compared from the points of view of families, occupations, firms, and the economy.

4

the theory
of labor supply:
family members in
the long run

In Chapters 2 and 3 we considered the theory of the labor supplied by family members in the short run and evidence bearing on the theory. We defined the short run as a period of time during which "long-run" conditions of labor supply such as education, occupational choice, and geographical location or residence are fixed. This distinction between the long run and the short run is similar to that used in the standard theory of the firm with which all readers are familiar; the long run is that period of time over which firms can adjust their inputs of all potentially variable factors of production. There is another very important similarity between the long- and short-run distinction for the firm and that for suppliers of labor: just as long-run output adjustments of firms involve investment decisions, so do the long-run labor supply decisions of family members involve decisions which may be treated analytically as investment in certain kinds of assets—human assets (human capital) in the case of labor supply. Labor supply decisions of family members in the long run are analogous to investment decisions of firms in that they involve actions which tend to increase the productivity of family members in the labor market over a long period of time. Productivity of suppliers of labor is raised in the long run by raising educational levels, moving to better labor market areas, and so on; nevertheless, such actions are costly, and the analytical treatment of costly decisions which may yield returns over time is the province of capital theory.

THE THEORY OF HUMAN CAPITAL[1]

present value

As soon as we begin to deal with labor supply decisions which have consequences over several time periods, it becomes convenient to treat them by means of a theory of human capital. At first it may seem morally wrong or factually incorrect to speak of human beings as though they were just so many machines, but nothing moral or ethical is implied in discussing human capital. The subject matter is quite relevant to situations in which workers have complete freedom of choice in their labor market decisions. In fact, the institutional requirement that human capital must be "owned" by the person in whom it is embodied is an important factor making the theory of human capital distinct from conventional capital theory. Whether the theory is "correct" can only be decided on the basis of its utility in explaining labor market phenomena.

In going from the implicit single time period analysis of the previous chapters (where all the relevant costs and benefits of decisions occur during the same time periods) to the multiple period analysis of human capital, we retain the assumption that individuals aim to maximize an index of utility. When all other characteristics of alternative labor market choices are the same, utility maximization coincides with maximization of some aspect of the wage rate. (A note of caution is called for here. Needless to say, the characteristics of alternative labor market choices are not always the same, and utility-maximizing individuals should be expected to consider these characteristics. Thus, long-run wage differentials may well contain elements

---

[1] The ideas contained in the theory of human capital have been known to economists in a more or less vague way since at least the time of Adam Smith, and many references to these ideas can be found in the writings of economists from Smith down to the present. However, only recently has the detailed analytical and empirical study of the theory of human capital been treated intensively in the mainstream of economics. The two most important references to the developing literature on human capital are Theodore W. Schultz, ed., "Investment in Human Beings," *Journal of Political Economy*, LXX, 5, Part 2, October, 1962; and Gary S. Becker, *Human Capital* (New York: Columbia University Press, 1964). The first reference contains several important articles on the theory of human capital and applications to various forms of human capital, including on-the-job training (by Jacob Mincer); migration (by Larry A. Sjaastad); information in the labor market (by George J. Stigler); education (by Burton A. Weisbrod and by Edward F. Dension); and health (by Selma J. Mushkin). The articles also contain a wealth of footnote references to the relevant literature. Becker's study is a modern classic treatment of the theory, with particular application to investment in education.

of "compensating differentials"—e.g., occupations which are "pleasant" will have lower wage rates relative to other occupations than can be explained on the basis of the assumption that occupations do not differ in the non-pecuniary conditions of work. The difficult problem in empirical work is to identify such nonpecuniary working conditions.)

What does it mean, however, to maximize one's potential money return in the labor market over the long run? Often, discussions of the total amount of earnings in alternative occupations take the form of urging young people to continue their education because high school degrees may add, say, $100,000 to their total lifetime earnings. Yet maximization of total lifetime earnings may not lead to utility maximization, even when we ignore all nonpecuniary aspects of labor market decisions. This is because a dollar received or paid out today is not the exact equivalent of a dollar tomorrow, except under very special circumstances. This is one of the essential points of capital theory. (To repeat, our emphasis here on the real money wage rate does not mean that capital theory is irrelevant to the nonpecuniary aspects of long-run decisions of labor suppliers. Surely the kind of work done, the climate of the area where it is done, working conditions such as cleanliness and hours, employment stability, occupational prestige, and so on, are job characteristics other than wage rates which the focus on utility maximization implies will be evaluated along with the wage rate in making long-run decisions. For analytical simplicity, however, we shall subsume all aspects of the real total returns to alternative long-run decisions in the real dollar returns per unit of time.)

To explore the importance of time to utility maximization, consider two alternatives: (1) to repay a $100 debt immediately; or (2) to repay the same debt one year from now. Which alternative would you prefer? If you think about it carefully, you will probably choose the second alternative. If you already have the $100, you can place it in a savings account or invest it for a year and earn interest—say 5 per cent. Thus, one year from now you can pay the $100 debt and have $5 left over. Alternatively, you could put a little over $95 in the bank now and spend the remainder; a year from now you would have $100 in your account which could be used to satisfy your credi-tors. In fact, if there were no transactions costs or uncertainty, you would probably choose to put off debt repayment so long as, at the end of the year, you would have to repay less than $105. The same analysis applies even if you would have to borrow money to repay the debt. For if you were to borrow $100 now, but placed it in your savings account for the year instead of repaying your debt, you would be better off at the year's end by the annual interest payment.

As long as there is an interest rate, decisions among economic alterna-tives must consider the *timing* of payments and receipts. A dollar today is not the equivalent of a dollar tomorrow—it is worth more than that. There is a simple technique for evaluating payments and receipts that occur through time. The technique is to express the value of a future payment or receipt in terms of a payment or receipt made today. The value today of a payment that will be made in the future is called the *present value* of the payment. In terms of the example given above, the present value of the $100 debt when due today is $100, but its present value when due one year from now is approximately $95, or $100/(1 + i)$, where i, the rate of interest $= .05$.

Consider the alternative of repaying the $100 debt *two* years from now. What is the present value of $100 in two years? We follow the same procedure as above; if you have $100 now, you can put it out at interest, earning $5 the first year, if the interest rate is 5 per cent. The second year, if you let the interest accumulate, you will earn $5 plus 5 per cent on the first year's interest, or $.25. Thus, you could repay the debt at the end of two years and have $10.25 left. Obviously, the longer you can delay repaying the debt, the better off you are; the present value of the $100 debt is smaller, the further away is the date of repayment. This is because the longer you can wait before paying out the $100, the smaller the sum of money you have to set aside today in order to have $100 when the debt is due. In the present example, in order to have $100 two years from now, you would have to set aside $100/(1 + i)^2$ today, or approximately $90. The present value of $100 two years from now is $100/(1 + i)^2$. The present value of a debt $100 one year from now *plus* a debt $100 two years from now is $100[(1 + i)^{-1} + (1 + i)^{-2}]$. Identically, a *creditor* views the present value of two payments of $100 each, one year from now and two years from now, as equal to $100[(1 + i)^{-1} + (1 + i)^{-2}]$.

Thus, in comparing labor market alternatives, such as occupations that require different levels of education and which promise different lifetime income streams, it is useful to note that the income expected in each year will have a present value as of today; the present values of the alternative income streams expected are merely the sums of the present values of the alternative incomes of each year in the future, with the present value of a payment occurring j years from now in alternative Y being equal to $Y_j(1 + i)^{-j}$ where Y_j is the expected income payment and i is the rate of interest. Algebraically, such a sum may be expressed as

$$\sum_{j=0}^{n} Y_j(1 + i)^{-j}$$

where $n =$ the number of years over which income is expected. The simplest treatment of the direct *costs* of labor market alternatives is to subtract them, in the relevant time periods, from the income payments. Thus, in expression (1) the Y_j's would be *net* of any direct costs (such as tuition, transportation, etc.) associated with receiving income. Clearly, the "better" of two alternatives is the one yielding the higher present value.

It is easy to see that since the weight $[(1 + i)^{-j}]$ attached to each year's income is smaller, the further in the future the year occurs, the alternative which promises the largest simple sum of income payments may not have the largest present value. Table 4-1 presents sample calculations of the present

Table 4-1

PRESENT VALUES OF ALTERNATIVE INCOME
STREAMS AT VARIOUS INTEREST RATES

Year ($j =$)	Net Income Received		$\frac{1}{(1+i)^j} \cdot Y_j$				$\frac{1}{(1+i)^j} \cdot X_j$			
	Alternative Y	Alternative X	$i = 0$	$i = .01$	$i = .05$	$i = .50$	$i = 0$	$i = .01$	$i = .05$	$i = .50$
0	$100	$1,000	100	100	100	100	1,000	1,000	1,000	1,000
1	50	900	50	49	48	33	900	891	859	600
2	500	600	500	490	480	330	600	588	545	267
3	600	500	600	582	512	178	500	482	429	148
4	900	50	900	864	736	178	50	48	41	10
5	1,200	100	1,200	1,140	936	158	100	96	78	13
Sum (Present Value)	$3,350	$3,150	$3,350	$3,225	$2,812	$977	$3,150	$3,105	$2,952	$2,038

values of alternative income streams, assuming various rates of interest. Note that if the interest rate is zero, the present value is equal to the simple sum of each income stream; the higher the interest rate, the more important the income occurring during the early years of each stream in determining present value.

rate of return

So far we have discussed the problem of deciding among alternative income or payment streams as though the alternatives to choosing, say, an additional four years of education were clearly defined in the market for factors of production and in the market for loanable funds. Thus, we have spoken as if one could borrow money to finance an investment in human capital much the same as one could finance the purchase of a new house. However, while some such transactions are possible and do take place, in general the human capital "market" behaves differently than conventional capital markets. The most important condition affecting the different behavior of the human capital market is not imperfect knowledge of alternatives and uncertainty about the future, which pervade many markets; rather, it is the nonnegotiability of its principal asset, human capital.

In a slave society, slave owners could probably borrow on their slave property just as on their real estate or personal property. When loans were not repaid, creditors could claim the slaves in lieu of payment. Furthermore, borrowers' uncertainty would be reduced because, even though the productivity over the lifetime of a single individual is uncertain, the law of large numbers would probably make predicting the results of alternative invest-ments in groups of slaves no more uncertain than the results of alternative investments in land clearance, new machines, etc. Thus, the slave owner would face the realistic alternatives of investing in his slaves, of lending or not borrowing the resources to do so, or investing in nonhuman, rather than human, capital. Since well-established markets could be expected to exist, the profitability of different investments could be expected to approach equality.

However, in our society, human capital is not collateral, because it cannot be bought and sold; furthermore, an individual investor cannot take advantage of the law of large numbers to reduce the uncertainty of investing (in himself, usually). Therefore, individuals who want to invest in human capital must usually find the funds to do so from their own savings or those of their families, or they may be forced to finance their consumption expendi-tures at consumer loan interest rates which are normally much higher than interest rates at which borrowers can finance business investments or the purchase of houses. Thus, what an average investor in human capital gives up in return for a relatively uncertain payoff is likely to be interest payments running to 15–20 per cent, or higher. An already-wealthy investor, however, may be able to finance his investment (or that of his children) by simply drawing down on his savings and sacrificing a rate of return of, say, 6 to 12 per cent. Thus, access to investible funds is much more likely to be a deter-minant of interpersonal differences in investment in human capital than in the case of physical capital. The implication is that the payoff (i.e., the rate of return) to further investment in human capital will tend to vary among individuals according to the amount of human capital invested in them; this presumably would not be the case if all individuals were able to invest in themselves up to the point where the payoff to an incremental amount of investment yielded the same return that would be obtained for any other investment with an equally certain outcome.

A method of estimating the value of alternative uses of resources invested by individuals in human capital is to assume that individuals attempt to maximize over time the utility they derive from their expenditures and to infer the value of these alternatives from observed behavior. This involves estimating the *rate of return* to investment in human capital, because we assume that individuals invest in themselves up to the point where the rate of return to further such investment is equal to the rate of return of investing in the best alternative.

To illustrate the concept of the rate of return (or the internal rate of return, as it is sometimes called), let us go back to the example of a debt to be repaid at some time. Let us suppose that you face the alternatives of paying $100 now, $105 a year from now, or $110.25 two years from now. First, compare paying $100 this year with $105 next year. In order to put off paying the debt for one year, you will have to pay an implicit interest rate of 5 per cent. This may be calculated by noting that

$$\$105 = (\$100)(1 + .05) \tag{1}$$

or, similarly, by finding r, the rate of return, such that

$$\$100 = \$105(1 + r)^{-1}. \tag{2}$$

The implicit interest rate, or rate of return, when we compare $100 now with $110.25 two years from now is also 5 per cent, which we derive from

$$\$100 = \$110.25(1 + r)^{-2}. \tag{3}$$

Now suppose that instead of a debtor who faces alternative dates of repayment or a creditor who faces alternative dates of collection, we consider an individual who has just graduated from high school and who faces two alternatives in the labor market. One alternative is to acquire no more education; this we assume would provide access to an occupation yielding a yearly income of X_j in each year, j, from now ($j = 0$) until the end of his life ($j = n$). The second alternative is to acquire one year of college education which will yield a net income of Y_j in each year. In terms of our previous simple example involving only two time periods, we may think of alternative X as that of receiving $100 in year zero (i.e., $X_0 = 100$; $X_1 = 0$), while alternative Y is that of receiving $105 in year one (i.e., $Y_0 = 0$, $Y_1 = 105$). Thus, the alternative income streams over the two-year period are, for X: $100 in year zero and nothing in year one; for Y: nothing in year zero and $105 in year one. The annual *differences* between the two income streams are: year 0, $X - Y = \$100$; year 1, $Y - X = \$105$. Thus, either equation (1) or (2) may be thought of as equating the *differences* between the two income (or payment) streams over their two-year periods. Similarly, for n years, we may define the rate of return for choosing Y, the year of college education, as r, where

$$X_0 - Y_0 = \sum_{j=1}^{n} (Y_j - X_j)(1 + r)^{-j} \tag{4}$$

But this may as well be written as

$$0 = \sum_{j=0}^{n} (Y_j - X_j)(1 + r)^{-j} \tag{5}$$

In other words, the rate of return is an implicit interest rate which makes the present value of the sum of the net income differences between Y and X equal to zero. Obviously, for r to be finite, some of the income differences must be negative, which they are, typically, for persons who may realistically choose between high school and college educations. That is, the income a typical high school graduate could earn if he were not attending college is larger than he could earn, less tuition, books, etc., while attending college. If it were true in general that $Y - X$ was never negative, then it would pay everyone to go to college, as it would be costless to do so. (If Y_j and X_j reflect only the relatively easily measurable *pecuniary* returns of Y and X, ignoring personal pleasure or displeasure that some people attach to the act of acquiring an education and the nonpecuniary returns of the occupations associated with Y and X, then the interpretation of r must be adjusted accordingly.)

Table 4-2

SAMPLE CALCULATION OF THE RATE OF RETURN

Year $(j =)$	Income Received		$Y_j - X_j$	Rate of Return (r) $= .04$
	Alternative Y	Alternative X		$(Y_j - X_j) \dfrac{1}{(1 + r)^j}$
0	$ 100	$1,000	−$ 900	−$900
1	50	900	− 850	− 185
2	500	600	− 100	− 93
3	600	500	100	89
4	900	50	850	732
5	1,200	100	1,100	909
Sum	$3,350	$3,150	$ 200	$ 79

$$\text{where } r = .03 \sum_{j=0}^{5} (Y_j - X_j)(1 + r)^{-j} = +88$$

$$r = .05 \sum_{j=0}^{5} (Y_j - X_j)(1 + r)^{-j} = -140$$

Table 4-2 illustrates the calculation of the rate of return, using the same numbers as employed in Table 4-1. The rate of return in the example is between .04 and .05.

Now, our profit-maximizing slave owner would invest in his slaves up to the point where the rate of return on a marginal, or last small, unit of investment was equal to the rate at which he could borrow money, or equal to the rate of return on his best alternative investment, which we assume is equal to the rate of interest. When the marginal rate of return is equal to the rate of interest, equation (5) holds true if i, the interest rate, is substituted for r; thus, when the rate of return equals the rate of interest, the present values of the alternative income streams are equal.

But what about an individual in a society which outlaws slavery and in which human capital cannot be used as collateral? In general, we would not expect to find that such an individual would invest up to the point where the rate of return on a marginal amount invested in himself or a member of his family equaled the rate of return achievable, say, in savings accounts or in investment in physical capital unless the investments are subsidized. From society's point of view, the rate of return to all investments taken together will tend to be greatest when the rates of return at any margin of investment (e.g., physical capital or human capital) of equal riskiness is the same as at any other margin; it is an idea such as this, however crudely formulated, which is *one* of the reasons why most progressive governments have fostered public aid to education.

By estimating the internal rate of return to incremental investments in human capital, we may derive some notion of the alternatives faced by individuals in deciding among different levels of education, leading to different occupations, and among other kinds of investment in human capital. As long as individuals have different degrees of access to resources for financing investment in human capital, we should expect to find, on the average, that those who invest a great deal in human capital will experience lower marginal rates of return (i.e., returns to their last increment of investment, such as college compared to high school) than those who invest relatively little. This is because we should expect the marginal rate of return to decline on the average as more investment accumulates relative to the fixed basic human resource. (This is not to deny that many individuals invest a great deal in themselves because they anticipate an unusually high rate of return due to ability or other personal factors.) In fact, this expectation has been generally confirmed by empirical studies.

The point of the three preceding paragraphs is this: if all investment in human capital were carried out under conditions similar to those describing the situation of a profit-maximizing slave owner, we would expect there to be no systematic relationship between observed *marginal* rates of return to investment in human capital among individuals and the amounts actually invested. However, since we believe that individuals in our society do not in general invest in human capital up to the point where the marginal rate of return equals a market rate of interest, the observed relationship between actual amounts invested and marginal rates of return is an approximation of the average relationship between the amount invested in human capital and the marginal rate of return for a typical individual, i.e., it is an approximation of the rates of return a typical individual *would* obtain *if* he invested in various amounts of human capital. Such a relationship is a demand relationship in that it answers the question, "How much investment in human capital will be demanded at various interest rates if loanable funds are freely available at such interest rates?" If the present distribution of investment suggests that the demand curve is downward sloping, then we may infer that providing easier access to resources for financing investment will increase its amount. Figure 4-1 is a hypothetical schedule relating the rate of return to various

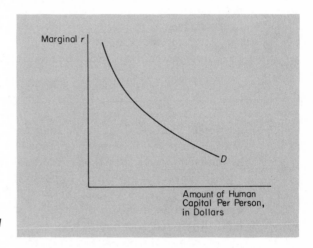

FIG. 4-1
Hypothetical Investment Demand Schedule for Human Capital

amounts of investment in human capital for a typical individual. It may be thought of as a typical individual's demand curve for human capital.

types of human capital

The analysis of human capital becomes much more complicated if we consider the different forms that investment in human capital can take. We have spoken as if formal education were the principal form of human capital, and it may well be. Nevertheless, direct and indirect costs of health, on-the-job training, apprenticeship programs, and geographical mobility constitute important elements of investment in human capital and must not be neglected. Each individual's total investment includes many if not all of these kinds of human capital. The method outlined in the previous section for estimating the rate of return to the investment in human capital arising from a year of college education ignored the other forms of investment in the human agent that would also influence observed earnings. Thus, the estimated rate of return to investment in education would be influenced by the rate of return to other forms of human capital that may be acquired previously, at the same time, or later. However, if the rates of return to investments in the various forms of human capital are nearly the same, the biases introduced in estimating actual rates of return by neglecting the various *forms of investment* in human capital are probably small if the time period over which earnings are observed is long enough to capture all the forms of investment and their returns, and if the most important cost elements are foregone earnings. A more serious source of bias, however, is the likelihood that amounts actually invested in human capital are correlated with "ability" and other personal characteristics which also determine earnings; thus, some estimated rates of return probably overestimate the rates of return that could be obtained by "typical" individuals if they acquired additional investment in themselves.

human capital and labor supply

The point of this section is to show how some important aspects of the long-run supply of labor can best be analyzed with the aid of the concept of human capital. There are some interesting questions that should be answered. For instance, in the long run, if families respond to rising wage rates by *reducing* the number of labor hours sold, how can economic growth (as conventionally measured) continue? In part, the answer seems simple enough: economic growth continues by means of the accumulation of physical capital and increased "productivity." But much of what passes as increased efficiency or productivity is the result of improvements in the *quality* of the labor force that is primarily due to investment in human capital; not only has growth of the physical capital stock been a principal cause of economic development, but growth of the human capital stock has been crucial as well.[2] Thus, despite the curtailment of European immigration after 1924, and despite an ever-shortening workweek, longer vacations, a declining labor force participation rate among youth and among the elderly, and a roughly constant participation rate among the population in general, the United States has been able to expand output greatly, in part because of the growth of the labor supply by means of the accumulation of human capital.

To look at the problem of long-run labor supply another way: in response to an ever increasing demand for labor, workers may in the long run reduce the number of hours they sell *and* increase the quality of their labor (because one of the theoretical effects of economic growth is, *cet. par.*, to widen the difference between the earning streams attributable to alternative amounts of investment in human capital without increasing the cost of investment proportionately).[3] Furthermore, even if the demand for labor were not increasing over the years, most individuals would realize that they could increase their earning power by acquiring more education and training and by increasing their labor productivity in various other ways. Thus, part of our

---

[2] Aspects of the role of investment in human capital in promoting economic growth are discussed in Chapter 13 of this book; also in Schultz *op. cit.*, and his article "Capital Formation by Education," *Journal of Political Economy*, December, 1960.

[3] Becker, *op. cit.*, pp. 53–54. See also Chapter 13 of this book, p. 224. This is a subtle point. The interested reader should consult Becker for further analysis.

rising standard of living has been the result of the gradual accumulation of human capital by individuals because it has paid them to do so. The result has been a growth in labor resources far in excess of the growth in population or the labor force.

POPULATION

An important aspect of the long-run labor supply is population. In response to an increase in the demand for labor, or to interregional differences in demand, labor may flow from one region or country to another. International migration was an important part of the increase in the labor supply of the United States before legislation restricted it in the 1920's. By and large, migration may be considered as part of the formation of human capital, with the alternative income streams being those in the source and receiving areas of migration. Of course, in order to take best advantage of migration, other kinds of human capital formation may be necessary as well. For instance, it may pay to move from one country or region to another only if the requisite skills and education have been acquired.

In the early days of the study of economics, the subject of population change via fertility was an important theoretical and empirical issue, although in recent years, this aspect of social science has been more closely studied by sociologists. Nevertheless, it is worthwhile to dwell briefly on fertility as an aspect of the long-run supply of labor. Malthus, simply interpreted, implied that human beings had a cost of production roughly equivalent to biological subsistence (although he recognized that "subsistence" levels of living might well rise above those necessary for the mere survival of life), and that when the standard of living rose above this level, the population would expand. Thus, the growth of the labor force was intimately tied to the rate of economic development; in fact, it was related in such a way as to assure that average per capita incomes would probably never rise for long periods of time above the subsistence level.

While today we do not accept Malthus' theory as accurately descriptive of Western European and American society, there is growing interest in the analysis of human fertility from an economic point of view.[4] Here we may view children as capital goods which yield utility to their parents in the form of consumption (in urban areas), and to some extent in the form of income (primarily in rural areas). It is implied by economic theory that expenditures on children are positively related to income levels, if children are "normal" goods, and negatively related to the cost of rearing them.

---

[4] For a provocative treatment of fertility from an economic point of view, see "An Economic Analysis of Fertility" by Gary S. Becker in *Demographic and Economic Change in Developed Countries*, A Conference of the Universities—National Bureau Committee for Economic Research (Princeton, N.J.: Princeton University Press, 1960).

The cost of rearing children, however, is not a well-defined concept. How, for instance, do we relate the cost of child-raising by a Mississippi sharecropper to that of a Chicago business executive? The Mississippian will not feel it necessary to send his children to school as long, spend as much on medical care, buy as many clothes, and so on, as the Chicagoan. Of course, the costs of *given amounts* of schooling, medical care, and clothing (as well as per capita income) are probably lower in Mississippi than in Chicago, but the principal difference in the amount spent per child in the two areas arises from differences in the ultimate "quality" of children, rather than from differences in the cost of raising children with the same inputs and character- istics. Whether we say the Mississippian spends less per child simply because his income is smaller and because of different attitudes toward the quality of children, or whether he is merely responding to different economically and culturally determined "costs" of child-rearing is an unsettled issue. Nevertheless, it is obvious that if, as economic growth occurs, people decide to spend more in raising each child, it does not necessarily follow that population will respond positively to a rising level of per capita income. Thus, Malthus turned upside down may have had a very good point—that *expendi- tures* on children rise as the demand for labor rises. These expenditures may, and probably do, have an important influence on the quality of the labor force via their effect on the stock of human capital. Thus, it is probably true that labor supply responds positively to labor demand in the long run, even if there is no easily ascertainable relationship between economic growth and population.

5

the theory
of competitive supply
of labor
to occupations, firms,
and the economy

In Chapters 2, 3, and 4 we concentrated on the subject of the amount of labor supplied by family members—that is, we discussed labor supply from the individual household member's point of view. We now briefly address ourselves to the question of the aggregated amounts of labor supplied to firms, industries, occupations, and the economy from the point of view of the business sector. Discussing labor supply from the point of view of the household members enabled us to formulate such questions as: How many hours will a household member supply to the market at alternative wage rates and income levels; and, What are likely to be important determinants of investment in human capital. However, we did not proceed to ask: If the demand for labor should grow in a firm, occupation, industry, or the entire economy, how will the multitude responses of individual household members be reflected in the supply of labor to these entities? In other words, how do the aggregate responses of individual household members appear from the point of view of demanders of labor? The answer depends, of course, on the way in which suppliers of labor need to be aggregated; this will vary depending on whether we concentrate attention on firms, industries, occupations, or the entire economy.

AGGREGATING SUPPLY BY OCCUPATIONS

the nature of occupations

We often think of working people as members of particular occupations. A man is known not only as John Smith, but as John Smith the pharmacist or as John Smith the plumber. Occupational categories are useful for labor market analysis. The principal reasons are that individuals who belong to one occupational group tend to be imperfect labor force substitutes for individuals who belong to others and that it is not in general costless for workers to change occupations. Of course, even *within* occupations interpersonal differences exist which make for imperfect substitutability among individuals who are members of the same occupation. But interoccupational differences in labor force characteristics of persons tend to outweigh intraoccupational differences. If this were not the case, differentiation of jobs by occupational categories wouldn't make much sense from the point of view of labor market analysis, although it might make sense from some other point of view. That is to say, for the questions of labor economics to which the concept of occupations is relevant, it does not make sense to define occupations in such a way that the members of one occupational group are freely substitutable for those in another, either from the point of view of individuals making occupational choices or from the point of view of production processes.

occupational choice and labor supply

Occupations pertain to the kind of work people do, and the principal reason for differentiating among individuals this way is to place in separate categories workers who are not perfect substitutes for each other in production because they differ significantly in attributes such as training, education, innate ability, attitude toward work vs. leisure, and so on. The concept of the supply of labor to an occupation has to do with the amount of labor of constant quality that workers are willing to offer at various wage rates to employers of that occupational category.

Clearly if it were costless for workers to change occupations, any tendency for the wage rate paid to workers in one occupation to rise relative to wage rates in other occupations would immediately attract utility-maximizing workers to leave occupations where wage rates were unchanging and enter the occupation where the wage rate is increasing. This would be consistent with the behavior of hours worked in the presence of wage rate changes which are expected to be transitory, because *given* the average number of hours per period individuals intend to work, it pays to work when *and where* the hourly rate of pay is highest, *cet. par.* However, it follows from the definition of occupations that individual decisions to change occupations are essentially *long-run* decisions because it is almost inevitable that some costs of education, training, lost wages in transition between jobs, and/or moving expenses, etc., will be involved. These costs are *investments* which will pay only if interoccupational differences in wages and associated nonpecuniary advantages are sufficiently large and of sufficiently long duration to compensate individuals for giving up alternative uses of invested resources and for undertaking the *risk* of investing in occupational change as opposed to other possible courses of action. In this sense, then, it follows from the theory of labor supplied by household members that the supply of workers to an occupation depends on the wage rate attainable.

Because the differences in worker characteristics, training, and education between major occupational groups are often large, many occupational "choices" are made, often with only vague intentions, while individuals are still quite young. In fact, *effective* choices during early life are made *only* between the broad occupational categories such as professional, skilled craftsman, or laborer. This is because a person attending high school who decides to become, say, a dentist rather than a doctor or other professional worker can do almost nothing about his decision except to prepare himself for college. If he wants to become *either* a dentist or a doctor or almost any other professional worker, much the same training in high school and early college is required. The kinds of occupational decisions that are effective between such broad occupational groups that college education is required for one group but not the other are typically made early in life for two reasons: (1) In terms of capital theory, limited life spans usually make it much less remunerative to change major occupational groups when one is beyond the age typical of college students; this is not only because the number of probable years of payoff is smaller than for younger persons, but also because the foregone earnings which are a large portion of the cost of education are much larger for individuals beyond typical school ages. (2) There is probably a correlation between the effective choices among broad occupational categories made at early ages and sociopsychological characteristics which determine attitudes toward schooling, deferred earnings and family formation, and knowledge of differences among alternative occupations and the necessary steps in achieving high occupational status. Thus, individual characteristics other than age mitigate against change among broad occupational categories for those past the ages at which such choices are usually made.

Among rather narrowly defined occupations, effective choices are typically made later in life; thus it is only after completing the first three or four years of medical school and an internship that a young doctor selects a speciality within medicine, and he may decide to change his speciality several years after beginning practice. Similarly, we can imagine a skilled carpenter deciding midway in his career to become a cabinet maker, and so on.

Thus, the nature of the aggregate supply response to changes in demand for workers in different occupational categories depends upon how broad the occupations are over which the individual responses are aggregated. Economic theory implies that in response to a persistent change in the demand for professional workers as opposed to skilled craftsmen, for instance, the amount supplied will change significantly only after several years, because of the changes in basic, early career decisions that are required. However, in response to a change in the relative demand for occupations within broad categories (such as a change in the demand for obstetricians relative to gerontologists or in the demand for physicians relative to dentists), the amount supplied can change significantly in a relatively short period of time because the relevant decisions are made at a relatively late stage in the process of occupational choice. The more narrowly occupational categories are defined, the greater will be the number of workers in related occupations who are close substitutes for workers in occupations where demand is changing, and the less relevant is a capital theoretic approach to occupational choice. However, some costs to workers are almost always involved in changing occupations, and it is difficult to conceive of useful occupational categories so narrowly defined that the aggregate supply curves to individual occupations would be highly elastic over short periods of time.

the supply of labor to occupations as a function of the wage rate

From a cursory analysis of the nature of occupations and the theory of investment in human capital, it is evident that we should expect wage rates to vary systematically among occupation categories, and they do. Table 5-1 shows median earnings and education of males in the experienced civilian labor force in 1959, by major occupational group. The earnings are not exactly equivalent to wage rates because they are influenced by the number of weeks worked per year and hours worked per week, which vary among occupational groups. However, the earnings differences provide an adequate approximation of the interoccupational wage rate differences. There is an obvious relationship between the educational level of the occupational categories and occupational earnings, although the relationship is not uniform; the relationship between occupations and earnings is discussed in greater detail in Chapter 13.

The reasons we should not expect persistent attempts by individuals to seek work where the pay is highest to create interoccupational wage equality should be fairly obvious. Not every individual is equally well suited by way of innate abilities and other personal characteristics to perform the tasks of every occupation. Furthermore, individuals differ in their access to

Table 5-1

EARNING AND EDUCATION OF MALES IN THE EXPERIENCED CIVILIAN
LABOR FORCE BY MAJOR OCCUPATIONAL GROUP

Occupation	Median Earnings[1] A 1959	Median Earnings[1] B 1965	Median Years of School[2] Completed by Employed Males 18+, 1959	Per Cent Who Worked 50–52 Weeks in 1959[3]
Professional, Technical, and Kindred Workers	$6,619	$7,668	16.4	77
Farmers and Farm Managers	2,169	2,630	8.7	79
Managers, Officials, and Proprietors, Except Farm	6,664	7,538	12.4	
Clerical and Kindred Workers	4,785	5,511	12.5	76
Sales Workers	4,987	5,552	12.6	75
Craftsmen, Foremen, and Kindred Workers	5,240	6,270	11.0	68
Operatives and Kindred Workers	4,299	5,046	10.0	63
Service Workers, Except Private Household	3,310	3,436	10.1	66
Farm Laborers and Foremen	1,066	2,274*	7.7	42
Laborers, Except Farm and Mine	2,948	4,651*	8.5	45

Source: [1] A-*U.S. Census of Population: 1960*, B-*Statistical Abstract of the United States*, (1967), I, 240.

[2] U.S. Department of Labor, *Monthly Labor Review*, May, 1963, p. 509 (based on data in the U.S. Census Bureau, *Current Population Reports*, Series P-20, No. 99).

[3] *U.S. Census of Population: 1960*.

* 1965 figures for these occupations refer to year-round full-time workers and are not comparable to the 1959 figures.

resources for investment in human capital and their attitudes toward and information about the relationship between education, training, and occupation. We observe, then, a relatively stable (but by no means unchanging) structure of wage rates among occupations. It is elements of this wage structure that reflect the interaction of the demand and supply of labor in the occupational categories. Economic theory implies that changes in elements of the structure reflect changes in demand and/or supply, and that the wage changes serve to bring about adjustments in the amount of labor supplied in response to changes in demand, and vice versa.

The supply curve of labor to an occupation answers the question, How much labor of a given quality will be supplied to this occupation at different wage rates, holding constant the wage rates in all other occupations? Thus, we view the occupational labor supply as a function of the wage rate of the

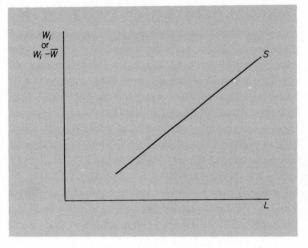

FIG. 5-1

Hypothetical Labor Supply Function for an Occupation (Expressed with Respect to W_i, the Occupational Wage Rate, and $W_i - \overline{W}$, the Occupational Wage Differential)

occupation, assuming that the wage rates of all other occupations are constant. At times it is more convenient to think of the labor supply of an occupation as a function of the *difference* between the wage rate in the occupation and, say, the average wage rate of other occupations. Figure 5-1 shows a hypothetical labor supply function for an occupation, using either the wage rate of the occupation (W_i) or the difference between the wage rate of the occupation and a suitable average wage rate ($W_i - \overline{W}$) as alternative independent variables. The supply curve shown illustrates a situation in which interoccupational adjustment costs induce a degree of inelasticity in the supply function (i.e., the supply curve is positively sloped rather than horizontal).

It should be clear from our discussion of the process of occupational choice that the longer the time period relevant to the labor supply curve of an occupation, the more elastic the supply curve is likely to be. This is because, as the time period grows in length, the relevant occupational choices can be made by a larger and larger number of individuals, since the effect of age on effective occupational choice becomes less and less important. In order to illustrate this point, consider the following hypothetical situation. Suppose the demand for atomic physicists were to increase, the demand curve for workers in other occupations remaining unchanged. In the very short run, an increase in the number of atomic physicists must come from men who work in closely related fields such as other branches of physics and perhaps engineering. But to change specialities is not costless even for these relatively close substitutes; some intellectual "retooling" would be required, such as reading past journal articles, understanding recent progress in the field, developing new lecture notes by university teachers. Nevertheless, an increase in the difference between salaries of atomic physicists and salaries in closely related occupations should induce some supply response.

As a result of rising salaries of fully trained atomic physicists, employers will have the incentive to find substitutes for them and to cut down on their use. Reasonably good substitutes for fully trained scientists may be partly trained scientists such as graduate students; thus, graduate students of atomic physics may find that it is easier to find industrial jobs and teaching and research assistantships; and the stipends for these positions will begin to rise as employers try to fill their vacancies. The increased ease which graduate students experience in obtaining financial aid and remunerative academic and nonacademic employment will attract additional students to the field of atomic physics; the attraction will be magnified as the news of increased salaries for fully trained scientists becomes more generally known. Finally, if the increased demand is great enough, it will spread to other fields, as they find their ranks depleted and recruiting made more difficult by men and women who have elected atomic science as their careers. Thus, by means of a chain of labor market substitutions and information flows young people will learn of the increasing financial attractiveness of science as a career and begin to consider this in choosing their academic curricula and other aspects of their long-run occupational choices.

The preceding discussion illustrates the principle that the supply curve of labor to an occupation will probably be upward sloping, and less elastic, the shorter the time period that is considered. In the long run, when full adjustment via investment in human capital occurs, the supply of labor to an occupation may be completely elastic, depending upon the size of employment relative to the labor force and the particular characteristics required of workers. In the long run, the costs of entering one occupation rather than another become lower and lower, as choices are made more among alternative *forms* of investment in human capital and less among alternative *quantities*. Only when the occupational categories considered are very broad might we expect the long-run supply curve to be significantly upward sloping, unless of course the occupation is one that requires some highly specialized characteristic of its members for which training is an imperfect substitute. Figure 5-2 depicts the short-run and long-run supply of labor to an occupation.

FIRMS

Firms hire members of different occupations and organize their activities in order to produce output. In the theory of competition, we assume that firms are too small, with respect both to the size of product markets and to the size of factors markets, to have any noticeable effect on prices. Therefore, we view the supply curve of labor to a firm as infinitely elastic, i.e., flat, at least in the long run. In the short run, expanding firms may have to raise wage rates in order to attract new workers, even if the firms are located in

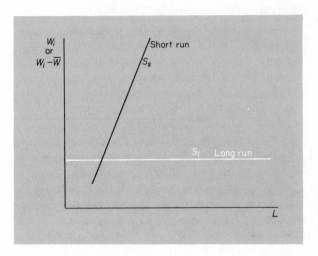

FIG. 5-2
Hypothetical Long-Run and Short-Run Labor Supply Function for an Occupation

relatively large labor markets. This is because workers may be unwilling to give up good jobs for the uncertainties associated with new jobs in return for only a few cents an hour more pay. Furthermore, even though a worker can change jobs between firms without changing occupations, there are bound to exist some initial costs of movement in most cases. These costs may be simply the psychological costs associated with leaving old acquaintances at one firm and making new acquaintances at another; however, pecuniary costs, such as loss of seniority (increased exposure to unemployment, fewer opportunities for overtime pay), and possible change of place of residence, are likely to be involved. The simple act of applying for work may cost a prospective employee a day's pay, and most workers would not pay such a cost, if already employed, unless they thought they could improve their situations more than just marginally. Thus, the capital theoretic considerations which apply to the occupational labor supply curve have relevance to the firm's labor supply as well. In the long run, however, a high proportion of workers seek new jobs because of layoffs, dissatisfactions with employers, geographic mobility which may be unrelated to wage differentials, entrance into the labor force, and so on. Therefore, the firm in a competitive market should be able to increase its employment in the long run without raising the cost of labor; the slower the rate of firm growth, the less likely will be the necessity of substantial increases in the firm's wages in order to attract new personnel.

Parenthetically, we should note that even though the firm's long-run labor supply curve is theoretically infinitely elastic, it does not follow that all firms in the same industry pay the same wage rate. Even if the output of firms could be so precisely defined that each industry produced a perfectly homogeneous output, the diverse characteristics of the various entrepreneurs in an industry might result in significant, if small, interfirm differences in production functions such that cost minimization by different firms might be achieved by employing somewhat different kinds of labor and cooperant factors of production. Equilibrium differences in the optimal skill mix of labor among firms in the same industry could well result in the coexistence of "high-wage firms" and "low-wage firms." Furthermore, at any moment of time, some firms may be expanding relative to others in the same industry, and this could produce interfirm differences in wage levels.[1]

An interesting illustration of the notion that interfirm entrepreneurial differences might result in interfirm differences in wage rates is the following: Suppose that some entrepreneurs in an industry are more "efficient" or skilled than others. Their firms would then have lower average and marginal costs of production. This implies that the industry will consist of marginal firms that earn little or no economic profits and more efficient firms that produce at higher than minimum (for them) average cost and earn economic profits, or rents. If the more efficient employers can produce most cheaply by using relatively high-grade labor, while the marginal employers can produce most cheaply with cheap labor, then the more profitable firms will also be high-wage firms. This might lead the casual observer to conclude that wages are higher in the profitable firms because the employers can "afford" to pay more, when the interfirm wage structure was the result of competitive forces, with all wage rates being equal in alternative employments for labor of given quality. A more careful observer would try to determine whether the labor supplied to the high-wage firm was of relatively high quality and, if so, whether it was in fact being paid more than it could earn elsewhere, and if in fact the relatively profitable firm had some particular advantage in using higher-grade labor. This example illustrates how the hypotheses to be confronted with data must be carefully derived from the underlying theory and a set of maintained hypotheses if inferences from observed behavior are to provide a meaningful test of whether a particular theory of behavior provides a useful framework for understanding actual events.

INDUSTRIES

Industries are defined by what they produce, not by the factors of production they hire, and the factors hired by one industry are likely to be similar to those hired by many others—especially when both factor and industrial categories are not defined extremely broadly. Therefore, if an industry is small, it is reasonable to expect its supply curve to behave similarly to that of the competitive firm, being less elastic in the short run than in the long run and highly elastic in the long run.

---

[1] These remarks are prompted by J. R. Hicks' *Theory of Wages* (2nd ed.) (London: Macmillan & Co., Ltd., 1964), Chap. II, Sec. III.

However, some industries may hire very specialized kinds of labor. In fact, as one thinks carefully about industrial categories, one becomes aware of the none-too-fine dividing line that sometimes exists between occupations and industries. Some examples of industries which tend to coincide with particular occupations are mining, construction, and certain kinds of food processing. Thus the conditions which contribute to an imperfectly elastic supply of labor to occupations (i.e., conditions other than these associated with *any* job change) can do the same thing for industries. Other industrial characteristics which may contribute to labor supply inelasticity are nonpecuniary differences in employment conditions (coal mining, for example, offering relatively disadvantageous conditions in this respect) and regional concentration, which implies that for some industries to expand it is often necessary to attract regional in-migrants. However, just as in the cases of firms and occupations, the conditions which contribute to the inelasticity of labor supply tend to be less effective, the longer the period of time during which adjustment to changing circumstances can take place. Thus, under any set of conditions, the industry labor supply curve is likely to be more elastic in the long run than in the short run. Effective empirical analysis of questions such as the degree to which the theory of competition is adequate for understanding labor supply responses to interindustry changes in labor demand is complicated by the characteristics of industries which contribute to interindustry differences in wage levels, to the speed of adjustment of the supply of labor, and to differences in labor supply elasticities over given adjustment periods.

THE ECONOMY

When immigration is not a large potential source of labor supply to the economy, any changes in the total number (and quality) of hours sold in the economy as a whole must come about from decisions made by family members regarding the number of hours they work and investment in human capital. These decisions have been discussed in Chapters 2, 3, and 4, and we need only review them here.

When plotted against "permanent" wage rates, we may expect the supply curve of labor hours (not necessarily of constant quality) to be backward bending. Evidence for this in the United States (discussed in Chapter 3) is the rather constant labor force participation rate, over time, accompanied by a trend toward earlier retirement, later labor force entrance, and reduced weekly and yearly hours of work. (A possibly important force working in the opposite direction is the increased life expectancy of the population.) On the other hand, forces working to increase education, training, and health probably serve to increase the quality of the labor force.

As was mentioned in Chapters 3 and 4, a part of the growing quality of labor hours sold is possibly itself induced by advancing productivity in the economy. The reason that productivity growth may induce a supply response contributing to increased labor force quality is that, if the productivity of all kinds of labor increases roughly in the same proportion, the return to human capital will grow. This is because as the marginal productivity of all kinds of labor grows, the absolute differences in the marginal products of labor of different qualities will grow as well. This may result in an increased rate of return to investment in human capital. To the extent productivity of other resources increases, the effect of growing productivity on the return to human capital is enhanced. Thus, when labor quality is taken into consideration, it is not unlikely that the labor supply curve for the economy is upward sloping, rather than backward bending.

When immigration is not severely limited, an increase in the demand for labor will induce immigration by raising wages relative to those in other countries where demand is growing less rapidly. Thus, the elasticity of the labor supply curve for an economy is surely higher when immigration is possible than when it is not.

FURTHER APPLICATIONS OF THE THEORY OF LABOR SUPPLY

So far, the principal empirical evidence bearing on the theory of labor supply has been presented in Chapter 3. There we examined some studies pertaining to family members' decisions to sell labor hours. We have not yet discussed in any detail evidence bearing on the theory of human capital or its application to the supply of labor to occupations, firms, industries, and the economy. Further applications of the theory of labor supply are relevant to the discussions of the wage structure, the general wage level, and unemployment. These subjects are dealt with in Chapters 13, 14, and 15. Some implications of the theory of labor supply under conditions of imperfect competition are discussed in Chapters 10, 11, and 12. Before proceeding to these discussions, however, it is important to complete the analysis of the labor market by treating the theory of labor demand and some evidence bearing on it; we proceed to do this in Chapters 6, 7, and 8.

PART II

the demand for labor: theory and evidence

6

the theory
of the demand
for labor:
the competitive firm

As you probably know, the demand for a factor of production is sometimes called a *derived demand*. That is, it is derived in part from the demand for the final goods the factor cooperates in producing. The relationship between the demand for final output and the demand for a productive factor depends crucially on the way in which the factor is used in production. The alternative combinations of factors that can be used in the production process—the relationship between factor inputs and the output of production—is formally described by a *production function*. In this chapter we shall explore at length the relationships between the demand for output, the production function, and the demand for labor. Demand will be analyzed assuming competitive conditions; in the next chapter, we apply the theory of demand developed here to a very interesting case study—the effect of minimum wage legislation on employment in Puerto Rico. In subsequent chapters we shall modify the assumptions of the theory of competition and consider demand under conditions where firms are not assumed to view prices as given in the product market and the factor market, and under conditions where firms are not assumed to maximize their profits. Finally, in the last section of this book, we bring together the theories of supply and demand in order to see how well they enable us to understand the behavior of wage rates and employment in the United States.

THE PRODUCTION FUNCTION OF THE FIRM (GEOMETRIC ANALYSIS)

The smallest and most basic unit we shall consider in analyzing labor demand is the firm. We assume that every firm possesses full knowledge of the technological relationship between inputs of the productive factors and output. This technological relationship is formally represented by a production function. Production functions may be described either algebraically or geometrically: the diagram in Figure 6-1 is a geometric representation.

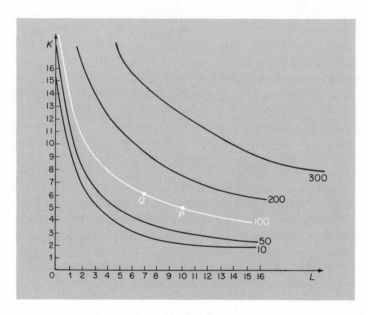

FIG. 6-1
The Production Function

The axes of the diagram measure quantities of factor services. The vertical axis is labeled K and measures the services of the factors other than labor; from now on we shall think of K as physical capital equipment or machinery. The horizontal axis is labeled L and measures the services of labor. We assume that all labor is of the same type and quality or that a suitable measurement system allows us to add up different kinds of labor. Our measurements are of *flows* of factor *services* per unit of time. That is, we might measure labor by manpower-hours per week and capital by, say, horsepower-hours per week; we are not interested simply in the number of men or the number of machines.

The production function is represented by a family of curved lines. Each line is numbered, and each number refers to a flow of output per unit of time. For instance, the line marked 100 represents an output of 100 units (e.g., pounds) per unit of time (e.g., weeks). The coordinates of each line represent the combinations of L and K which are capable of producing each amount of output. For instance, point P shows that 5 units of K plus 10 units of L are capable of producing 100 units of output. Point Q shows that 100 units of output may also be produced with 6 units of K and 7 units of L. Each line is called an *isoquant*, meaning equal quantity, because the output along each line is everywhere the same. Each isoquant describes all the factor combinations which will produce each quantity of output (only parts of the isoquants are drawn—for convenience).

The production function illustrated in Figure 6-1 conveys one of the most important ideas in economics—that *a given level of output can be produced in alternative ways, using various combinations of the productive factors.* There are many examples of the use of alternative production techniques to produce a certain product. In heavily populated Asian countries, for instance, crops are produced on little land with a great deal of labor, whereas in California, where labor is very expensive, similar crops (e.g., rice) are produced with relatively large inputs of land and machinery. In business offices, accounting can be done with relatively intensive use of bookkeepers working with adding machines or relatively little use of human inputs and heavy reliance on complicated computers, and so on. Thus, the existence of a production function implies that a firm must choose among alternative production techniques; we proceed now to investigate how firms make such choices and how these choices help determine the demand for labor.

The most important characteristics of the isoquants are their slopes and shapes. As a rule, the isoquants have *negative* slopes; their shapes are generally *convex* to the origin. This is the way the isoquants in Figure 6-1 are drawn. The isoquants have negative slopes because of the *principle of substitution*. According to this principle, to hold output constant, when one unit of a factor is taken away in production, a quantity of the other factor must be added. The slope of the isoquants at each point describes exactly the substitution relationship between the factors; for instance, if the slope is minus 1/3, three units of labor must be added for every unit of machinery taken away. The slope of an isoquant is named the *marginal rate of substitution* between the factors (MRS).

Convexity is the characteristic that, along each isoquant, as the ratio of labor to machinery grows, the amount of labor that must be added for each unit of machinery taken away becomes larger. That is, the slope becomes smaller and smaller (absolutely) as the labor-to-machinery ratio grows larger and larger. Convexity represents the *principle of imperfect substitution*, or the *principle of variable proportions*. While the factors are substitutes for each other, they are not perfect substitutes, and the degree of substitutability depends on the factor ratio.

THE AVAILABILITY OF FACTORS

In order to go from the firm's production function to the demand for labor, we need to know not only the firm's choices of production techniques, but also what options the firm faces in regard to obtaining the factors. In competition, the firm's purchase options are determined by conditions outside its control—by the interaction of supply and demand in the factor markets. Thus, each firm feels (correctly) that it may elect any option it chooses without affecting the conditions under which it may purchase any of the productive factors. The essentially important condition of purchase is, of course, the factor price. Thus, we express the purchase options of the firm by saying that under competitive conditions the supply of each factor is infinitely price elastic, i.e., the firm may buy as little or as much as it wants of each factor at the going price, which is determined in the market.

The concept of the infinitely elastic supply of labor to each firm is shown graphically in Figure 6-2. The vertical axis measures the price of labor

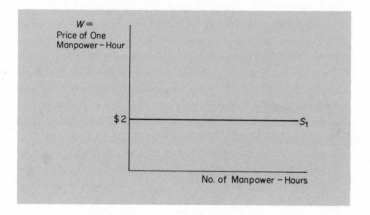

FIG. 6-2
The Firm's Labor Supply Curve

(in dollars), and the horizontal axis measures manpower-hours per week. The labor supply curve is parallel to the horizontal axis—implying an elasticity of infinity (that is, the percentage change in quantity divided by the percentage change in price, along the curve, is infinite). The supply curve of machinery services may be drawn similarly.

DERIVING THE DEMAND CURVE: THE SHORT RUN

We are now in a position to derive the firm's demand curve for labor. First of all, let us consider the very short run. Suppose a firm experiences a change in the price of labor. There are two reasons for supposing the firm will be quite cautious in adapting to the change. One reason is that it doesn't know how permanent the change in supply conditions will be; indeed it may have good reason for suspecting that it will be temporary, if the change is due to well-known seasonal or cyclical movements in the economy. The second reason is that many kinds of adaptation are expensive and would be worth-while only if the price change is to be semipermanent. The most expensive kinds of adaptation involve investing in new plant and equipment; consequently, in the short run we may expect firms to change their inputs of labor (and raw materials) more readily than their inputs of machinery. It is reasonable, therefore, as a first approximation to the short-run demand for labor, to assume that the input of machinery is fixed.

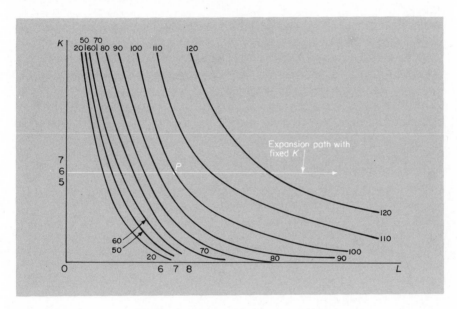

FIG. 6-3
The Production Function (Inputs of K Fixed at 6)

If the input of machinery (factor K) is fixed, we do not need to know its supply conditions. Let us redraw Figure 6-1 and suppose that the firm is producing an output of 100 units per week, as shown in Figure 6-3, with an output of 6 units of K and 7 units of L. This situation is represented by point P in Figure 6-3. Now, suppose the wage rate falls because, say, there is an influx of inexpensive labor. This reduces the firm's cost of production, and it has an incentive to expand output. But by how much?

As you know, the firm will maximize its profits if it expands output so long as the value of the additional production is greater than the cost of producing it. As far as the firm is concerned, the value of additional production is measured by the amount of additional output multiplied by its price. Price, in the theory of competition, is constant with respect to the output of the firm, and the crucial determinant of the firm's demand for labor will be the behavior of output as additional labor is added to the fixed inputs of machinery.

We can discover the relationship between production and additional inputs of labor, with machinery fixed, by examining the production function along a ray extending from 6 on the K axis, parallel to the L axis. All the points along this ray represent the levels of output that correspond to various inputs of L, with the inputs of K held fixed at 6 horsepower-hours per week.

In examining Figure 6-1, we noticed that along any isoquant the ability to substitute L for K diminishes as the ratio of the inputs $L:K$ increased. Similarly, holding K constant (rather than output), the ability of L to contribute to additions to output falls as we move outward along the ray, as the ratio $L:K$ increases. Or, to put it another way, in order to increase output by equal amounts, larger and larger additional inputs of L must be added as the ratio $L:K$ rises. We call the additions to output that correspond to each constant small addition of L, the *marginal product* of L. As Figure 6-4

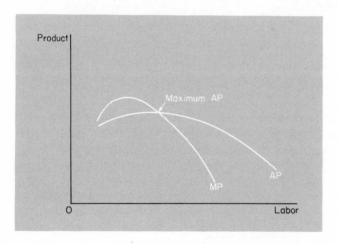

FIG. 6-4
Marginal and Average Physical Product of Labor

is drawn, the marginal product of L declines as the $L:K$ ratio increases *over a certain range*. This range is reached after a critical level of output (50). The reason that the critical level of output is greater than zero is that it is not unrealistic to suppose that when the ratio $L:K$ is very low, additions of L, holding K constant, have an increasing marginal product. Consider, for instance, a farmer with 100 acres of land. If he tries to do all the farming himself, he must be a "jack of all trades," and will be handicapped by the fact that he can be in only one place at a time. But if the farmer hires a helper, the product of the farm may more than double, because some specialization will be possible. Furthermore, if there is a hole in a fence at the same time as there is a leak in the barn, both emergencies can be taken care of at once;

the labor resources of the farm will be employed more flexibly, as well as with specialization. This increasing efficiency of labor may continue as the farmer hires a second, third, and even a fourth helper. However, as the number of workers on the same piece of land grows larger, the marginal product of labor must eventually fall. This is the effect of the principle of variable proportions.

In Figure 6-4, the relationship between output and labor, holding machinery constant, has been redrawn. We measure output on the vertical axis and units of labor on the horizontal axis. The curve labeled *MP* is drawn simply by plotting the changes in output (differences between the isoquants) along the ray in Figure 6-3 against the corresponding amounts of labor. The *MP* curve represents the *marginal physical product* of labor. *Marginal product* and *marginal physical product* are identical concepts, as far as we have gone in our analysis at this point.

It will make the following analysis easier if we convert the relationship between output and labor into value terms. That is, since we want to find out how much labor the firm will hire in order to maximize its profits which are generally measured in units of money, it is convenient to multiply the marginal physical product by its price in order to have all quantities measured in the same units. Of course, the competitive firm can sell as much output as it would like at the going price, determined by the forces of supply and demand in the market. Therefore, we merely have to multiply the marginal physical product by a single price in order to find the *value of marginal product of labor* (*VMP*). Since we are multiplying by a constant to obtain value of marginal product, the *VMP* has the same shape as *MP*; this is shown in Figure 6-5. In Figure 6-5 we also plot the supply curve of labor, which was originally drawn in Figure 6-2. This, of course, is also expressed in terms of dollars.

Now, how much labor will the firm hire in order to maximize its profits? You should already know the answer. In competitive conditions, firms maximize their profits by producing up to the point where marginal

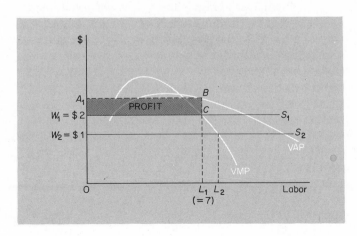

FIG. 6-5
Value of Marginal Product and Average Product

cost (MC) is just equal to marginal revenue (MR) which, in the case of competition, is equal to price (P). Similarly, the firm will hire labor, the only variable factor of production in this simple example, until the marginal cost of labor (i.e., the wage rate) is equal to the marginal revenue it produces (i.e., VMP). Thus, the firm's original desired quantity of labor is given by $L_1(= 7)$, the amount of labor which represents the point at which the labor supply curve intersects the VMP curve. In response to the decline in the price of labor, the firm will recognize that the supply curve has fallen from the original curve, W_1S_1 to W_2W_2, and it will increase its employment to L_2.

We proceed now to express the profit-maximizing *hiring* policy of the firm algebraically in terms of the profit-maximizing *output* policy of the firm and to show they are equivalent. Algebraically, we may state the firm's profit-maximizing hiring policy as

$$W = VMP \tag{1}$$

and its profit-maximizing output policy as

$$P = MC. \tag{2}$$

In order to show that the firm's profit-maximizing output is consistent with its profit-maximizing input of labor, we need to demonstrate that (1) and (2) amount to the same thing.

The equivalence of (1) and (2) can be shown as follows: we derive MC in terms of MP by using the concept of the marginal product of labor to develop the concept of the additional amount of labor required to produce one more unit of output. Suppose, for instance, that the marginal product of labor is 3 units of output. Then, it would take approximately 1/3 additional unit of labor to produce one more unit of output. That is to say, the marginal cost of output *in terms of labor* is $1/MP$. For convenience we name $1/MP$ a *marginal input* of labor. It follows that a marginal input of labor multiplied by the wage rate is the cost *in dollars* of one more unit to output. Thus, all we have to do to relate MC to MP in terms of dollars is to multiply $1/MP$ by W, obtaining $W/MP = MC$. Therefore, we may rewrite (2) with an equivalent formulation,

$$P = W/MP. \tag{3}$$

It is now simple to show that (1) is the equivalent of (2). Equation (3), which is an equivalent formulation to (2), can be transformed into (1) by multiplying both sides by MP and recognizing that $P \cdot MP = VMP$. Thus, the conditions under which a firm will maximize its profits in the hiring of labor are identical to those under which it will maximize its profits in determining the amount of its output.

In what sense is the *VMP* curve a demand curve for labor? In order to answer this question, let us note that a demand curve answers the question, How much labor will the firm wish to hire at various wage rates? Over most of its range, the *VMP* curve answers this question. However, over part of its range (the part that lies above *VAP*, as we shall see) it does not. Let us pursue this point. Figure 6-5 also shows the *value of average product of labor* curve (*VAP*). This curve is derived by dividing the value of total output by the number of units of labor required to produce it. As you learned in your economics principles course, an average curve always rises as long as the corresponding marginal curve lies above it; it falls as long as the marginal curve lies below it; therefore, the marginal curve crosses its corresponding average curve at the average curve's minimum or maximum point. In the case of product curves, the *VMP* crosses *VAP* at maximum *VAP*.

In Figure 6-5, the firm hires L_1 units of labor at wage rate W_1 and L_2 at W_2. The value of average product when L_1 is hired is A_1; by definition, the total value of output is $A_1 \times L_1$, or the rectangle OA_1BL_1. Similarly, total variable cost is $L_1 \times W_1$, or the rectangle OW_1CL_1.

You also know from your economics principles that the firm will stay in business only so long as total revenue exceeds total variable cost. The amount by which total revenue exceeds total variable cost when the firm maximizes its profits at wage rate W_1 is represented by the rectangle W_1A_1BC. It is possible to construct such a rectangle for any profit-maximizing output greater than the output corresponding to maximum *VAP*. When the wage rate equals maximum *VAP*, the area of the rectangle representing the excess of total revenue over total variable cost is zero. Thus, so long as the wage rate is less than *VAP*, the firm will maximize its profits (or minimize its losses) by hiring up to the point where $W = VMP$. However, if the wage rate should rise above *VAP*, the firm will minimize its losses by not producing at all. *Hence, the VMP curve is the short-run demand curve for labor wherever it lies below maximum VAP.*

DERIVING THE DEMAND CURVE: THE LONG RUN

Once we pass from the short run to the long run, in which the firm may, and chooses to, vary the inputs of both labor and machinery, it is necessary to reconsider the demand curve for labor.

The first step is to represent the firm's purchase options on the same diagram as the production function. This involves portraying the factor prices. In the production function diagram, we measure physical quantities of the factors along the axes; there is no place to represent the units in monetary terms. However, if we know the supply prices of labor and machinery in terms of dollars, we have all the information we need to express the price of labor in terms of machinery, and vice versa. For instance, if the price (wage rate) of labor is $1 per manpower-hour and the price of machinery is $2 per horsepower-hour, then we know that the price of labor in terms of machinery is 1/2. That is, if the firm decides not to purchase some additional labor, but to purchase instead some more machinery, it can get 1/2 horse-power-hour of machinery services for every manpower-hour of labor it gives up. The price of labor in terms of machinery—1/2—is the *relative price* of labor in terms of machinery. More concisely, one may simply refer to the relative price, keeping in the back of one's mind that the relative price refers to the quantity of one factor that may be exchanged for the other. Conversely, the relative price of machinery is 2.

Obviously, if the dollar prices of labor and machinery do not depend upon how much of either factor the firm buys, the relative price of the factors is independent of purchases as well. The relative price of labor and machinery is a *rate of exchange* between the two factors. The rate of exchange is formally similar to the rate of substitution that is represented by the slopes of the isoquants, but it refers to substitution in purchases, not to substitution in the production process. Just as the variable degree of substitutability in production is represented by convex isoquants, constant substitutability in

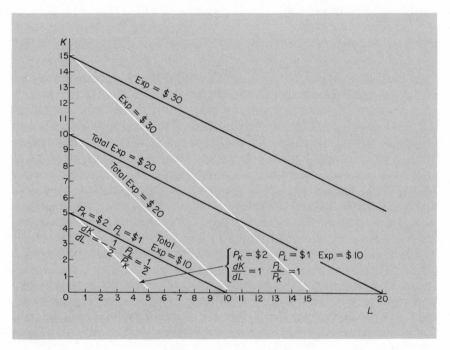

FIG. 6-6a
Two Families of Isoexpenditure Lines

purchasing is represented by straight lines. Figure 6-6a shows graphically the purchase options available to the firm. The purchase options are represented by a family of parallel straight lines; they are often called *relative price lines*. Each line represents a fixed number of dollars spent on the factors L and K; for this reason they are also called *isoexpenditure lines*. Consider the isoexpenditure line $10, in which $P_K = \$2$ and $P_L = \$1$. This is the solid isoexpenditure line nearest the origin. It represents all the combinations of L and K that can be purchased for $10 if the price of K is $2 and L is $1, such as $8L$ and $1K$, $6L$ and $2K$, $4L$ and $3K$, and so on. Note that each time the firm decides to purchase one more unit of K, it must purchase two less units of L, if it wants to keep its expenditures unchanged. As they move away from the origin, the solid isoexpenditure lines represent successively higher levels of expenditure on the factors. (If the price of L rises to $2, then the dashed $10 isoexpenditure line represents all the factor combinations that can be bought for $10.) The lines have negative slopes. The slopes represent the amount of K that must be given up to purchase one more unit of L, and vice versa. Since the slope of the solid lines is $-1/2$, $1/2$ unit of K must be given up to purchase one unit of L.

Note that we can derive the family of relative price lines if we know the dollar prices of the factors; we cannot, however, infer the dollar prices from a knowledge of the relative price. A change in the relative price lines from $1/2$ to, say, -1 could come about either from a *decline* in the price of machinery to $1 or from a *rise* in the price of labor to $2 (or from any other of an infinitely large set of changes in dollar prices). While such changes have identical effects on relative factor prices, they have substantially different effects on the cost of production.

When more than one factor is variable, we must consider how the firm minimizes its cost of production. It is essential that the firm minimize the cost of producing whatever level of output is selected if it is to maximize its profits; in the case of the short run and only one variable factor, cost minimization did not require special analysis, because there was only one possible method of producing each level of output. However, when all of the points on each isoquant represent possible production methods, we must inquire how the firm is to choose among them. In Figure 6-6b, the isoquants have been added to Figure 6-6a, so that it is easy to see how the firm minimizes its costs by comparing its purchase possibilities with its production possibilities. In order to see how the firm would minimize the cost of a given output, start at one end of an isoquant such as 100, and proceed along it until you reach the isoexpenditure line representing the lowest possible level of expenditure on factors consistent with producing 100 units of output. This will be at point Q at which isoexpenditure line $10 is tangent to isoquant 100. Note that 100 is also the highest level of output that can be achieved by spending $10 on the factors of production. Most readers will recognize that the condition of minimizing the cost of producing 100 units of output at Q is similar to the

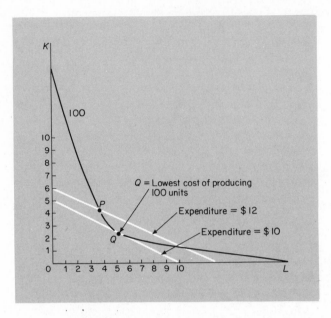

FIG. 6-6b
*The Least Cost of Producing
100 Units*

condition of utility maximization by a typical household member in determining his hours of work.

The firm minimizes the cost of producing any level of output (or
maximizes the output achievable with any given expenditure) by producing
at a point where an isoexpenditure line is tangent to an isoquant. There is
one, and only one, such point for each isoquant and for each isoexpenditure
line, except in rather rare cases where an isoquant and isoexpenditure line
intersect at one of the axes, with there being no point of tangency between
them in the quadrant northeast of the K and L axes. Where such an intersection occurs, we say that the least cost of producing that level of output is
represented by a "corner solution"; recall that corner solutions were possible
in the case of utility-maximizing household members deciding how many
hours to work as well. Note that a corner solution is possible *only* if the
isoquants intersect an axis. If they do not, then some small amount of each
factor is always required in production, and corner solutions are precluded.

Let us examine more closely the proposition that the point of tangency
between an isoquant and an isoexpenditure line represents a minimum cost of
production. Suppose the firm attempted to produce 100 units with combination P, which does not represent a point of tangency between the $10 iso-
expenditure line and the 100 isoquant. The isoexpenditure line going through
point P represents an expenditure of $12. Why should the competitive firm
spend $12 to produce 100 units when it can produce them for $10? There is
no reason at all. Thus, let the firm give up one unit of K and purchase just
enough L to compensate in production for K's loss. Since the slope of the

isoquant at P is steeper than the slope of the iso-expenditure line, by sub-stituting L for K, the firm can reduce its cost of production. The firm will continue to reduce production cost by substituting L for K until it reaches the tangency point, Q.

Let us now discuss the nature of the tangency, least cost, position somewhat more formally. We redraw Figure 6-6b in Figure 6-7, giving special

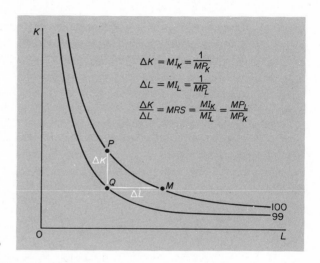

FIG. 6-7

Definition of MRS, MI, and MP

consideration to two isoquants which differ by only one unit of production—100 and 99. Consider point P on the 100 isoquant and point Q, vertically below it, on isoquant 99. These points differ by one unit of output and by just enough K (ΔK) to account for the difference in production (the input of L is the same for both outputs). Consider also point M on the 100 isoquant. This differs from point Q on isoquant 99 by one unit of production and just enough $L(\Delta L)$ to account for the output difference. The line segment PQ is defined as a *marginal input* of K (MI_K) [See page 126], and QM as a marginal input of $L(MI_L)$. Thus, the slope of isoquant 100 may be thought of as MI_K/MI_L. This is in general true for every isoquant: the slope is the ratio of the marginal inputs of the factors at a particular point. Formally:

$$\Delta K/\Delta L \text{ (isoquant)} = MI_K/MI_L. \qquad (5)$$

Remember that on page 126, we noticed that the marginal product of a factor is the reciprocal of its marginal input. Similarly,

$$MI_K/MI_L = MP_L/MP_K. \qquad (6)$$

It follows that

$$\Delta K/\Delta L \text{ (isoquant)} = MP_L/MP_K. \qquad (7)$$

It follows from (6) to (7) that the marginal rate of substitution between the factors may more usefully be thought of as the ratio either of the marginal inputs or of the marginal products of the factors.

Recall now that on page 128, the slope of the isoexpenditure line was defined as measuring the relative prices of the factors. Formally,

$$\Delta K / \Delta L \text{ (isoexpenditure)} = P_L / P_K. \tag{8}$$

Thus, at any point of tangency between an isoexpenditure line and an isoquant, the *relative* price of the factors is equal to the *ratio* of their marginal products. That is, from equations (7) and (8) we have

$$P_L / P_K = MP_L / MP_K \tag{9}$$

as the condition of cost minimization.

An alternative way of viewing what is implied by cost minimization is to rewrite (9) as

$$\frac{P_L}{P_K} = \frac{MI_K}{MI_L}. \tag{10}$$

By cross multiplication, we see that (10) implies

$$P_L MI_L = P_K MI_K. \tag{11}$$

That is, when cost is minimized, the cost of increasing output by one unit is the same, whether a marginal input of L or of K is added. If this were not so, the firm could lower its cost by reducing its input of the appropriate factor and adding more of the other. When the firm is minimizing the cost of production, $MC = $ *either* $P_L MI_L$ or $P_K MI_K$.

Do not confuse the condition of cost minimization with profit maximization! Equation (9) defines the condition of cost minimization, but there is such a condition for each level of output. At only one of these outputs will the firm also maximize profits! Cost minimization is a *necessary* condition of profit maximization, but it is not *sufficient*.

In order to go from the concept of cost minimization to the concept of labor demand when both labor and machinery are variable inputs, we must introduce still one more concept. Let us once again redraw Figure 6-6b, in Figure 6-8. In Figure 6-8 we have a set of isoquants and two possible sets of isoexpenditure lines which are tangent to them. The two sets of isoexpenditure lines represent two possible relative prices of labor and machinery. (Let us suppose, as in our short-run example, that inexpensive labor enters the market, lowering the wage rate and causing the isoexpenditure lines to have shallower slopes.) Thus, the flatter set of isoexpenditure lines represent the

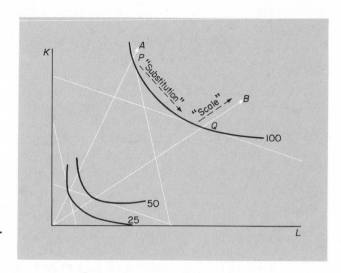

FIG. 6-8
The Firm's Expansion Paths—
The Substitution and Scale
Effects

same price of machinery, in terms of dollars, as the steeper set, but a lower price of labor. The loci of the tangency points between the two sets of iso-expenditure lines and the set of isoquants form two lines extending outward from the origin. Along these lines, we observe the least-cost combination of factors to produce any level of output, depending on relative factor prices. These are the firm's *expansion paths*[1] (sometimes called *scale lines*). There is a different expansion path for each set of relative prices. Obviously, and sensibly, as the relative price of labor falls, the expansion path moves in a clockwise direction, implying that the cost-minimizing input combinations involve a higher proportion of labor, the lower labor's relative price. For simplicity, the expansion paths have been drawn as straight lines, although this is not necessary. (Recall that in our analysis of the demand for labor in the short run, the firm's expansion path was a ray extending parallel to the *L* axis along the ordinate corresponding to the fixed input of machinery; see Figure 6-3.)

Let us now suppose that the firm is in equilibrium at some point, *P*, on expansion path *A* (which represents the higher price of labor). At point *P*, the firm is maximizing its profits by equating marginal cost with marginal revenue and, hence, the value of the marginal product of each factor with its price. Suppose now the price of labor falls, so that the firm's expansion path becomes *B*. Two kinds of adjustments take place. First, each level of output can now be produced most cheaply with a higher proportion of labor.

---

[1] We implicitly assume in constructing the expansion paths that increases in output are associated with increases of all productive factors at all output levels. This is not a necessary assumption, as demonstrated by D. V. T. Bear, "Inferior Inputs and the Theory of the Firm," *Journal of Political Economy*, LXXIII, No. 3 (June, 1965). Ignoring the possibility of inferior inputs does not affect the generality of the ultimate inference that factor demand curves are negatively sloped with respect to the factor price, *cet. par.*

We may think of the firm as moving along isoquant 100, where P is located, to Q, where expansion path B crosses the 100 isoquant. This hypothetical movement holds output constant, but changes the proportions in which the factors are used. L is substituted for K, and the marginal product of L falls while the marginal product of K rises. This is the *substitution effect* of a change in the relative prices of L and K. The substitution effect implies that even if a firm did not change its rate of output, the change in relative input prices would lead it to change the way it combined inputs, more of the relatively lower-priced input being used in place of the relatively higher-priced input.

We know that the relative price of L has fallen because its dollar price fell while the dollar price of K remained the same. Therefore the cost of production is less than it used to be. The cost of production at P is less than it used to be, because the dollar price of L has declined; *a fortiori*, the cost of production at Q is less than it used to be at P, because the firm is using more of the now cheaper factor and less of the factor whose price has remained unchanged. Since the price of output has not changed, but the cost of production has fallen, the firm can increase its profits by expanding output. Consequently it proceeds northeast along expansion path B until marginal cost is once again equal to marginal revenue, and the value of the marginal product of each factor once again equals its price. The movement from Q along expansion path B is called the *scale effect* of the change in the price of L.

In the analysis of the short-run demand for labor, we demonstrated that in equilibrium, the profit-maximizing firm hires labor up to the point where VMP equals W. In the long run, this condition holds for every variable factor of production. The statement that when the firm is in equilibrium, the VMP of each factor is equal to its price, may be demonstrated algebraically as follows. From equation (10) and the remainder of the paragraph in which it appears, we know that both of the following equations hold in equilibrium:

$$MC = MI_K P_K \qquad (11)$$

$$MC = MI_L P_L. \qquad (12)$$

From (2) we also know that in equilibrium,

$$MC = P.$$

Thus,

$$P = MI_L P_L. \qquad (13)$$

From (13) it follows that

$$P/MI_L = P_L. \qquad (14)$$

Thus

$$VMP_L = P_L; \qquad (15)$$

which follows from the fact that MI_L is the reciprocal of MP_L and from the definition VMP_L. The proof for K is identical.

We are now in a position to diagram the long-run demand curve for labor. Let us return to Figure 6-5, and redraw it in Figure 6-9. In this figure

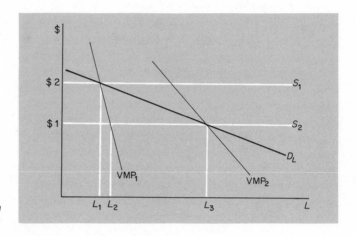

FIG. 6-9
The Short-Run and Long-Run
Demand Curves of the Firm

we draw only the part of the *VMP* curve which is the demand for labor in the short run—that part which lies below maximum *VAP*. Let us suppose, as in the original example, that the price of labor falls from $2 to $1. We can see what will be the quantities demanded at these prices in the short run by examining the *VMP* curve. In the long run, the firm not only has an incentive to expand its output because of the decline in the price of labor, but it has a greater incentive than in the short run, because it can further reduce the cost of production by moving from expansion path *A* to expansion path *B*. Both the substitution effect and the scale effect assure that the amount of labor demanded will increase if its price falls, or decrease if its price rises. Their combined action in the long run assures that the long-run response of the quantity of labor demanded to a change in its price will be greater than the short-run response. Thus, the curve labeled D_L represents the firm's long-run demand for labor; it has a smaller slope and a greater elasticity than the *VMP*, or short-run demand curve. Thus, immediately after the price falls to $1, the firm will increase its employment of labor from L_1 to L_2. But after enough time has elapsed to allow for all possible substitution of labor for machinery, the amount demanded will grow to L_3.

Note that each point on D_L passes through a different *VMP* curve. At every point on the firm's long-run demand curve, the wage rate is equal to VMP. Since a VMP *curve* is drawn with respect to a fixed input of K, and since the input of K is in general different at different points along D_L, each point on D_L corresponds in general to a different input of K and, hence, a different VMP curve. The VMP curve is drawn with respect to a given *quantity* of machinery inputs, while the demand curve is drawn with respect to a given *price* of machinery. It so happens that in the short run the VMP curve and the demand curve coincide; but in general when we refer to the labor demand curve we shall be thinking of one that is drawn with respect to a given *price* of machinery, but not necessarily with respect to a fixed *quantity*.

It is important to remember that while the substitution and scale effects both work in the same direction with respect to the factor whose price has changed, they work in *opposite* directions for the factor whose price has remained unchanged. Thus, in Figure 6-8 we see that the amount of K used might well have been either greater or less after adjustment to the decline in the price of labor, since while the substitution effect worked to reduce the amount of K demanded, the scale effect worked to increase the amount demanded of both L and K. In theory, there is no way to predict whether the scale effect or the substitution effect will have the greater influence on the amount demanded of the factor whose price has not changed. An important implication is that one cannot predict the direction of the change in the amount of a factor demanded if one knows only how its *relative* price has changed (in our example, the relative price of K went up); one must know what happened to its price in terms of dollars as well.

The most important implication of the past two sections, however, is that despite whether we consider the long run or the short run, or whether a great deal or only a little substitution between the factors is possible, *the demand for labor slopes downward with respect to its price in terms of dollars.* The substitution and scale effects assure us that this is an unequivocal implication of the theory of competition. This is one of the most important (and often one of the most controversial) hypotheses of labor economics; in Chapter 8 we shall examine evidence bearing on this demand hypothesis.

7

the theory of the demand for labor: the competitive industry

We proceed from our discussion of the competitive firm's demand for labor to the demand of a competitive industry. A competitive industry is a collection of firms, each of which is too small to have any noticeable effect on the price of output or the factors of production. In deriving an industry's demand curve for labor, one is tempted simply to add up the demand curves of the firms. Before adopting this simple approach, which has a certain appeal to common sense, it would be wise to ask the question, Are the conditions that we hold constant when discussing the firm's demand curve also relevantly held constant when discussing the demand curve of an industry? The opposite may also be asked, Are conditions which are constant for an industry also constant for individual firms?

The answers to both of these questions is usually No, and therefore, it would be incorrect to say that the industry's labor demand curve is simply the sum of the demand curves of the individual firms.

Recall that in Chapter 6 we discussed the firm's demand curve as an answer to the question, How much labor will the firm demand at various wage rates? We wish to ask the same question for an industry. But think now of what happens if the labor supply conditions should change for a whole industry. If there is a decline in the price of labor to each firm, as assumed for an individual firm in Chapter 2, each firm will use more labor per unit of machinery. Each will also expand its output, because it will pay to produce more at the going selling price of output. But will the price of output remain unchanged? No. While each firm faces an infinitely elastic demand curve for its product, an industry does not. If all the firms at once attempt to sell more output as a result of a decline in the price of labor, they will be able to do so only if the price of output falls, inducing consumers to purchase greater quantities. A decline in price will lower the firms' demand curves for labor because the value of marginal product will fall. Thus, it is not proper to assume that price of output, held constant in analyzing the behavior of an individual firm, may also be held constant for an industry. In general, as a result of an industry's declining product demand curve, its labor demand curve will be less elastic than the sum of the demand curves of the individual firms.[1]

A second factor which was held constant for the individual firm, but which may not be constant when an industry changes its output, is the supply price of labor and of other factors. It may well be that an industry uses rather specialized factors of production, including labor, which have an upward-sloping supply curve to the industry, because the industry uses a rather large proportion of the available supplies. As an industry expands its output, the price of specialized labor resources may rise, curtailing both the substitution and scale effects and lowering the industry's response to a change in labor supply conditions. Note, however, that an upward-sloping labor supply curve does not affect the slope or elasticity of the industry's demand curve. This point is demonstrated in Figure 7-1. The change from S_1 to S_2 represents an increase in labor supply when the supply curves are imperfectly elastic. The change from S_1' to S_2' represents an identical change in supply when each curve is perfectly elastic.

The responsiveness of an industry to a change in the supply conditions of labor (i.e., the elasticity of the demand curve) *does* depend in part upon the supply conditions of the other factors of production. The interaction of labor demand with the supply conditions of machinery is complex, but it is possible to gain an intuitive grasp of the essential features of the relationship by means of a literary explanation.[2]

Consider first the case in which the scale effect of a change in labor's

---

[1] It is probably simpler to compare the *elasticities* of the demand curves for the firm and the industry than their *slopes*. This is because, if the industry demand were simply the sum of *n* identical firm demand curves, its slope would be ndL/dW, greater than the slope of the firms' demand curves by the factor *n*; on the other hand, its elasticity would be $ndL \cdot P/dP \cdot nL = dL \cdot P/dP \cdot L$, which is identical to the elasticity of each firm's curve.

[2] This subject is treated neatly by J. R. Hicks in *The Theory of Wages* (2nd ed.) (London: Macmillan & Co., Ltd., 1964), pp. 241–45. See also Joan Robinson, *The Economics of Imperfect Competition.* (London: Macmillan & Co., Ltd., 1965), pp. 261–62.

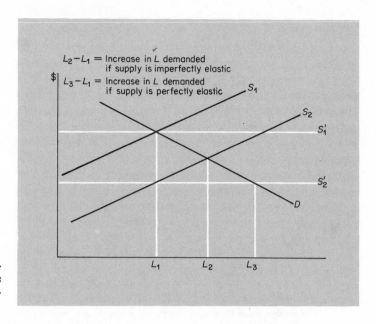

FIG. 7-1

Change in Labor Demanded When Supply Is Perfectly Elastic or Imperfectly Elastic

In the figure:

$L_2 - L_1 =$ Increase in L demanded if supply is imperfectly elastic

$L_3 - L_1 =$ Increase in L demanded if supply is perfectly elastic

S_1, S_2, S_1', S_2', D, L_1, L_2, L_3

price on the amount of machinery demanded outweighs the substitution effect. Then, if labor's price falls, there will be an increase in the demand for machinery. Since the scale effect predominates, the resulting rise in the demand for machinery may cause an increase in its price. Now, the increase in machinery's price will cause the entrepreneur to try to substitute more labor for machinery, but it will also raise production costs and cause him to increase his output less than if the price of machinery had not changed. Thus, there are two opposite feedback effects of an increase in the price of machinery on the demand for labor. It is true, but it will not be proven here, that if the scale effect outweighs the substitution effect of a change in the price of labor on the demand for machinery, the same is true for a change in the price of machinery on the demand for labor. Thus, the increase in the price of machinery will have a negative scale effect on the demand for labor that will outweigh the substitution effect, and an imperfectly elastic supply curve of machinery will cause the amount of labor demanded to increase less than it would if the supply were perfectly elastic, when the scale effect outweighs the substitution effect.

When the substitution effect predominates, the price of machinery will fall when the price of labor falls, if the machinery supply curve is imperfectly elastic. For the same reasons that were set forth in the preceding paragraph, a decline in the price of machinery will have the effect of causing a smaller substitution of labor for machinery, which outweighs the larger-scale effect induced by the decline in machinery's price.

To summarize, when the scale effect outweighs the substitution effect, a decline in the price of labor will cause an increase in the price of machinery, which damps output expansion; hence, the demand for labor is less elastic than it would otherwise be. When the substitution effect outweighs the scale effect, a decline in the price of labor will cause a decline in the price of machinery, which damps the substitution of labor, and which also causes the labor demand curve to be less elastic.

Finally, the production function of the industry may be quite different from that of the firm. Essentially, the firm's demand curve for a productive factor must slope down for the same reason that the size of competitive firms must remain small compared to the size of the industry—diseconomies of scale. Once the firm has moved to its new expansion path, the value of marginal product is made equal to marginal factor cost (marginal cost is brought to equality with marginal revenue) as the firm moves northeastward along the path, because we implicitly assume some factor (entrepreneurship?) which is fixed in amount for each firm and which ultimately limits the size of each firm. Thus, if there were a change in the labor supply curve for a particular firm, the firm would be prevented from expanding to take over the entire industry by inherent limits to its size, which limits act primarily to lower the marginal productivities of all variable factors as the firm expands.

On the other hand, an industry expands in two ways: (1) Each firm may expand its output in the short run. (2) In the long run, new firms enter the industry if the existing firms earn positive economic profits. Provided that new firms which enter the industry as demand grows are as efficient as the old firms, the only factors limiting industry growth are demand for output and the supplies of the variable factors of production. If the industry is small, or does not use highly specialized factors, demand is the only limiting factor.

Thus, in a simple model of a competitive industry, only demand limits industry size and its demand for productive factors, while diseconomies of scale limit size and factor demand for the firms making up the industry. In such a simple case, it appears ambiguous whether the industry's labor demand curve would, on balance, be less or more elastic than the demand curves of its component firms.

The most crucial aspect of our analysis of the industry's labor demand curve is not whether it is more or less elastic than the firms' but whether the general shape of the industry demand curve is anything but negatively sloped. Just as in the case of the competitive firm, *the competitive industry's demand curve for labor slopes down*, and this hypothesis has important implications for economic theory and policy.

Throughout the economy, industries producing the multitude of goods and services which make up national product compete with each other for labor resources. In the next chapter, we consider evidence bearing on the nature of industries' labor demand curves.

evidence
on the demand
for labor

INTRODUCTION

Testing the theory of the demand for labor can be done in more than one way. One of the best ways would be to estimate demand functions for labor along with the production functions of the relevant economic units (firms, industries, etc.).[1] This is a good method because one may explicitly inquire to what extent firms or industries hire labor up to the point where the value of the marginal product of labor (or marginal revenue multiplied by marginal product) equals the wage rate. However, it is also a difficult method. It is important to be able to specify the quality of labor and other inputs in the production process; this is difficult. The mathematical and statistical procedures used in estimating production functions are highly technical. Therefore, it would not be consistent with the technical level of this book to examine the empirical evidence regarding the demand for labor using techniques involving the estimation and manipulation of production functions.

---

[1] A description of a method of estimating the demand for labor this way is found in George H. Hilderbrand and Ta-Chung Liu, *Manufacturing Production Functions in the United States, 1957* (Ithaca, N.Y.: The New York State School of Industrial and Labor Relations, 1965), especially pp. 53–57.

However, we are not completely at a loss. We shall fall back on the less precise procedure of testing the hypothesis that demand curves for labor slope downward, i.e., that increases in wage rates cause the quantity of labor demanded to decline, *cet. par.* Indeed, the principal implication of the theory of the demand for labor discussed in Chapters 6 and 7 is that the amount of labor demanded by firms and industries is a negative function of labor's price. In testing this hypothesis, we may shed light on the parameters of some labor demand functions, even though we shall not employ the most correct procedure for doing so.

Testing the hypothesis that labor demand curves slope downward involves us in an area of controversy that at times has been heated indeed. (At this point, the reader may wish to review Section II of the appendix to Chapter 1.) The issue revolves about whether or not increases in wage rates do in fact cause declines in the amount of labor demanded. At times, such controversy has included arguments about the macroeconomic effects of wage increases and about the importance of monopsony elements in the economy, but the most important and pervasive feature of the arguments surrounding this issue centers on the relevance of the economic theory of the firm. Those who argue that the hypothesis of the downward-sloping demand curve is not useful for predicting many, of even most, effects of increases in wage rates on the quantity of labor demanded most often assert that the basic fault of the hypothesis is its derivation from the assumptions that firms attempt to minimize their costs and to maximize their profits. For some reason—probably historical accident—similar arguments about labor *supply* have not been as heated when they have occurred (which seems to have been less frequently than in the case of labor demand). Thus, while the following discussion is applicable to the discussion of labor supply as well, it is included in this chapter because of the nature of many of the discussions and controversies that have taken place regarding labor demand.

Indeed, it can frequently be "established" merely by asking firm owners or managers that they do not engage in cost minimization, marginal cost pricing, or profit maximization. Rather, they are interested in paying "fair" wages and producing "quality" products, and they do not know or care what "marginal cost" or "marginal revenue" means. Some firms that employ the most modern computing and accounting techniques may indeed attempt to operate in a way that looks something like the economist's description of the representative firm of economic theory, but by and large, such examples are hard to find. Thus, critics of the hypothesized downward-sloping labor demand curve, relying principally on rejection of all or part of the competitive theory of the firm, assert that no such precise relationship as the labor demand function exists, at least for "small" changes in wage rates. As was noted previously, one often hears the expression that "the labor demand curve should be drawn with the broad side of the chalk," meaning that the theoretical implication of a negative slope is perhaps useful for understanding the effects of very large changes in labor supply and/or wage rates, but not little changes.

But what is the difference between "big" and "little" changes in wage rates? To what extent does the apparent lack of explicit attempts to minimize costs and maximize profits make the theory of labor demand not very useful? One can attempt to answer these questions in two ways. One way is to recognize the role of theory in leading to useful statements about the behavior of prices and quantities. Thus, if the economy is essentially competitive, firms may be *forced* to minimize their costs, even if they do not aim to or know how to do so precisely, because firms that don't minimize their costs will be eliminated by the competition of those that do. Similarly, if suppliers of productive factors—particularly nonhuman factors—tend to sell their services to the highest bidders, firms which don't engage in cost-minimizing and profit-maximizing behavior may well lose out in their attempts to purchase inputs necessary for production. This way of dealing with criticism of the standard labor demand hypothesis states that it is not *necessary* that firms engage in what their owners or managers *consider* to be cost minimization and profit maximization; it is only necessary that they act as if they did, and competition will tend to force firms to behave in such a manner. In other words, firms competing with each other for sales revenues will find one of their most effective tools of competition to be offering goods of given quality at the lowest prices. Thus, firms that do not engage in what is effectively cost-minimizing behavior will be relatively ineffective in attracting customers, whether or not managers wish or aim to discover the lowest costs of producing their output.

Another and extremely important consideration in dealing with the questions posed above is to recognize that economic theory typically is developed in deterministic terms, assuming constant all variables but those included in the theoretical structure. Thus, the relationships discussed are exact, allowing for no deviations from the predicted effects of changes in the independent variables. In the real world, of course, economic relationships are inexact, and the *ceteris paribus* assumption cannot be maintained. However, the *ceteris paribus* assumption has, as its stochastic (i.e., relating to inexact behavior) counterpart, the assumption that variables not included in the theory, but nevertheless affecting the behavior of the dependent variables in which we may be interested, are related randomly (are essentially uncorrelated) to the independent variables which are included in the theory. It is an asumption like this that underlies most attempts to measure economic relationships with modern statistical tools. Thus, the notion that "the demand curve ought to be drawn with the broad side of the chalk" can be reinterpreted in terms of conventional statistical inference—that we expect to observe a scatter of labor demand observations whose averages are the real world counterparts of the points on a theoretical demand curve.

But once we recognize the basic stochastic problem of measuring demand curves—whether they be demand curves for labor or for any other factor of production or commodity—the broad side of the chalk criticism loses its force. This is because the criticism is ordinarily made to support the statement that "small" changes in wage rates will have no predictable effect on the quantity of labor demanded, e.g., a successful attempt by a union to raise wage rates, or effective minimum wage legislation, will not have a predictable effect on the quantity of labor demanded if the wage increase lies within the width of the figurative broad chalk line. How small is small is not usually specified, but the point we must accept is that once the stochastic nature of empirical demand curves is recognized, it is necessary to modify economic theory only to the extent that we predict that *on the average* wage increases will result in a decline in the amount of labor demanded; we would not base a test of the hypothesis on only one or a few observations, because we do not claim to be able to predict each individual event—only the average of a reasonably large number of events. What is a large number is specified by statistical considerations.

The preceding remarks do not deal explicitly with arguments that rely on the presence in the economy of monopsony or monopoly elements which may force us to modify the predictions of competitive economic theory regarding the effects of wage rate changes but, once again, one must ask whether the existence of some element of control over prices of commodities sold and bought requires the rejection of competitive theory. The question is, Is there a way in which knowledge of the presence of "imperfect" competition can be incorporated into our analysis to yield more usable predictions of labor market behavior? Sometimes the answer is Yes, and sometimes it is No. We must be aware, however, that to observe simple relationships such as evidence of downward-sloping labor demand curves does not shed much light on whether such demand curves are generated by competitive, monopolistic, or monopsonistic firms or industries. On the one hand, it may not be necessary to know precisely how far firms and industries deviate from the behavior postulated in a competitive model in order to derive some useful insights into the behavior of labor demand; on the other hand, the observation of such simple relationships cannot yield us any more than evidence pertaining to the hypotheses being tested. If the hypothesis of a downward-sloping demand curve for labor is derivable from models of competitive and monopolistic firms, we cannot infer, if we think we observe such demand curves, that the firms or industries which generated them are competitive; in order to do that, we should have to decide just how steep a labor demand curve would be if it were generated by a firm with monopoly power in the sale of its output, compared to a demand curve of a firm or group of firms without such power, and so on. We cannot get any more out of testing a hypothesis than the reasoning that has been put into relating the hypothesis to the underlying theory and to the data bearing on it. For the remainder of this chapter, we shall deal with the very simple hypothesis, derivable from competitive and some noncompetitive theories, that the amount of labor demanded is a negative function of the wage rate. Our purpose is to demonstrate how the hypothesis can be tested. We deal with one such test, and we do not claim that the empirical validity of the hypothesis is thereby established; rather, we claim that the method is instructive and that the results shed important light on the hypothesis.

A TEST OF THE THEORY OF DEMAND

In order to test the hypothesis that labor demand curves slope downward, we shall look at a study of the response of employment to minimum wage legislation. Such studies have the advantage of observing the response of the quantity (and sometimes the quality) of labor demanded to *exogenous* changes in wage rates caused by legislation. When such legislation in fact establishes a legal minimum higher than that which would have prevailed in the absence of legislation, economic theory implies that an excess supply of labor will result. This means that employers can hire all the labor they desire at the going wage rate and that the amount of labor employed is equal to the amount demanded, depending only on the position of the labor demand curve.

An especially useful study of this kind is that of the effect of minimum wage legislation in Puerto Rico, reported by Reynolds and Gregory.[2] The Puerto Rican case has many advantages from the point of view of testing the hypothesis that the demand curve for labor is negatively sloped: (1) In Puerto Rico, unlike the mainland United States, there are different minimum wage rates for each industry, and they are adjusted frequently. (2) The wage minima in Puerto Rico are substantially higher relative to average wage rates in the covered industries than in the United States, and there is a substantial evidence, reported by Reynolds and Gregory, that minimum wage rates in most industries have been the principal factor forcing wage rates to rise over at least the past ten to fifteen years. (3) The unemployment rate in Puerto Rico has been greater than 10 per cent of the labor force—sometimes substantially so—since at least the end of World War II; thus, for many and perhaps most of the firms in Puerto Rico, we may think of an almost infinitely elastic supply of labor at whatever the going wage rate happens to be.

---

[2] This summary is based on the study by Lloyd G. Reynolds and Peter Gregory, in their book *Wages, Productivity, and Industrialization in Puerto Rico* (Homewood, Ill.: Richard D. Irwin, Inc., 1965), pp. 41–103.

Figure 8-1a characterizes the relationship between wage rates and employment in Puerto Rico described in the preceding paragraph. In Figure 8-1a, Wa, Wb, and Wc are the minimum wage rates in representative industries A, B, and C, respectively, whose labor demand curves are so labeled, and La, Lb, and Lc are the respective quantities of labor demanded in the three industries at the going wage rates, which are essentially determined by the wage minima. During a period of time, say, four years, the minima are raised, and we observe data such as those characterized by Figure 8-1b,

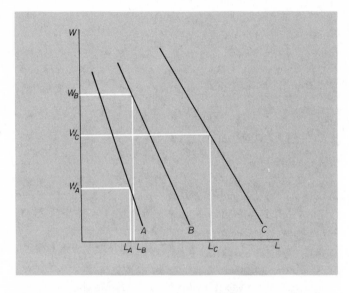

FIG. 8-1a

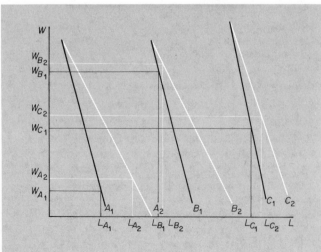

FIG. 8-1b

Reynolds and Gregory's Method of Estimating the Employment Effect of Minimum Wage Rates Using the Linear Homogeneity Assumption

in which the dotted demand curves are those of the terminal year of such a period of time and the solid lines correspond to the demand curves in Figure 8-1a (the first year). The subscripts 1 and 2 associated with the wage rates and quantities demanded correspond to magnitudes in the first and last years of the period, respectively. Since the minimum wage rates have been raised by different amounts in the different industries and since there is no reason to believe that these wage rate increases are related in any way to inter-industry differences in changes in the prices of nonhuman inputs, we are in a position to estimate the average net effects of wage rate changes on the amounts of labor demanded. As we shall attempt to demonstrate, we can make use of our knowledge of the frequency with which minimum wage rates are changed in Puerto Rico, the different amounts by which they are changed, and the apparent fact that the minima are very high relative to what the going wage rates would be in their absence to conduct a simple test of the hypothesis that labor demand curves slope downward, using data with a rather wide range of variation. We shall describe a method of estimating, *on the average*, the effect of wage increases on the quantities of labor demanded in a large group of industries, such as industries *A*, *B*, and *C* in Figures 8-1a and 8-1b.

Reynolds and Gregory studied most closely the relationship between wage rates and employment in narrowly defined (3- or 4-digit) manufacturing industries. Data were available for a group of between thirty-seven and fifty such industries. A very important (and probably not unrealistic) assumption underlying the study is that the production functions for the *industries* (as distinct from the firms) studied are *linear and homogeneous*. The meaning of linear homogeneity will be well known to many readers; it is a simple concept, implying that for each industry studied, any change in output at constant factor prices will necessitate increases in the inputs of productive factors in the same proportion as output has changed. (Recall our discussion of the industry's demand for labor in Chapter 7.) This further implies that factor proportions (the ratios of the quantities of factors used in production) depend only on relative factor prices and are the same at every level of output, given factor prices; also, there are no economies or diseconomies of scale for the industries, which implies that the industries' long-run output supply functions are infinitely elastic.[3] For the kinds of manufacturing industries typically found in Puerto Rico (footwear, clothing, light durable

---

[3] The following two production functions are examples of linear homogeneous functions. (1) $Q = \alpha_1 K + \alpha_2 L$; $Q = \alpha_0 K^{\alpha_1} L^{1-\alpha_1}$; where Q = output, K and L are productive factor inputs, and the other symbols are constants. It can easily be seen that multiplying each factor input in either of the two functions by a constant, b, will result in multiplying output by the same constant. Consider function (2), for instance. If each input is multiplied by a constant, b, then output becomes $Q' = \alpha_0 (bL)^{\alpha_1}(bK)^{1-\alpha_1} = \alpha_0 b^{\alpha_1} L^{\alpha_1} b^{1-\alpha_1} K^{1-\alpha_1}$. Thus the proportionate increase in output, $Q'/Q = \dfrac{\alpha_0 b L^{\alpha_1} K^{1-\alpha_1}}{\alpha_0 L^{\alpha_1} K^{1-\alpha_1}} = b$.

goods manufacturing, etc.), the assumption of linear homogeneous production function is probably a useful one.

The purpose of using the linear homogeneity assumption can be seen by referring to Figure 8-1b. Since we are going to estimate the average net effect of wage rate increases in different industries over time, we need a method of controlling for the effect of output growth on the amounts of labor demanded in each industry. We ignore the impact on output of adjustments to the minimum wage rates in each industry, and using the data of output in each of the years 1 and 2, we can estimate what the quantities of labor demanded would have been in year 2 at the wage rates prevailing in year 1, or the quantities of labor demanded in year 1 at the wages of year 2. Thus, we shall attempt to estimate the effect on the amount of labor demanded, *at a given level of output*, that comes about from changing factor proportions which result from rising wage rates.

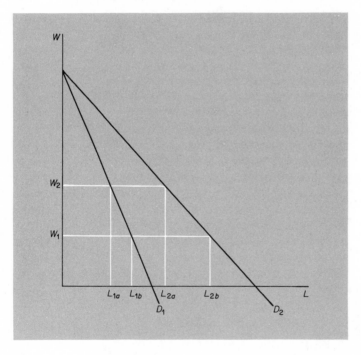

FIG. 8-2

Further Illustration of Reynolds and Gregory's Method

The procedure is illustrated more clearly in Figure 8-2, which represents the demand curve for labor in each of years 1 and 2 for one of the industries shown in Figures 8-1a and 8-1b. In year 1, we actually observe wage rate W_1 and the quantity of labor employed L_{1b}. In year 2, we actually observe wage rate W_2 and quantity L_{2a}. In order to estimate the effect of the wage increase from W_1 to W_2, we must estimate either L_{1a}, the quantity that would have been employed in year 1 at wage W_2, or L_{2b}, the quantity that would have been employed in year 2 at the wage W_1. We estimate either of these quantities by multiplying L_{1b} by the ratio of output in year 2 to that in year 1, to obtain L_{2b}; or by multiplying L_{2a} by the ratio of output in year 1 to that in year 2, to obtain L_{1a}. This is done for every industry in the sample studied; then the change in the quantity of labor demanded for each industry can be measured along either demand curve 1 or demand curve 2.

As was pointed out above, this method does not provide a measure of the impact of wage rate changes on the amount of labor demanded via the effect of wage rate changes on industry output. It is probably true that some firms did not open plants in Puerto Rico and that others closed down or failed to expand operations because of rising labor costs. To this extent, Reynolds and Gregory's analysis underestimates the response of the amount of labor demanded to wage rate changes. On the other hand, there may be an element of overestimation if neglected economies of scale and/or exogenous increases in efficiency (due to, say, "learning by doing") would in any event have caused labor inputs to rise less than in equal proportion to output.

In order to estimate the average effect of wage increases, two samples of industries were examined. One included thirty-seven industries for the period 1949–54 and the other fifty industries for the period 1954–58. For each of these samples, output was measured by value added,[4] and the amount of labor demanded by the employment of production workers in each industry. (Hours of work per week changed little over the periods studied.) Employment in the first year of each period was "inflated" by the proportionate change in value added for each industry, so the demand elasticity was estimated as the average response along curves like D_2 in Figure 8-2.

To summarize, L_{1b} in Figure 8-2, for each industry is multiplied by the ratio of value added during the second year of observation to that during the first year in order to estimate L_{2b}; i.e., $L_{2b} = L_{1b} \dfrac{X_2}{X_1}$ where X_1 is value added in either 1949 or 1954, and X_2 is value added in either 1954 or 1958 respectively. In order to estimate the *average* response of labor demanded to wage rate changes, the following regression equation was estimated for each of the two periods, 1949–54 and 1954–58:

$$\frac{L_{2b} - L_{2a}}{\frac{1}{2}(L_{2b} + L_{2a})} = a + b \frac{W_2 - W_1}{\frac{1}{2}(W_2 + W_1)} \tag{1}$$

---

[4] Value added is the total sales of an industry less purchases of partially processed goods and depreciation allowances. It essentially measures the input of all productive factors plus profit. For the period 1949–54, value added in each industry was deflated by the appropriate price indexes; for 1954–58, output prices changed little, and no deflation was performed.

Obviously, the left-hand term is the proportionate change in the quantity of labor demanded along demand curve D_2 for each industry, and the right-hand term is the proportionate change in the wage rate for each industry, between either 1949 and 1954 or between 1954 and 1958, depending on which regression is being estimated. Note that if both sides of (1) are divided by $\dfrac{W_2 - W_1}{\frac{1}{2}(W_1 + W_2)}$, we derive

$$\frac{L_{2_b} - L_{2_a}}{W_2 - W_1} \frac{W_2 + W_1}{L_{2_b} + L_{2_a}} = \frac{a}{\dfrac{W_2 - W_1}{\frac{1}{2}(W_2 + W_1)}} + b \tag{2}$$

that is, we have a measurement of the arc elasticity of demand,[5] which may be seen more clearly if we rewrite (2) as

$$\frac{\Delta L}{\Delta W} \frac{W^*}{L^*} = b$$

in which we assume a is statistically indistinguishable from zero, and b is thus an estimate of the arc elasticity. (If a is significantly different from zero, then the elasticity must be evaluated at particular values of W, as can be seen in (2).)

The results of estimating (2) are that for both the periods 1949–54 and 1954–58 the estimated constant terms (a) are statistically indistinguishable from zero; the estimated elasticities (b) are -1.1, with a standard error of .2; and $-.92$, with a standard error of .2, respectively. The standard errors are small relative to the estimated elasticities, suggesting that the estimates are reliable.[6]

The estimates suggest that, on the average, minimum wage increases resulted in equiproportionate declines in employment; thus, total wages paid in manufacturing industries tended to be unaffected by wage rate increases. To obtain some idea of the possible magnitude of the effect of wage increases on employment and unemployment, consider the following: Reynolds and Gregory estimate that had wage rates not risen from 1954 to 1958, actual employment of production workers in manufacturing would have been greater by 29,000 workers.[7] This is about one-half of the actual

---

[5] Most readers will recall that the arc elasticity of demand is a measure of the average elasticity between two separate points on a demand curve.

[6] These estimates of elasticity were supplied by Professor Gregory and represent a corrected version of the results originally reported in the work cited in fn. 2 (p. 145).

[7] *Ibid.*, p. 101. One needs to be careful in interpreting these results, however. For instance, to the extent that the characteristics of the unemployed, such as education, age, health, reliability, etc., are less desirable to employers than those of the employed, a *given* reduction in wage rate would have a smaller impact on employment.

employment of production workers in manufacturing in that year.[8] Manu-facturing constituted somewhat less than 15 per cent of total employment in Puerto Rico at that time, so it is reasonable to conclude that minimum wage rates had an important role to play in maintaining unemployment at the high level of about 15 per cent of the labor force.

The Reynolds and Gregory study provides evidence consistent with the hypothesis that the amount of labor demanded is a negative function of the wage rate, *cet. par.* In addition, the test of the hypothesis yields an estimate of the value of the elasticity of demand for the samples of industries used in the study. The purpose of discussing this study has been to demonstrate a simple method of testing the most important hypothesis about labor demand curves derived from economic theory.

---

[8] *Ibid.*

PART III

the interaction of supply and demand: theory and evidence

9

the interaction of supply and demand in competitive labor markets

THE MARKET

The interaction of the forces of labor supply and demand takes place in labor markets. The concept of a labor "market" is sometimes criticized because it is sometimes thought to be irrelevant to the real world. That is, since labor is not bought and sold under quite the same conditions as, say, cotton, for which a visible, organized exchange exists, it is sometimes implied that to use the term in the context of labor economics may convey a misleading impression of how labor supply and demand behave.

As it is used in economic theory, however, the term "market" refers to an idea, or concept, which is analytically convenient. It does not refer to a particular economic institution but is instead like the word "cause"—an analytical concept used to help organize the ideas which make up a theory. Here we describe a market formally by means of a geometric diagram depicting the interrelationship of labor supply and demand curves; however, we can also represent markets by means of mathematical descriptions of the supply-demand interrelationship or by means of verbal descriptions. Thus, a labor market may be thought of as a "place" in economic theory where labor supply and demand interact. That the market is an adaptable theoretical

155

tool is shown by its broad applicability to geographical regions (e.g., the labor market of Chicago), industries, and occupations (e.g., the labor market for industrial engineers). Ultimately, the usefulness of the market concept must be judged by its contribution to the efficient formulation of economic theory with predictive value, and not by its representation of observable economic institutions.

EQUILIBRIUM

From previous work in economics you are by now aware of the concept of equilibrium in a market. Equilibrium is used to describe the effect of supply and demand upon the price and quantity of (in this case) labor hours bought and sold. A common definition of equilibrium is that it exists when the amount of labor hours family members wish to sell is just equal to the amount business firms desire to purchase. This occurs, of course, where the demand curve and supply curve intersect, as shown in Figure 9-1. If the wage rate is

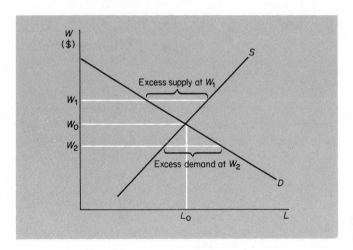

FIG. 9-1
Labor Market Equilibrium

higher than w_0, the equilibrium wage rate, a number of forces tend to reduce wage rates. Similarly if the wage rate is below w_0, the wage rate tends to rise.

It is worthwhile to describe some of the market forces which tend to promote equilibrium in labor markets. Suppose changes in demand or supply conditions leave the wage rate above its equilibrium level. Then, the amount of labor demanded will be less than the amount supplied. Employers will begin to notice that it is easier to hire labor of given quality to fill vacant positions and they may respond in a number of ways. One way is to raise hiring standards, thus attempting to get higher-quality labor without raising wages. This would imply, of course, a lower wage rate for the more able workers than had previously been offered and reduced labor costs for the employer, because higher-quality labor is presumably more productive. On the supply side, workers will begin to notice that it is harder to find a job and to keep one; they may notice that employers are demanding more of them and are becoming less lenient about vacations, coffee breaks, sloppy work, and so on. Finally, employers will find that they can fill their job openings satisfactorily and reduce wages at the same time, and workers may become willing to accept jobs of given characteristics even if wage rates are reduced. Thus, wage rates will tend to approach w_0, the equilibrium rate.

The equilibrium wage rate will persist so long as there is no economic incentive for anyone to alter his behavior. If, however, the equilibrium achieved in one market (e.g., a geographical region) implies a wage rate such that employers can increase their profits by buying labor elsewhere (if w_0 is higher than equilibrium wages elsewhere) or workers can increase their welfare by seeking employment elsewhere (if w_0 is lower than equilibrium wages in other markets), then w_0 will not represent a long-run equilibrium. If we neglect the costs of seeking and choosing alternative employers and employees (which in the long run may be very low but in the short run significant),[1] all labor markets will be in equilibrium only when the wage rate of a given quality of labor is the same in all alternative employments of given nonpecuniary characteristics. When there is wage inequality among labor markets, excess supplies will persist in markets where wages are high, and excess demands where wages are low. These excesses will cause wage rates to tend to move toward their long-run equilibrium values.

The speed with which labor markets approach equilibrium has important implications for the effectiveness of the economic system in allocating resources. Slow market adjustment may manifest itself in one or both of two ways: (1) "Short-run" inelasticities of supply and demand may persist for long periods of time; thus, changes in demand and supply conditions may induce undesirably wide swings in wage rates (and unemployment, which is considered in later chapters). (2) The impact of conventional pricing policies and economic institutions may hinder the responsiveness of wage rates to changing demand and supply conditions, resulting in excess supplies (gluts) and excess demands (shortages). The role of labor market adjustments in determining the allocation of labor and the structure of wage rates among different occupations and industries, as well as the average level of real wage rates, is discussed in Chapter 13.

---

[1] Some of the effects of positive information and adjustment costs on labor markets are treated in Chapters 14 and 15.

It is almost certainly true that labor markets do not adjust to changing conditions as rapidly as the markets for some other factors and commodities with which labor markets are often compared. Consider the markets for financial assets: information about relevant alternatives in these markets is widespread, and transaction costs are small; therefore prices adjust rapidly to changing conditions, and interregional and interasset anomalies in price behavior are rare. The markets for some commodities such as grain, beef, pork, cotton, etc., behave similarly. By comparison the adjustment of labor markets is sluggish indeed. However, in evaluating the efficiency of labor markets, it is necessary to consider the causes of sluggish adjustment and the nature of alternative methods of eliminating them; it is not sufficient to conclude from the observation of some other markets that labor markets function badly relative to their potential.

The role of market adjustments to changing demand and supply conditions in determining the general level of unemployment and the general level of money wages is discussed in Chapters 14 and 15.

ECONOMIC WELFARE

When each competitive labor market is in equilibrium, the value of the marginal product of labor is equal to its wage rate, and the wage rate of labor of a given quality must be the same everywhere, except for "equalizing" wage differences that arise due to nonpecuniary differences in the characteristics of different kinds of employment. Thus, the value of the marginal product of labor will be equal in all of its alternative employments. This equality of the value of the marginal product of labor in alternative employments leads to what is called economic efficiency. To understand what this means, consider that if the value of the marginal product of labor were unequal in different employments, the national income could be raised by a reallocation of labor. Suppose, for instance, that labor's VMP in the manufacture of automobiles was $5 per hour and in the manufacture of trousers, $10. Then, taking away one manpower-hour of labor from the automobile industry and adding it to the trouser industry would raise the national income by $5. The transfer of labor from automobiles to trousers would continue to increase national income until the VMP discrepancy was eliminated.

Other things, including the distribution of income, being the same, most people would agree that it is good to maximize the national income in the sense described above. However, forces which interfere with the economy's attaining a *competitive* equilibrium (apart from constant changes in factor supplies, technology, and tastes) usually change the income distribution, and it is impossible to say on scientific grounds that such interferences are therefore bad, unless we also believe that the resulting income distribution is bad. Labor unions and minimum wage legislation are examples of attempts to change the price and quantity solutions of the labor market in an effort to alter the distribution of income. We shall consider the effects of labor unions in Chapters 11 and 12. Other institutions which may prevent the economy from achieving a competitive equilibrium are the existence of monopolistic and monopsonistic firms; we shall discuss their effects in the next chapter.

the labor market under conditions that interfere with competition

Economists have frequently discussed the effects on labor markets of four conditions that interfere with competition. These are (1) monopoly power in product markets; (2) monopsony power in factor markets; (3) monopoly power in factor markets; (4) employer (and employee) behavior which is due to irrationality or lack of full knowledge of relevant alternatives. In the following sections, we shall discuss these sources in turn.

INTERFERENCE WITH COMPETITION IN PRODUCT MARKETS

Under competitive conditions, each point on a labor demand curve represents the value of the marginal product of labor, which is the product of the price of output and marginal physical product. When a firm has monopoly power, however, it maximizes its profit by producing at a point where marginal revenue (which is less than price in the case of monopoly) is equal to marginal cost. Consequently, when monopoly is present each point on the labor demand curve is *marginal revenue* multiplied by marginal physical product, or *marginal revenue product* (*MRP*). Since marginal revenue is always less

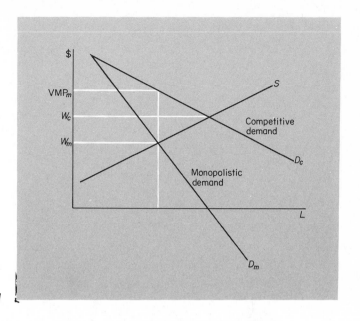

FIG. 10-1

Competitive and Monopolistic Demands Compared

than price for monopolistic firms, *MRP* is always less than *VMP*, and the labor demand curve when monopoly is present will always lie below the competitive demand curve. (We assume that the monopolist's production function is identical to that of competitive industry.) This is illustrated in Figure 10-1.

If some labor markets in the economy are dominated by monopolistic firms, they will use less labor than they would if competition prevailed; this is because if competition prevailed, they would hire labor up to the point where the wage rate equaled *VMP*, which obviously implies more employment than hiring up to the point where the wage rate equals *MRP*. If the labor supply curve to markets where monopoly is present has any degree of inelasticity, so that it is upward sloping, it is obvious from Figure 10-1 that the equilibrium wage rate as well as employment will be lower than if competition prevailed. The effect of monopoly in product markets upon the equilibrium wage rate is sometimes called *monopolistic exploitation*.

Economic welfare, in the sense of Chapter 9, is not maximized when monopoly exists in product markets. In the labor market, economic welfare could be increased by transferring labor from the relatively competitive sectors of the economy to the relatively monopolistic sectors, as the *VMP* of labor will be greater in the latter sectors than in the former, and the national income would thereby be increased.

MONOPSONY

It is possible that while competition prevails in the product market, it does not in the factor market (the two forms of interferences with competition may coexist, of course, but we shall examine their effects one at a time). When a firm is the only buyer of labor in a market, we say that it is a *monopsonist* (single buyer). Just as in monopoly, there need not be just a single firm in a market for monopsonistic power to exist; the essential feature of monopsony is the realization by firms that in order to increase the amount of labor they employ, they must raise wage rates. That is, each firm feels that its labor supply curve is imperfectly elastic. Thus, the marginal cost of adding more labor is greater than the average cost, and there is a marginal labor cost curve which lies above the labor supply curve. Monopsonistic firms maximize their profits by hiring up to the point where marginal labor cost is equal to *VMP*. The equilibrium position for a labor market when monopsony is present is shown in Figure 10-2.

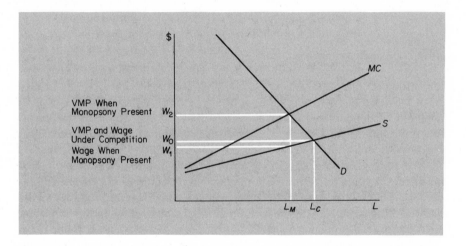

FIG. 10-2
*Competitive and Monopsonistic Labor
Markets Compared*

Relatively monopsonistic markets will employ less labor, at a lower wage rate, than relatively competitive markets. *VMP* will be greater than the wage rate in monopsonistic markets, and the value of national income could be raised by transferring labor to monopsonized forms of employment from other parts of the economy, just as when monopoly is present in product markets.

MONOPOLY IN FACTOR MARKETS

It is possible for monopoly to exist among sellers of labor. To take a rather unrealistic, but simple, example, let us suppose that a firm specializes in procuring workers and selling their services to employers in a labor market and that this firm has a license guaranteeing its position as the sole seller of labor. If this firm, which acts as a labor broker, faces a perfectly elastic supply curve, it will maximize its profits by selling labor up to the point where the curve marginal to the market's labor demand curve intersects the labor supply curve of the broker. That is, the labor demand curve of the market is the broker's demand curve; like any other monopolist, the broker firm maximizes its profits by "producing" up to the point where marginal revenue equals marginal cost. If the broker firm is also a monopsonist, it will sell labor up to the point where its marginal cost curve (now lying above the imperfectly elastic labor supply curve faced by the firm) intersects the marginal revenue curve. These possibilities are shown in Figures 10-3a and 10-3b.

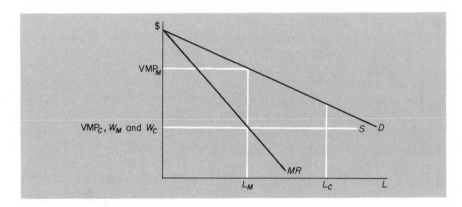

FIG. 10-3a
Labor Monopolist without Monopsony Power

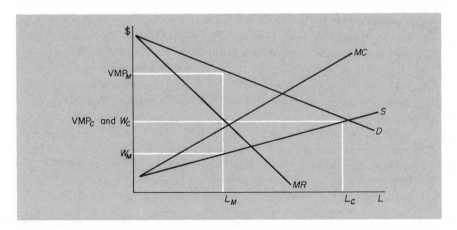

FIG. 10-3b
Labor Monopolist with Monopsony Power

When labor monopoly of this kind exists, less labor will be employed than in a competitive situation, and the effects on economic welfare and wage rates are similar to those described in Sections I and II.

A not unrealistic case of labor monopoly is that of an individual who possesses a special talent or some kind of training for which there are few readily available substitutes. (Imperfect ability of consumers to judge among alternatives, as may be the case in the consumption of medical care, may produce situations similar to this kind of labor monopoly. This is because the availability of substitute labor services is not relevant unless consumers can judge among them.) Let us assume that Figure 10-4 describes such a

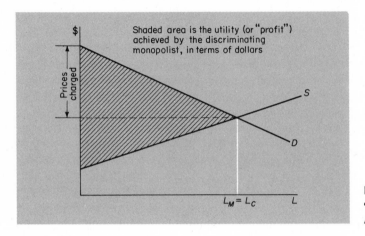

FIG. 10-4
"Discriminating" Labor Monopolist

situation. We draw the individual's labor supply curve upward sloping for convenience, and we assume that he faces a negatively inclined demand function for his services. A utility-maximizing individual in such a situation might sell his services up to the point where the curve marginal to the demand function (not shown) intersects the supply curve. (Note that we do not consider the curve marginal to the supply function. This is because the seller in this case benefits from the entire difference between the supply curve and marginal revenue. That is, each point on his supply curve is "marginal cost" at that point.)

If, however, the seller can provide his services in such a way that one buyer cannot sell the service to another (a doctor or lawyer would be able to do this, but a performer giving a concert in a hall in which there were no reserved seats would not), it would pay him to discriminate among buyers, i.e., "charge what the traffic will bear." If the seller can distinguish buyers according to the maximum amount they are willing to pay for his services, he will maximize his utility (or "profits") by charging that price, represented by each point on his demand function, to each individual served. Since in this case the seller's marginal revenue equals price at any quantity of sales, he will sell up to the point where the demand curve and supply curve intersect. His "profit" is represented in this case by the triangular area between the demand curve and supply curves, to the left of their intersection, and it is maximized by selling labor services up to the point of intersection of the two curves.

Finally, we should consider briefly the role of labor unions as monopolists. Since Chapters 11 and 12 are devoted to unions, we shall consider them only briefly here.

Labor unions cannot be treated simply as monopolists. Even under circumstances of the closed shop, unions cannot be described simply as organizations which buy and sell labor in order to maximize profits. To begin with, unions do not buy or sell labor; they represent groups of individual sellers in collective bargaining over wage rates and other employment conditions. It is not at all clear that attempting to maximize the union's "profits," even if they could be conceived and measured, would be consistent with maximizing the utility of union members. This is because the union members are not indifferent to the amount of employment available for each member, and unions do not in general have the power to bargain over the quantity of labor employed. Even if unions did have such power, there would be a tradeoff between the levels of wages and employment achievable. Furthermore, union leaders are undoubtedly concerned about the size of their membership, and optimum union size may not be consistent with an optimal economic package to be delivered to members as a result of bargaining.

Nevertheless, it is reasonably clear that one of the important goals of unions is to achieve higher wage rates and related benefits for their members. In order to achieve these goals, unions must have something akin to monopoly power in order to force employers to bargain with them. Insofar as unions are able to achieve wage bargains that are more favorable than individual workers would achieve under competitive conditions, much of the analysis of this section is relevant. It is impossible, however, to assign to the theoretical effect of unions on wages and employment anything quite so precise as we have assigned to the effects of utility- or profit-maximizing monopolists discussed previously.

Finally, we should note that it is theoretically possible for labor monopoly to offset some of the effects of monopsony. If a monopolist faces a monopsonist in the labor market, the monopolist *may* set a price for the services he sells between w_1 and w_2 in Figure 10-2, allowing the monopsonist to buy as much as he would like at that price. This converts the monopsonist's imperfectly elastic labor supply curve to a perfectly elastic one, and he now maximizes his profits by hiring more labor—at a higher wage rate—than when he faced a multitude of individual sellers. This would result in a wage rate–employment equilibrium that lies somewhere between that of monopsony and that of perfect competition. Whether in fact the monopolist would have an incentive to set his price between w_1 and w_2 is another matter, however, for that may not be consistent with his profit or utility maximization.

IMPERFECT KNOWLEDGE AND NONMAXIMIZATION OF PROFITS

It is often argued that the competitive model is irrelevant to the real world because employers and employees do not have full knowledge of the alternatives available to them and do not always desire to maximize profits or wage rates.

Let us take the second point first. It is indeed conceivable that no one, or very few people, behaves sufficiently in accord with the maximization assumptions of competitive economic theory; thus, the theory may not describe reality sufficiently well. However, a sufficiently good description of reality depends upon alternative descriptions available. In order to argue against competitive theory on the basis of the nonmaximization of utility and/or profits it should be shown that competitive theory leads to predictions about the economy which are useless or not as good as the predictions of an alternative theory which is based on different assumptions about underlying human behavior. Regarding the postulate of profit maximization, however, it might not be necessary that each firm attempt to maximize profits for the assumption of profit maximization to prove fruitful; if *some* firms attempt to maximize profits, those that don't may find themselves undersold or outproduced unless they behave more competitively. Thus the economy could behave *as if* profit maximization were general, and this may be all that is necessary for competitive theory to be a good description of reality. Regarding the postulate of utility maximization by family members, we must be careful to distinguish among three cases: (1) Assuming utility maximization, we can infer hypotheses which are sufficient to predict a substantial proportion of the labor market behavior of individuals. (2) When other factors, such as psychological and sociological characteristics, are taken into consideration, "economic" variables (relative prices, and costs, wage rates, incomes, and the like) are useful in predicting behavior, but they do not account for much observed variation. (3) "Economic" variables have little predictive value under any circumstances. Only situation (3) is clearly inconsistent with the usefulness of economic theory as it has been developed in the text so far. Situations (1) and (2) are consistent with it.

To come back to the first point—that information about alternatives is not pervasive—the economics of information has increasingly been incorporated in modern economic analysis—particularly as part of the theory of human capital. Information may be considered as a (costly) factor of production or as a consumer's durable good, which yields productive services or utility. Once one realizes that information requires scarce resources, it becomes subject to economic analysis; its scarcity suggests hypotheses about observable behavior but does not imply that the competitive model is a bad one. Once it is recognized that information is a commodity subject to economic analysis, the apparent lack of correspondence between real world behavior and economic theory which ignores the cost of information often disappears. It then becomes relevant to ask whether it would be worthwhile in terms of costs and benefits to reduce all kinds of unemployment to zero, to move workers instantaneously to regions where they would be most productive, and so on. The analysis of the influence of information cost is increasingly being recognized as crucial to understanding the behavior of wage differentials, the wage level, employment, and unemployment, and we attempt to incorporate some of the analysis at several points throughout the remainder of the book—particularly in Chapters 14 and 15.

THE RELEVANCE OF COMPETITIVE THEORY

This chapter has been devoted to enumerating circumstances in which the theory of competition may not apply. In Sections I through IV we have discussed the effects of dropping one or more postulates of competitive theory, and particularly in Sections I–III we have suggested the kinds of observations that might be generated if the competitive model is deficient in one or more respects. It is apparent, however, that in regard to much of the currently available data of the economic system and techniques for analyzing them, the predictions of competitive theory differ little from those of the theories discussed in Sections I through III. Even when we drop the postulate(s) of price-taking behavior, the resulting theories lead to hypotheses that demand curves slope down and supply curves to firms and industries slope up; none of the competitive or non-competitive theories developed here suggest critical hypotheses about the steepness of the slopes of labor demand and supply curves at the industry level, and even at the firm level in the short run. Although we may predict how much labor would be employed in particular markets if competition prevailed, actually measuring the value of the marginal product of labor is difficult; furthermore, how can we distinguish between a disequilibrium situation and a non-competitive one? Nor do we have good measures of monopolistic or monopsonistic power. It is usually difficult to distinguish among alternative economic theories empirically, and many economists are inclined to ignore noncompetitive theories of economic behavior because of this.

On the other hand there are cases in which critical hypotheses, distinguishing between the implications of the theory of competition and other theories, may be formulated. For instance, if we found that over long periods of time and over a wide selection of industries, the variation in concentration of firms (a proxy for monopoly power) "explained" a significant proportion of the variation in the wage rates of employees, when differences in labor quality and nonpecuniary aspects of employment were taken into consideration we would be led to suspect that the economy contains a significant amount of monopoly power. If we should find that "economic" variables such as productivity, the cost of training, and obvious nonpecuniary considerations have little to do with explaining wage rates and employment, then we should possibly be forced to conclude that theories (competitive or otherwise) which postulate profit and utility maximization are not useful and that a theory not based on the maximization of profits and utility may be more relevant to the real world.

In the remainder of this book we discuss three very important topics: (1) labor unions; (2) the behavior of real wage rates and the wage structure; and (3) the behavior of the level of money wage rates and unemployment. All three of these topics bear on the relevance to behavior of the competitive theory of labor markets, and they are treated as such. Not only does the subject matter bear on the theory, but more important, the theory, especially when we are able to contrast its implications with those of alternative theories, provides a sound basis for understanding the observed labor market behavior.

11

the economics
of
unions—I

INTRODUCTION

In this and the next two chapters we shall be concerned with the important and challenging question: How can we understand the behavior of wage rates in terms of their purchasing power over goods and services and in terms of each other? In attempting to answer this question, we shall make use of the body of theory developed throughout the preceding chapters; however, one of the most important agents involved in the process of wage determination is often a labor union, and we have said almost nothing about unions until now. Therefore, it is essential to consider the role of unions in the economy before going further.

The subject of labor unions is one of the most pervasive in the study of labor economics. If one takes a historical view, this is not surprising, because the issues of the right to strike and to bargain collectively were hotly contested in American history. On the one hand, many workers have felt that unions are the only means by which the living standards of the labor force can be raised and the individual dignity and rights of workers protected. On the other hand, many employers have felt that the compulsion to bargain with workers in groups infringed upon their property and moral rights.

These issues, while still occasionally arising in current discussions, have by and large ceased to be important. The employers of most workers recognize at least in principle the right of workers to organize for purposes of collective bargaining; on the other side, unions have for the most part limited their activities to attempts to raise wages and to improve working conditions via collective bargaining and through influencing legislation. Furthermore, legislation over the past thirty years has provided labor and management with a fairly clear and stable set of ground rules which simultaneously protect the property rights of employers and the organizing and bargaining rights of employees.

All of this is not to say that the problems causing disagreement between labor and management have disappeared or that new ones will not arise. Currently, the controversial "right-to-work" laws are an important political topic; and the issue of the right of public employees to strike has not been resolved. Nevertheless, one feels that time and evolutionary, rather than revolutionary, change will see these debates settled. Bargaining over wages, working conditions, and employment standards will continue to be the principal activity of American unions in their relationship to employers, and attempts to influence legislation will be the principal activity in their relationship to society at large.

THE GOALS OF UNIONS

In our discussion of unions, we shall concentrate on the interrelationship between union behavior and the economy. In order to understand this relationship, it is illuminating first of all to consider the goals of unions. Recall that in the discussion of labor demand and supply, we proceeded a long way on the assumptions of the goals of profit maximization on the part of firms and utility maximization on the part of households. What goals can we ascribe to unions?

Students of unions do not agree precisely on what the goals of unions are. However, speculation about the likely nature of these goals appears to be fruitful and suggestive of an outline of union motivation which, if it does not fully describe the driving forces of unionism, is nevertheless consistent with many of the more obvious aspects of union behavior. Principally, we assume that the primary goal of labor unions is to improve the economic welfare of union members, mainly by raising wage rates. (Included in the concept of wage rates are fringe benefits, paid holidays, working conditions, rest periods, and the like, which have more or less easily calculable wage rate equivalents as far as employers are concerned.) However, the relationship between increases in wage rates and increases in the economic welfare of union members is not as simple as it may at first seem. Reasoning from the situation of the individual laborer may be quite misleading. For the individual, any increase in wage rates, other things remaining unchanged, is bound to improve economic welfare. However, for a group of workers, other things are not likely to remain unchanged, because the firm or industry's demand curve for labor is not likely to be horizontal, but rather downward sloping, with respect to the wage rate. In other words, wage increases gained by unions are likely to reduce the amount of union labor demanded by employers. This would tend to counteract the influence of wage increases on improvements in the welfare of union members.

It sometimes happens, of course, that unions bargain not only for wage rate increases, but also for a satisfactory employment level. From the employer's point of view, however, having to hire more labor than is desired is like having to pay a higher wage rate than is necessary to attract a given amount of labor: both raise labor costs above what is most profitable. Therefore, the union is limited in achieving both its wage rate and employment goals by the relationship between wage rates and the maximum amount of labor the employer is willing to hire, and we can simplify our analysis without doing much damage to its relevance by assuming that collective bargaining agreements are struck on the wage rate only and that employers are then free to hire as much labor as they like.

Not only do unions have the goals of raising the wage rates of their members, they usually have the power to do so,[1] at least for a short period of time. In competitive equilibrium, firms earn zero profits (excluding, of course, a "normal" return to entrepreneurship and to invested capital). However, even a competitive firm, facing a completely elastic demand for its output, would be willing to pay something more than the competitive wage rate rather than shut down operations as long as some of its plant and equipment is fixed in supply. In response to a union's threat to withhold labor altogether, thereby forcing the firm to shut down, the firm would be willing to pay a higher wage rate so long as it could keep its average variable cost per unit of output below selling price. Of course, the firm would not replace its plant and equipment if it could not earn a normal rate of return, but in the short run it would minimize its losses by remaining in business so long as the union did not force wages to the point where variable costs exceeded revenue.

To the extent that a union can control the supply of labor to a firm with monopolistic power, to an industry, or to a large group of firms, its power to raise wages is increased, compared with its power when facing a competitive firm. This is because the relevant demand curve for output is no longer horizontal, but downward sloping, and the supply of competing labor and

---

[1] It is elucidating to treat the wage gains of labor with an analysis identical to that of the incidence of excise taxes. Such a treatment is found in George W. Hilton, "The Theory of Tax Incidence Applied to the Gains of Labor Unions," in M. Abramovitz *et al.*, *The Allocation of Economic Resources* (Stanford: Stanford University Press, 1959), pp. 122–33.

other factors is likely to be less elastic. Still another condition which would allow unions to obtain higher wage rates without a severely adverse employment effect is monopsony. Parenthetically it should be noted that the demand for higher wage rates—and getting them—might stimulate (non-profit-maximizing) firms to become more efficient than they had been and thus provide the wherewithal to pay the increased labor costs without cutting down on labor demanded. We shall explore the conditions which allow unions to raise wage rates above competitive levels in more detail later on; it is sufficient now merely to point out that even under competitive conditions, it may be consistent with profit maximization on the part of firms to accede to union demands for higher wage rates—at least in the short run.

Now that we have seen that unions have the power to obtain wage increases if they can effectively control the supply of labor to firms or industries but are limited in power by the fact that as wage rates rise, firms are likely to demand less labor, we may proceed to analyze the effect of unions' attempts to increase wage rates on the welfare of union members. We begin by assuming that a union represents its members' interests as though it were a super-family trying to maximize group welfare. We simplify the analysis by assuming that the union members have identical tastes for market goods, home goods, and time, and that they have equal relative productivities in the home and in the market. We assume also that wages and employment are shared equally among the members. It follows, then, that what increases the welfare of any member of the union increases the welfare of all members.

The analysis of the behavior of unions in this context is illustrated in Figure 11-1, which shows a typical worker. Dollars of constant purchasing power are measured along the vertical axis. The horizontal axis measures hours *not* worked (going from left to right). H_m is the maximum number of hours available (e.g., 168 per week); therefore, measuring from H_m to the left denotes the number of hours worked. Consider a situation in which a certain number of hours $(H_m - H_1)$ are bought from each worker by a firm or industry in competitive equilibrium. Total earnings per worker equal OC. A union is formed including all of the workers, and any changes in employment conditions and the wage rate affect all members equally. The union is successful in raising the wage rate, and this is shown by a change in the budget constraint from H_mA to H_mB. It is quite clear that if each member were free to choose any point on H_mB, the new wage rate would be unequivocally preferable to the old wage rate; every union member would be better off than he had been. However, we know that employment is likely to fall from $(H_m - H_1)$ per worker to some level, say $(H_m - H_3)$, represented by point k. The likely reduction in employment would occur because the employers want less labor than they did prior to the wage increase.

It is not certain whether the union members will want to work more or less than before. It is consistent with our knowledge of the income and

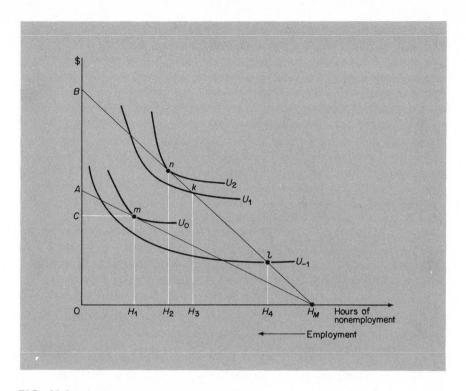

FIG. 11-1
*Utility Maximization of a Union Member
When There Is an Employment Constraint*

substitution effects of wage rate changes, however, to presume that after
wage rates are raised, the union members will want to work less than before.
A possible point of equilibrium which each member would try to attain is n,
indicating increased earnings (consumption of market goods) and increased
leisure. But, if n lies to the northwest of k, rationing of work among the
union members will be required. (If n lies to the southeast of k, there will be an
excess demand for labor, and no rationing will be required. In this case,
the union may have to admit more members, or compulsory overtime may be
necessary.) When rationing is required, the level of welfare is indicated by the
indifference curve passing through k. As long as U_1 is higher than U_0,
the indifference curve through m, each worker will be better off with the
higher wage rate than with the old wage rate. However, if l (any point on
H_mB below U_0) were the best attainable point on H_mB, the workers would
be better off with the lower wage rate. The change in the welfare of workers
as a result of the increased wage rate depends on two factors: (1) the elasticity
of demand for labor, which determines the horizontal distance between
n and k or l; and (2) the workers' marginal rate of substitution between

173

leisure and market goods (i.e., the curvature of the indifference curves). The flatter the indifference curves—indicating that a relatively greater amount of leisure is required to compensate for the loss of a given amount of market goods—the more likely it is that the best attainable point will be below U_1. The greater the elasticity of demand for labor, the greater the horizontal distance between n and k or l, and hence, the greater the probability that an increase in the wage rate will reduce welfare.

While the above analysis is a beginning of a model of union behavior, it is perhaps overly simple and leaves much to be done. For instance, we have assumed that the number of union members is constant. Now, it is obvious that reducing the number of members would increase the welfare of remaining members if work rationing is necessary, other things remaining unchanged. This is because reducing the number of members would move k or l closer to n, allowing the remaining members to improve the allocation of their time between labor and leisure. However, if a union allows its membership to decline, it may increase the elasticity of demand for its members' labor, as workers no longer in the union (or prevented from joining the union) may offer their services to firms whose output competes with that of unionized employers. The existence of nonunion workers would thus reduce the effectiveness of unions in securing higher wage rates, because firms that would be willing to sign contracts would also fear the competition of nonunion rivals. Therefore, unions may not be anxious to let membership dwindle, even though the short-run result could be to improve the welfare of remaining members.

We should also bear in mind that unions have goals other than the maximization of the economic welfare (narrowly defined) of members. Prestige of the members, especially of the leaders, and the salaries of leaders may be associated positively with union size. Political power may be prized and aided by large membership. These goals may well conflict with the goal of achieving increased welfare for union members through higher wage rates won via collective bargaining.

an application of the analysis of union goals: union membership

In the preceding section, union goals were treated, assuming that the principal aim of unions is to maximize (or increase) the economic welfare of union members; at the same time it was recognized that the interrelationship between wage gains and the size of union membership imposes a constraint on behavior. If this approach is a useful way to talk about union goals, it should aid understanding various aspects of union behavior. There are two obvious areas of behavior to which the theory may be applicable: (1) the effect of unions on wages; and (2) the ability of unions to organize the labor force.

We shall devote considerable attention to (1) in the next chapter and concentrate on (2) here.

Presumably, the proportion of the labor force that is unionized at any moment in time depends on three things: (1) the benefits that workers enjoy because they are union members; (2) the tastes and attitudes of workers toward union membership as such; and (3) the costs of organizing and maintaining worker participation in unions and collective bargaining arrangements with employers. According to the preceding analysis, the benefits enjoyed by union members largely depend upon the elasticity of demand for the labor of unionized workers. Factors (2) and (3) determining union membership depend on the general social, political, and legal framework within which unions must operate.

The economic theory of the demand for labor developed in Chapters 6 and 7 suggests that four conditions influence the elasticity of demand for the labor of unionized workers: (1) the elasticity of demand for the commodities produced; (2) the importance of union labor in production cost; (3) the ease of substituting other factors of production (including nonunion labor) for union labor; and (4) the elasticity of supply of the cooperant factors of production. The greater is any of the factors (1) through (4), the greater should we expect to be the elasticity of demand for union labor; thus, the more severe would be the adverse employment effects of union wage gains and the smaller would be the benefits enjoyed because of union membership.[2] While we do not have a well-formulated theory of the determinants of attitudes of workers toward union membership or of the costs of organizing and maintaining union membership, we can attempt to identify those periods of history during which these conditions were relatively conducive to the growth and maintenance of union membership.

We address ourselves now to the analysis of the behavior of union membership in the United States over time. The data pertain to union membership in relation to total labor force since 1900. The year 1900 is a convenient starting point because it marks roughly the beginning of the growth of modern American unionism, which is associated with the growing importance of the AFL (now the AFL–CIO). Since 1900, the attitude of the American public toward unions has been characterized by a trend of increasing acceptance and toleration—with important discontinuities and fluctuations. This, along with the disappearance of the frontier and perhaps the

---

[2] Probably the best formal treatment of the relationship between the elasticity of demand for a factor of production and the four conditions listed is contained in the appendix to Chapter 6 of J. R. Hicks' *Theory of Wages* (2nd ed.) (London: Macmillan & Co., Ltd., 1964), pp. 241–47. There it is shown that the four factors are related to factor demand elasticity in the way specified, in the presence of a linear homogeneous production function; an exception is condition (2), which holds only when the elasticity of demand for output is greater than the elasticity of substitution between the factors.

decline in the importance of foreign labor, is a good explanation of the increase in union membership from less than 5 per cent to over 20 per cent of the labor force during the last sixty years. Deviations from the trend in union membership appear to be consistent with a hypothesis relating the extent of union organization to the elasticity of demand for union labor, the sociopolitical situation, and the costs of organizing unions.

The data in Table 11-1 show that over the first six decades of this

Table 11-1

UNION MEMBERSHIP AS A PERCENTAGE OF
THE CIVILIAN LABOR FORCE, 1900–1962

Year	Union Membership (per cent)	Interdecade Changes (percentage points)
1900	3	
1910	6	+3
1920	12	+6
1930	6	−6
1933	5	
1940	13	+7
1945	22	
1950	22	+9
1953	26	
1962	21	−1

Source: Leo Troy, "Trade Union Membership, 1897–1962,"
National Bureau of Economic Research, *Occasional
Paper No. 92* (New York, 1965), p. 2.

century, union membership as a fraction of the labor force grew on the average by about 3 percentage points every ten years. Thus, the decade 1900–10 was one of about average union growth, 1910–20 greater than average, 1920–30 less than average, and so on.

Between 1900 and 1920, union membership increased at a moderate pace, doubling from 3 per cent of the labor force in 1900 to 6 per cent in 1910, and doubling again to 12 per cent in 1920. The relatively rapid rate of growth from 1910 to 1920 was undoubtedly aided by World War I in two ways; the demand for labor was high during the latter half of the decade, and the war situation rather severely curtailed European migration to the United States. These two factors together changed the alternatives faced by employers who were threatened with unionization of their labor forces.

Three events appear to have contributed to the decline in the proportion of the labor force consisting of union members during the 1920's. The first was the severe, though brief, depression of prices and economic activity in 1921–22. Periods of high general unemployment have traditionally been difficult ones for unions because of the unusually good alternatives to union labor available to employers during such times and because of the high risk of unemployment borne by workers who dare to agitate or strike, especially when there are few or no legal guarantees of workers' rights to organize or strike. Between 1920 and 1922, union membership dropped from 18.5 per cent of nonagricultural employment to 15.6 per cent.[3]

A second event had to do with major changes in the structure of the United States economy. The 1920's marked a tremendous increase in the productivity of inputs (as conventionally measured) in agricultural production. The data in Table 11-2 suggest that during the period 1923–29 the productivity

Table 11-2

CHANGES IN OUTPUT AND INPUT IN AGRICULTURE
IN THE UNITED STATES

Period	Output (per cent)	Input (per cent)	Proportion of Additional Output Accounted for by Additional Input (Assuming Constant Returns) (per cent)
1900–20	25	18 to 21	72 to 84
1910–20	15	17	100
1923–29	7	3.7	53

Source: Theodore W. Schultz, "Reflections on Agricultural Production, Output and Supply," *Journal of Farm Economics*, V, 38 (August, 1956), pp. 748–62.

of factors employed in agriculture nearly doubled on the average, while at the same time output growth declined compared with the preceding twenty years. As a result, rural-to-urban migration was undoubtedly substantially greater than it otherwise would have been. The increase in internal migration was great enough to provide a net increase over the previous decade in total net movement of native and foreign-born whites, and of nonwhites, to the states which, in 1950, contained the eleven largest standard metropolitan statistical areas. This increase in total migration took place despite legal restrictions on international immigration that were imposed beginning in 1924. According to Table 11-3, net population increase due to migration to these states was about a third greater in the 1920's than it was during the previous decade. Further evidence that economic conditions contributed to a "buyers' market" for labor during the 1920's is the course of real wage rates shown in Table 11-4, where the behavior of wage rates in the 1920's

---

[3] Leo Troy, "Trade Union Membership, 1897–1962," National Bureau of Economic Research, *Occasional Paper No. 92* (New York, 1965), p. 2.

Table 11-3

MIGRATION TO STATES CONTAINING THE 11 LARGEST SMSA's (1950)

Period	Native Whites	Native Nonwhites (Negroes)	Foreign-Born Whites	Total
1910–20	530,100	392,000	1,775,900	2,698,000
1920–30	1,143,200	661,800	1,828,300	3,633,300

Source: Everett S. Lee et al., Population Redistribution and Economic Growth in the United States, 1870–1950 (Philadelphia: The American Philosophical Society, 1957), Vol. I, Table PI, pp. 115–99.

Table 11-4

AVERAGE HOURLY EARNINGS IN MANUFACTURING, 1914–1929

(1) Year	(2) Average Hourly Earnings of Production Workers	(3) Consumer Price Index (1947–49 = 100)	(4) (2) ÷ (3) × 100
1914	$.223	42.9	$.52
1919	.477	74.0	.64
1920	.555	85.7	.65
1929	.566	73.3	.77

Source: Historical Statistics of the United States, Colonial Times to 1957, pp. 92, 126.

is compared with this behavior during the period 1914–19. According to the data summarized in Table 11-4, average hourly earnings of production workers in manufacturing, divided by the consumer price index, increased about 5 per cent per year from 1914 to 1919, but grew slightly less than 2 per cent annually between 1920 and 1929. Thus, it seems fairly clear that during the 1920's, economic forces were at work which tended to intensify the adverse employment effects of union-obtained wage increases and, therefore, probably made organization more difficult than it might otherwise have been.

A third event involved the sociopsychological and political reaction to the end of World War I which contributed to the difficult circumstances of organized labor during the 1920's. In general, this reaction was characterized by a desire to return to "normalcy," i.e., to reinstate pre-World War I attitudes, morals, and behavior. Associated with, and part of, this general set of social attitudes, the courts were increasingly disposed to grant antiorganizational and antistrike injunctions to employers threatened by labor unions. During this period, the courts continued to interpret the antitrust acts as applying to crucial forms of union activities, and they upheld and enforced the so-called "yellow dog" contracts (agreements between employers and employees in which employees agreed not to join labor unions as a condition of employment). Thus, the social environment of the 1920's reinforced economic circumstances by contributing to a high cost of organization and collective bargaining during the period.

In 1932, passage of the Norris-LaGuardia Act greatly restricted employers' use of injunctions as a weapon against union organization and collective bargaining and made the yellow-dog contract unenforceable in the courts. There followed a substantial increase in union membership, despite the fact that the economy was in the midst of the Great Depression, and economic depressions have traditionally been bad for union activity. This seems to be clear-cut evidence that legislation and social environment do matter to the success of unions. Note, however, that the really big increase in union membership did not occur until much later—in the 1940's during the tight labor market conditions of World War II.

The effects of the Norris-La Guardia Act on union membership were reinforced by the provisions of the Wagner Act in mid-to-late 1930's. This act ushered in the era of union legislation in which we still find ourselves (particularly insofar as legislation affects the right to strike and organize), in that the National Labor Relations Board was established, unfair labor practices were defined, etc. Thus, the rights of unions to organize, bargain, and strike were given clear legal sanction, and the NLRB was established as a court for the settlement of many labor-management disputes.

By 1940, the proportion of the labor force consisting of union members stood at 13 per cent, roughly equal to the figure for 1920 (see Table 11-1). The tight labor market conditions of World War II, along with a social and political environment that was relatively favorable toward unions, contributed to a rise in membership of 9 percentage points between 1940 and 1945. Favorable economic and social circumstances contributed to maintenance of union membership at about 22 per cent of the labor force during the remainder of the decade.

During the 1950's, union membership rose slightly to its peak of nearly 26 per cent of the labor force in 1953. Whether the economic circumstances associated with the Korean War contributed a great deal to this increase is difficult to say, but the evidence from past events suggests that the timing of the peak is not fortuitous. Since 1953, union membership in proportion to total labor force has declined by about 6 percentage points. One suspects that the relatively high unemployment rates of the latter half of the 1950's and early 1960's (see p. 260) contributed to this; however, other economic and legal factors were also changing during this period.

In 1947, the Taft-Hartley Act, aimed at restricting some aspects of union activity, was passed. Perhaps the feature of the act which conceivably could have had the greatest effect on union membership is the controversial Section 14 B, which allows states to pass "right-to-work" laws. These laws essentially outlaw the union shop. However, few industrial Northern states have passed such laws, and as of mid-1968, no major industrial state had such a law.

In addition to high unemployment during the late 1950's and early 1960's, economic factors which may have contributed to the relative decline in union membership were the changing occupational and sex mix of workers. Between 1950 and 1960, the "manual worker" or "blue-collar" occupations of craftsmen, operatives, and nonfarm laborers dropped from 41 per cent to 38 per cent of the labor force; between 1910 and 1950, this percentage had changed little, rising slightly from 38 per cent to 41 per cent.[4] (While these changes may seem small, consider the following: if 50 per cent of all manual workers are union members, and, say, 10 per cent of all others are members, then the "effect" of a 3 percentage point decline in the proportion of manual workers in the labor force would mean a decline of 1.2 per cent in union membership as a proportion of the labor force—or about a fifth of the decline between 1953 and 1962.) Female employees rose from 28 per cent of the labor force in 1950 to over 32 per cent in 1960. To the extent that women are less committed to full-time labor force participation than men, they may feel less inclined to join unions. However, the most important source of impact of females on union membership may be via occupational and industrial channels. That is, women are more likely than men to be school teachers, secretaries, and other types of white-collar workers, who, regardless of sex, are less likely to be union members.

---

[4] *Historical Statistics of the United States, Colonial Times to 1957*, p. 74; *U.S. Census of Population*; *1960, Detailed Characteristics*, T. 201.

12

the economics of unions—II

INTRODUCTION

In this chapter, we explore the effects of unions on wages. To the extent that unions raise the wage rates of their members above the levels that would have prevailed in the absence of the unions, the economic welfare of members is probably increased. (Needless to say, unions may improve the economic welfare of members through such means as fringe benefits, working conditions, seniority rules, and the like. However, the major effect is probably via wage rates, and one's impression is that success in obtaining other benefits for members seems to be highly correlated with success in obtaining higher wage rates.) The efforts of unions to raise the wage rates of their members may also affect wage rates elsewhere in the economy, and these indirect effects need to be considered when estimating the impact of unions on wages.

We defer until Chapter 13 a more general discussion of wage rates in the American economy and until Chapter 14 a general treatment of the level of money wage rates and inflation. Thus, the reader is urged to view this and the following two chapters as a unit which applies the approach taken throughout this text to the important subject of the determination of wage rates.

CONCEPTS OF THE EFFECTS
OF UNIONS ON WAGES

**the effect of unions on the wage
rates of union members, compared
to what they would have been in
the absence of unions (absolute
real wage effect)**

Perhaps the most interesting kind of union wage effect is the impact on real hourly wage rates relative to what they might have been in the absence of unions. Unfortunately, this is the aspect of union wage effects that is most difficult to measure. The reason is that when union membership accounts for a significant proportion of the labor force, the general real wage level may be changed in such a way as to eliminate any benchmark against which the effect of unions on the absolute real wage rates of their members can be measured. That is to say, in order to conclude that unionism, or any other force, has changed the wage rates of union members, we have to be able to discover what such wage rates would have been in the absence of unions. However, the very presence of unions in the economy is likely to make this kind of comparison very difficult by changing the wage rates of many workers *besides* those who are union members.

To demonstrate this difficulty simply, imagine that we can divide the economy into a unionized sector and a nonunionized sector, and suppose that the unionized sector of the economy is more labor intensive that the non-unionized sector (i.e., the share of labor in production cost is higher in the unionized sector than in the nonunionized sector). When the now unionized sector of the economy first became organized by unions, two things may be assumed to have happened: (1) There was a shift to more capital-intensive methods of production, reducing the labor intensity of the sector. (2) The production costs (and selling prices) of the output of the unionized sector increased relative to the nonunionized sector, and demand consequently shifted toward the output of the nonunion sector of the economy, the extent of the shift depending on the elasticity of demand. Concomitantly, the demand for all productive factors increased in the nonunion sector, while the demand fell in the union sector (holding the factor proportions constant). Whether wage rates went up or down, on the average, depends on the growth of labor demand in the nonunion sector relative to the decline of demand in the union sector.

In the present example, since the union sector is *assumed* to be relatively labor intensive to begin with (we are not stating this as a fact but merely to demonstrate an argument), it is possible that the wage rates of both union and nonunion labor fell as a result of unionization. (We should expect the wage rates of unionized workers *relative* to nonunion workers to have risen in any event.) Applying this example to the actual effect of unionization of part of the labor force, we see that unionization, while it probably has had a nonnegative effect on the relative wage rates of union workers relative to other workers may have raised, lowered, or left unchanged the average wage rate of all workers. Consequently, the absolute real wage rates of unionized workers may also have ended up either higher or lower than they would otherwise have been.[1]

There is presently little work which provides empirical evidence of the effect of unionization on the absolute real wage rates of union members. We are thus left in the position of having to point out that, paradoxically, the effect may be positive or negative, but we do not know which is more likely.

the effect of unions on the share of labor in national income

The functional distribution of the national income has often been thought to be important because of its implications for equity and for macro-economic behavior. However, the share of total output going to labor appears only tenuously related to either of these issues. This is because it is not necessarily correct to think in terms of a clear relationship between the size and type of income and because it is *size*, rather than type, that is important for equity considerations; furthermore, there is no evidence which substantially supports the importance for macroeconomic behavior of the functional distribution of income.

Nevertheless, it is intriguing to explore the possible influence of unions on the functional income distribution, if only because some people think it is important.

Theoretical Considerations. We first must consider how unions could possibly alter the functional distribution, particularly "labor's share," of national income. Let us temporarily ignore the problems created in trying to attribute certain incomes (such as the income accruing to the owners of unincorporated enterprises) to the productive factors which yield them, and speak as if the national income can be divided accurately into income derived from labor and from capital, these two categories totally exhausting the amount to be divided.

It is quite clear that in a competitive economy the amount of income accruing to each factor is the factor's value of marginal product multiplied

---

[1] This analysis is based on "The Effects of Unionization: A Geometrical Analysis," an unpublished paper by Harry G. Johnson.

by the *amount* of the factor employed. It follows that the success of unions in raising the wage rate of their members is neither a necessary nor a sufficient condition for raising the *share* of labor in national income. First of all, it was pointed out in the preceding section that the ultimate effect of unions might be to raise, lower, or leave unchanged the average wage rate of all workers. Secondly, even if the effect of unions is to raise wage rates on the average, whether this would result in an increase in the share of labor in national income depends on the degree to which, on the average, capital is substituted for labor as a result. The degree of substitutability between labor and capital is measured by the *elasticity of substitution* between them. The elasticity of substitution is the percentage change in the relative quantities of the factors used divided by the percentage change in their marginal product, measured along an isoquant. Geometrically, the elasticity of substitution can be demonstrated in Figure 12-1. The elasticity of substitution at a point *b* on the iso-

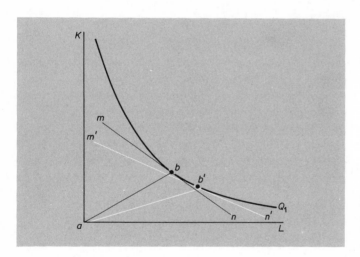

FIG. 12-1

Diagrammatic Representation of Elasticity of Substitution

quant Q_1 is the proportionate change in the slope of line segment *ab* (the relative quantities of the factors used) divided by the proportionate change in the slope of Q_1, going from *b* to another point, *b'*, which is infinitesimally close.

If the effect of unions is to raise wage rates generally, then labor's share will rise if the average elasticity of substitution is less than unity. However, if the effect of unions is to lower wage rates, labor's share will rise if the average elasticity of substitution is greater than unity. At present there is no clear-cut evidence bearing on the average value of the elasticity of substitution for the economy as a whole. Perhaps it is more accurate to say that there is no persuasive evidence that it is substantially different from unity. Furthermore, the elasticity of substitution has to differ from unity substantially before important changes in the functional income distribution would result from any likely effect of unions on the average level of real wage rates. (Moreover, the moderate size of the unionized sector of the economy leads one to believe that not only would the elasticity of substitution have to deviate from unity rather widely, but also the effect of unions on wage *rates* would have to be quite large before any noticeable effect on the functional distribution of income occurred.) On *a priori* grounds, therefore, one would not expect to observe a significant relationship between the influence of unions on wage rates and labor's share of national income.

The Data. It is difficult to specify a method of measuring the influence of unions on labor's share, since we do not know in which periods the effect of unions on average real wage rates has been greatest, or, indeed, what the sign of the effect has been. The approach we use here is to hypothesize that the effect of unions on wage rates depends on the level and rate of growth of the proportion of the labor force consisting of union members. If this is true, and if unions have tended to raise labor's share, we should observe labor's share to be relatively high and/or growing rapidly in 1910–19, 1930–39, and 1939–48 (based on the level and growth of union membership in the economy discussed in Chapter 11). However, the data in Table 12-1 suggest that only during 1930–39 is there any evidence of a positive correlation between the level or growth of union activity and a relatively high or rising

Table 12-1

LABOR'S SHARE OF NATIONAL
INCOME, 1900–1957

Period	Labor's Share of National Income
1900–09	.694
1910–19	.681
1920–29	.716
1930–39	.766
1939–48	.757
1949–57	.762

Source: I. B. Kravis, "Relative Income Shares in Fact and Theory," *American Economic Review*, December, 1959, p. 919 (Table I, Col. 10). Kravis' estimates are based on those of D. G. Johnson, "The Functional Distribution of Income in the United States," *Review of Economics and Statistics*, May, 1954, pp. 175–82.

share of labor in national income. If one ignores the basic upward trend in both union membership and labor's share over the past sixty years, there is no observable stable relationship between the two series.

The absence of a relationship (except for a common upward trend which is difficult to interpret) between union membership and labor's share can be interpreted in two ways. One is that the effect of unions on labor's share is negligible, and the other is that while it may be significant and important, other factors influencing the share of labor in national income have also been important and may have dominated whatever the effect of unions has been. Both interpretations are consistent with the assertion that union activity certainly has not constituted the dominant influence on labor's share; this is an assertion with which most economists would probably agree.

the effect of unions on the wage rates of union workers relative to nonunion workers

The effect of unions on wage rates about which we have the most extensive and reliable information is the effect on relative wage rates. While the question of the effect of unions on the absolute real wage rates of union and nonunion workers may be more intriguing, the question of their effect on relative wage rates is nonetheless important. It is important because knowledge of this effect gives us some clue about the likely size of the economic impact of unions on absolute real wage rates (if not the direction) and upon the functioning of labor markets.

It is hard to imagine how unions could have any effect on absolute real wage rates or on labor's share except via an influence on relative wage rates. Recall that in the discussion on the effect of unions on absolute real wage rates, the analysis was carried out using the conception of a two-sector economy—one sector unionized and the other sector not unionized. If any of the effects of unionization discussed there were to take place, the wage rates of union workers would first have to rise relative to those of other workers. Finally, we should expect to observe a continuing positive influence of unions on relative wage rates of their members if there has been *any* effect on real wage rates, and even if there has not been any such effect, the relative wage effects of unions tell us something about the impact of unions on the distribution of economic welfare among workers.

Estimating the relative wage effect of unions is difficult, but nevertheless it is a more tractable problem than estimating the effect on real wage rates or on labor's share. The procedure is to compare, over space or time, the relative wage rates of two or more groups of workers which differ in extent of unionism. Unionism is a measure of the importance of union membership among a group of workers, such as the proportion of the group that consists of union members or the share of the wages of union members in the total wages of the group. After the relative wage rate data have been adjusted for the influence of conditions other than unionism, the remaining differences are attributed to the effect of unions on relative wage rates. Thus, estimates can be made of the relative wage effects of unions over time, from place to place, and in different occupations and industries.

Most of the estimates of the relative wage effects of unions have been brought together, made comparable, summarized, and in some cases enlarged upon by H. G. Lewis in his book *Unionism and Relative Wages in the United States*.[2] In order to see what is involved in estimating relative wage effects, we shall discuss in some detail one of the studies summarized by Lewis.

In his summaries, Lewis has been extremely careful to make comparable all of the studies summarized. His aim is to provide an estimate of the effect of unions on the wage rates of union workers relative to nonunion workers. This effect is measured as of a particular date, and it is " . . . the percentage difference between the average relative wage of the group [directly affected by a union] in the presence of unionism · · · and the corresponding average in the absence of unionism."[3] Thus Lewis tries to "net out" of the relative wage effect estimates the relative wage differences that would exist even if there were no unions in the economy.

In order to demonstrate one of the methods used to estimate the effect of a union on the wage rate of its members relative to other workers, we review here part of a study summarized by Lewis, that by Elton Rayack of workers in men's clothing manufacturing.[4] By way of background to the study we quote Lewis:

> Unionization of wage-earners employed in the manufacture of men's, youth's, and boys' suits, coats and overcoats—in short, men's clothing—began in 1914 with the formation of the Amalgamated Clothing Workers of America (ACWA). By 1919 the ACWA had organized well over half, perhaps three-fourths, of the wage-earners in the industry. During the 1920's and until 1933, however, the extent of unionism in the industry declined and in 1933 may have been less than 50 per cent. With the coming of the New Deal the union quickly organized most of the industry; since 1935, nonunion employment in the industry has probably accounted for less than 10 per cent of total wage-earner employment in the industry.[2]

---

[2] Chicago: University of Chicago Press, 1963.

[3] *Ibid.*, p. 10.

[4] *Ibid.*, pp. 90–99; a condensed version of the original Rayack study appears as "The Impact of Unionism on Wages in the Men's Clothing Industry, 1911–56," *Labor Law Journal*, IX (September, 1958), pp. 674–88.

[5] Lewis, *op. cit.*, p. 90.

Table 12-2 contains some of Rayack's data. The major producing cities are classified by their union status. In each city, the wage rate in men's clothing manufacturing was divided by an index based on average annual earnings in manufacturing. This was a crude attempt to adjust the wage data for factors other than unionization. Note that before unionization (1911–13), there was little dispersion in the adjusted wage rates among the cities, but that afterwards (1922 and later), the adjusted wage rates in unionized cities (denoted "u") rose substantially relative to those in cities where unionization was negligible (denoted "n"). Rows 11 and 12 in Table 12-2 are employment-weighted means of the adjusted wage rates in union and nonunion cities, by year. Line 13 (line 11 divided by line 12), is a measure of the union's average effect on relative wage rates. The effect appears to have been substantial—ranging between 17 and 39 per cent (i.e., line 11 divided by line 12 varies between 1.17 and 1.39).

In this study as in others, Lewis makes further adjustments so that all the diverse results can be expressed as a percentage wage differential per percentage point difference in the degree of unionism between the observed group and some benchmark group. This is desirable because the unionized group is not usually 100 per cent unionized, and the benchmark group often has some union membership; thus, the estimated effect of unionism on relative wages will be affected by differing degrees of unionism if the actual effect per percentage point difference in the degree of unionism between the unionized group and the benchmark group varies from case to case and no adjustment is made for this source of error. (In this case, the benchmark group is nonunion men's clothing workers.) While these adjustments alter the measurement of the relative wage effect in men's clothing somewhat, the degree of alteration is reasonably small and need not concern us here.

Lewis has brought together many of the estimates he summarized in order to provide some idea of the interindustry differences in the relative wage impact of unions as described above. These estimates are the most recent available for the industries (except that 1945–49 estimates were not used; this was a period of rapid inflation, during which the relative wage effects of unions were by and large negligible). The estimates are presented in Table 12-3.

On the basis of the work summarized in Table 12-3 and on other evidence, Lewis judges that the majority of workers have been ". . . employed in industries whose average relative wages have been raised or lowered by unionism by no more than 4 per cent." However, the effects in some industries have been ". . . as large as 20 per cent or even larger."[6]

One of the interesting results of some of the studies summarized by Lewis is support for the hypothesis that during periods of unusual general

---

[6] *Ibid.*, p. 282.

Table 12-2

ADJUSTED AVERAGE HOURLY EARNINGS IN MEN'S CLOTHING MANUFACTURING, MAJOR PRODUCING CENTERS, 1911–1932

Line Number	City	1911–13 Average	1919	1922	1924	1926	1928	1930	1932
1	New York[a]	25.2n	52.7u	84.7u	88.9u	87.6u	85.9u	79.9u	58.3u
2	Chicago	23.2n	46.3u	78.1u	87.8u	92.3u	93.4u	84.9u	57.9u
3	Rochester	25.0n	50.1u	65.4u	75.7u	81.4u	79.4u	80.8u	62.8u
4	Boston	—	57.6u	67.4u	79.9u	85.6p	83.0p	82.7p	55.8p
5	Cincinnati	24.5n	40.1n	70.4n	78.6n	83.0p	87.0u	81.8u	55.9u
6	Baltimore	25.1n	61.1u	89.1u	83.6u	82.6u	64.0n	59.0n	38.8n
7	Philadelphia	24.8n	44.6n	64.2n	70.3n	77.6n	71.3n	73.5u	57.0u
8	Buffalo	—	37.4n	—	—	67.3n	58.8n	64.4n	40.2n
9	St. Louis	—	41.3n	—	—	67.8n	66.8n	61.1n	43.0n
10	Cleveland	—	39.4n	—	—	66.2n	64.8n	60.5n	46.6n
11	Mean of "u" cities[b]	—	51.7	79.8	85.7	87.6	87.4	80.7	58.4
12	Mean of "n" cities[b]	24.6	41.8	66.5	73.4	72.3	67.0	60.2	42.0
13	Line 11 ÷ line 12	—	1.24	1.20	1.17	1.21	1.30	1.34	1.39

[a] The letter "u" denotes strongly unionized cities; "n" weakly unionized or nonunion cities; "p" denotes partial unionization.

[b] The average wage rates are weighted averages, using as weights a 1923–29 average of each city's relative employment in the Men's Clothing Industry.

Source: H. G. Lewis, *Unionism and Relative Wages in the United States* (Chicago: University of Chicago Press, 1963), Table 15, p. 91.

Table 12-3

ESTIMATES OF THE RELATIVE WAGE EFFECT OF UNIONS
(WAGE RATE OF UNION WORKERS RELATIVE TO NONUNION
WORKERS, ADJUSTED FOR DEGREE OF UNIONIZATION, LESS ONE)

Industry	Date	Estimate
Contract construction	1939	0.180
Bituminous coal mining	1956–57	0.424
Men's clothing manufacturing	1956–57	0.000
Local transit	1958	0.117
Hotels	1948	0.076
Paints and varnishes, footwear, cotton textiles and auto parts manufacturing	1950	0.000
Wooden furniture, hosiery, and women's dresses manufacturing	1950	0.068
Barbers	1954	0.174
Commercial air transportation	1956	0.242
Seamen	1950's	0.179
Rubber tire manufacturing	1936–38	0.130

NOTE: The estimates here refer to the effect of unions on the relative wage rates of union workers in percentage points per percentage point difference in the degree of unionism. Thus, the estimates imply that, in comparison with a completely non-unionized group of workers, a 100 per cent unionized group of workers would experience a percentage increase in its *relative* wage of 100 times the estimates shown here.

Source: H. G. Lewis, *Unionism and Relative Wages in the United States* (Chicago: University of Chicago Press, 1963), p. 280, Table 80.

price increases, unions may actually lower, rather than raise, relative wages. The hypothesis is suggested by reasoning along the following lines: in periods of unusual price increases, employers realize that the *VMP* of labor is rising, but they are uncertain by how much. This uncertainty makes unionized employers less willing to grant wage increases that they might otherwise have been forced to give in order to maintain an adequate number of employees. The reason is that unions tend strongly to resist reductions in the money wage rates of their members. Thus, if employers overestimate the rate of inflation and grant wage increases that are too large, they cannot rectify their mistakes as easily when there is a union to bargain with as when there is not; therefore wage increases in unionized industries during periods of inflation are likely to lag behind increases in nonunionized industries.

Evidence supporting this hypothesis is that during periods of inflation the relative wage effects of unions tend to be lower than average. The outstanding example is the period 1945–48, when there was a very rapid inflation of prices in the United States. During this period, the relative wage effects of unions appear to have been negligible, or even negative. Evidence of a negative effect is found in the steel industry where labor shortages were prevalent and attributable to a lag of wage adjustment behind other industries, which lag is attributed to the negative influence of the steel workers' union on relative wage rates during the immediate postwar period.[7]

---

[7] The study of wage behavior in basic steel manufacturing was conducted by Albert Rees, "The Effect of Collective Bargaining on Wage and Price Levels in the Basic Steel and Bituminous Coal Industries, 1945–48" (unpublished Ph.D. dissertation, University of Chicago, 1950); also *idem*, "Postwar Wage Determination in the Basic Steel Industry," *American Economic Review*, XLI, No. 3 (June, 1951), pp. 389–404.

13

real wage rates
and
wage structure

INTRODUCTION

In this chapter we discuss wage rates in the American economy. The purpose is twofold. The first reason for studying wage rates is to view important aspects of the principal immediate source of economic welfare; the reader should develop some idea of the way in which wage rates have behaved historically and how they relate to each other now. The second reason is to see how well we can explain the behavior of wage rates using the competitive theory of the labor market developed in Chapters 1 through 9 and the extent to which the competitive theory must be modified to incorporate assumptions which are not part of the theory of competition.

In the first section of this chapter, we treat the behavior of real wage rates[1] throughout a long stretch of the history of the United States. In doing

---

[1] Real wage rates are wage rates measured in terms of the goods and services they can buy; theoretically they are measured by the slope of the budget constraint relating hours of leisure to the amounts of market goods for which hours can be exchanged in the market. In practice, real wage rates are usually estimated by dividing a measure of nominal wage rates (i.e., wage rates as conventionally stated in terms of dollars) by an index of the cost of living (e.g., the consumer price index). Thus real wage rates are usually measured in terms of dollars, with reference to a base period when the "purchasing power" of a dollar is taken to be unity; a simple numerical example follows: a man who earns $2.00 per hour

this, we show how the rate of exchange between hours of leisure and the goods and services for which these hours can be exchanged has grown over the years; we also attempt to outline what some of the basic causes of wage rate growth are likely to have been. In the second section we treat aspects of the wage structure—i.e., relative wage rates or wage rates in terms of each other. In doing this we concentrate attention on the structure of wage rates among the various industry groups in the economy and among the various occupations or skill levels; we do not treat the wage rate distribution by size class, nor do we treat the geographical structure of wage rates, although these subjects are interesting and worthy of attention. We do attempt to show how the industrial and occupational or skill wage structures are related to hypotheses derived from competitive economic theory and to what extent noncompetitive elements must be considered in interpreting their behavior. The tasks we attempt are difficult, and this is an area of economics where there is probably less agreement among economists than in many others discussed in this book. At almost every point we are required to relate wage data to hypotheses derived from an underlying theory—usually the theory of competition—with the aid of many stated and unstated maintained hypotheses. Thus, we are often left in the position of being able to say only that the behavior of wage rates is not inconsistent with the theory of competition, but we are not often able to state that we have strong confirmation of the theory. Hopefully, those who read this chapter will not only benefit from learning something about the nature of real wage rate growth over the years and of the interrelationships that make up aspects of the wage rate structure but also gain some idea of what is needed if we are to discover the forces that interact to determine wage rates.

We do not attempt to treat the general level of money wage rates in this chapter, as that subject is discussed at length in Chapter 14.

THE HISTORICAL BEHAVIOR
OF REAL WAGE RATES IN
THE UNITED STATES

According to economic theory, wage rates in a competitive economy will tend to equal the value of the marginal product of labor. Even in an economy

---

in 1965 and $2.00 per hour in 1968, while the consumer price index has risen from 1.00 to 1.10 (conventionally the consumer price index is multiplied by 100 and would be recorded in standard sources as having risen from 100 to 110), will have experienced a *decline* in his *real* wage rate of ($2.00 − $2.00/1.10) ≅ $0.18. That is, his real wage rate in 1968, in terms of a price index equal to 1.00 in 1965, would be approximately $1.82, while his nominal or money wage rate would still be $2.00. The usual method of measuring real wage rates tends to ignore wages paid in kind. Since the importance of wages paid in kind has declined over the years, a positive bias is imparted to many historical wage series, especially those measuring wages before the late nineteenth century.

which is not competitive but is permeated with deviations from competitive behavior in the form of monopoly power, monopsony power, and the like, wage rates should be expected to rise as the productivity of labor rises. Thus, we shall explore the historical behavior of real wage rates in the United States along with the behavior of factors influencing labor productivity. The most important influences on labor productivity, according to the predictions of economic theory, are: (1) growth of the stock of nonhuman capital relative to human capital; (2) rising investment in human capital per person; and (3) "technological change," which is a catchall phrase referring to conditions which cause rises in productivity (such as "improvements in the organization of production") but which are not easily measured as part of the growth of human or nonhuman capital. It is an interesting and important question whether labor unions and/or labor legislation aimed at setting minimum wage rates have been important causes of wage rate growth. Addressing ourselves to this question, we attempt to evaluate their effects in promoting wage rate growth as compared with investment in human and nonhuman capital.

Data on real wage rates prior to 1890 are hard to find; for wages prior to 1860, they are both hard to find and unreliable. However, what information there is suggests a moderate and unsteady secular (long-term) increase prior to 1860 and a rather steady increase from around 1880 to 1920; except for the period of approximately 1930–38, the secular increase in wage rates has continued over the past $4\frac{1}{2}$ decades.[2]

Table 13-1 shows some indicators of real wage rates up to 1890. It is important to remember that prior to 1860 the proportion of free men who were wage recipients was much smaller than it is today, and that a large proportion of those who today would be wage earners were slaves. Slavery and self-employment accounted for much of the labor performed in that period, especially in agriculture.[3] Furthermore, a large portion of wages was paid in kind, in the form of room and board and in goods produced. Therefore, the data must be interpreted with appropriate caution. For what they are worth, the data of real wage rates prior to 1860 suggest an average annual rate of growth in the neighborhood of 1 per cent. Real wage rate growth seems to have halted during the 1860–80 period, but it apparently resumed a rate of about 1 per cent annually through 1890.[4]

---

[2] Stanley Lebergott, *Manpower in Economic Growth*, (New York: McGraw-Hill Book Company, 1964), pp. 137–64.

[3] *Ibid.*

[4] Clarence Long's figures in *Wages and Earnings in the United States, 1860–90* (Princeton, N.J.: Princeton University Press, 1960), Tables A-11 and A-12, suggest that real wage rates rose between 1870 and 1880 as well as from 1880 to 1890. Thus we are very unsure of the behavior of real wage rates, by decade, between 1860 and 1890.

Table 13-1

SOME INDICATORS OF REAL WAGE RATES
IN THE UNITED STATES: 1832–1890

	(1)	(2) a	(2) b	(3)	(4)	(5)	(6) a	(6) b
1830				100				
1832	$313	$0.62				$313	$0.62	
1840				91				
1849	292					400		
1850		0.61	$0.87	73			.84	$1.19
1859	346					444		
1860			1.06	78	78			1.35
1869	524		1.55			430		1.27
1870					122			
1879	394					410		
1880			1.23		96			1.28
1889	522				95*	549		
1890			1.46		95*			1.54

Definition of Columns:

(1) Full-time and full-time equivalent average annual earnings in iron and steel manufacturing.
(2a) Average daily earnings of common labor, with board.
(2b) Average daily earnings of common labor, without board.
(3) Weighted index of retail prices of textiles, shoes, rum and whiskey, coffee, and tea (1830 = 100).
(4) Consumer price index (1830 = 100); *1889 and 1890 figures are the author's estimates.
(5) (1) ÷ (3) and (4) (× 100).
(6a) (2a) ÷ (3) and (4) (× 100).
(6b) (2b) ÷ (3) and (4) (× 100).

Source: Stanley Lebergott, *Manpower in Economic Growth* (New York: McGraw-Hill Book Company, 1964), pp. 541, 545, 548–9.

Wage rate data in manufacturing for the period since 1890 are shown in Table 13-2. These data are considerably more reliable than those of Table 13-1. They show that the growth of real wage rates continued at about 1 per cent per year through 1915. Subsequently, the growth rate increased sharply, and it has been increasing more than 2 per cent annually since 1915.[5] If we consider the period 1890–1965, over which the best data are available, we see that real wage rates in manufacturing were about $4\frac{1}{2}$ times as high in 1965 as in 1890. The average annual rate of growth was about 2.3 per cent.

---

[5] *Ibid.*, p. 109. This source reports average real wage increases of about 1.5 per cent annually from 1860 to 1890 and about 2.8 per cent from 1914 to 1953. While the level of these figures is higher than those derived from Tables 13-1 and 13-2, the change circa 1915 is similar.

Table 13-2

REAL WAGE RATES IN MANUFACTURING
IN THE UNITED STATES: 1890–1965

	(1)	(2)	(3)	(4)	(5)
1890	$.199		91	.219	
1895	.200		84	.238	
1900	.216		84	.257	
1905	.239		89	.269	
1910	.260		95	.274	
1915	.287		101	.284	
1920	.663	.555	200	.331	.278
1925	.645	.547	175	.368	.313
1930		.552	166		.333
1935		.550	137		.401
1940		.661	140		.472
1945		1.023	179		.572
1950		1.465	240		.610
1955		1.88	267		.704
1960		2.26	294		.769
1965		2.60	311		.836

Definitions of Columns:

(1) Average hourly earnings in manufacturing.
(2) Average hourly earnings of production workers in manufacturing.
(3) Consumer price index (1914 = 100).
(4) Col. (1) ÷ Col. (3) (× 100).
(5) Col. (2) ÷ Col. (3) (× 100).

Sources: Col. (1): *Historical Statistics of the United States, Colonial
Times to 1957*, p. 91.

Col. (2): *Ibid.*, p. 92 (through 1955); *Statistical Abstract
of the United States, 1965*, p. 237 (1956–65).

Col. (3): *Historical Statistics of the United States*, p. 127,
Rees index through 1914, p. 126; consumer
price index, all items 1915–1965 (1960 and 1965
from *Statistical Abstract, 1965*, p. 361). The
indexes were adjusted to 1914 = 100.

some possible explanations
of wage rate growth

In what sense is the historical rate of growth of real wage rates consistent with the theory of competition? Does this economic theory provide
important insights into the growth process? Can the theory help explain the
apparent increase in growth after 1915? As we have seen, the theory of
competition predicts that real wage rates will grow when the value of the
marginal product of labor increases. An increase in the value of the marginal

product could come about in a number of ways; the two we shall dwell on being: (1) an increase in the ratio of nonhuman (i.e., physical) to human capital in the economy; and (2) an increase in the amount of human capital embodied in each worker. The first force mentioned as tending to raise the marginal product of labor in the economy—an increase in the ratio of nonhuman to human capital—is an implication of the principle of variable proportions; we assume that the marginal productivity of labor rises when the factor ratio rises. The second force may seem to contradict the first: if the amount of human capital per worker increases, holding population and the amounts of other factors in the economy constant, wouldn't this lower the marginal product of a given amount of human capital and thus lower its remuneration per unit? Quite possibly; but when we speak of wage rates, we are speaking of the rate of pay per unit of a worker's time, and we are not usually thinking of the rate of pay per unit of human capital per time period. Thus, it is entirely consistent that the rate of pay per worker per hour should rise while the rate of pay per unit of human capital per hour falls; all that is required is that the "quality" of labor (i.e., the amount of human capital embodied in each worker) rise fast enough to offset the possibly declining marginal product per unit of human capital.

Needless to say, it is conceivable that *both* the ratios of nonhuman to human capital *and* the amount of human capital per worker rise concurrently; then both of these forces would work toward increasing wage rates. An increase in the ratio of physical to human capital could occur due to a relatively high rate of investment in physical capital or to a slowdown in the rate of population growth and/or immigration, to name two likely causes. Increasing the stock of human capital per worker could come about through rising educational levels, increased training of workers, improved health, and so on. It has the effect of making each member of the labor force capable of producing an output of greater value than he could otherwise; some of the effects on total output of increasing the investment in human capital per worker may be similar to increasing the number of workers with given investment per man. However, we do not know much about this at present.

Growth of the Ratio of Physical Capital to Human Capital. Since we do not have precise measures of the stock of human capital over the entire period we wish to examine, we look first at the growth of the stock of physical capital with respect to the labor force, at first not considering the growth in the quality of labor. However, temporarily neglecting the rate of growth of the quality of the labor force does not destroy our chances of saying something worthwhile about the probable role of the growth of the physical capital stock relative to the human capital stock in affecting the acceleration of wage rate growth that took place sometime around the First World War. This is because, as we shall see, the evidence suggests that the ratio of physical to human capital slowed down its rate of growth about that time, while the growth of human capital per person was probably occurring at a faster rate than previously. Thus, if we had good estimates of the actual rate of growth of the stock of human capital, we would probably find that the ratio of physical to human capital grew more slowly after about 1915 than before and that this slowdown was probably more pronounced than that in the growth of the ratio of physical capital to the labor force.

Data on the stock of reproducible tangible assets in constant prices provide an indicator of the amount of physical capital in the United States for the period 1850–1956.[6] This stock increased at an average annual rate of slightly more than 5 per cent from 1850 to 1912. From 1912 to 1956, the average annual rate of growth was only 2.3 per cent. During similar periods the labor force grew at rates of 2.5 per cent (1850–1910) and 1.3 per cent (1920–1956), respectively. Thus, in both periods, the rate of growth of the capital stock was about twice as great as the rate of growth of the labor force. If there was any difference between the two periods, the ratio of capital stock to labor grew more slowly after 1915 than before; this is so since the rate of growth of the capital-labor ratio is $\frac{1+r}{1+i}$ where r is the rate of growth of the capital stock and i is the rate of growth of the labor force, and $\frac{1.05}{1.025}$ is greater than $\frac{1.023}{1.013}$.

The capital stock data are extremely interesting, because one is tempted to attribute the rise in the rate of growth of wage rates to the decline in European immigration that occurred at about the same time.[7] The decline of immigration was caused first by World War I and subsequently by restrictive legislation in the 1920's. Presumably, low levels of immigration would have caused the denominator of the physical-to-human capital ratio (as measured crudely by the capital-to-labor ratio) to grow slowly, thus increasing the growth of the ratio. However, we have seen that the numerator of the ratio also grew more slowly when immigration declined, the reason being perhaps that the rate of physical capital accumulation was not independent of the rate of growth of the labor force. That is, immigration may have made many kinds of investment projects more profitable than they otherwise would have been, by providing inexpensive labor complementary to new investment projects. Thus, whatever influence the decline of European immigration may have had on wage rates in the United States, it seems

---

[6] *Historical Statistics of the United States, Colonial Times to 1957*, p. 152.

[7] The number of international immigrants arriving in the United States dropped from 5.2 million in 1910–14 to 1.2 million in 1915–19. (*Ibid.*, p. 56.)

unlikely that such an influence was by means of stimulating an increase in the growth of the economy's capital-to-labor ratio.

A clue to one of the causes of the pronounced increase in the growth of real wage rates after about 1915 is provided by information on the course of education in the United States. There is evidence that a significant increase in labor force quality took place at roughly the same time that immigration declined. One bit of evidence is that between 1870 and 1910 the proportion of the 17-year-old population graduating from high school rose from 2.0 per cent to 8.8 per cent, or about 2.2 percentage points per decade, while from 1910 to 1930, the proportion rose to 50.8 per cent, or by slightly more than 10 percentage points per decade. Further evidence that the United States was increasing its rate of investment in human capital per person is that the fraction of gross national product going into direct educational expenditures rose sharply during the last four decades of the nineteenth century, as shown in Table 13-3. Even though there was no tendency for

Table 13-3

FRACTION OF DIRECT EDUCATIONAL
EXPENDITURES IN GROSS NATIONAL
PRODUCT—UNITED STATES:* 1840–1900

Year	
1840	.006
1850	.007
1860	.008
1870	.013
1880	.011
1890	.015
1900	.017

* Includes public school expenditures at all levels.

Source: Albert Fishlow, "American Investment in Education," *Journal of Economic History*, December, 1966, p. 430.

the share of direct educational expenditures in national product to slow down its rate of growth toward the end of the century, the rate of growth of the 10–19-year-old population fell sharply after 1890. The interdecade rate of growth of this age group had been around 25 per cent following the Civil War, but it declined to 15 per cent in 1890–1900 and had fallen to 10 per cent by 1910–20.[8] Judging from data on direct educational expenditures in the

---

[8] *Ibid*, p. 10.

twentieth century,[9] the rising trend of the share of such expenditures in gross national product continued throughout the first three decades at least. In addition to rising educational expenditure levels, declining immigration probably contributed to the rising educational level of the labor force. Counting persons 10 years of age and over, 4.6 per cent of the native white population was illiterate (defined as being unable to read and write either in English or a foreign language) in 1900, while 12.9 per cent of the foreign-born white population was so classified.

What were the actual increases in labor force quality at the time the change in the growth of real wage rates took place? Data on labor force quality are even scarcer than those on wage rates. However, a study by Edward F. Denison[10] provides interesting and useful data for the period 1909–1960. Between 1890 and 1957, the growth of the labor force, *adjusted for quality change*[11] (principally via change in education level), was about equal to the growth of physical capital. The growth of quality via education was about twice as high between 1929 and 1957 as it was from 1909 to 1927.[12] Denison estimates that labor force quality (as effected by education and factors contributing to quality which were correlated with education—measured by the association between education and earnings in given years) rose slightly less than 1 per cent per year from 1929 to 1957. This was about one-half a percentage point more than from 1909 to 1929. Thus, it is plausible that one-half, and perhaps more, of the one percentage point rise in the growth rate of real wage rates after 1915 was due to improvement in labor quality, rather than to the direct effect of curtailed immigration on the supply of labor relative to the demand for it.

Note that we are *not* asserting that all of the growth of real wage rates was due to an increase in the growth rate of human capital per worker. This would be implausible on the face of it because the amount of physical capital

---

[9] T. W. Schultz, "Capital Formation by Education," *Journal of Political Economy*, December, 1960, p. 578.

[10] The study is reported in Denison's article, "Education, Economic Growth, and Gaps in Information," *Journal of Political Economy*, October, 1962 (supplement), pp. 124–28.

[11] The essential feature of adjusting the size of the labor force for quality change is as follows: The labor force members are categorized by educational level and earning power. Earning power is taken to be a measure of marginal productivity, and if a high school graduate earns, say, twice as much as an eighth-grade graduate, he is given twice the weight in counting the size of the labor force. Other correlates of productivity in addition to education can be used to help measure labor force quality when sufficient information is available. Thus, if the proportion of highly productive labor force members grows over time, the labor force adjusted for quality change grows more rapidly than the labor force not so adjusted.

[12] Denison, *op. cit.*, pp. 124–26.

per worker was rising over the entire period 1832–1965, and the invention of new production techniques contributed to rising productivity of most productive factors. However, a substantial amount of the *increase* in wage rate growth after 1915 appears attributable to acceleration of investment in human beings.

Are there other factors which could provide additional or alternative explanations of real wage rate growth and changes in the rate of growth? At least three suggest themselves. One is that we have not allowed for improvements in the quality of physical capital as well as human capital. Therefore, the ratio of physical capital (adjusted for quality change) to labor (adjusted for quality change) surely has risen faster than suggested by the figures adjusted only for changes in labor quality. In fact, this rationalization is probably substantiable in the light of our knowledge of how quality changes have been incorporated into available data on the stock of physical capital.[13]

A second alternative explanation is that important aspects of the process of economic growth, such as economies of large-scale enterprises and contributions of education to the value of production which are not reflected in differences in earnings among workers of different educational attainment (such effects of education on output are called external economies), have been left out of account. The results of studies not discussed here, as well as Denison's work,[14] suggest that such factors have contributed to the growth of the average level of real wage rates and may have been rather important.

Finally, we could resort to a rationalization which denies that overall market forces associated with changing factor endowments have been crucial in raising real wage rates. Such a rationalization would explain wage rate growth largely as a result of labor union activity, declining monopsony power of employers, and legislation. It is unlikely that such factors played an important role in determining the growth of real wage rates (although it is not improbable that the declining importance of immigration to the labor force after the mid-1920's reduced the overall degree of monopsony power of employers, and this contributed to wage rate growth). The effects of unions on wage rates were discussed in greater detail in Chapter 11. Briefly, our argument that unions contributed little to wage growth over time revolves around the fact that there was very little pro-labor legislation prior to the 1930's, and union membership didn't approach 20 per cent of the labor force until the 1940's. Nevertheless, wage rates have increased throughout the century; there seems to be little correlation between the level of union membership (relative to the labor force) and the *rate of growth* of real wage rates. Real wage rates don't appear to have grown more rapidly during

---

[13] *Ibid.*, pp. 146–47.

[14] *Ibid.*

recent decades, when union membership has been high, than in earlier decades, when membership was much lower.

Are we now in a position to answer the question of whether the historical growth of real wages is consistent with the economic theory of essentially competitive markets? You should be able to see that this is a difficult question to answer. The theory is stated in the form: *if* certain events occur (such as an increase in the ratio of physical to human capital), *cet. par.*, then certain others will follow (such as an increase in wage rates). However, we have been able to make only rather uncertain statements about the antecedent events: What was the rate of growth of human capital prior to 1890? Were additional factors, not correlated with education, important influences on the growth of human capital after 1890? How has failure to account for quality change of nonhuman capital influenced our estimates? Are there other productive factors, left out of account (e.g., land or "innovative activity") which have influenced wage rate growth? What is the importance of external economies of education? In addition, our real wage rate series is rather unreliable prior to 1890. However, if we are heroic (foolish) enough to ignore these uncertainties, we can say that the historical growth of real wage rates is consistent with competitive economic theory; but such consistency is not proof that this is the only theory capable of rationalizing our observations.

We would have stronger reasons for asserting consistency if we had formulated our theory in sufficiently precise terms to enable us to bound more narrowly the range of relationship that would be consistent with it. For instance, by *how much* should we expect wage rates to rise if the capital-to-labor ratio changes by 1 per cent? Nevertheless, we haven't done that, and we must still ask, with *which* theory may the observed wage rate data be consistent? A variety of theories predict that if physical or human capital per worker rises, wage rate will also rise. For example, the prediction can be derived from theories which assume pervasive competition, from those which assume varying degrees of monopsony and monopoly, from theories which do not stem from the assumptions of utility and profit maximization, and even from those which stress the role of legislation and collective bargaining in determining wage rates. Because of the long historical period we have examined, during much of which union power and the influence of "pro-labor" legislation have been very small compared with the present, we can be reasonably sure that the data are inconsistent with a theory that stresses the importance of unions and legislation in determining wage rates in the long term. However, we are not yet in a position to test the validity, or usefulness, of several alternative theories which imply the historical changes we observe. Such testing awaits more careful formulation of the alternative theories, which emphasize the *differences* in the relationships they predict; it also awaits, probably, more extensive data than are now available.

THE WAGE STRUCTURE

introduction

The second aspect of real wage rates we shall discuss is their relationship to each other among various subcategories of the labor force at a moment in time. The relationships among wage rates of subcategories of the labor force such as occupational groups, industry groups, and the like, constitute what we call the *wage structure*. The wage structure has occupied a great deal of the attention of economists. There are two reasons for this interest. One is a concern with the determinants of income inequality; the other is a concern about how well the labor market functions to allocate labor among alternative employments and, concomitantly, to determine the wage rates of workers in accordance with their marginal products. These two concerns are not unrelated, the reasons being: (1) If one wishes to alter the income distribution, a knowledge of how it is generated is essential. (2) One's evaluation of the desirability of an existing wage structure may depend in part on the degree to which workers are paid according to their productivities.

Reason (1) may not be immediately obvious. If it is not, consider the following. Suppose it is decided that the earnings of executives are too high relative to the earnings of production workers and that a progressive income tax is imposed. *If* the earnings of executives are high because executives are remunerated for specialized skills acquired through education and training and for a willingness to assume risk and responsibility, a tax may eventually reduce the willingness of workers to supply these qualities. If so, the (pretax) remuneration of executives will have to increase, and after an adjustment period, the pretax income distribution may be more unequal than it was before the income tax was levied. If, on the other hand, the relatively high remuneration of executives occurs because executives possess special talents which are inborn traits whose only use is in executive activities, an income tax would reduce the "rents" (i.e., payments in excess of the value to executives of their most attractive alternative employments) executives receive for these talents, but it would probably not reduce in the long run the amount of executive talent supplied. Or, if executives receive high wages because of their social class, nepotism, or prejudice on the part of employers, again a tax might well reduce the rent component of executives' wage rates.

The question we ask seeks information about the behavior of wage rates relative to each other over long and short periods of time. If everyone had equal access to resources for investment in human capital and similar information and attitudes toward the risk and uncertainty associated with such investment, we should nevertheless expect to observe wage rate inequality due to interpersonal differences in intelligence, other forms of ability, and such investments in human capital as education that complement them (that is to say, the marginal rate of return to investment in human capital, given the level of investment in each person, probably depends on conditions such as intelligence and ability). We should also expect to observe wage rate differences which are due to nonpecuniary differences in the employment conditions associated with various jobs. In the world as it is, interpersonal differences in access to resources for investment in human capital and in the perception of opportunities for such investment no doubt contribute to differences in investment in forms of human capital such as health, geographical mobility, education, and other forms of training, and hence in wage rates. We shall not in this chapter look deeply into the question of what determines interpersonal differences in investment in human capital, although the issue is touched upon at various points. We shall, of course, inquire into the role played by investment in human capital—especially formal education—in helping to determine aspects of wage structure.

In addition to conditions which affect the cost of training workers for different kinds of jobs and nonpecuniary differences in working conditions among jobs, short-run factors such as recent changes in the demand for particular goods and services and the stage of the business cycle will affect wage structure at any moment in time; we shall also look at the role of such short-run factors in determining the relationships among wage rates. Finally, we hope to gain some insight into the question of whether the wage structure behaves as if it were generated by the interaction of supply and demand for different kinds of labor in competitive markets or whether it more clearly reflects the interplay of custom, unions, legislation, monopoly, and monopsony.

the kinds of wage structure and their long-term characteristics under competitive conditions

The wage structure can be defined in a number of ways; in the next few paragraphs we discuss a few of these and some of the implications of the theory of competition for their behavior.

The Occupational or Skill Wage Structure. Almost by the very definitions of skill or occupation, we expect to observe wage differences among workers in the different skill and occupational categories. Since occupations are defined, by and large, according to the nature of the tasks performed (rather than, as with industries, according to the kind of output produced), the various occupations can be categorized according to the amount of training and education they require, according to their relative pleasantness, usual location of work, and so on, all of which may be expected to have an effect on wage rates.

The Industrial Wage Structure. In a competitive economy, inter-industry wage rate differences (in equilibrium) should reflect only inter-industry differences in skill requirements and employment conditions such as region, pleasantness of work, cyclical variability of employment, etc. There should be no persistent interindustry wage differentials due to conditions such as difference in capital-to-labor ratios (because workers will seek employment where their wage rates are highest, and because employers will seek workers of given quality who are willing to work at relatively low wage rates; both of these activities produce forces which tend to equalize wage rates). Nor should there be an association (*cet. par.*) between wage rates and the amounts of labor and capital employed. Trying to judge when other things are in fact equal or have remained unchanged, so that economic theory in its simplest (usually competitive) form can be applied and tested, is one of the most difficult parts of empirical work in economics.

Other Wage Structures. There are other kinds of wage structures that we might fruitfully consider. One is the interfirm wage structure. Within local labor markets, economic theory implies much the same about the inter-firm wage structure as about the interindustry structure: in the long run, wage rates should differ among firms in a competitive economy only because of differences in the quality of workers employed and because of differences in the nonpecuniary conditions of employment. There should be no differences attributable to firm size per se, profits, or industry. However, in the short run, expanding firms would be expected to have to increase the wage rates they pay relative to other firms, while declining firms should be able to allow their wage rates to decline.

Competitive economic theory implies that, except for interregional cost of living differences (broadly conceived), interregional wage differences should tend toward zero. The forces which theory implies will promote interregional wage rate equality are: (1) the movement of workers *from* regions of low wage rates (for labor of given skills) to regions of high wage rates; and (2) the movement of firms (i.e., physical capital) *toward* regions of low wage rates (for labor of given skills). These forces are properly analyzed by means of capital theory, because investment in initial costs of moving either workers or firms is undertaken in the anticipation of increased wage rates or returns to physical capital over time. Counterforces slowing down the adjustment of wage rates toward interregional equality are those which make it difficult for workers or firms to finance investment in mobility and those which make for costly information and uncertainty about relevant alternatives and future payoffs to mobility. We shall not discuss mobility and the interregional wage structure at length, although this is a very important and interesting subject.

In the remainder of this chapter, we shall focus primarily on the determinants of interoccupational and interindustry wage differences, trying to find out to what extent the wage structures examined behave as if they were generated by competitive market forces.

the theory of occupational and industrial wage structures

In this section we review and elaborate the implications of the theory of competition that was developed earlier for the behavior of the occupational and industrial wage structures.

The Relationship Between Industry, Occupation, Skill, and Wages. Industries are defined according to what is produced and, hence, economic theory implies that in equilibrium there should be no differences among wage rates for the same kind of labor according to industry per se except for working conditions that vary systematically among industries. On the other hand, classifying workers by occupation and/or skill is to classify them by characteristics which, according to economic theory, should be among the most important determinants of wage rates. The principal occupational categories differ essentially in the kind of work performed, and there is a general agreement between kind of work performed and what most people would consider to be the degree of skill—as measured by formal education, on-the-job training, experience, and natural ability—needed to perform the necessary tasks adequately.

Occupations and industries occasionally differ in characteristics required of workers such as race, religion, and possibly sex. Such requirements are not consistent with competitive economic theory, unless we incorporate desires to employ or to work with persons of particular races, religions, or sex (for reasons other than those which are intrinsic to the work performed) in the production functions of firms and the supply functions of workers.

The Long Run and the Short Run. Occupations and industries also differ among themselves in respect to recent changes in the demand for workers. When there is a change in demand for workers in a particular occupation or industry, we cannot in general expect the supply response of workers to be instantaneous. This is because it takes time and money to acquire information about changing labor market conditions and to engage in any formal and informal training that may be required when workers change jobs. Furthermore, some characteristics required of workers in certain occupations (such as manual dexterity, unusual physical strength, great facility with numbers, etc.) may be in part congenital characteristics, for which training is an imperfect substitute. Perhaps most important, workers are by and large loath to give up jobs about which they have a certain degree of knowledge, in which they have acquired seniority, and the leaving of which may require moving to a new place of residence, for only a slight improvement in wage rates. Finally, trade unions may act to limit the number of workers in particular industries and occupations (often through restricting membership to whites, males, etc., and/or by charging high entrance fees and/or requiring long periods of apprenticeship). Therefore, at any moment of time there will probably have occurred enough recent changes in the demand for labor in different occupations and industries so that some of the wage differences observed will not be explainable in terms of differences in worker characteristics and nonpecuniary employment conditions but rather in terms of short-run deviations of actual wage rates from their long-run equilibrium values; consequently certain workers are likely to be earning considerably more than they could in alternative pursuits (i.e., earning economic rents), and others considerably less. (Do not fall into the trap of concluding that such rents, if observed, reflect a misallocation of resources. If workers respond to wage differentials in the long run, the short-run rents perform a vital allocative function. Furthermore, they signal employers to use relatively less of resources in high demand and more of others.)

However, new workers with no previous labor market attachments are continually entering the labor force, and there are always some experienced workers who for one reason or another seek to change jobs; therefore, the less rapidly employers attempt to expand their work forces, the greater advantage they can take of the availability of job seekers and the lower will be the wage premiums they need to pay. Also, the conditions which enable unions to demand and obtain relatively high wage rates tend to deteriorate over time as employers change methods of production and geographical locations. In the long run, we expect competitive forces to predominate and to eliminate wage premiums paid by industries that have expanded relative to the economy. That is to say, we hypothesize on the basis of the theory of competition that long-run labor supply curves to occupations and industries are highly elastic.

Similarly, industries whose employment is contracting can maintain their desired work forces, in the short run, at lower wage rates than are paid elsewhere. In the long run, however, economic theory predicts that their work forces will continue to shrink unless they pay competitive wages.

Some Methodological Considerations.   Before going on, it should prove worthwhile to reflect a bit on the nature of the tools we shall employ in the investigation of wage structure, most of which are covered in pages 20–36 of the appendix to Chapter 1. In the remainder of this chapter we shall adopt the methodology discussed in the appendix to apply the theory of the competitive determination of wage rates to observed behavior.

In applying the competitive theory, we are forced, because of limited information about all the conditions affecting wage behavior, to test very simple hypotheses derived from the theory, assuming many variables left out of the analysis to be uncorrelated with the independent variables included. Another condition which forces us to test simple hypotheses derived from competitive theory is the low level to which we have developed the contrasting implications of the theory of competition, on the one hand, and theories with noncompetitive postulates (such as non-price-taking behavior), on the other. Thus, we are not in a position to confirm or refute competitive theory with a high degree of certainty. Nevertheless, testing simple hypotheses derived from competitive theory does provide insights into the determinants of wage behavior and shed some light on the theory's explanatory power. A convenient expression summarizing what we intend to do is that we intend to test competitive *hypotheses* about wage behavior, derived from the theory of competition under assumed restrictive conditions.[15]

the behavior of skill and industry wage differentials

Occupational and Industrial Wages—1959. Table 13-4 shows the distribution of earnings and education by major occupational group for employed civilian males in 1959. (There are also data for 1965 to give some idea of the growth of earnings since the last census.) Table 13-4 also shows average weekly earnings of production workers in selected industries for 1964. There is an obvious relationship between the educational level of various occupations and occupational earnings, but the relationship is not perfect. For instance, the median earnings of nonfarm laborers are greater than those of farm managers, although median education differs by only 0.2 years, with farm managers having higher median education. If the earnings are corrected for the difference in the average number of weeks worked per year in 1959,[16] the discrepancy becomes much greater. Undoubtedly, some of this discrepancy is due to the neglect of important components of income in kind of farmers' earnings. However, an important part of the discrepancy is surely due to an *industrial* difference between the two occupational groups. No matter how hard we try, we cannot define "pure" occupations which have no industrial connotations. Thus, agricultural occupations, located in an industry in which there is an excess supply of labor that has persisted for at least forty-five years, tend to have lower earnings than occupations in nonagricultural industries with seemingly similar or less exacting requirements.

---

[15] Such a procedure in respect to wage structure is outlined by Melvin W. Reder in an article entitled "Wage Differentials: Theory and Measurement," in *Aspects of Labor Economics* (Princeton, N.J.: Princeton University Press, 1962), pp. 257–317.

[16] *U.S. Census of Population: 1960*, Vol. I.

Table 13-4a

EARNINGS AND EDUCATION OF MALES IN THE EXPERIENCED
CIVILIAN LABOR FORCE BY MAJOR OCCUPATIONAL GROUP

Occupation	Median[1] Earnings A	B	Median Years of School[2] Completed by Employed Males 18+, 1959	Per Cent Who Worked 50–52 Weeks in 1959[3]
	1959	1965		
Professional, Technical, and Kindred Workers	$6,619	$7,668	16.4	77
Farmers and Farm Managers	2,169	2,630	8.7	79
Managers, Officials, and Proprietors, Except Farm	6,664	7,538	12.4	
Clerical and Kindred Workers	4,785	5,511	12.5	76
Sales Workers	4,987	5,552	12.6	75
Craftsmen, Foremen, and Kindred Workers	5,240	6,270	11.0	68
Operatives and Kindred Workers	4,299	5,046	10.0	63
Service Workers, Except Private Household	3,310	3,436	10.1	66
Farm Laborers and Foremen	1,066	2,274*	7.7	42
Laborers, Except Farm and Mine	2,948	4,651*	8.5	45

Sources: [1] A—U.S. *Census of Population: 1960*, B—*Statistical Abstract of the United States*, (1967), I, 240.

[2] U.S. Department of Labor, *Monthly Labor Review*, May, 1963, p. 509 (based on data in the U.S. Census Bureau, *Current Population Reports*, Series P-20, No. 99).

[3] U.S. *Census of Population: 1960*.

* 1965 figures for these occupations refer to year-round full-time workers and are not comparable to the 1959 figures.

Another discrepancy in the relationship between occupational earnings and education is found between clerical or sales workers and craftsmen. This discrepancy would also appear larger if it were corrected for the difference in the average number of weeks worked per year by each worker. Craftsmen, whose earnings are 10 per cent or more greater than those of clerical workers, have median formal education of 1.5 years less. Part of the educational difference is no doubt made up by a greater amount of apprenticeship training among craftsmen. Another likely cause of the high relative

Table 13-4b

AVERAGE WEEKLY EARNINGS OF
PRODUCTION WORKERS IN SELECTED
INDUSTRIES: 1964[4]

Industry	Earnings
Mining	$118.01
Contract Construction	132.06
Manufacturing	102.97
Durable goods	112.19
Nondurable goods	90.91
Transportation and Public Utilities	
Class I Railroads	120.37
Local Transportation	104.58
Motor Freight Transportation	
and Storage	122.18
Wholesale and Retail Trade	79.87
Laundries, Cleaners, and	
Dyeing Plants	55.73

Source: [4] Statistical Abstract of the United States,
1965, pp. 238–240.

earnings of craftsmen is the relatively high degree of union strength and effectiveness among skilled manual workers.[17]

The next step in our analysis of industrial and occupational wage structures is to express wages as a function of age, education, and other personal characteristics which, while they may not themselves represent qualities which are relevant to productivity, nevertheless may be correlated with such qualities. We wish to test the following competitive hypothesis about the wage structure: at any moment in time the wage structure looks as if it represents relationships among long-run competitive equilibrium wage rates. The degree to which such an hypothesis is consistent with the data is reflected in: (1) the degree to which characteristics associated with worker quality and nonpecuniary employment conditions can account for the observed variation in wage rates (the R^2 statistic[18] of a regression of wage rates on such variables is important in measuring this; so is the "reasonableness" of the regression coefficients); and (2) the degree to which systematic

---

[17] However, the data of Table 13-5 suggest that when industry, age, education, and other variables are held constant, the discrepancy disappears.

[18] In the appendix to Chapter 1, we noted that economic theory has little to say about the R^2 statistic. Thus, it is *not* inconsistent with competitive economic theory as we have developed it to find the R^2 statistic "low." However, the *competitive hypothesis* we wish to test implies, among other things, that we can account for a "substantial" proportion of wage rate variation with a manageable number of independent variables, which variables are consistent with the theory of perfect competition.

differences in wage rates among industries and occupations are eliminated when the influence of variables thought to represent worker quality and nonpecuniary employment conditions is accounted for.

Table 13-5 shows the partial results of study which can be used to examine wage structure in the light of a competitive hypothesis. The study regressed annual earnings[19] of a random sample of male workers on the variables shown in the table, plus variables representing place of residence, birth and family characteristics, residential characteristics, and weeks worked. The sample, from the 1:1,000 sample of the 1960 *U.S. Census of Population*, consists of 34,180 males aged 25–64 who worked, and had mean earnings of $5,530.60 in 1959. The unit of measurement of the coefficients is dollars per year.

Note that almost all the occupations and industries have large and significant deviations in annual earnings, despite the fact that education, age, race, sex, and other relevant worker characteristics are held constant.[20] Furthermore, the R^2 statistic suggests that only slightly more than one-third of the variation of earnings among individuals has been "explained" by the regression. The author of the study from which the table is derived states:

> One could expect a considerable portion of this variance to be "unexplainable," due to transistory and random effects on individual earnings. However, this would probably account for up to 30 per cent of the variance [this statement is based on the results of a previous study by the author quoted]. The remaining 35 per cent of the variance, unexplained by our variables, should be attributed to all the intractions that were not accounted for, as well as to the missing variables, such as ability and non-pecuniary returns.[21]

One should add to the quoted author's list of missing variables those which possibly influence wages in ways not accounted for by the economic theory

---

[19] Earnings *not* adjusted for weeks or hours worked were used. The regression results shown, however, included weeks worked as an independent variable (even though it is not shown in Table 13-5). *Not* including weeks worked as an independent variable would be justifiable on the grounds that systematic differences in weeks or hours worked persist over time among groups of workers who differ in their occupational and industrial attachments and in their personal characteristics; if these differences in amount worked reflect differences in permanent *real* income, then to that extent their effect on earnings should be reflected in evaluating interoccupational and/or interindustrial wage differentials. However, to the extent that individuals value hours not worked equally to hours worked we would, by not holding weeks constant in the regression, understate the real income of those who work fewer hours compared to those who work more. Since weeks worked *was* held constant in the regression, the reported coefficients refer to the estimated effects of the included variables on earnings, holding weeks worked constant.

[20] All the variables shown in Table 13-5, which are a subset of the variables used in the regression, are dummy variables. The meaning and use of dummy variables is discussed on pp. 33–34 of the appendix to Chapter 1.

[21] Giora Hanoch, "Personal Earnings and Investment in Schooling" (unpublished Ph.D. dissertation, University of Chicago, 1965), pp. 26–27.

Table 13-5

ESTIMATES OF THE WAGE FUNCTION: MALES OF AGE 25-64 WITH EARNINGS IN 1959

Variable	Coefficient (in dollars)	St. Error	Variable	Coefficient (in dollars)	St. Error
Constant Term	-1,750	282	Occupation		
			Professional, etc.	414	93
Schooling (years)			Farmers & Farm Mgrs.	-1,966	270
0-4	-1,073	106	Managers, Officials, Prop.	1,821	83
5-7	-938	76	Clerical & Kindred plus Sales	-38	77
8	-755	69	Craftsmen, Foremen, etc.	0	
9-11	-446	61	Operatives	-402	65
12	0		Service & Private HH	-677	101
13-15	650	78	Farm Laborers	-383	285
16	1,886	98	Not Reported	760	118
17+	3,191	115			
			Industry		
Age			Agriculture	-747	238
25-34	0		Contract Construction	-20	75
35-44	789	55	Manufacturers	0	
45-54	941	61	Transportation	-81	76
55-64	782	74	Trade	-816	66
			Services & Industry	-936	74
			Not Reported		
Race Region			Public Administration	-848	88
Southern Whites	-410	52			
Northern Whites	0				
Southern Nonwhites	-1,069	105		$R^2 = .345$	
Northern Nonwhites	-725	106			

NOTE: The sample, from which the 1:1,000 sample of the 1960 U.S. Census of Population, consists of 34,180 males with mean earnings of $5,530.60 in 1959. The unit of measurement of the coefficients is dollars. Variables included in the regression whose coefficients are not reported here, but whose influence is therefore not reflected in the coefficient reported, are: residence (rural, urban, etc.), family characteristics, weeks worked, marital status, and others.

Source: Giora Hanoch, "Personal Earnings and Investment in Schooling" (unpublished Ph.D. dissertation, University of Chicago, 1965), pp. 24-25.

of competitive labor markets (such as union membership and nepotism).

When occupation and industry variables *and* weeks worked are left out of the regression reported in Table 13-5, the R^2 statistic falls by 8 percentage points, to .265. Thus, it seems that while personal chracteristics cannot account for all of the interoccupational and interindustry wage differences, they account for perhaps 40 per cent of the variation of *normal* wage rates (excluding the influence of transitory or random effects) among males aged 25–64 who worked in 1959. (*Normal* refers to the wage rate a man in given circumstances could expect to earn *on the average*, or normally, not taking into consideration temporary deviations due to special circumstances such as unusually low or high demand for his services.) Furthermore, inter-industry and interoccupational factors systematically influencing wage rates reduce the degree of unexplained variation by only about 12 per cent.

What about the variation of normal wage rates that remains un-explained? One suspects that some of the factors which are sometimes thought to determine wage rates and which are inconsistent with a com-petitive hypothesis, such as unions, custom, nepotism, monopsony, and monopoly in product markets, are partially reflected in the occupation and industry variables. Others, such as plant size, personal tastes of employers, and so on, may not be reflected at all. However, the opinion of the author of the study, that the unexplained variation is due to ability and other factors, consistent with a theory of competitive labor markets, is probably defensible if not at present testable. Thus, competitive economic theory gives us insights into which variables are likely candidates for explaining interoccupational and interindustry wage differentials. While the competitive hypothesis that the wage structure at a moment of time looks as if it represents the relationships between competitive equilibrium wage rates doesn't fare too badly when confronted with the data, someone who strongly held the opposite view probably would not find the evidence we have presented so far very persuasive.

Another View of Wage Differences—the Rate of Return to Education. The study we have been discussing was designed to provide information about the rate of return to investment in formal education. The way this was done was to view the coefficients of age and education on earnings as estimates of the influence of these variables, holding constant other variables which also influence, or are correlated with, earnings. The procedure involved is fairly simple, but it is not without its difficulties. For instance, certain conditions (such as marital status and family size) would normally change with age; thus one doesn't really wish to hold such variables constant in estimating the relationship between age and earnings. Nevertheless, a number of variables were included in the regression whose results were used as the basis of Table 13-6, many of which have not been discussed here in detail nor shown in Table 13-5. For purposes of calculating the earnings figures shown in Table 13-6, variables which one would normally expect to vary with age were allowed to vary in calculating the estimated earnings, and the figures in the table therefore reflect the expected earnings for men with (for instance) a larger number of children at age 42 than at age 20. On the other hand, other variables included in the regression (such as place of birth or residence) were held constant not only in the regression but in calculating the estimated earnings shown in Table 13-6 as well. The estimates in the table are based on the results of a regression similar to that whose partial results are shown in Table 13-5, with one important exception: the occupation and industry variables were *not* included, because it is believed that one of the ways education enables a man to improve his earnings is through movement toward jobs in higher-paying occupations and industries. Therefore, it would be improper to hold occupation and industry constant in estimating the influence of education on earnings. A useful way of viewing the estimated earnings figures shown in Table 13-6 is that the calculations were designed to

Table 13-6

SELECTED ESTIMATED EXPECTED
EARNINGS (DOLLARS PER YEAR) BY
AGE AND SCHOOLING, PERSONS OUT
OF SCHOOL, 1959, BY RACE AND REGION

	Years of School Completed		
Age	8	12	16
	Whites/North		
20	1,737	2,233	—
42	4,934	6,222	9,561
62	3,667	5,239	8,298
	Whites/South		
20	1,337	1,883	—
42	4,004	5,792	8,821
62	3,127	4,798	7,557
	Nonwhites/North		
20	1,038	1,519	—
42	3,543	4,291	5,395
62	3,046	2,414	1,481
	Nonwhites/South		
20	832	1,134	—
42	2,158	2,750	4,040
62	1,649	1,305	1,054

Source: Giora Hanoch, "Personal Earnings and Investment in Schooling" (unpublished Ph.D. dissertation, University of Chicago, 1965), pp. 55–56.

Table 13-7

ESTIMATES OF PRIVATE INTERNAL RATES OF
RETURN BETWEEN SCHOOLING LEVELS,
BY RACE AND REGION

Higher Level of Schooling (Years)	Lower Level of Schooling (Years) 8	12
	Whites/North	
12	.161	
16	.115	.096
	Whites/South	
12	.186	
16	.128	.101
	Nonwhites/North	
12	.23	
16	.07	no data
	Nonwhites/South	
12	.11	
16	.08	.06

Source: Giora Hanoch, "Personal Earnings and Investment in Schooling" (unpublished Ph.D. dissertation, University of Chicago, 1965), p. 71.

produce estimates which reflect the *expectation* which a typical man of, say, age 20 would hold with respect to the effects of alternative levels of additional schooling on his future earnings.

Earnings estimates which include those shown in Table 13-6 were crudely adjusted for the estimated direct costs of schooling (e.g., tuition, transportation, and books), and following a procedure like that outlined in Chapter 4, rates of return to different levels of schooling were estimated. Some of these rates of return are shown in Table 13-7. The estimated rates of return are between 5 and 23 per cent for white and nonwhite high school and college graduates in the North and in the South. The rate of return table should be read as follows: the number appearing in the column corresponding to 8 years of schooling and the row corresponding to 12 years in the estimated rate of return to completing high school for an eighth-grade graduate. The number immediately below is the rate of return to completing *both* high school and college for an eighth-grade graduate. The number in the 12-year column and 16-year row is the rate of return to completing college for a high school graduate.[22]

---

[22] Rates of return to education have been estimated in a similar way by Gary S. Becker in *Human Capital*, (New York: Columbia University Press, 1964), and by W. Lee Hansen, "Total and Private Rates of Return to Investment in Schooling," *Journal of Political Economy*, April, 1963.

It is difficult to relate the rates of return to a competitive hypothesis about wage structure. For instance, it would be deceptively simple to infer from theory that, if the estimated marginal rates of return to education and other forms of human capital were roughly equal to the rate of return to investment in nonhuman capital (10 per cent is a defensible figure), this would be evidence that the human capital market works pretty well and that wage differentials in this regard behave in accordance with economic theory.

However, while the condition stated above—equality between the marginal rates of return to physical and human capital—may be a necessary condition of competitive equilibrium, it is not sufficient. (This is not the only condition which would prevail with respect to rates of return in competitive equilibrium, of course. Another would be equality among the marginal rates of return to all forms of investment in human capital, *cet. par.*) The reason is that since one of the most important costs of investment is *foregone earnings*, any market imperfection which impinges upon wages of persons at different educational levels, making wages deviate widely from competitive equilibrium rates, might nevertheless only slightly alter the estimated rate of return. This is clear if one considers the formula

$$0 = \sum_{j=0}^{n} \frac{Y_j - X_j}{(1 + r)^j}$$

where Y and X are alternative earnings streams attributable to different levels of educational achievement, and r is the rate of return. (See Chapter 4 for the derivation of this formula.) Suppose interregional labor market disequilibrium lowers wages in the South at all educational levels. How will $Y - X$ be affected? You can see that the rate of return might end up higher, lower, or unchanged in the South, even though wages there are low, due to interregional disequilibrium. In fact, migration from South to North should be thought of as a kind of investment in human capital that would help restore interregional labor market equilibrium. The fact that such investment only slowly eliminates interregional disequilibrium could very well make regional rate of return estimates misleading indexes of how well labor markets function.

Consider another example. Suppose unions successfully raise above competitive levels the wage rates of high school graduates, and monopoly power and trade and professional organizations do the same for college graduates. The rate of return to college education might well be unaffected and fail to reflect these market imperfections.

Nevertheless, while rate of return estimates such as those in Table 13-7 cannot by themselves provide good evidence to test a competitive hypothesis about wage structure, they can, if interpreted with care, shed some light on behavior in labor and human capital markets. For instance, why do the rates of return seem to decline with increasing amounts of investment? While one cause of the apparent decline may be the failure of earnings to reflect the consumption value of higher education and the effect of ability on earnings, it is probably true that an important part is due to interpersonal differences in access to funds for financing investment in human capital (see also Chapter 4, p 100).

Consider first the effect of ability, which may be as follows. The differential degree of ability among persons of different educational attainment is probably greater, the lower the level of education at which differential attainment is measured. For instance, lack of ability is probably a more important reason for failure to complete grammar school than failure to enter college. If ability also affects earnings, the earnings differentials due to ability between groups differing in educational attainment may be larger at lower educational levels than at high levels, imparting a downward bias to the relationship between estimated rates of return and the level of education.

The effect of access to funds for financing investment in human capital probably arises because most higher education is at least partly financed out of the savings or earnings of the individuals being educated, or those of their families. Thus the amount invested per person often depends on personal and family financial resources, and, those people who are financially able to invest in themselves do so and others do not—not regardless of rates of return but sometimes in spite of them. To the extent this is true, the declining marginal rates of return reflect in part the effect of adding different amounts of education to fixed basic human capacities.

As mentioned above, another factor possibly influencing the estimated rates of return may be the failure of earnings to reflect the consumption value of education. But it is not clear why the consumption value of education (the influence of education on personal welfare, not reflected in earnings) should vary with educational level in such a way as to cause the *estimated* marginal rates of return to decline as the level rises.

To conclude this brief discussion of the rate of return to formal education, we consider an intriguing objection to the relevance to labor market behavior of the rate of return concept. The objection is that perhaps we aren't observing the effect of education on earnings at all, but rather the reverse. That is, one might assert that earnings are determined by social standing and custom—rich men's sons get rich men's jobs, etc.—and that people of high social standing also customarily complete high school and go to college. In this case, high earnings and high education would be correlated by virtue of their response to a common cause, but there would be no causal relationship between them. However, this argument seems implausible. If it were true, it would be difficult to explain some important phenomena: (1) the behavior of real wage rates in the United States after 1915 (see Section I of this chapter); (2) the great emphasis on education as a means of achieving economic development in such countries as the Soviet Union; (3) the relationship between the earnings of college graduates and college dropouts.

The third phenomenon requires some elaboration. Note the 1959 earnings of male college graduates as contrasted with the earnings of men who had some college, as shown in Table 13-5. While men with some college averaged $650 per year more than those with only a high school diploma (holding occupation constant), an average college graduate earned $1,886 more than an average high school graduate. According to data prepared by the Commission of Human Resources from the 1950 Census of Population,[23] 22 per cent of high school graduates had fathers who were in professional, semiprofessional, or managerial occupations, while about 45 per cent of the fathers of college graduates or college dropouts were in those occupations. Thus, the difference in earnings between college dropouts and college graduates cannot easily be attributed to family background. Most of it is probably due to a combination of differential ability (college graduates have higher measures of ability than do college dropouts)[24] and educational achievement.

Secular Changes in Skill Differentials. It is generally but not universally agreed that wage differences among occupations requiring workers with different degrees of skill have narrowed secularly. Table 13-8 presents data on skill differentials for manufacturing, steam railroads, and the building trades for various years from 1890 to 1947. All these data indicate a long term, but not continuous, decline in *relative* skill differentials (i.e., wage rates of skilled workers divided by those of unskilled workers). However, even when account is taken of the change in the price level that occurred over the period covered (see Table 13-2, column *3*), the *absolute* difference in *real* rates appears to have widened. Column (10) of Table 13-8 implies a tripling of the cents per hour difference in wage rates between 1907 and 1947, while the cost of living approximately doubled during the same period.

Other studies provide further evidence that *relative* skill differentials have narrowed. One study, by Paul G. Keat,[25] is particularly thorough. Keat examined the behavior of the coefficient of variation[26] of over 100

---

[23] Reported in Becker, *op. cit.*, p. 80.

[24] *Ibid.*, pp. 80–83.

[25] "Long Run Changes in Occupational Wage Structure 1900–56," *Journal of Political Economy*, December, 1960.

[26] The coefficient of variation is the standard deviation divided by the mean. The standard deviation of a set of numbers is a measure of dispersion. Let X_i, $i = 1 \cdots n$, represent one of a set of n numbers. The standard deviation is defined to be

$$\sigma = \left[\frac{\sum_{i=1}^{n} (X - \bar{X})^2}{n} \right]^{1/2}$$

Table 13-8

SKILL DIFFERENTIALS, UNITED STATES

Year	(1)	(2)	(3)	(4)	(5)	(6)	(7)
		Average Annual Earnings					
	Wage Earners		Clerical Workers in Manufacturing and Steam R.R.	Relatives of (1), (2) and (3) [1890 = 100]			[(6) ÷ (4)] × 100
	Manufacturing	Steam R.R.					
1926	$1,309	$1,613	$2,310	298	288	274	95
1920	1,358	1,817	2,160	309	324	255	83
1910	558	677	1,156	124	121	136	110
1900	435	548	1,011	99	98	119	120
1890	439	560	848	100	100	100	100

RELATIONSHIPS BETWEEN EARNINGS OF SKILLED AND UNSKILLED
OCCUPATIONS IN MANUFACTURING AND BUILDING TRADES
(AVERAGE EARNINGS OF UNSKILLED OCCUPATIONS = 100)

Year	Manufacturing (8)	Building Trades (9)	Building Trades (10)
1907	205	185	20
1918–19	175	182	32
1931–32	180	179	59
1937–40	165	170	59
1945–47	155	148	61

Sources: Cols. (1)–(7): *Historical Statistics of the United States, Colonial Times to 1957,* pp. 91–92.
Cols. (8)–(10): Harry Ober, "Occupational Wage Differentials, 1907–1947," *Monthly Labor Review,* August, 1948, pp. 127–134. Cols. (8) and (9) represent relative earnings differentials; Col. (10) is expressed in cents per hour.

occupations (not confined to production workers) in a large number of industries. He found that while the occupations which were relatively high-paying in 1903 were also relatively high-paying in 1956 (the correlation coefficient is about .8), the coefficient of variation fell by about one-third, implying a narrowing of skill differentials. Keat's data, as well as the data in Table 13-8, provide evidence that real absolute differentials have widened. While the coefficient of variation declined by an annual average of 0.8 per

where $\bar{X}$ is the arithmetic mean of the set of numbers. The coefficient of variation is $\frac{\sigma}{\bar{X}}$.
Thus the standard deviation of the set of numbers 1, 2, 3, 4, 5 is $\left(\dfrac{4 + 1 + 1 + 4}{5}\right)^{1/2}$, which

equals $(2.00)^{1/2}$. The coefficient of variation would thus be $\dfrac{(2.00)^{1/2}}{3}$.

cent, the real standard deviation rose by an average of 1.2 per cent per year.[27]

The secular decline in relative skill margins appears to be consistent with a competitive hypothesis. Two events of major importance have probably been the principal causes of the decline. The more important of the two causes has been the increase in the educational level of the labor force; the second, and not completely unrelated, event was the restriction of foreign immigration by legislation. Both rising education and declining immigration probably have affected the wage structure by changing the relative supplies of workers in different skill categories. First, we shall explore briefly how education and immigration may have affected skill differentials, and then we shall consider alternative explanations.

We can be fairly confident that one of the principal causes of the rising educational level of the labor force has been rising per capita income. By enabling the relatively poor to invest in more education than they would otherwise have been able to afford, rising income increases the proportion of the labor force that possess relatively high skill or can be trained in skilled occupations relatively easily. (Keat noted that the typical length of apprenticeship has declined considerably over the years. He attributed this in part to the reduced need for lengthy apprenticeships as a result of the rising educational attainment of the labor force.) Note that we are assuming that the relative demand for workers of different skill levels has not shifted enough to offset the change in relative supplies.

However, economic growth may have contributed to increasing investment in human capital in still another way. As productivity rises, wage rates tend to increase, and *absolute* real wage differences tend to widen. (See the discussion of this process in Chapter 4, pp. 102.) Since absolute real wage differences are positively related to the rate of return to investment in human capital, rising productivity may well have contributed to rising investment in human capital through an increasing payoff to investment, as well as by providing additional resources available for investment.[28] The fact that relative skill differentials have declined while absolute real differentials have risen suggests that not all the increased educational level of the labor force has come about because more abundant resources increased

---

[27] The behavior of the real standard deviation is reported by Becker in *Human Capital*, p. 54. The real standard deviation is the standard deviation of wage rates adjusted for price level changes.

[28] This point is emphasized by Becker, *op. cit.*, pp. 53–54, and it was mentioned in Chapter 4, pp. 102. Incidentally, we should not completely rule out the possible role of rising ages of compulsory school attendances as a cause of increased educational attainment over the years. However, it seems unlikely that the minimum ages of school leaving could have risen without a great deal of law enforcement effort if the age of voluntary school leaving was not rising constantly. The same remarks apply to child labor laws. These and other possible alternative explanations are discussed in the text below, pp. 221ff.

the amount of investment, given the rate of return. Some of the increase has probably been a response to a tendency of the rate of return to increase.

It is not unlikely that rising income levels and the response to a tendency of the rate of return to increase have caused investment in education and other forms of human capital to rise sufficiently to keep the rate of return more or less constant over the last sixty years or so. Becker estimates[29] that there was no decline in the rate of return for high school education or college education from 1939 to 1958—there possibly was an increase. Keat has estimated that, if the rate of return to investment in human capital has remained roughly constant, a substantial part of the decline in skill differentials is attributable to the decline, between 1900 and 1950, in the time of apprenticeship training and the foregone earnings of apprentices per year of training. This decline he attributes to greater efficiency of training and a substitution of formal education for on-the-job training.[30] Increasing education has also worked to reduce skill differentials by reducing the supply of youthful workers, a principal source of unskilled labor.[31]

Immigration probably tended to widen skill differentials by contributing heavily to the unskilled labor force. To the extent that there was discrimination against foreign labor and to the extent that foreign workers were paid less because they could not speak and read English well, these factors added to supply pressures tending to reduce the wages of unskilled workers relative to skilled workers. Keat has estimated that a small but significant part of the decline in skill differentials is attributable to the decline in the importance of immigration to labor force growth after the mid-1920's, because immigrants (particularly those from Eastern and Southern Europe, who predominated in late nineteenth and early twentieth century immigration) tended to be less skilled than native workers.[32]

There are additional explanations of the decline in skill differentials, not all of which are inconsistent with the preceding explanations. Consistent with the preceding explanation is the possibility that one of the ways in which workers enjoy the benefits of economic progress is through a substitution of pleasant jobs for unpleasant ones. To the extent that this substitution occurs and to the extent that relatively pleasant jobs are those whose skill requirements are relatively high (which seems a likely relationship), downward pressure will be exerted on skill differentials as economic progress occurs.[33]

---

[29] *Op. cit.*, pp. 128–30.

[30] Keat *op. cit.*, p. 600.

[31] Reder, "Wage Differentials, Theory and Measurement," p. 265.

[32] Keat, *op. cit.*, pp. 593–94. See also this chapter, p. 200.

[33] This argument is not novel. It is mentioned by, among others, Reder, *op. cit.*, p. 267.

Somewhat less consistent with the preceding arguments is the possibility that legislation limiting child labor, establishing compulsory school attendance, and providing for minimum wage rates has been responsible for the decline in skill differentials. The effect of child labor laws would have been much the same as the effect of legislation limiting immigration. However, it is an important question whether the reduction in child labor and the increased school attendance that have occurred were responses to rising income levels and rates of return to investment in education or whether they were primarily the results of legislative pressure.

Surely, to some extent child labor and school attendance laws reflect tendencies which would have reduced the labor force participation of young people in any event. Minimum wage legislation has never had a substantial impact on the American economy in the aggregate because the rates have always been set at a low level relative to the wage rates received by most workers. We are not yet in a position to evaluate the relative effects on skill differentials of declining immigration, rising income levels, and a rising tendency of the rate of return to increase investment in human capital, on the one hand, and legal restrictions on child labor, school leaving, and minimum wage rates, on the other.

Still another explanation of the secular behavior of skill differentials, inconsistent with a competitive hypothesis, is the hypothesis that unions—especially industrial unions—have exerted pressure toward disproportionately large wage increases for unskilled workers, relative to skilled workers. Whether it is true or not can only be resolved by an appeal to the facts; however, a prioristic argument sheds some light on the issue. As Reder puts it,

> Taken literally, this argument [that unions have successfully demanded, or governments have imposed, "equal cents per hour" wage increases for all workers] is analogous to saying that the incidence of a tax is determined by the fiat of the levier, and is vulnerable to the same question, i.e., "What if the buyer refuses to pay"?[34]

In other words, the analysis of union wage gains should be treated within a framework like that suggested in Chapter 11, where the desire of unions to demand and obtain higher wage rates is constrained by the demand of employers for labor, which is a negative function of the wage rate.

As a matter of fact, unions appear to have had very little effect on the interoccupational wage dispersion. Keat found that the degree of unionization in 1946 had little correlation with the changes in occupational wage dispersion among the twelve industries for which he had sufficient data; he noted, however, that the industries organized by industrial unions tended

---

[34] M. W. Reder, "Theory of Occupational Wage Differentials," *American Economic Review*, December, 1955, pp. 849–50.

to show greater declines in dispersion than those organized by craft unions.[35] Keat also found that, making allowance for the *interindustrial* effect of unions on wages, there was no ascertainable effect on the occupational dispersion If anything, the effect of unions on the wage rates of different industries may have been to increase the occupational dispersion.[36]

Finally, we should comment on the fact that throughout this discussion. of the secular change in occupational wage differentials, we have had nothing to say about the possible role of changes in the demand for labor of different degrees of skill except to note that we have tacitly assumed that such changes in demand have not been sufficient to offset the changes in the supply of and quality of labor that we have outlined. One reason for this neglect of demand is that we know very little about whether and how much the demand for different skills has changed over the years. We cannot determine this simply by looking at the skill mix of the labor force now and comparing it with the skill mix of fifty or sixty years ago, because the skill mix can more or less easily be explained in terms of the supply of educated workers, as we have in fact attempted to do. To find out what changes in production functions and substitutability among workers of different skill levels have occurred over the past half century would be very difficult and beyond the scope of this book. We thus are virtually forced by lack of information to ignore the role of secular changes in demand. However, a more fundamental reason for neglecting demand is the implication of the theory of competition that in the *long run* (maintaining the hypothesis that in the long run information and adjustment costs do not influence behavior), the labor supply curves to occupations differing in skill level are highly elastic; this is how such supply curves were described in Chapters 4 and 5. Clearly, if the supply curves are highly elastic, then changes in demand, *cet. par.*, would have no effect on the skill structure of wage rates in the long run. Thus, while we cannot rule out the possibility that the changes in skill differentials described in this section have been due more to changes in the demand for labor than in the supply, as we have asserted, we should note in defense of the supply explanation that for changes in demand to have predominated they would have to have been of sufficient magnitude to make misleading the hypothesis of highly elastic long-run labor supply curves to occupations of different skill levels.

Short-Run Behavior of Skill Differentials. In this section we consider very briefly the short-run behavior of skill differentials. This behavior is interesting and important, because it sheds some light on the process by means of which the long-run contraction of relative differentials has occurred. (It also sheds light on the relationship between the general level of money wage rates and unemployment discussed in Chapter 14.) The most interesting

---

[35] Keat, *op. cit.*, p. 592.

[36] *Ibid.*, p. 593.

feature of the short-run behavior of skill differentials for our purposes is that during periods of very high labor demand, such as during wartime, wage rate differences between skills tend to contract, more or less irreversibly.[37] It is this tendency for the skill differential to contract during periods of unusually high labor demand that needs to be explained, and we shall show how the explanation can be tied in with the explanation of the behavior of skill differentials over the long run.

The explanation of the short-run behavior of skill differentials seems to lie mainly in a combination of the theory of investment in human capital, and in the way employers adjust to short-run changes in labor requirements. The explanation also makes use of the concept of a *social minimum wage*. The application of this concept to the explanation of skill differentials has been developed by M. W. Reder.[38] Reder defines the social minimum wage rate (*SM*) as follows.

> SM is the minimum (straight-time) hourly wage rate at which a business firm or government—as distinguished from a household or family farm—can hire an hour of labor. SM may be set by statute (e.g., a minimum wage law), by social custom and/or by trade union policy. SM is also related, indirectly, to the assistance from social security, friends, family, etc., that a wage earner can obtain. However, when SM is not effectively set by statute or union policy, it becomes a very slippery concept. Therefore, we shall treat SM as established by statute or effective union policy, although its bases are far more complicated that this assumption would suggest.[39]

The existence of the SM creates a kind of reserve labor force of persons who would like jobs at the SM but cannot get them. This reserve labor force contracts during periods of high labor demand and expands during period of low demand. Thus, the unemployment and labor force participation rates, rather than SM, adjust the amount of employment to the amount of labor demanded in the short run.

Applying the theory of human capital to the short-run behavior of skill differentials leads us to modify the implication of the theory of competition that profit maximization will lead firms to hire labor up to the point where the wage rate equals the value of the marginal product. This is because in the theory of human capital we distinguish between training which is general (equally productive in a large number of alternative jobs) and that which is specific (useful in a limited number of jobs—perhaps only one). While workers are paid the value of the marginal product of *general* training, they will in general be paid *less* than the marginal product of *specific* training.[40] That is,

---

[37] Evidence may be found in Ober, *op. cit.*, p. 130, and Keat, *op, cit.*, p. 584.

[38] Reder, "Theory of Occupational Wage Differentials," pp. 833–852.

[39] *Ibid.*, p. 839.

[40] This point may not be obvious. The interested reader may thus wish to pursue it further and is referred to Becker, *op. cit.*, p. 80.

specific training is viewed by employers as an investment which yields a return to employers measured by the excess of the value of marginal product over the wage rate. An employer who has invested in the specific training of all or some of his workers will thus not wish to lose them because he would also lose the return to their specific training. Thus, if we postulate that specific training exists, we must alter the hypotheses we derive from the theory of competition about the behavior of the firm's demand for labor. Furthermore, there are certain fixed costs involved in hiring workers which affect employers' attitudes toward the amount of labor demanded similarly to the existence of specific training. It is thought the costs of specific training and hiring are positively related to the skill level of workers.[41]

We modify our hypothesis about labor demand, based on including the idea of specific training in the theory of competition, as follows. As a result of the existence of specific training and hiring costs, employers are not always willing to lay off workers in response to temporary declines in their need for labor. The reason is that in laying off workers, employers increase the risk that the workers will seek jobs elsewhere, destroying the employers' investments in the costs of hiring and specific training. To the extent that fixed costs are positively associated with skill level, relatively unskilled workers (whose wage rates are closest to *SM*) are more likely to be laid off when demand declines, and relatively skilled workers may be used to fill temporarily the jobs normally held by less skilled employees. Note that to the extent specific training is associated with the length of employment in a job, the existence of seniority rights is not inconsistent with the behavior we have been describing, and the effect of seniority rights on wages and employment may be much the same.

Conversely, during the periods of high labor demand, relatively unskilled workers are upgraded and used to fill jobs normally reserved for more skilled personnel. This is what happens, for example, during wartime. During such periods of very high labor demand, the reserve labor force may be so nearly exhausted that the *SM* and the wages of the least skilled workers rise relative to the wages paid to workers in higher-skilled jobs (and the upgrading of employees further increases the wages paid to workers who move up from lower occupational levels). The upgraded workers inevitably acquire training, so that the skill mix of the labor force is permanently altered, and this acts as a force to narrow skill differentials, preventing or retarding the reestablishment of the old differentials when the period of high demand is over. As the general level of educational attainment rises over time, the ease with which upgraded workers learn new skills probably also rises, and thus an important part of the effect of a rising level of education on skill differentials may well

---

[41] Walter Oi, "Labor as a Quasi-Fixed Factor," *Journal of Political Economy*, December, 1962.

operate through making it easier for employers to "upgrade" workers during the periodic increases in labor demand relative to supply.

The Long-Run Behavior of Industrial Wage Differentials. There is a considerable body of data on productivity, factor ratios, and wage rates of different industries for the period beginning in the late nineteenth century. These data are not inconsistent with the competitive hypothesis that wage rates and the demand for labor should be uncorrelated over time. As we pointed out in Chapter 5 and in the discussion of the long-run behavior of skill differentials, a very simple interpretation of the theory of competition implies that industries face infinitely elastic long-run labor supply curves. However, we can conceive of situations where particular industries employ a large proportion of some specialized type of labor or have unusual working conditions, such that inelasticity of their labor supply curves could persist over long periods of time. Our competitive hypothesis is derived by maintaining the hypothesis that such situations are empirically unimportant. Another maintained hypothesis imposed upon the theory of competition in order to derive a competitive hypothesis is that changes in the demand for labor are uncorrelated with changes in the skill mix of labor demanded, among industries. To examine the correlation between wage rates and labor demand over time, M. W. Reder has examined data for thirty-three industries (including farming, manufacturing, transportation, and communications industries) and has found that between 1899 and 1953 the percentage *changes* in wage rates are insignificantly (but positively) correlated with percentage changes in employment for thirty-three industries.[42]

Economic theory implies that workers of the same skill level will earn the same wage in every industry (*cet. par.*). Since changes in the capital stock of industries cannot themselves affect the skills of the workers employed (and we maintain the hypothesis that changes in the capital stock are uncorrelated with changes in employers' desired skill mixes), a competitive hypothesis implies that changes in the capital stock of industries should not in the long run be correlated with changes in the wage rates. That is, to the extent interindustry differences in the growth of the capital-to-labor ratio raised the marginal productivities of labor of given skill in the same direction, labor market adjustments under competition should, in the long run, have reallocated labor in the direction of growing productivity, thus tending to keep wage rates growing at equal rates everywhere. Reder also found an insignificant but positive relationship between percentage changes in real wage rates and percentage changes in tangible capital input among industries

---

[42] "Wage Differentials, Theory and Measurement," p. 286. Data are those of S. Fabricant, "Basic Facts on Productivity Change," National Bureau of Economic Research, *Occasional Paper 63*, (New York, 1959), and John W. Kendrick, *Productivity Trends in the United States* (Princeton, N.J.: Princeton University Press, 1961).

over the period 1899–1953.[43] This relationship is shown in Figure 13-1, and it is consistent with our competitive hypothesis. On the other hand, changes in output per worker may be due to changes in the ratio of capital to labor inputs and/or to changes in the skill of workers employed. Thus, one would not as strongly expect, as in the two cases discussed above, to find the correlation between wage rates and output per worker to be near zero. Nevertheless for the same thirty-three industries referred to above, the correlation between wage rates and output per man were insignificantly (but positively) correlated for the period 1889–1953.[44]

The Short-Run Behavior of Industrial Wage Differentials. Following up on our discussion of the long-run behavior of occupational and industry wage differentials, where we were concerned with evidence that long-run labor supply curves are highly elastic, it seems an obvious step to look for evidence of supply curve inelasticity in the short run. An hypothesis that in the short run interindustry differences in changes in labor demand do account for a significant part of changes in wage rates among industries is clearly consistent with the theory of competition. However, such an hypothesis does not perform consistently when confronted with the data. There have been several studies which, among other things, related interindustry differences in wage rate changes to differences in employment changes over periods ranging from one to eleven years.[45] While the results of some of these studies suggest that changes in labor demand are more important in determining wage rate changes in the short run than they are in the long run, the results are not all consistent with each other, some indicating no correlation (or even negative correlation) between short-run employment and wage rate changes among industries.

There are a number of hypotheses that have been advanced to explain interindustry wage rate behavior in the short run, besides the demand hypothesis put forward in the preceding paragraph. Some of these hypotheses are not inconsistent with the theory of competition and some are.

Perhaps the most prominent among alternative hypotheses says that wage rate changes can be explained by the behavior of profits, product market monopoly power, and unionism. Typically, this explanation of wage behavior says that employers pay high or rising wage rates when they can afford to do so (rather than paying the market wage as competitive theory implies)

---

[43] "Wage Differentials, Theory and Measurement."

[44] For eighty manufacturing industries, changes in wage rates and output per unit of input (labor and capital inputs together) were barely significantly correlated with each other. A relevant and important contrast with the correlation discussed above is a strong negative correlation between changes in the price of output and productivity as measured by output per unit of input. (*Ibid.*, p. 201.) This is what a competitive hypothesis would lead one to expect.

[45] Some of these studies are summarized by Reder, "Wage Differentials, Theory and Measurement."

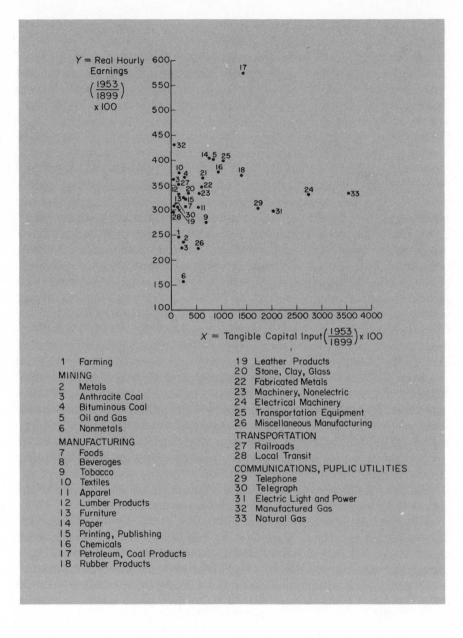

FIG. 13-1

Ratios of Real Hourly Earnings (1953 ÷ 1899) and Tangible Capital Input (1953 ÷ 1899) Compared by Industry

Source: S. Fabricant, "Basic Facts on Productivity Change,"
National Bureau of Economic Research, Occasional Paper 63 (New York, 1959), pp. 44–47.

and that unions influence wage rates more in monopolistic industries (i.e., those industries with high concentration ratios) than in others; that is, unions and monopolistic employers "share" monopolistic profits.

It is important to remember at that point that merely to observe a correlation between high profits and rising wages is not to observe a phenomenon necessarily inconsistent with competition. An expanding, competitive industry would undoubtedly earn unusually high profits *and* be forced to pay unusually high wage rates in the short run. The argument above, on the other hand, implies that industries in which monopolistic power assures supernormal profits in the long run possess *and exercise* the discretionary power (perhaps encouraged to do so by a labor union) to pay unusually high wage rates. What bothers one about the argument is that while monopolistic industries may have the resources to pay unusually high wages, they also have the resources to withstand unions, and the theory does not explain why employers should use monopolistic profits in part to raise wages. This is not to say that *no* monopolistic industry has *ever* paid higher wage rates than it needed to; rather it is an attempt to point out that there is no compelling theoretical reason to believe that it is in the best interest of a monopolist to pay more than a competitive wage rate or that unions can always do best bargaining with a monopolist.

The best available evidence pertaining to the effect of product market monopoly on wage rates has been analyzed by Leonard Weiss.[46] Using the 1:1000 sample of the 1960 *U.S. Census of Population*, Weiss examines the wage rates of different occupations in a large number of industries. He tests two forms of the "monopoly wage hypothesis," much as it was outlined above. In Weiss' words,

> [The monopoly wage hypothesis takes two forms:] (1) that concentrated industries pay high incomes for given occupations, and (2) that these incomes exceed the alternative costs of the labor involved.[47]

Weiss used the information from the 1960 census by performing regression analysis in which he attempted to discover whether interpersonal wage rate differences can be explained by differences in worker "quality" (as measured by education, age, and other characteristics), or whether the variables implied by the monopoly wage hypothesis can do equally well or better. Weiss found that, indeed, highly concentrated industries do pay unusually high wages, but he found that once worker characteristics are taken into account, the "effect" of concentration on wages disappears. That is, concentrated industries seem to get better (or at least more attractive) workers for their

---

[46] "Concentration and Labor Earnings," *American Economic Review*, March, 1966, pp. 96–117.

[47] *Ibid.*, p. 114.

money. This is not inconsistent with a competitive hypothesis, but Weiss' tests cannot establish that the workers hired by firms in concentrated industries represent the least-cost combination of skills. To the extent that the workers are high-quality employees, the high wage rates are offset; however, noncompetitive factors which we have not taken into consideration may induce firms in concentrated industries to pay higher wage rates (and thus have access to a different mix of workers) than they would under competitive conditions. Our knowledge of the labor market is this regard is still quite incomplete.

Contrary to the hypothesis that unions and firms in concentrated industries share monopolistic profits, Weiss found that there is no evidence of a positive interaction between the degree of concentration and the importance of unions. That is, Weiss' results "support the notion that it is unionism or the threat of unionism [not concentration itself] that produces high wages in concentrated industries."[48] In fact, Weiss' results suggest that unions may have a greater power to raise wages in industries where concentration is low. This would be because unions can in such cases gain from exploiting the unused monopoly power (i.e., the *industry's MR* will in general be less than *MC*) inherent in the industry demand function.

Weiss' study also presents significant evidence that industries in which employment grew most rapidly between 1950 and 1960 paid high wages, *cet. par.* This is one bit of evidence that is consistent with the competitive hypothesis that industries' short-run labor supply curves are relatively inelastic and that interindustry variation in wage rate growth can be explained by differences in the growth of labor demand.

CONCLUSION

What have we learned from this rather long and detailed discussion of the behavior of wage rates? Hopefully, we have been able to see somewhat more clearly the ways in which economic theory lends insight into economic events. It is important to know how real wage rates have behaved over the past fifty years and what the structure of wage rates among occupations and industries looks like. But in order to draw conclusions about how the labor market works from such information, we need to know how to interpret wage rate data as evidence bearing on theories of economic behavior. Thus, we have tried carefully to apply some of the implications of competitive economic theory (conditioned by various maintained hypotheses) to some available data.

One of the most pervasive findings is the importance of the role of education and other forms of human capital related to it in explaining wage

---

[48] *Ibid.*, p. 115.

behavior. We found that education and worker characteristics presumably associated with worker quality have an important role to play in explaining existing wage differentials. We also found that significant parts of the long-term growth of real wage rates and the narrowing of relative skill differentials are attributable to the rising educational level of the population. Furthermore, the long-term behavior of both the occupational and the industrial wage structures behave in a manner consistent with the competitive hypothesis of highly elastic labor supply curves to occupations and industries.

The short-run behavior of the occupational and industrial wage structures is more difficult to interpret in terms of competitive theory than behavior in the long run; but it is difficult to find an alternative theory that makes interpretation easier or which promises to yield fruitful insights into wage behavior. On the basis of the material in Chapter 12 as well as in this chapter, it is clear that labor unions, certain kinds of conventional wage-setting behavior (e.g., the "social minimum" wage), the existence of control over product prices in the hands of some firms or industries, and other forces not considered in the theory of competition play a role in determining the short-run behavior of the wage structure. Nevertheless, we do observe in some aspects of the short-run behavior of the occupational and industrial wage structures the working of processes which seem to characterize the long-run behavior. Thus, we observed that the short-run behavior of occupational wage differentials by degree of skill fits in with the tendency toward the long-run decline in relative skill differentials. We also observed some evidence of the tendency of labor to move in the direction of relatively high marginal productivity (which is consistent with the working of competition) in the short-run behavior of wage rates in different industries.

While we cannot yet with great certainty answer the question of whether wage rates behave as if they were the real world analogs of equilibrium wage rates in the theory of a competitive economy, it appears that seeking the answer leads us toward a fuller understanding of wage behavior.

the level
of
money wage rates

INTRODUCTION

Up to this point we have considered only the determinants of real and relative wage rates. However, important questions of economic policy often center on the level of money wage rates. The reasons for concern with money wage rates are varied, but they are related to the connection between money wage rates and the price level. Whether we think the economy is characterized by pervasive competition or by varying degrees of monopoly power, there is a more or less direct link between money wages and the price level via the cost of production and the aim of firms to earn profits. Thus, a theory of the determination of wages is part of a theory of the price level or, to put it slightly differently, a theory of inflation.

In a closed economy, the principal reason for concern with the price level would be to avoid unintended and undesired income redistribution resulting from unanticipated inflation; an additional reason would be to avoid an atmosphere of uncertainty among businessmen which could contribute to economic inefficiency. In an open economy (one in which trade with foreign countries is important) inflation is often undesirable because, if exchange rates are fixed by law, it may cause unwanted loss of gold and foreign currency reserves. Similarly, unanticipated deflation of the price level can have undesirable economic effects. Over the past forty years, however, inflations have been much more frequent than deflations, and we shall for simplicity of expression refer to price level changes as inflation.

In this chapter, we attempt to develop a theory of how the level of money wage rates is determined. We do this in order to deal with what may seem to be a contradiction between the traditional theory of the wage level, which ascribes no causal role in the theory of inflation to the process by which workers and firms "set" their wage rates, on the one hand, and more recent notions which treat the wage-setting behavior of workers, unions, and firms as crucial to an adequate theory of the level of money wage rates, prices, employment, and unemployment, and to an adequate policy to deal with inflation, on the other hand. In order to reconcile the traditional theory, which treats the quantity of money as the essential determinant of the level of money wage rates, with the currently popular and appealing emphasis on the apparent discretionary power of buyers and sellers of labor to set particular wage rates and, hence, to influence the general level of wage rates, we first outline briefly and crudely the traditional approach (Section II). Next, (Section III) we develop a theory about how firms and workers decide among alternative courses of action in choosing wage rates, prices, jobs, employment levels, and output levels when uncertainty exists and information is costly.

The theory developed in Section III leads us to expect to observe, even in a competitive economy with freely (in a legal sense) mobile labor, the co-existence of job vacancies and unemployment. The theory also helps explain the behavior of wage rates and prices which in the short run do not in general reduce excess supplies and demands to zero. Furthermore, on the basis of the theory, we should expect to observe a negative relationship between the rate of unemployment and the rate of change of the levels of money wage rates and prices. However, even though the theoretical framework of Section III helps explain our observation that inflation and unemployment are negatively correlated, it is also used to show that the rate of inflation should not for most purposes be viewed as causally related to the rate of unemployment despite the observed correlations between these variables. The theory of Section III also helps us to see why the *traditional* theory of the determination of the levels of money wage rates and prices is not inconsistent with such a correlation or with situations where individual workers appear to have the power to raise their wage rates without immediately losing the opportunity to work, where unemployed workers may lower the wage rates they demand (their reservation wage rates) without immediately ending their unemployment, and where employers may similarly adjust their wage offers without immediately filling all their job vacancies or losing all their employees.

In Section IV we treat some recent empirical evidence relating to the observation of a negative relationship from one time period to the next between unemployment rates and the rate of change of wage and/or price levels—the so-called "Phillips Curve" relationship—again emphasizing that the observed relationship should not be used as evidence to support the notion that unemployment can be permanently reduced by means of an acceptable degree of inflation or that some degree of inflation is a necessary—or even a feasible—price to pay for maintaining "full" employment.

THE TRADITIONAL THEORY
OF THE WAGE LEVEL

Traditionally, the theory of the determination of the wage level was developed in terms of the comparative static analysis of the price level. In comparative static analysis, the cost and speed of adjustment from one position of static equilibrium to another is ignored and assumed to be unimportant for deriving useful predictions about the behavior of the economic phenomena considered; most of the theory of the labor market developed so far in this book has been of this type, and it is often quite useful, particularly when one is concerned with long-run behavior. The simplest form of the traditional theory of the price level has its roots in classical economics. Most students are familiar with the equation

$$MV = PT$$

or one of its variants, in which T is the level of transactions in the economy (in real terms) or real national income, V is the "velocity" of money, assumed constant or a function of variables, such as the interest rate, which may not be included in the above equation or one of its variants; M is the supply of money in nominal terms; and P is the price level. In this simple model, increases in the quantity of money are necessary and sufficient for the price level to rise; the level of money wage rates (W) is proportional to the price level, and real wage rates (W/P) are determined by the supply and demand for labor in real terms. A sometimes crucial and often implicit assumption of the theory is that changes in the money supply are exogenous—that is, they are not a function of changes in the demand for money that occur for example, when there are autonomous changes in the price level.[1] A second important implicit assumption is that no amounts of labor and commodities demanded and supplied are affected by "money illusion." Money illusion occurs, for instance, if workers decide how many hours per week to work on the basis of money wage rates rather than on the basis of wage rates in terms of their purchasing power over goods. Similarly, money illusion would occur if firms did not consider the price at which output is sold in determining

---

[1] See, for instance, R. G. Lipsey and P. O. Steiner, *Economics* (2nd ed.) (New York: Harper & Row, Publishers, 1969), Chap. 36.

the amount of labor demanded at alternative wage rates (i.e., if they considered W, rather than W/P to be the relevant cost of a unit of labor, or, if in evaluating marginal product to compare with the money wage rate, they consistently used the wrong price of output), or if they felt that only the wage rates they pay, not their wage rates *relative* to those of other firms, were relevant to their optimal hiring policies.

As it is generally accepted by economists now, the traditional theory of the price level has incorporated the notion that over some range the money supply may not be an exogenous variable because fractional reserve banking provides a basis from which commercial banks can, within limits, increase the quantity of money to accommodate increases in the demand for it. Nevertheless, reserve requirements limit the supply responsiveness of the money stock, and to the extent that the profit motive induces banks to be "loaned up" at almost all times, conditions approximate those that would exist under a system of 100 per cent reserve requirements.

However, the declared goal of the federal government to limit the magnitude of unemployment in the economy casts a new light on the problem of the price level because price-setting actions by sellers of labor and/or commodities which ordinarily would raise prices, reduce the quantity of real money and, thus, raise unemployment rates, would be met by economic policies aimed at reducing unemployment and hence tending to expand the money supply if the government attempted to keep unemployment from rising under such circumstances. An important question that has arisen therefore is, if our monetary system interacting with the expressed economic goal of preventing unemployment rates from rising "too high" makes it *possible* that the monetary authority is forced to expand the money supply when the demand for money grows, thus facilitating inflation, *is this process likely to take place*?

Economists who conclude that the traditional theory of the price and wage level is sufficient to answer most questions about inflation often state that it is unlikely that a process of monetary expansion in response to sellers' price-setting behavior will occur. That is, they say that unilateral actions of sellers of labor and commodities raising their prices are not likely to be an important cause of inflation. Granted, they say, monopoly elements may be significant; but monopoly power can explain only relatively high prices in some parts of the economy—not rising prices generally. At any moment of time, monopolists (unions may be thought of as attempting to maintain and exert monopoly power) set prices which are intended to maximize profits or some index of private economic welfare which depends on wages or profits. Thus, once such prices have been found, there is no reason to attribute continuously rising prices to monopoly power, unless there is reason to believe that the degree of monopoly power increases over time. Such an increase is rejected as an implausible and certainly as an improbable explanation of changes in the levels of wages and prices that have occurred since the early 1950's. Rather, it is argued, the direction of causation has typically run from changes (or acceleration) in the money stock to changes in aggregate demand (which outpace the growth of supply) to rising prices and wages. The view that the process by which firms set wage rates and prices has itself an independent influence on the course of the wage and price levels and—because of attempts to maintain low unemployment—on the money supply is rejected as unlikely.

On the other hand, many economists today reject the relevance of the traditional theory of the price level, at least in the short run, on two grounds we have mentioned: (1) There are important elements of monopoly power in labor and product markets—at least in the short run—which give sellers of labor and commodities discretionary power over the prices they charge. (2) The argument from the degree of monopoly, and monopolistic equilibrium, given above is irrelevant if sellers feel that their demand curves will be increased by monetary and fiscal policies designed to combat unemployment when they raise their prices. Thus it is asserted that the general level of wages and prices leads a life of its own rather independently of autonomous actions of the monetary authorities. If inflation *and* unemployment are simultaneously to be maintained at acceptable levels, therefore, actions other than standard monetary and fiscal policies may be required. This is because there is alleged to be a "tradeoff" between the level of unemployment and the rate of inflation that results from the organization of markets and the goal of maintaining a low level of unemployment by means of monetary and fiscal policies.

A THEORY OF WAGE ADJUSTMENT, EMPLOYMENT ADJUSTMENT, AND THE WAGE LEVEL

In this section we attempt to show how an analysis of the way wage rates and prices are decided upon by profit- and utility-maximizing decision-making units (i.e., firms and households) in essentially competitive markets can reconcile the short-run existence of monopoly and monopsony power with the long-run applicability of the comparative static theory of perfect competition. In particular we wish to demonstrate that what at times is taken to be evidence of the pervasiveness of discretionary power over wage rates and prices in the presence of a government policy to maintain low unemployment rates—namely, a negative correlation between the rate of change of the general wage level and the economy's unemployment rate (and/or its rate of change)—is consistent with the theory of perfect competition, *if the costs of*

*information and the adjustment of resources allocation to alternative uses are
assumed to be positive and important.*

The Role of Information and Adjustment Costs in the Short Run. The
theories discussed above are difficult to reconcile because they do not consider
explicitly the implications of the cost to workers and firms of adjusting to
a constantly changing environment, and therefore neither approach is capable
of explaining how prices and wage rates are actually set. In Chapter 10, we
noted that one of the reasons some competitive and noncompetitive economic
theories are sometimes thought to be inapplicable to understanding real
world behavior is that they assume perfect knowledge of all alternatives. That
is, they include postulates that there are no costs of acquiring information
and adjusting the allocation of resources to maximize profits and utilities
in the presence of changing and incomplete information about the environment. There is probably little wrong with assuming away the costs of information and adjustment for many problems which require comparing positions
of long-run equilibrium. However, analyzing the determination of employment and the wage level in the short run often involves us in inquiring into the
day-to-day actions of firms and family members in deciding what wage rates
and prices ought to be. Up to now, we have ignored this problem by assuming
that prices are "determined" by the intersection of supply and demand
curves, ignoring the obvious fact that price decisions are made by human
beings acting on the basis of limited information. We proceed now to
incorporate into the discussion of the joint determination of the general
level of wage rates, employment, and unemployment, the idea that acquiring
information and adjusting the allocation of resources involve the use of
scarce resources and are thus subject to economic analysis. We thus hope to
arrive at a theory of the wage level that is based on the postulates of competition and is also consistent with the observation that many buyers and
sellers in our economy appear to have some discretion over prices in their
day-to-day operations.

Basically, incorporating the role of information in economic theory
proceeds along the following lines:

> If complete information about all job possibilities and all workers and all
> goods were free and instantly available, there would be no point to shopping
> or waiting for better offers. One would instead instantly take the best one.
> But information is neither free nor complete, despite the existence of markets
> which certainly do help to lower the costs · · ·
> · · · we state four central propositions.
> (1) *Information is not free.* (2) *The more rapidly it is obtained, the greater
> the cost of information.* Making the search less hastily is less costly per unit
> of new information obtained. Production and acquisition of information,
> as with any other good, conform to the general laws of production. More
> rapid acquisition may or may not be worth the extra costs, as we shall see.
> (3) *Adjustment of resource uses to new jobs is costly, and the more rapidly a*

move is made the more costly it is. Again, moving from one place to another or from one job to another uses up productive effort and resources. As with other production, moves are not free goods. They involve costs. (4) *Information about other jobs is sometimes cheaper to obtain while "unemployed."*[2]

Let us analyze statements (1) and (2) of the preceding quotation in some detail. (1) *Information is not free.* This means that acquiring knowledge about one's alternatives in markets requires the expenditure of resources. These resources take the form of time and materials spent in shopping for better buys or better markets, time and materials spent in advertising in its various forms, contacting people who are thought to be "in the know" about the market situation, and so on. Why, therefore, do people try to acquire or disseminate information? Consider a businessman who experiences a sudden upsurge in the number of new orders he receives for his product. If he has difficulty in meeting the orders, given his current number of employees, work shifts, and plant size, he faces at least the following alternatives: (1) He can do nothing, essentially letting all of his costs of adjusting to the new situation arise from the foregone profits of an unknown "correct" adjustment and from annoyed customers, who may possibly seek other suppliers not only for current orders but for future orders as well. (2) He can raise his selling price enough to keep new orders from accumulating any faster than in the past (or "too fast"); this procedure would have costs similar to those of (1) and might raise profits. (3) He can require his workers to work overtime at the cost of paying overtime premium wage rates and probably the cost of reduced efficiency; also, his workers may not wish to work overtime indefinitely, and he therefore risks a higher labor turnover rate, which would be costly; however, he can possibly increase his profits by raising output and incurring a concomitant increase in unit production costs. (4) He can add a new work shift, if his plant is not currently being used twenty-four hours a day, at a cost of hiring new workers and reduced time for machine maintenance. (5) He can add new plant and equipment and hire new workers to go

---

[2] Armen A. Alchian and William R. Allen, *University Economics* (2nd ed.) (Belmont, Calif: Wadsworth Publishing Co., Inc., 1967), p. 497. (Italics in the original.) The theory of the wage level (and unemployment) presented in this section is based partly on ideas contained in various works of Charles C. Holt and Edmund S. Phelps as well. This theory is applicable to a wide variety of markets—not just labor markets. For a cogent statement, see K. J. Arrow, "Toward a Theory of Price Adjustment," in Moses Abramovitz and others, eds., *The Allocation of Economic Resources* (Stanford, Calif.: Stanford University Press, 1959), pp. 41–51. The discussion presented here is also similar in some respects to those by R. G. Lipsey, "Structural and Deficient Demand Unemployment Reconsidered," in Arthur M. Ross, ed., *Unemployment and the Labor Market* (Berkeley and Los Angeles: University of California Press, 1965), pp. 210–55; and Milton Friedman, "What Price Guideposts," in G. P. Shultz and R. F. Aliber, eds., *Guidelines, Informal Controls, and the Market Place*, (Chicago: University of Chicago Press, 1966), pp. 17–39. A recent article which approaches the subject in the spirit of this chapter is by M. W. Reder "The Theory of Frictional Unemployment" in *Economica*, N.S., 36, No. 141, pp. 1–28.

with them, at the relatively high costs of designing and financing the new plant and equipment and searching for and hiring (at possibly higher wage rates than he is currently paying) an additional group of workers to go with them. Clearly, which (combination) of these alternatives he adopts depends on how long he expects the increased demand for his product to persist, how greatly demand has increased, and the expected costs and benefits of the alternative procedures for meeting the increased demand. Thus, the business-man is willing to pay something for information that will help him reduce the uncertainty and risk involved in choosing among his alternative courses of action.

(2) *The cost of information per unit of information is an increasing function of the speed with which it is acquired.* Thus, the businessman may rely on his past experience, luncheon conversations with business associates, casual reading of the newspapers and trade journals, much as he would in the ordinary course of business, to choose among his alternatives for meeting the demand increase. Indeed, if the increased demand is typical of the season of the year, the businessman can acquire the information he needs virtually without cost. On the other hand, if the increase in demand bewilders the businessman, or is a novel experience, he may wish to engage in a more intensive search for information, involving search procedures he is not accustomed to. Thus, he may hire the services of a market analyst, travel to other cities to confer with businessmen there, and so on. Now, he eventually could acquire the information he needs at a lower cost if he simply waited long enough; but by that time he may have lost too many customers impatient with his growing list of back orders, or he may have made a major mistake in setting the wrong price, hiring new workers, or building a new plant, etc., and therefore it may indeed be worthwhile for the businessman to acquire information rapidly at a relatively high cost per unit in the presence of an unusual change in the number of new orders he receives (or some other substantial change in his business conditions).

Consider Figure 14-1. In the upper diagram, we depict the businessman we have been discussing, who at price P_0, the old price at which he had been producing and selling Q_0, now has orders for output Q_1.[3] Among the businessman's many alternative courses of action, he could raise his price to P_2 (the exact value of which he probably does not know) and still (for a certain period of time and not without risk of losing old customers to his rivals) maintain his sales at Q_0; or he could raise his price to P_1 (the exact value of which he probably does not know) and sell an output Q_2 somewhat less than Q_1; either of these two alternatives could increase the businessman's profits for a while, depending on the alternatives faced by his customers (also not known certainly by the businessman). In the lower part of Figure 14-1,

---

[3] We ignore the question whether the businessman produces at an output where $MC = P$ or whether he produces where $MC =$ marginal revenue.

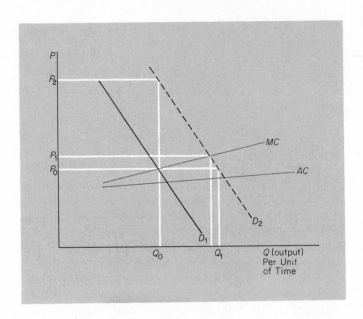

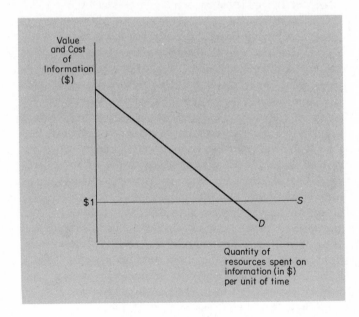

FIG. 14-1

Environmental Change and the Demand and Supply of Information

we diagram the businessman's demand and supply curves for resources to acquire information per period of time. We define a unit of resource spent to acquire information in terms of an expenditure of $1 on obtaining information, and the value of information as the expected present value of the businessman's increased profits if an expenditure of $1 on information acquisition is made. Clearly, if the increase in demand depicted in Figure 14-1 has been anticipated as a normal seasonal fluctuation, the businessman feels that a

240

minimum output or price adjustment is required (perhaps because he has been building up inventories to meet the seasonal increase), and this would be reflected by the businessman's estimate on the basis of prior experience that P_2 and P_1 lie very close to P_0 and that Q_1 lies close to Q_0 if the Q's are taken to represent current production. Thus, the expected present value of an additional expenditure of \$1 to acquire information will be relatively low, and his demand curve for information lies toward the southwest of the lower diagram in Figure 14-1. On the other hand, if the increase in demand is large and unanticipated, the business man feels that some adjustment (the nature of which he is uncertain) will increase his profits substantially over what they might be if no adjustment is made; thus, his demand curve for resources to acquire information will lie toward the northeast of the diagram. Clearly, the longer the increase in demand is expected to last, the longer will be the payoff period of obtaining good information, and the higher will be the present value of the information. The higher is the present value of information, the farther to the right will lie the information resource demand curve. On the other hand, if the demand increase is large and anticipated but nonseasonal, the businessman, by his anticipation through whatever channels he acquired his information, had reduced the probability that further resources spent to acquire information will increase the present value of his profits by a given amount; and his demand for information will be relatively low. Thus we have defined the demand curve for information to be the relationship between the expected yield of an additional dollar's worth of resources spent on information and the total amount spent per time period. This relationship is negatively inclined in accordance with statement (2) that the more information which is acquired per unit of time, the more costly will it be per unit; we have drawn the demand curve in such a way that the additional expenditure of resources required to increase the *expected value* of profits by \$1 rises with the amount of information acquired per time period. The technology of obtaining information is similarly reflected in the demand curve, because when resources used to acquire information can be used relatively productively, the demand curve will lie relatively farther to the right, and vice versa. The supply curve we have drawn as infinitely elastic at \$1; i.e., the businessman is assumed to be able to buy one dollar's worth of resources to acquire information for \$1, no matter how much he buys per time period. The intersection of the demand and supply curves for information describes the amount of resources the businessman uses per time period to acquire information. This analysis implies that the businessman will use resources to acquire information up to the point that the information produced by the last dollar's worth of resources will increase the expected present value of profits by \$1.

The businessman's decisions concern not only what to do about output and the price of his product, but the best method of increasing production, if he decides to increase it. The best method will depend in part on his knowledge of his alternatives in the labor market, and we can apply the analysis of the preceding paragraphs to the businessman's procedure in deciding among his labor market alternatives, given a change in his circumstances. Just as in the case of the increase in demand for output where the businessman may decide after considering the information he obtains that it is best simply to let orders accumulate, because he may feel the demand increase will be short-lived, he may also feel that if he does decide to increase output, it is best to fill the resultant job vacancies either slowly or rapidly, given his information about the labor market and the profitability of letting job vacancies go unfilled rather than advertising for more workers, raising wage rates, or lowering hiring standards. *Thus, resources spent to acquire information are factors of production, just as labor and machinery, and when used in the optimal combination with the other productive inputs, they contribute to the minimization of production cost and the maximization of profits.*

We see from the preceding analysis, then, that the decision to establish a price at which he is willing to sell output or a wage rate at which he is willing to hire labor of given quality is but one of several decisions a businessman makes in the face of changing market conditions. The act of changing a price or a wage rate is the result of a decision based on information about the product market, the factor markets, and the production process, *and it is itself an action which is a substitute for investing more resources in gathering information or taking no action at all*. That is, the very act of price and wage setting should be viewed as one part of the production process—the aim of which on the part of the firms engaged is to maximize their profits.

So far we have spoken only of the price and wage decisions made by businessmen or firms. But we may analyze similarly the decisions of households. Thus, household members must decide at which wage rates they are willing to accept alternative jobs, and whether active job search (implying being unemployed if search cannot be carried on while workers are employed) is worthwhile as an alternative to accepting available jobs or leaving the labor force. They must make decisions as consumers about the purchases they are willing to make at various prices. We may analyze these decisions of households as part of the process of utility maximization, just as we analyzed the price, wage, employment, and output decisions of firms as part of the profit-maximization process.

Thus, on the basis of this brief analysis of the role of information in the allocation of resources and in consideration of statements (3) and (4) of the quotation on p. 237, we conclude that in a changing environment, in which profit-maximizing firms deal with family members who are allowed to choose freely the form of employment (or nonemployment) and consumption they most desire, we should expect to observe simultaneously, at all times, prices and wage rates which change but not in such a way as always to eliminate excess demands and supplies of goods in product markets and unemployment and job vacancies in labor markets. Even if it were humanly possible for employers and workers to adjust their decisions in such a way as to eliminate all apparent excess supplies and demands, it is almost certain that it would be economically inefficient to do so. Furthermore, in searching for their profit- and utility-maximizing prices, output, wage rates, employment, and consumption, firms and household members will not respond instantaneously to price and wage rate differentials; therefore, firms and household members will in general appear to face less than infinitely elastic demand and supply curves in the short run. That is to say, elements of monopoly and monopsony will appear to be pervasive in the short run.

It should be fairly clear by now that the application of the idea of positive search and adjustment costs to the analysis of price and wage rate determination proceeds along lines that are quite similar to the discussion in Chapters 2, 4, and 6 of the distinction between the short-run and long-run demand for and supply of labor. Indeed, once we recognize that the acquisition of information and the making of adjustments are *investments* whose (uncertain) payoffs are worthwhile only if the conditions about which information is acquired and to which adjustments are made are expected to persist, we see once again that we distinguish between the long run and the short run by the criterion of the variability of all inputs in the production process. In the presence of continuous change in the environment, it does not pay sufficiently in the short run for firms or workers to acquire enough information so that they behave like picture-book representatives of the typical firms and workers of the theory of "perfect" competition; on the other hand, over *long* periods of time, workers move about and acquire information in the natural course of work and leisure, and business firms have to replace plant and equipment that wears out, so that adjustment to a changing environment is less costly relative to the benefits obtained.

Thus, for purposes of analyzing short-run wage setting procedures, firms may be thought to have a degree of monopsony power in the sense that they can pay more than the wage rate that would prevail under long-run competitive equilibrium conditions and still not obtain all the workers they would like (at the wage rate they are paying), and pay less without losing all of their workers. Similarly, workers have a degree of monopoly power, in that they can affect the time it takes to find suitable employment by raising or lowering the minimum (reservation) wage they are willing to accept for a given kind of job. It follows that as long as environmental conditions are changing (which is all the time), it is consistent with competitive economic theory to observe the simultaneous existence of unemployed workers and unfilled job vacancies; furthermore, it is consistent to observe firms and workers who act as if they believe they face downward-sloping demand curves and upward-sloping supply curves for their output and services. Nevertheless, over such long periods of time, information can be gathered at relatively low cost per unit, and its present value is likely to be higher when based on considerable experience; thus workers and firms can be expected to behave more in accord with the implications of the theory of "perfect" competition where the economics of information and adjustment are ignored.

Application of the Role of Information and Adjustment Costs to the Theory of the Wage Level and Employment.   We proceed now to apply our discussion of the role of information and adjustment costs in the short run to analyze how firms set wage offers to potential employees and wage rates paid to existing employees; we also discuss the forces that determine the reservation wage rates of workers seeking jobs and apply our analysis to the problem of the general level of money wages and employment.

Firms' decisions about how much labor to hire and which wage rates to pay are assumed to depend on the expected gains and costs of filling the job vacancies that exist at a moment of time or are expected to exist in the future. Firms may select among alternative courses of action to reduce vacancies or prevent them from occurring in the future. Raising wage rates is only one possible way to attract workers; alternatively, firms may wait until by chance and with the passing of time, sufficient job applicants appear to satisfy the firm's needs. The costs of this procedure include the cost of possible lost sales revenues if vacancies become too large and output cannot be maintained. A third method of reducing vacancies is to engage actively in search and advertising for new workers. The cost of this method includes extra wages to personnel and agencies engaged in the search process, in addition to whatever costs are involved when vacancies are not reduced immediately. A fourth method is to improve the nonwage aspects of the firm's offer to employees. This might involve allowing workers to put in more or less overtime hours as they desire, increasing fringe benefits such as pension and health plans, improving the physical surroundings on the job, and/or improving personnel policies such as grievance procedures, providing better supervisory personnel, and the like. The costs of increasing nonwage benefits include the direct expenditures required, as well as the costs of possibly delayed reduction of vacancies.

Of course, any combination of the four methods can be adopted, and we presume firms do adopt and adjust them simultaneously as conditions change. However, we concentrate here on the decision to adjust wage rates and/or lower hiring standards at given wage rates, both of which affect the average level of money wages in the economy.

Workers, on their side, face alternative methods of obtaining work or finding better work. One is to lower their reservation wage rates or broaden the range of jobs they will accept at given wage rates. A second method is to engage in more intensive search. Another is to improve their skills. All of these methods are costly, and again we concentrate on the reservation wage rate adjustment. We assume that workers, in deciding which jobs are acceptable at particular reservation wage rates, consider their own tastes and attitudes toward work, leisure, and alternative jobs; wage rates received by acquaintances; the general level of difficulty in finding jobs; and the length of time they have been looking or waiting for acceptable jobs. In general, we expect that the longer workers have been waiting and searching for acceptable jobs, the further reservation wage rates will have declined, until the point is reached where it seems no longer worthwhile to seek such work or even to learn much about alternative jobs. As long as workers are allowed to change jobs at will and as long as information is a scarce resource, costly to obtain, we expect to observe unemployed workers searching for jobs at the same time that firms are searching for workers and job vacancies exist. The proportion of workers thus unemployed should tend to approach some equilibrium level, given real wages, real information costs, and the normal rate of depreciation of information once obtained. (The rate of depreciation of information is determined mainly by the rate of change of the parts of the environment to which the information applies; that is, information depreciates if and only if the environment is changing.)

The theory of wage adjustment applied to wage levels incorporates the above ideas as follows. Consider an economy experiencing equilibrium or normal unemployment and an event, such as an increase in government spending, which tends to raise the level of aggregate demand for goods and services. Firms will notice their sales rising and depending on their decisions to adjust, their vacancy rates will tend to increase. In attempting to restore vacancies to their desired levels firms will, among other actions, attempt to raise their wage rates *relative* to those paid by competing firms. Of course, it is literally impossible for *all* firms to raise their wage rates relative to each other, and the general level of wage rates will rise. (Similarly, we expect also that product prices will tend to rise as firms become aware of rising unfilled orders, declining inventories, and rising costs.) *If* there is a lag between increases in wage rates and product prices, *or if* workers do not immediately adjust their reservation wage rates to changes in the consumer price index (money illusion), *then*, as wage rates go up workers in the pool of unemployed and those out of the labor force find more jobs with offered wage rates equal to or greater than reservation wage rates. Thus, vacancies tend to fall from their unusually high level, unemployment tends to fall, and labor force participation tends to rise. A slightly different way of describing this process, consistent with our analysis of the role of information costs, is to note that one of the effects of the hypothetical unforseen change in government spending is to cause firms' and consumers' stocks of information to depreciate more rapidly. It would be too costly or even impossible for workers and firms to obtain all the information that would be necessary to eliminate behavior which has the appearance of money illusion; thus, for a short period of time, changes in the general wage level, relative to the cost of production and to the consumer price index, will have little influence on workers' and firms' decisions. Firms and workers will act as if the nominal wage rates, rather than wage rates relative to product prices or relative to those paid by competing firms, were relevant to profit and utility maximization.

Now, it is implausible that workers and firms do not eventually respond to changes in prices and costs, and therefore the price of output will after a time reflect changes in labor costs, and reservation wage rates will reflect changes in the consumer price index and in the reduced length of time it takes to find suitable jobs. Employed workers can also be expected to respond by being increasingly ready to quit their current jobs when dissatisfied, risking unemployment, as the apparent probability of finding better work rises. Thus, as unemployment rates tend to decline, quit rates may be expected to increase, dampening the decline in unemployment rates. Thus, job opportunities which attracted workers while unemployment was still relatively high and before prices had increased, or while decisions were influenced by money illusion, will cease to be as attractive, and the unemployment and labor force participation rates will tend to return to their old levels, unless firms continue to increase their wage offers. Firms presumably will do so if aggregate demand and vacancies remain high (demand will tend to remain high if the government offsets the increase in the price level with an increase in the quantity of money and expenditures) since they will be unsuccessful in maintaining their desired labor forces if they do not increase their wage offers, and this will induce, instead of a once-and-for-all increase in the price level, a continuing inflation. However, just as we assumed that money illusion would eventually disappear with respect to a once-and-for-all general increase in wages and prices, so we may assume (with considerable empirical support) that workers and firms will eventually come to anticipate the rate of inflation and adjust their reservation wages and wage offers accordingly. Thus, unemployment and labor force participation will eventually return to their equilibrium levels in the presence of a constant inflation, rather than a stable price level, if the government continues increasing expenditures and the money supply *pari passu*. It is only during the period in which product prices have not fully adjusted to changes in costs and/or money illusion persists that inflationary pressures on the economy lower unemployment and increase labor force participation. Eventually, according to our theory, labor force participation, employment, unemployment, and output are functions of real wage rates and prices in terms of costs, and even a constant rate of inflation is incorporated into decisions determining reservation wage rates, wage offers, employment, and output decisions. The values of reservation wage rates, wage offers, employment, unemployment, and output so determined are equilibrium values. An implication of the theory is that if the government wishes to reduce the rate of unemployment permanently below its equilibrium level by means of inflation, it may be able to do so in the long run, but only if it promotes a *continuously increasing rate of inflation*. It remains to be seen, of course, just what level of unemployment is the equilibrium level, and how much persistent deviation below it will actually induce such an accelerating inflation.

Our application of the role of information and adjustment costs to the theory of the wage level and employment has led us to infer that in the short run changes in the level of money wage rates and unemployment will be negatively correlated, but in the long run the level of unemployment and employment will be determined by real wage rates and other relative prices, not by the rate of inflation. The cornerstones of this theory are the postulates of positive costs of information and adjustment in the short run, but acquisition of sufficient information to anticipate the future course of wage rates and prices in the long run. There are good reasons to suppose that an inflation or deflation will eventually become anticipated, because it is in peoples' interest to acquire the information necessary for such anticipation. It pays workers and firms to attempt to anticipate inflation or deflation, because it is costly to bear the effects of unanticipated price level changes. Workers who have negotiated formally or informally will receive lower real wage rates than they planned on if they have not anticipated a rise in the price level that takes place during the course of the wage agreements; employers will experience higher than anticipated vacancies if wage rates in their firms fall relative to those in other firms during a formal or informal contract period. Furthermore, given a change in the course of wages and prices that tends to persist, the cost of information about the future course of these variables tends to decline. Thus, it is likely that once inflation or deflation occurs over a period of time, the anticipated rate of price change will be added to wage offers and reservation wage rates, and there will be little or no effect on the rates of employment, unemployment, or output.

There is as yet rather little if any empirical evidence pertaining to the relationship between anticipations and wage offers or reservation wage rates; however, studies of inflation and the demand for money suggest strongly that the quantity of money demanded depends on anticipated changes in the price level.[4] It seems plausible that anticipations are as important in the labor market as in the money market.

Thus, to go back to the controversy discussed in Section II, regarding whether it is likely that autonomous changes in wage rates and prices bring about responsive changes in the quantity of money, we must conclude that such a possibility is probably consistent with the theory of wage, price, and employment adjustment we have discussed, and such responsiveness does not necessarily depend on the economy's being essentially noncompetitive.

---

[4] One of the best-known studies is that of Philip Cagan, "The Monetary Dynamics of Hyperinflation," in Milton Friedman, ed., *Studies in the Quantity Theory of Money* (Chicago: University of Chicago Press, 1956), pp. 25–117.

It is not within the scope of this book, however, to attempt to judge the quantitative importance of such a possible endogenous characteristic of the money supply to an explanation of the levels of wage rates and prices.

EVIDENCE BEARING ON THE THEORY OF WAGE ADJUSTMENT

One of the principal implications of the theory of wage, price, and employment adjustment presented in Section III is that we tend to observe a negative correlation between changes in the general level of money wage rates and/or prices and the general unemployment rate over short periods of time. This implication is consistent with observed relationships, particularly in England and the United States, between the rate of change of wage rates (and/or prices) and unemployment rates. Such relationships are known as Phillips curves.[5] However, the theory is a complicated one to express in terms that can conveniently be subjected to empirical test, because the correlation between unemployment and changes in the wage level is also consistent with a theory that makes use of the importance of monopoly elements as crucial to price and wage-setting behavior. It would not be correct to say that as yet anyone has confirmed the wage adjustment theory empirically.

The theory suggests that there is a stable short-run relationship between the general level of wage rates, vacancy rates, and unemployment rates, such that wage level changes are positively correlated with the level of vacancy rates and negatively with unemployment rates. Furthermore, when vacancies are high and the wage level rising, the theory implies that unemployment will be *falling*; so the theory has implication for relationships between the rates of change of wages, vacancies, and changes in unemployment as well.

In the United States, vacancy rates are virtually unobtainable. Nevertheless, increases in aggregate demand which cause vacancies to fall below their usual level should induce reductions in unemployment rates, and vice versa. Therefore, it probably sheds some light on the theory of wage adjustment to observe the relationship between wage rate changes, unemployment, and the change in unemployment, and, perhaps, prior changes in wage rates and prices (to reflect the effect of anticipated wage changes on wage decisions). Various studies have established that such a relationship exists. One such study is by Albert Rees and Mary Hamilton[6] for data covering the period 1900–57.

---

[5] The impetus to current interest in the relationship between inflation and unemployment as discussed in this section was given by an article of A. W. Phillips, "The Relation between Unemployment and the Rate of Change of Money Wage Rates in the United Kingdom, 1861–1957," *Economica* N.S., November, 1958, pp. 283–99.

[6] "The Wage-Price-Productivity Perplex," *The Journal of Political Economy*, February, 1967, pp. 63–70.

Without elaborating in detail the statistical methods used, we may discuss briefly the quantitative nature of the results and their consistency with the wage adjustment theory. A regression equation typical of those estimated by Rees and Hamilton is shown at the top of Table 14-1. Columns (2), (3), and (4) contain postulated values of the unemployment rate, the change in the unemployment rate from the previous year, and the lagged change in the consumer price index. On the basis of these values and using the equation shown at the top of the table, the figures in column (1) representing the annual

Table 14-1

A TYPICAL RELATIONSHIP BETWEEN WAGE LEVEL
CHANGES, UNEMPLOYMENT, AND THE PRICE LEVEL
(BASED ON ANNUAL DATA, 1900–1957)

$$\frac{W_t - W_{t-1}}{W_{t-1}} = .039 - .09U_t - 1.32(U_t - U_{t-1}) + .67\frac{P_{t-1} - P_{t-2}}{P_{t-1}}$$

(1) $\dfrac{W_t - W_{t-1}}{W_{t-1}}$	(2) U_t	(3) $U_t - U_{t-1}$	(4) $\dfrac{P_{t-1} - P_{t-2}}{P_{t-2}}$
.035	.04	.0	.0
.022	.04	+.01	.0
.048	.04	−.01	.0
−.005	.04	+.03	.0
+.075	.04	−.03	.0
.037	.02	.0	.0
.024	.02	+.01	.0
.050	.02	−.01	.0
−.003	.02	+.03	.0
+.077	.02	−.03	.0
.049	.04	.0	+.02
.036	.04	+.01	+.02
.062	.04	−.01	+.02
.011	.04	+.03	+.02
.089	.04	−.03	+.02
.025	.155	.0	.0

The subscripts refer to time periods (years); $W =$ the average money wage rate, U the unemployment rate and P the consumer price index. Thus $W_t =$ the wage rate in year t, while $W_{t-1} =$ the wage rate during the preceding year, and so on.

NOTE: The equation above has been slightly modified in form to facilitate presentation. Therefore the t-ratios are not shown. However, the original coefficients appeared highly significant.

Source: Albert Rees and Mary Hamilton, "The Wage-Price-Productivity Perplex," *The Journal of Political Economy*, February, 1967, p. 65, row 7.

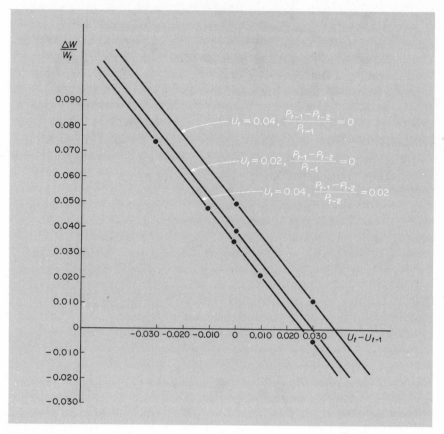

FIG. 14-2

*An Estimated Relationship Between the
Rate of Change of Money and
Wage Rates Unemployment*

Source: Same as Table 14-1

rate of change of the average level of money wage rates are calculated. The results suggest that a 1 percentage point change in the rate of decrease of unemployment has a much greater effect on the rate of wage increase than does a decline of 1 per cent that takes place between one year and the next that is followed by no subsequent changes. Note, for instance, that the results shown in Table 14-1 imply that if the unemployment rate is 4 per cent, having *risen* from 3 per cent (by 1 percentage point), the rate of wage change will be 2.2 per cent when past price level changes are zero; however, if the unemployment rate has *fallen* by 1 percentage point (from 5 per cent), the implied rate of wage change is more than twice as high—4.8 per cent. If, on the other hand, the *level* of unemployment is halved from a permanent level

of 4 per cent to a permanent level of 2 per cent, the implied change in the
rates of change of wages is very small (i.e., from .035 to .037); thus the effect
of *changes* in the unemployment rate dominates the effects of the *level* of
unemployment. This is inconsistent with the theory because the wage
adjustment theory implies that the wage-setting behavior of firms depends
on vacancy rates, which are influenced by the demand for labor and the supply
available. Whether unemployment is rising or falling at particular unemployment levels depends on whether vacancies are low or high, and thus the rate
of change of wage rates should be more strongly associated with the rate of
change of unemployment than with the unemployment level.

At first it might seem that there is nothing in the results obtained by
Rees and Hamilton consistent with the notion that if the unemployment level
is permanently maintained below its equilibrium level, a runaway inflation will
result. For instance, the regression coefficient of the unemployment rate is
only .09, which does not imply high inflation at low unemployment rates.
However, the equation is a simple one, and it does not explicitly include a
feedback from unemployment changes and levels, through wages to prices, to
the determination of unemployment and vacancy rates. Note, however, that
the lagged rate of price change is an important correlate of wage rate changes.
Therefore, the Rees-Hamilton results cannot be construed as inconsistent
with the wage adjustment hypothesis as regards the notion of equilibrium
unemployment. The results do illustrate the kind of short-run relationship
the hypothesis suggests between wage rate changes, vacancy rates, and unemployment rates.

IMPLICATIONS OF THE THEORY

Perhaps the most important implication of the adjustment theory of the
wage level is a negative one: namely, economists who have observed statistical
relationships between the level of unemployment and the rate of wage and
price change have often concluded that such relationships imply a long-run
"trade-off" between inflation and unemployment. This implication means that
those whose responsibility it is to control the levels of inflation and unemployment have a choice to make between unemployment rates and inflation
rates and that at some rate of unemployment, inflation would be continuously zero, and at some rate of continuous (and constant?) inflation,
unemployment would be acceptably low. One of the reasons that much
attention has been paid to such estimates of the alleged tradeoff is that the
estimates often imply that a rate of unemployment permanently near 4
per cent is attainable only in the presence of continuous inflation, and zero
inflation is consistent only with an unacceptably high long-run unemployment
rate. For instance, if the Rees-Hamilton study were taken to provide estimates
of such a tradeoff (which the authors did not intend it to provide), the implication is that a permanently maintained unemployment rate of over 15 per cent

would be necessary to keep the rate of change of wage rates in line with historical increases in productivity, thus providing the basis for an unchanging price level. On the other hand, the Rees-Hamilton study implies that a permanently maintained rate of unemployment of 4 per cent implies an annual increase of money wage rates of 3.5 per cent if there is zero price inflation (assuming that we can ignore the accelerating effect that such wage increases could have on further wage increases via the price level).

It would be an important question, if such a tradeoff existed, whether we should attempt to maintain an unemployment rate of, say, 3 or 4 per cent, and thus "choose" a corresponding positive rate of inflation, or whether we should strive to reduce inflation to zero. However, the wage-adjustment theory implies that such a question is inappropriate, because there is no tradeoff between any *permanently maintained* unemployment rate and a constant rate of inflation. Rather, *permanent* deviation from equilibrium unemployment (i.e., that unemployment which results from the rate of change of the economic environment, search costs, adjustment costs, and utility and profit maximization) could be maintained only in the presence of an accelerating inflation or deflation. Therefore, the wage-adjustment theory implies that one should be skeptical of any such tradeoff one may be tempted to infer from observed correlations between unemployment rates and changes in wage and price levels.

An important point to note in closing is that much of the discussion of the so-called wage-price guidelines is explicitly or implicitly based on an assumed permanent relationship between inflation and unemployment which such guidelines are allegedly able to "improve" if they can be enforced. If the wage-adjustment theory presented in this chapter is correct, however, the need for such guidelines appears to be very doubtful, especially if monetary and fiscal policies can be used to promote economic stability rather than to accentuate the fluctation in activity inherent in our economy.

15

unemployment

INTRODUCTION

Unemployment, like wage rates, is one of the most important determinants of economic welfare. In Chapter 14, we analyzed the way in which information and adjustment costs interact with changes in the economic environment to determine the general level of wages, prices, employment, and unemployment. The analysis implied, among other things, that we should expect to observe unemployed household members at all times and that there is an "equilibrium" unemployment rate determined by the rate of economic change, information and adjustment costs, and the aims of firms and household members to maximize their profits and utilities. In this chapter we explore in greater detail the behavior of unemployment in the United States and its uneven incidence among individuals.

It is implied by the analysis of Chapter 14 that the markets of all commodities and productive factors will frequently exhibit discrepancies between amounts demanded and supplied; however, it is not obvious that discrepancies between amounts demanded and supplied in labor markets are paid more attention than those in other markets because labor markets themselves perform less efficiently than others. Rather, it is probably true that the *social consequences* of a given degree of excess supply in labor markets are thought to be less desirable than elsewhere.

"unemployment" other than in labor markets

Consider briefly how well labor markets function compared with other markets. In the housing market, for instance, the length of time between the date a house becomes available for sale and the date it is actually sold is highly variable and can be quite long. Houses are highly immobile; their characteristics are expensive to alter; the transaction costs involved are high; sellers and buyers are often uncertain just what price the next buyer will offer or the next seller ask. All these factors contribute to a low probability of matching a buyer to a seller in a given short period of time—a probability which nevertheless rises as the price of a given house declines (as long as the house is offered for sale). If an economic decline affects a city, causing fewer people to want to live there, houses will probably decline sharply in value, and many people who want to move away may have to assume very large losses on houses they wish to sell; indeed there may be no positive price at which some houses can be sold. Just think of the ghost mining towns of the American West. The miners moved away long ago, but the derelict houses still remain!

Housing data suggest that any moment of time a significant number of housing units are in a sense "unemployed." At the time of the *U.S. Census of Housing* in 1960, 6.7 per cent of available rental units were vacant, and 1.6 per cent of units occupied by owners or available for sale were vacant. Vacancies accounted for 6.1 per cent of total housing units; this group was broken down as follows: 0.4 per cent were rented or sold, awaiting occupancy, 1.5 per cent were being held off the market, 0.9 per cent were for sale only, 2.5 per cent were for rent, and 0.9 per cent were dilapidated (long-term unemployment?).[1] Table 15-1 shows some interesting data for Columbus, Ohio, for the years 1959–66. Column (1) shows the number of buildings which came through the multiple listing service in each year, and column (2) shows the number of such transactions consummated during each year; the difference, shown in column (3), is the number of attempted building sales not completed during each year. There were about 200,000 dwelling units in the Columbus area in 1960, which is an overstatement of the number of buildings containing dwelling units but does not include buildings used solely for business purposes. The amounts in Column (3) equal about 5 per cent of this figure. It is significant that in every year the failures outnumber the successes by a substantial margin. Of course, not all unsuccessful attempts to sell result in "unemployed" housing, as households may well continue to occupy

---

[1] Housing data are from the *U.S. Census of Housing, 1960* and the *Current Housing Reports*, as reported in the *Statistical Abstract of the United States, 1965*, pp. 757 and 758.

Table 15-1

BUILDINGS AND HOUSES LISTED AND
SOLD: COLUMBUS, OHIO

Year	(1) No. of Multiple Listings	(2) No. of Closings	(3) (1) − (2)
1959	5650	1801	3849
1960	5682	1517	4165
1961	6056	1916	4140
1962	6378	2288	4090
1963	7041	2670	4371
1964	7683	2964	4719
1965	8155	3454	4701
1966	8577	3551	5026

Data courtesy of Columbus Board of Relators.

houses that are not sold, and firms may continue to rent space in buildings whose owners would like to liquidate their assets. Yet it is obvious that matching of buyers and sellers is not an easy task, and it is probably a costly one.

Similarly, inventories of manufactured goods show significant fluctuations with respect to the shipments of goods. Much of such fluctuation is undoubtedly unintended and probably represents the accumulation of unsold goods when sales do not rise as rapidly as expected and decumulation when sales rise faster than anticipated. Table 15-2 shows how year-end inventories of finished durable manufactured goods as a proportion of yearly shipments have behaved since 1954. These fluctuations probably underestimate the differences between actual and desired sales, as part of the discrepancies are no doubt reflected in production changes. Even so, the difference between the lowest and highest ratio of inventories to shipments is .011, which is about 25 per cent of the average figure. (Year-end unfilled orders in proportion to shipments varied from about .21 to .33, or about 45 per cent of the average figure.) Unemployment during the same period varied by about .03, a considerably higher proportionate variation than that of the inventory-shipment ratio.

Unemployment in Labor Markets

Why does unemployment affect economic welfare more than excess supplies in other markets? The answer is tied to the fact that each person owns his own labor power, and we place a high value on the economic welfare of individuals. Since the greater part of economic welfare is derived from the sale of labor power, unemployment can be and is a source of social concern.

Table 15-2

DURABLE GOODS MANUFACTURING AND U.S. UNEMPLOYMENT RATE

	(1)[a]	(2)[b]	(3)	(4)	(5)	(6)[c]
Year	Shipments	Finished Goods Inventories	Unfilled Orders	(2) ÷ (1)	(3) ÷ (1)	U.S. Unemployment Rate
1954	141.9	6.0	45.2	.042	.32	.050
1955	168.9	6.3	56.4	.037	.33	.040
1956						.038
1957						.043
1958	162.9	7.6	45.7	.047	.28	.068
1959						.055
1960	189.8	9.0	43.2	.047	.23	.056
1961	186.4	8.9	44.8	.048	.24	.067
1962	206.2	9.4	43.7	.047	.21	.056
1963	216.8	10.1	46.2	.047	.21	.057
1964	230.8	10.6	53.0	.046	.23	.052
1965	252.2	11.0	61.5	.044	.24	.046
1966	276.1	12.7	75.3	.046	.27	.039

[a] Billions of dollars per year.
[b] Billions of dollars on December 31.
[c] Persons 14 years and older, annual average.

Source: Statistical Abstract of the United States, 1967, p. 753.

A large proportion of the individuals and families who are considered to be living in conditions of poverty in the United States experience a great deal of unemployment which contributes substantially to their low incomes. Note that it just so happens that unemployment is a phenomenon which disproportionately affects the poor. This need not be so: one could conceive of unemployment being a phenomenon of the rich. Why unemployment and poverty happen to be related is a question we shall deal with later on.

If we did not value highly individual economic welfare, then unemployment in labor markets would probably not be of any greater social concern than would many other kinds of excess supply. Moreover, the individualism we value highly in the labor force may contribute somewhat to the degree of unemployment actually experienced as well as to its undesirable effect on social welfare. For comparison, consider a slave society. In such a society, slave owners would derive their revenues from the employment, rental, and sale of slaves, much as manufacturers of equipment derive their revenues. Excess labor supply would occur less frequently than it does under free labor conditions, because slave owners would be able to take advantage of scale economies in labor market information, in avoiding the uncertainties of training and retraining workers, and so on. Furthermore, slave owners probably would not consider the psychological disadvantages of regional relocation of workers to the same extent as do individual workers in a free labor market. Thus, the unemployment rate of slaves would probably be lower than that of free workers. Furthermore, while an individual worker, if unemployed, suffers a substantial decline in his income, a slave owner would have far greater resources, and the unemployment of part of his workers at any moment of time would inflict no greater economic harm to him than would the unemployment of part of his plant and equipment to the owner of a manufacturing company. (It would in general be in an employer's interests, even if it were not prescribed by law, to maintain his slaves, even when they were "unemployed.") While the bad effects of unemployment on economic welfare would not be absent in a slave society, they would be more comparable in magnitude with the effects of excess supply in other markets than they are in a society characterized by free labor.

Conceptually, measured unemployment could equal zero. As a matter of fact, measured unemployment is always positive, although we should surely find, if adequate statistics were available, that the number of people looking for work sometimes falls short of the number of job vacancies; thus, the excess supply of labor as measured by the number of unemployed less the number of unfilled vacancies would sometimes be negative. However, the deviation from equality between the number of people unemployed and the number of job vacancies is hardly a good measure of the social consequences of unemployment, since if workers cannot find employment, the effect on their welfare is virtually the same, whether jobs actually exist somewhere or not; it would be of little consolation to men and women who cannot find work to know that vacancies minus unemployment is positive. As far as the unemployed are concerned, they are out of jobs, and the fact that there are unfilled vacancies doesn't by itself put any money in their pockets. We do not mean to imply that no one is ever "voluntarily" unemployed. Sometimes a worker who wants to change jobs can do so most efficiently if he quits his old job first. Nevertheless, the unemployed bear important costs of economic change and labor market mobility, and we wish to explore the nature and causes of unemployment in some detail.

THE VARIETIES OF UNEMPLOYMENT AND THEIR CAUSES

We have seen that unemployment is an excess supply of workers in labor markets and that its causes are probably to be found among the causes of excess supplies in general. It is convenient to categorize types of unemployment in accordance with its various causes. This should aid in understanding the determinants of unemployment and the appropriate policies which may be taken to "cure" unemployment when desired and to reduce its bad effects on social welfare. For at least one reason already discussed, namely the positive costs of acquiring information and adjusting the allocation of resources, the amounts demanded and supplied in labor markets do not in general match each other in the presence of changing market conditions which tend to make them unequal. Sometimes, such a tendency toward excess demand or supply is labeled a "market imperfection," but this is a term that is used very loosely—often too loosely. The relevant consideration is, Is there any *economical and socially desirable* means by which the market process can be speeded up or improved upon? If there is, then it makes some sense to speak of market imperfections; if there is not, it makes little sense, since no desirable alternative to market force presents itself. Under circumstances when no alternative to the market for reducing unemployment seems worthwhile, the best thing to do may be to supplement the incomes of those who are unemployed, if their incomes are thought to be undesirably low from a social point of view.

"frictional" unemployment

Frictional unemployment is so called because it is that part of excess labor supply presumably attributable to market "frictions" and not to the more or less severe declines in particular industries as a result of economic change or declines (in the rate of growth) of aggregate demand that cause periodic economic recessions and depressions. *Frictional unemployment* is not an altogether fortunate term, for all unemployment can in some sense be thought of as a result of "frictions," or "stickiness," or what we have chosen to call information and adjustment costs, in one form or another. As the term is commonly used, however, frictional unemployment refers to unemployment in its most benign form—a form which it no doubt would be impossible to eliminate entirely while preserving the freedom of workers to leave jobs when they please and to seek work when and where they most desire it. It is probably not the equivalent of what we conceive to be equilibrium unemployment, because even if there were no business cycles, the continually changing structure of the economy would generate unemployed workers who find it very difficult to locate new satisfactory jobs, and furthermore it is impossible to conceive of eliminating completely fluctuations in aggregate demand, in the normal course of events.

The Nature of Frictional Unemployment. Frictional unemployment comes about because it takes time and resources for workers to change jobs, either voluntarily or involuntarily, even though suitable job vacancies exist and can be found without workers' having to adjust their accustomed types of work or their reservation wage rates. Workers who want to change jobs (or who are dismissed) often find new jobs fairly easily. Nevertheless, two, three, or more weeks may elapse between leaving one job and starting a new one, and during this time workers may be counted as unemployed, depending on just how they answer the questions put to them in labor force surveys. Even during the Second World War, the unemployment rate never fell below 1 per cent of the labor force, even though finding a job then was a relatively simple task. Indeed, during such periods of strong labor demand, frictional unemployment resulting from *voluntary* separations (and entry into the labor force) may well be higher than during normal periods, because workers who want to change jobs need not fear quitting their old jobs without having first obtained new positions. The unemployment of such workers constitutes part of the price paid for job changing; during periods of high labor demand, the unemployment component of the price of job changing is lower (i.e., shorter) than at other times, and workers might therefore "spend" more on job changing in the aggregate than when the price is high—that is, the price elasticity of demand for job changing may be greater than unity, where the price is measured in terms of time spent unemployed before a new job is found. Moreover, during periods of high labor demand, it may be difficult for some workers to take all the time off they desire, and periods spent apparently unemployed between jobs may be in part a substitute for vacations. Evidence that when jobs are relatively easy to find (as measured by the overall rate of unemployment), workers are more prone to quit their jobs is found in Table 15-3 and Figure 15-1 where the number of quits per 100 employees in manufacturing is compared with the rate of unemployment in the economy. The relationship is clearly negative.

We have defined frictional unemployment to be that which involves sufficiently little expenditure of resources (in terms of foregone earnings while unemployed and direct expenditures on travel, etc.) that functionally unemployed workers are not forced to adjust their customary types of work or lower their reservation wage rates in order to find jobs. It is likely that if frictional unemployment is to be reduced, it is by reducing the costs involved in finding a new job, once it becomes desirable or necessary to leave an old job (or to find a first job for new labor force participants). That is, the unemployment cost of changing jobs can be reduced by substituting for it other costs—costs of search before job leaving, advertising by both workers and employers, and so on. In fact, workers and employers both find it worthwhile, to a greater or less extent, to devote time and money to the goal of reducing the length of time between needing a job and finding one, or needing an employee and finding one. Workers differ in the extent to which they can take advantage of nonunemployment costs of job search.

An employed worker who wants to change jobs may be able to do so without experiencing any unemployment if his occupation is one in which potential employers are readily identifiable and if he has easy access to

Table 15-3

UNEMPLOYMENT RATES: 1947–1967

Year	(1)	(2)	(3) (1) × (2)	(4)
1947	.039	.745	.029	4.1
1948	.038	.792	.030	3.4
1949	.059	.721	.043	1.9
1950	.053	.671	.036	2.3
1951	.033	.778	.026	2.9
1952	.030	.809	.024	2.8
1953	.029	.817	.024	2.8
1954	.055	.684	.038	1.4
1955	.044	.678	.030	1.9
1956	.041	.729	.030	1.9
1957	.043	.720	.031	1.6
1958	.068	.590	.040	1.1
1959	.055	.632	.035	1.5
1960	.055	.660	.036	1.3
1961	.067	.588	.039	1.2
1962	.055	.631	.032	1.4
1963	.057	.646	.037	1.4
1964	.052	.659	.034	1.5
1965	.045	.694	.031	1.9
1966	.038	.742	.028	2.6
1967	.038	.775	.029	2.3

(1) Fraction of the labor force aged 16 and over unemployed (annual averages).
(2) Fraction of the unemployed who were unemployed
10 weeks or less at time of survey (annual averages).
(4) Number of quits per 100 employees manufacturing
(1967 figure is a preliminary estimate).

Source: Manpower Report of the President, 1967, pp. 201,
219, 256; 1968, pp. 221, 240, 278.

information about their employment needs. One seldom hears these days of
college professors who may be described as frictionally unemployed, for
instance, because of the easy identifiability of employers of college professors
and because of the ease of ascertaining when and where job openings exist.
At the other extreme, a boy trying to earn some money by cutting lawns
may spend a considerable amount of time going from door to door seeking
employment, and it is unlikely that extensive use of alternative means, such
as newspaper ads, search by telephone, or the use of an employment agency
would be economical (i.e., reduce the cost of finding jobs). Since the boy is
not a salaried employee, he is unemployed when he cannot find lawns to cut.

There are many workers who, because they are salaried, are not

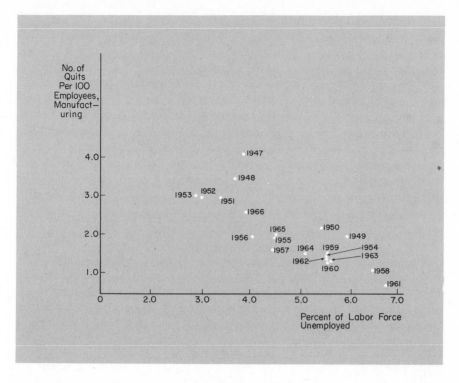

Source: Manpower Report of the President, 1967, pp. 201, 219, 256;
1968, pp. 221, 240, 278

FIG. 15-1

*Relationship Between Quits and Unem-
ployment Rate in the U.S., 1947–1966*

considered unemployed when they are not producing anything for their employers, so long as they receive their monthly salary checks. Nevertheless,
frictional unemployment in an economic, if not official, sense can exist for
such persons, especially salesmen and other kinds of business representatives.
For instance, an advertisement in *Time* magazine (August 18, 1967) by the
American Telephone and Telegraph Company advises businessmen that "A
waiting agent gathers no green . . . , " and that use of the telephone will save
unnecessary agents' calls on customers. Under certain circumstances it may
pay employers to instruct their salesmen to use the telephone instead of
making personal calls, and in other cases it may not; similarly for the employee seeking information. If making personal calls is precluded by current
employment, experiencing a period of unemployment may be a prerequisite
for changing jobs.

All workers bear the risk of dismissal due to the vagaries of demand
for the output of particular firms and industries, technological change, and
so on, and it therefore pays to have accumulated a more or less extensive and
up-to-date body of information about employment alternatives even if

voluntary changes are not anticipated. Such a stock of knowledge can be viewed as part of a worker's investment in human capital. In part, the extent to which workers acquire such information will depend on their opportunities for doing so, the rate at which information once accumulated deteriorates over time, and the effect of acquiring information on lowering the probability of unemployment. Such knowledge is valuable to workers, because it reduces the expected costs of job changing. Since the knowledge is also costly, it will not necessarily pay to reduce to zero or near zero the expected probability of unemployment; rather, like other aspects of investment in human capital, investment in information about the job market pays only so long as marginal benefits are greater than marginal costs.

Similarly, employers have incentives to provide information which helps reduce frictional unemployment, because advertising job vacancies and other (costly) means of spreading information about available employment opportunities reduce the wage rate at which employers can hire a given number of workers of given quality in a specific time period.

How important is search effort on the part of workers as a means of reducing actual or potential unemployment? We have no data bearing directly on this question; however, there is evidence that search costs and returns play an important role in labor markets. Searching for alternative employment opportunities may pay off not only by reducing actual and potential unemployment, but by revealing sources of employment where wages are relatively high. If workers search for high-wage employers, and/or employers search for workers willing to work at low wages, we should expect to observe the variation of wages among regions to have declined over time as means of communication have improved. We should also expect to observe that the variation of wage rates is greater among older workers who, because of the limited length of expected working life, have a shorter period of time in which the benefits of search on the part of either workers or potential employers can pay off. In fact, George Stigler has found that between 1904–09 and 1947–54 the average coefficient of variation of average earnings in selected manufacturing industries among a set of identical states declined by about one-third; data of monthly earnings of engineers, by age, in 1929, show that the coefficients of variation increase with age. Stigler also found evidence of a higher coefficient of variation of wage rates among women (who typically are in the labor market a shorter time and, therefore, to whom the rate of return to a given expenditure on search is probably lower) than among men in the same occupation.[2] Stigler's findings do not provide conclusive proof of the importance of information in the labor market. His findings are consistent with its importance, however; they are consistent with a competitive hypothesis about search.

---

[2] George J. Stigler, "Information in the Labor Market," *Journal of Political Economy*, October, 1962 (Supplement), pp. 99–100.

The Behavior of Frictional Unemployment. How important is frictional unemployment in total unemployment? This is a hard question to answer, because we do not have information about the composition and amount of all resources spent by the unemployed in obtaining jobs; we cannot usually measure what happens to given workers after experiencing a given period of unemployment—that is, whether they find work, what kind they find, or whether they leave the labor force. However, we can exclude from any count of the frictionally unemployed those individuals who at any moment of time have experienced a very long period of unemployment. Therefore, a reasonable approximation of the behavior of frictional unemployment is likely to be the behavior of short-term unemployment, which we do measure continuously. Let us define frictional unemployment operationally to be that portion of total unemployment which consists of individuals who, at the time of observation, have been unemployed for ten weeks or less.[3]

Table 15-3 shows the behavior of total and short-term unemployment (ten weeks or less) from 1947 through 1967 for the noninstitutional population aged 16 and over. The table also shows the quit rate in manufacturing industries over the same period of time. The per cent of the labor force unemployed ten weeks or less ranged from a low of 2.4 to a high of 4.0 during the 1946–67 period, while the average total unemployment rate ranged from 2.9 per cent to 6.7 per cent. The differences between the maximum and minimum rates were 1.6 and 3.8 percentage points respectively.

Short-duration employment as a proportion of the labor force varies less, both absolutely (in percentage points) and relatively, than does total unemployment, and it varies positively with total unemployment. This seems to be plausible behavior for what we have defined frictional unemployment to be. The causes of frictional unemployment should be relatively stable over the business cycle, but it is reasonable that the unemployment associated with a given amount of effort spent gathering information about available jobs is higher during periods of relatively low labor demand. Thus, what could well be classified as frictional unemployment may rise with the general unemployment level. (This would not necessarily be the case, because we

---

[3] Albert Rees uses a ten-week cutoff as a "possible device for distinguishing frictional unemployment from other types." Albert Rees, "The Meaning and Measurement of Full Employment," *The Measurement and Behavior of Unemployment.* (Princeton, N.J.: Princeton University Press, 1957), p. 27. However, many government publications often make an important distinction between unemployment that is 15 or fewer weeks in duration and that which has greater duration. Rees notes, and it is clearly true, that the unemployment duration statistics available to us do not match perfectly our most desired operational definition of unemployment by type. This is because the available statistics provide information only on the length of time those who are currently unemployed have been in that status. We should like to know how long it has taken to find work, for workers who have just been unemployed and have started new jobs, and how long it will take the currently unemployed to find work.

have remarked above that the voluntary separations may increase enough when labor market conditions are tight to increase the contribution of voluntary job changing to the level of frictional unemployment. That this does occur is consistent with column 4 of Table 15-3. However, the unemployment data suggest that the contribution of involuntary job changers to the level of frictional unemployment more than offsets any anticyclic contribution of voluntary changes, in that the amounts of short-term and long-term unemployment appear positively correlated. See, however, footnote 3 before drawing a firm conclusion on this issue.)

An alternative measure of frictional unemployment is the lowest level of unemployment reached during periods of high labor demand. The lowest recorded unemployment rates since the depression of the 1930's were 1.2 per cent in 1944, 1.9 per cent in 1943 and 1945,[4] and about 3 per cent or slightly less during the Korean War. The Korean War period was one of sufficiently high labor demand to justify accepting the unemployment rate then as being purged of almost all but frictional components. The near equality between short-term and total unemployment when the latter is low and the rather mild increases in short-term unemployment during periods of relatively slack labor suggest that 3.25 per cent of the labor force aged 16 and over is probably not too inaccurate an estimate of average frictional unemployment in the economy.

structural unemployment

"The cause of a man's being unemployed is not that which led him to lose his last job but that which prevents him from getting another job now." Loss of a job for any cause results in frictional unemployment *if there are other jobs available reasonably well suited to the worker's abilities.*[5] (Italics added.)

We might add to the quotation the provision that not only must jobs as described be *available*, but workers must be able to discover them with a "reasonable" expenditure of time and other search costs. Whereas frictional unemployment occurs when the time and resource costs required to match workers to existing jobs to which they are by and large well suited can be "afforded" without undue difficulty, structural unemployment results when this matching process takes an unreasonably long period of time (e.g., more than ten weeks) and/or large expenditures of other resources and when it is specific to the labor force of particular industries, occupations, or regions rather than an economy-wide phenomenon. Obviously, the line between the two kinds of unemployment is fuzzy because the point at which a worker

---

[4] *Historical Statistics of the United States, Colonial Times to 1957*, p. 73. These are for the population aged 14 and over, rather than 16 and over.

[5] Rees, *op. cit.* p. 27, quoting William H. Beveridge.

decides to lower his reservation wage, change his criterion of an acceptable job, or give up looking entirely depends on his financial resources, his physical strength, attitudes toward adjusting to a new type of work and/or place to live, and so on. Thus, whether individuals fall into the category of the structurally unemployed depends not only on demand conditions and available job vacancies, but also on the characteristics of household members looking for work. Some workers, for instance, would change places of residence or type of work relatively rapidly in response to the loss of a job and be difficult to distinguish from the frictionally unemployed, while others in the same situation would "stick it out" and could be identified as structurally unemployed. We define structural unemployment operationally to be included in unemployment of more than ten weeks' duration. We must bear in mind, however, that it is the *causes* of such unemployment in which we are ultimately interested, because only through a knowledge of the causes of unemployment can we reasonably discuss its cures.

The Nature of Structural Unemployment. Structural unemployment derives its name from the idea that it is caused by changes in the industrial, occupational, and demographic structure of the economy. Indeed, sometimes it is useful to think in terms of the relationships between the *structure* of unemployment and the structure of wage rates.[6] (This is an issue we shall discuss briefly later on and which is relevant to the discussion of the short-run behavior of the wage structure developed in Chapter 13.) The question is, given the industrial and occupational structures of the economy and the changes that occur in them, why doesn't the economic system adjust enough to eliminate structural unemployment? Of course it would be wrong to think that structural unemployment always results when changes occur in the demand and supply of different kinds of labor; it does not. Most economists would agree that the economy adjusts reasonably well even to rather major changes in conditions; sluggish responses are the exception rather than the rule. Nevertheless, such situations warrant careful attention. When adjustments of labor markets to changing conditions occur too slowly to keep structural unemployment from reaching undesirably high levels, the causes can be classified into three or four groups. First of all, all adjustments to a changing economic structure are costly, often requiring relocation and/or reeducation of workers, installation or alteration of plant and equipment, production slowdowns until new methods are effectively incorporated into the production process, and so on. Thus, neither firms nor workers will take steps to adjust to changing conditions unless the changes are thought to be permanent enough to justify the necessary expenses; in the presence of

---

[6] For a discussion of the relationship between the structures of unemployment and wage rates, see M. W. Reder, "Wage Structure and Structural Unemployment," *The Review of Economic Studies*, XXXI, No. 4, pp. 309–322.

uncertainty, it takes time to decide whether the investment in information and adjustment will pay. In addition to the adjustment and information costs which are more or less directly measurable in terms of money, the psychological costs of adjustment, especially when the migration of workers is involved, may also be a serious deterrent preventing structural adjustments. Still another cause of structural unemployment is the interdependence of the supply of and demand for labor. That is, adjustment of the labor force to changing demand conditions, for instance, moving from a declining community to an expanding one, often further reduces the demand for labor in the declining area. Finally, the customary setting of wage rates (recall the concept of the social minimum wage) and other institutionalized sources of wage rigidity (unions, minimum wage rates, and so on) may hinder or prevent adjustment of the wage structure from doing its part to bring about reasonable equality between the amounts of labor supplied and demanded.

Let us consider a hypothetical illustrative example to help clarify the possible causes of structural unemployment. Suppose there is a small agricultural and mining community in the Appalachian region of the United States and technological changes make the introduction of laborsaving mining machinery economical at existing wage rates. Even in the absence of conventional and institutionalized restrictions on reducing wages, introduction of the new machinery may be economical, and men are thrown out of work because the ensuing reduction in the price of coal does not bring about a sufficient increase in the amount of coal demanded to restore mining employment to its old level. There will, of course, be some smaller mines in which the introduction of the new machinery is not feasible, and any decline in wage rates that does occur may make previously marginal mines economical to operate. However, we may imagine that substantial unemployment remains. Some of the unemployed may find work in agriculture, but agriculture typically cannot absorb large numbers of such workers.

As some of the unemployed emigrate from the area, repercussions are felt in industries which have supplied local needs (services, construction, etc.) as the demand for their output falls. Thus, a decline in demand for labor in mines has the effect of reducing the demand for labor in other industries in the area. Workers who are in the prime working age group, who have few or no children, and who have favorable attitudes toward moving will leave the area and find jobs in more prosperous locations. Thus, the remaining population tends to be made up disproportionately of those who for reasons having to do with their age and the likelihood of their finding work elsewhere, the size of their families, or their attitudes toward moving *per se* have remained in the declining area despite the increasing difficulty of earning a living.

Now, if this area happened to be previously marginally attractive to some industry (e.g., textiles or apparel) that had not yet located there, the declining wage rates and the increasing availability of workers might be sufficient to induce a change in the local industrial structure and to restore the demand for labor to a level high enough to keep unemployment reasonably low. This is more likely to happen if the unemployed workers are of a relatively high skill level and/or are readily adaptable to new kinds of jobs. Workers are more likely to have such characteristics if they are relatively well educated and have been employed in jobs where the work contributes to adaptability. Alternatively, high unemployment may persist with no new industries being attracted; able workers continue to leave until the community is indeed depressed, with few readily employable workers among the unemployed. Gradually, discouraged workers leave the labor force, lowering both the labor force participation and the unemployment rates of the community.

Some Examples of Structural Unemployment in the Early 1960's. Examples of communities with something like these alternative kinds of behavior can be found in the United States. Table 15-4 shows recent data for three labor markets—San Diego, California; Johnstown, Pennsylvania; and Fall River, Massachusetts. All three of these areas experienced higher than average unemployment during the period 1960–67; all three suffered from declining employment in one or more important industries; but the three communities differed in important ways in the adjustment of their labor markets to the changing conditions. Two of the labor markets, Fall River and Johnstown, were classified as "chronically depressed" for some time prior to 1960. According to the definitions employed, therefore, they had a great deal of unemployment of more than fifteen weeks' duration.[7]

The difference in behavior between San Diego and Fall River is striking. Each labor market experienced approximately a 50 per cent decline of employment in an industry which accounted for a substantial proportion of nonagricultural employment. While ordnance and aircraft manufacturing accounted for over 20 per cent of nonagricultural employment in San Diego in 1960, textile manufacturing accounted for 16 per cent of nonagricultural employment in Fall River. By 1965, ordnance and aircraft employment had fallen to 10 per cent of nonagricultural employment in San Diego, and textiles accounted for only 8 per cent of nonagricultural employment in Fall River. The striking differences in response are reflected in a 3 per cent rise in total nonagricultural employment in San Diego during the five-year period, on the one hand, and a 3 per cent decline in Fall River, on the other. In other words, rising employment in other industries was sufficient to keep total labor demand buoyant in San Diego, while in Fall River, no such rise took place.

---

[7] U.S. Bureau of Labor Statistics, "The Structure of Unemployment in Areas of Substantial Labor Surplus," *Study Paper No. 23*, Washington, 1960, p. 34.

Table 15-4

EMPLOYMENT AND UNEMPLOYMENT IN THREE LABOR AREAS

Year	San Diego, California					Fall River, Mass.				Johnstown, Pa.			
	(1)	(2)	(3)	(4)	(5)	(6)	(7)	(8)	(9)	(10)	(11)	(12)	(13)
1960	.064	260.1	48.2	67.9	.086	44.1	7.1	25.3	.129	71.7	6.4	7.0	7.9
1961	.075	264.4	49.9	70.7	.095	44.2	7.2	25.2	.182	65.2	5.4	6.7	8.3
1962	.079	261.3	40.5	62.0	.097	43.6	5.6	24.1	.151	65.5	5.1	7.4	8.6
1963	.077	259.7	34.8	56.4	.104	42.9	5.1	23.3	.106	67.0	4.8	7.6	8.8
1964	.075	261.2	29.3	50.5	.104	42.0	3.9	21.5	.071	70.0	4.9	7.7	9.1
1965	.072	268.0	26.1	49.5	.080	42.7	3.3	21.3	.057	72.6	4.9	7.9	9.4
1966	.052	288.3	29.9	56.2	.063	44.2	3.3	21.7	.046	75.4	5.1	7.9	10.1
1967*	.047				.061				.054				

Columns: (1) Unemployment rate
(2) Total Nonagricultural Employment ('000)
(3) Ordnance and Aircraft Employment ('000)
(4) Manufacturing Employment ('000)
(5) Unemployment Rate
(6) Total Nonagricultural Employment ('000)
(7) Textile Mill Products Employment ('000)
(8) Manufacturing Employment ('000)
(9) Unemployment Rate
(10) Total Nonagricultural Employment ('000)
(11) Mining Employment ('000)
(12) Nondurable Goods Manufacturing Employment ('000)
(13) State and Local Government Employment ('000)

* 1967 Unemployment rates are preliminary and based on an 11-month average.

Sources: Cols. (1), (5), (9); Manpower Report of the President, 1967, Table D-7 (pp. 263–4) (1968, pp. 287–88).
Cols. (2)–(4), (6)–(8), (10)–(12); Employment and Earnings, BLS Bulletin 1370-3, 4.

Johnstown, Pennsylvania, occupied an intermediate position between the labor market experiences of San Diego and Fall River, although it experienced a smaller initial decline in demand for a crucial industry. In 1960, mining accounted for almost 10 per cent of total nonagricultural employment in Johnstown; by 1965, employment in mining had declined by more than 20 per cent. Nevertheless, rising employment in nondurable goods manufacturing and in state and local government was sufficient to keep total nonagricultural employment from declining.

As a result of these changes, San Diego has experienced moderately high unemployment, which is declining; Fall River has experienced rather high unemployment which, although declining, is still high; and Johnstown, which experienced the extremely high unemployment rate of 18.2 per cent, by 1965 had the lowest of the three cities—4.6 per cent. (By 1967, however, Johnstown's experience turned out to be less favorable than San Diego's; Johnstown's unemployment rate lay between that of the other two cities.) It remains unanswered why these labor markets responded so differently to declines of employment in principal industries. Perhaps the most unequivocal implication of the data is that diverse responses occur to sharp changes in industry mix. At no time, for instance, did San Diego experience a total unemployment rate as high as occurred in Fall River, even though the two cities experienced similar proportionate declines in industries accounting for about 20 per cent of total unemployment.

The answers to the question about why these differences appear is to be found ultimately in a useful theory of the labor market. At present there is no tested and accepted set of hypotheses about the adjustments of labor markets to changing demand and supply conditions which enables us to predict which areas will experience structural unemployment and which will not. However, we are in a position to speculate fruitfully about the crucial conditions which make for relatively rapid adjustments to changing circumstances. These conditions are found in different degrees in the three areas we have examined. (We do not mean to generalize on the basis of this sample of three labor markets but rather simply to illustrate a possible explanation of why structural unemployment occurs in some places and not in others.)

Potentially, one of the most important variables explaining the response of labor markets to changing conditions is the educational attainment of the labor force. The reason for this is probably that a high degree of educational attainment is associated with a high degree of general training, that is, training acquired formally and on-the-job which is useful in a wide variety of alternative types of work and which no doubt facilitates the acquisition of information. Thus, in response to a decline in the demand for one kind of skill, well-educated workers rapidly adapt to new demands. Furthermore, it is probably true that the kind of work done by many well-educated workers varies less from industry to industry than that done by less well-educated workers. To use a rather extreme example for illustration: it is often observed that executives move among jobs in a variety of unrelated industries. This is because the managerial functions of salesmanship, production control, cost control, and the like are similar in industries producing dissimilar products. On the other hand, a stockyards worker who has spent the last twenty years of his working life smacking cattle on their heads with a hammer is unlikely to be able to fit well in the production of women's hosiery. Thus, it is not surprising that one of the principal factors contributing to the comparatively successful adjustment of the labor markets in Johnstown and San Diego appears to be the relatively higher educational attainment of their labor forces. Among persons 25 years of age and over, the rates for completion of four years of high school or more were: San Diego Standard Metropolitan Statistical Area, .55; Johnstown SMSA, .33; and Fall River SMSA, .24.[8]

The prevailing wage level is another characteristic of the three labor markets which, while it reflects conditions which caused differences in adjustments to changing demand conditions, to some extent probably played a causal role in the adjustment process. In 1960, gross average hourly earnings of production workers in manufacturing were as follows: San Diego, $2.73; Johnstown, $2.54; and Fall River, $1.66.[9] Thus, while in the first two areas, manufacturing wages were high compared to the rest of the United States, wage rates in Fall River were among the lowest in the country. (In 1960 average gross hourly earnings in manufacturing for the United States were $2.26.[10]) These wage figures reflect the training and skill mix of the respective labor forces as well as the recent history of supply and demand conditions in the areas. If the concept of social minimum wage (see p. 224) is valid, it may help to explain the slow disappearance of unemployment in Fall River. For despite the fact that high unemployment has persisted in Fall River longer than in the other two areas, between 1960 and 1966 manufacturing wage rates rose by 23 per cent there, compared to 25 per cent in San Diego and only 15 per cent in Johnstown.[11] The federal minimum wage during this period rose to $1.15 from $1.00 in September, 1961, and by February, 1967, it had risen to $1.40; almost certainly, a larger proportion of Fall River's workers were affected by the minimum wage and were at or near the social minimum than in the other two cities. During this period, average gross hourly earnings in manufacturing in the United States rose about 20 per cent,

---

[8] *U.S. Census of Population: 1960*, Vol. 1, "Characteristics of the Population," Part 6, p. 219; Part 40, p. 275; and Part 23, p. 119.

[9] U.S. Bureau of Labor Statistics, Bulletin No. 1370–4.

[10] Bulletin No. 1312–4.

[11] Bulletin No. 1370–4.

to $2.71 in 1966.[12] If the social minimum is proportional to the federal minimum wage, then we may estimate that it rose about 25 per cent between 1960 and 1966. Of the three cities, only Johnstown experienced an average wage increase less than either the estimated increase in the social minimum or in manufacturing wages. San Diego's employment may have been able to grow as it did with wages rising relative to the rest of the country because of the high quality of its labor force, while unemployment in the Johnstown area may have fallen partly because wage rates increased less rapidly there than in the rest of the nation. It is not unreasonable to speculate that social and legal factors were responsible for the comparatively high growth of the average wage rate in Fall River and that this growth has been an important factor contributing to prolonged high unemployment.

Additional Data on the Behavior of Structural Unemployment. We have been searching for possible causes of differences in labor market adjustments to changing economic conditions, and these seem to include the characteristics of workers and of the wage structure which contribute to the adaptability of workers to change and to wage rate flexibility. We cannot attempt a thorough analysis of the causes of structural unemployment here, and the preceding remarks must be considered suggestive and tentative. However, there is readily available additional information about the characteristics of workers in labor market areas considered by the U.S. Department of Labor to be chronically depressed, i.e., suffering from a high degree of structural unemployment. Some of these data for 1959 are shown in Table 15-5, and they are broadly consistent with the evidence bearing on the causes of structural unemployment presented up to this point. In chronically depressed areas (designated as "class III"), a higher proportion of the workers were in blue-collar occupations, and of these, disproportionate numbers were operatives, rather than craftsmen or foremen; a higher proportion were aged 35 years and over. Thus, education, occupational training, and age seem to have mitigated against labor force adaptability in chronically depressed areas. (Of course, the data in Table 15-5 may exaggerate these tendencies of depressed areas to the extent that selective migration had already taken place.)

Furthermore, older workers and operatives constitute a disproportionately large number of the long-term unemployed in all areas taken together. This is demonstrated in Table 15-6, with data for 1960. While males aged 45–64 constituted 17.5 per cent of the total unemployed in that year, they constituted over 24.3 per cent of those unemployed fifteen weeks or more. Similarly, operatives constituted a larger proportion of the long-term unemployed than of total unemployed.

---

[12] *Monthly Labor Review*, April, 1967, Table C-1.

Table 15-5

*CHARACTERISTICS OF WORKERS BY LABOR
MARKET AREA CLASS:* SPRING 1959*

Fraction of Workers with Stated Characteristics

Characteristic	Labor Market Area Class	
	Class I	Class III
Blue Collar	.341	.410
Operatives	.154	.214
Age less than 35 years	.41	.38

* Class I areas are "areas of continued tight, or balanced, labor supply-demand relationships."

Class III areas are "areas of chronic labor surplus. . ."

Source: U.S. Bureau of Labor Statistics, "The Structure of Unemployment in Areas of Substantial Labor Surplus," *Study Paper No. 23,* pp. 2, 13–15.

Table 15-6

*CHARACTERISTICS OF THE UNEMPLOYED BY
DURATION OF UNEMPLOYMENT: 1960*

Fraction of Unemployed with Stated Characteristics

Characteristic	Total Unemployed	Unemployed 15 weeks or over
Males 45–64 years old	.175	.243
Operatives and Kindred Workers*	.265	.290

* Experienced workers only.

Source: U.S. Department of Labor, *Manpower Report of the President, 1967,* pp. 217, 220, 222.

deficient-demand unemployment

Modern concern with unemployment dates from the Great Depression of the 1930's, and we still tend to associate the principal problem of unemployment with the economy's periodic reductions in the rate of growth of aggregate demand and the demand for labor, causing periodic rises in the overall unemployment rate. It is these periodic declines in the rate of growth of labor demand which have been most responsible for the various periods of mass unemployment that have occurred.

The Nature of Deficient-Demand Unemployment. That there is a strong inverse relationship between aggregate demand and unemployment is made quite clear by the data in Table 15-7 and in Figures 15-2 and 15-3. Figure 15-2

Table 15-7

PER CAPITA GNP, DEVIATIONS FROM TREND,
AND UNEMPLOYMENT RATE,
UNITED STATES: 1946–66

Year	(1)	(2)	(3)	(4)
1946	$1,998	$1,927		
1947	1,959	1,963	−4	.039
1948	1,999	2,001	−2	.038
1949	1,962	2,039	−77	.059
1950	2,097	2,078	19	.053
1951	2,216	2,117	99	.033
1952	2,253	2,157	96	.030
1953	2,313	2,198	115	.029
1954	2,236	2,240	−4	.055
1955	2,376	2,283	93	.044
1956	2,383	2,326	57	.041
1957	2,385	2,370	15	.043
1958	2,304	2,416	−112	.068
1959	2,420	2,461	−41	.055
1960	2,435	2,508	−73	.055
1961	2,436	2,555	−119	.067
1962	2,544	2,605	−61	.055
1963	2,597	2,654	−57	.057
1964	2,701	2,705	−4	.052
1965	2,829	2,756	73	.045
1966	2,959	2,808	151	.038

Column (1): Per capita gross national product, 1954 prices (dollars).

Column (2): "Predicted" values of col. (1) based on estimated trend, $Y = 7.55e^{.0188t}$ [t = 0 in 1946].

Column (3): Col. (1) − Col. (2).

Column (4): Proportion of civilian labor force, 16 years and older, unemployed.

Sources: Col. (1) 1946–62; U.S. Census Bureau, *Historical Statistics of the U.S., Colonial Times to 1957 and Continuation to 1962*, pp. 20, 114; 1963–66, U.S. Department of Commerce, *Survey of Current Business, 1967*, p. 44.
Col. (4) U.S. Department of Labor, *Manpower Report of the President, 1967*, p. 201.

shows per capita gross national product in 1954 prices for the period 1946–66. A trend line, assuming a constant growth rate, has been fitted to this series ($Y_t = 7.55e^{.0188t}$, where Y is per capita gross national product in 1954 prices and t is time, equal to zero in 1946).[13] The deviations of per capita gross national product from this trend are negatively correlated with the aggregate unemployment rate, as shown in both Figures 15-2 and 15-3. This suggests that when aggregate demand for goods and services is higher than average, the demand for labor is generally higher than average, and unemployment is low. Similarly, when aggregate demand is lower than average, unemployment is high.

We beg a crucial question, however, if we assume that fluctuations in aggregate demand inevitably cause similar fluctuations in labor demand without a decline in labor supplied—resulting in unemployment. While such an association may indeed be very likely to occur, it is instructive to inquire, why must it?

The answer probably lies once again with information and adjustment costs. When aggregate demand declines, firms may be hesitant to reduce prices and wage offers (they may not be able to reduce wage offers significantly in any event if they have signed collective bargaining agreements) without a great deal of information that it would be worthwhile in the long run to do so, and it probably would require a prolonged period of declining demand before it would seem worthwhile to invest in accelerated acquisition of information and in the actual wage adjustments. One reason for this is that firms will be reasonably certain that the general level of demand will rise again; at that time they will need approximately their current volume of employment and they may feel that to reduce wage rates now would expose the firms to an undue risk of losing valued employees to other firms, necessitating additional hiring and training costs when demand returns to its normal level. The firms can reduce such a risk, and still reduce labor costs, by laying off unskilled workers and filling their jobs with relatively skilled workers, who are most difficult to replace. (That changes in the skill mix of unemployment are correlated with the overall level of unemployment is borne out in the unemployment data discussed later in this section. See also Chapter 13,

---

[13] The equation used is a "constant rate of growth" equation, because the proportionate rate of growth of national income over time is $\dfrac{dY}{dt}\dfrac{1}{Y}$, by definition. This expression, in the equation used, happens to be the coefficient of t. To verify that this is true, take the natural logarithm of both sides of the equation, obtaining

$$\ln Y = .0188t \ln(e) + \ln 7.55$$

Since $\ln e \equiv 1$,

$$\frac{d \ln Y}{dt} = \frac{dY}{dt}\frac{1}{Y} = .0188$$

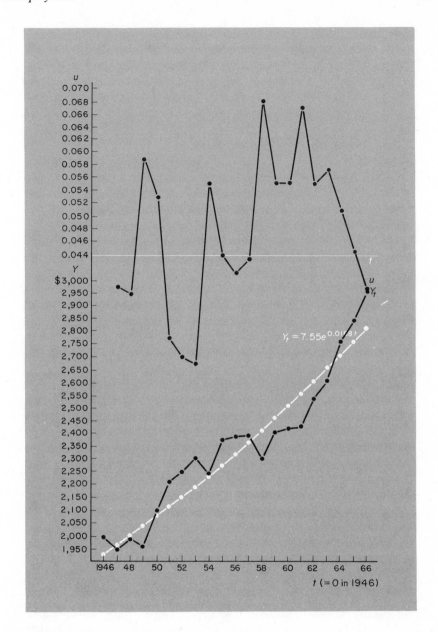

Source: Table 15–7

FIG. 15-2
Unemployment and Gross National Product:
1946–1966

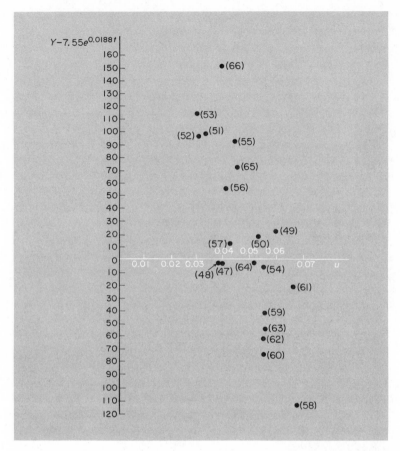

Source: Table 15–7, Cols. (3) and (4)

FIG. 15-3
Unemployment and Deviations from Trend
of GNP: 1946–1966

p. 263.) Certainly, if firms believe the demand decline to be short-lived, they will not feel it is worthwhile to invest in new kinds of equipment that would enable them to substitute labor for machinery, even if wage rates tended to decline relative to other factor prices. On the supply side, workers will not be induced in the short run to engage in intensive revaluation of their labor market alternatives when they know labor market conditions are bad all over—and there is small probability of finding good alternatives to their expected long-run possibilities. Furthermore, to offer to accept lower wage rates in their current jobs, rather than risk unemployment, might adversely affect their long-run wage rates prospects and thus not be worthwhile. Even when unemployed workers do engage in intensive search, it will be extremely difficult for workers to find jobs that they will accept, and workers near the bottom of the occupational ladder probably will often find nothing when labor market conditions are bad, no matter how hard they search for jobs.

In addition, it is well brought out in most courses in macroeconomics that even if substantial wage changes were to take place in the presence of declines in the demand for labor associated with declines in aggregate demand, speculation that further wage reductions might occur, and the effect on debtors of a rising value of money in terms of goods, might well prolong the existence of deficient labor demand. In other words, the causes of deficient-demand unemployment are somewhat similar to the causes of structural unemployment: they center on the understandably sluggish responses of wage offers and reservation wage rates to excess supply and upon the response of excess supply to wage reductions when and if they occur. The principal differences between deficient-demand and structural unemployment is that the former results from occasional reductions in overall demand, while the latter results from changes in the structure of the economy that reduce the demand for labor in particular industries, areas, and/or occupations.

This is not to say that deficient-demand unemployment affects all industries, areas, and occupations identically; it does not. This makes it extremely difficult at times to identify whether high unemployment rates are the result of structural changes in the economy or of deficient aggregate demand. The difficulty in discerning between the types of unemployment is important, because the types of policies which should be effective in reducing one type are probably less effective (although not ineffectual) in reducing the other.

Further Aspects of the Behavior of Deficient-Demand Unemployment, 1947–67. The similarity between deficient-demand and structural unemployment caused great arguments among economists during the period following 1957, until the Viet Nam War and other causes reduced unemployment to below 4 per cent of the labor force for the first time in several years. It is now evident in the data shown in Figures 15-2 and 15-3 that the period 1957–61 was one of low economic growth; the level of aggregate demand remained below its long-run average (assuming constant growth potential) from 1958 through 1963. Consequently unemployment rates were abnormally high during this period, as shown in Table 15-7. At the same time, and beginning prior to 1957, there evidently was taking place a long-run process that involved a relative decline in the importance of goods-producing industries (manufacturing, construction, mining, and the related transportation and utilities industries) in the economy and a relative increase in the importance of service industries. In addition, the goods-producing industries were engaged in a long-run process of substituting machinery for labor. Thus, although total employment increased in all but two years between 1953 and 1962, substantial employment declines took place in the goods-producing industries. Concurrently, unemployment rates were relatively high in these industries, and they were also high in occupations characterized by manual labor. (See Tables 15-8 and 15-9.)

The period 1958–63 was one of subnormal business activity, and from the point of view of that time, it appeared that the high unemployment rates in goods-producing industries and in manual occupations might be due to an increase in the proportion of structural unemployment in total unemployment. Actually, unemployment rates almost always rise more in goods-producing industries than elsewhere during periods of depressed business activity; this is a feature of the structure of the economy and of business cycles. So do unemployment rates in manual occupations; this is probably due to the concentration of manual occupations in goods-producing industries and to the relationship between general training, wage structure, and unemployment which we discussed in the section on the short-run behavior of wage differentials between workers differing in degree of skill (Chapter 13, pp. 223–26). Thus, in 1957, a year of more or less normal business activity, the total unemployment rate was .043, the unemployment rate of experienced laborers was .094, and that of workers in manufacturing was .050. The differences in the unemployment rates between laborers, workers in manufacturing, and the general average were, respectively, .049 and .007. However, during 1961, the worst year of the depressed period, these differences had risen to .078 and .010. If the previously mentioned changes that were taking place in goods-producing industries and in manual occupations had been the principal causes of high unemployment rates, then we might have expected to see these more recent unemployment rate differences persist; however, they did not. By 1966, the difference between the unemployment rate of laborers and the general average had fallen to .034, and the difference between the unemployment rate in manufacturing and the average unemployment rate had declined once again to .007.

Indeed, it was apparent as early as 1962 that there had occurred no significant change in the interindustry or interoccupational differences between unemployment rates that was not common to previous periods of depressed economic activity.[14] The behavior of unemployment rates has been consistent with the hypothesis that the high rates that occurred from 1958 through 1964 were due to low aggregate demand, rather than to an

---

[14] Walter W. Heller, "The Administration's Fiscal Policy," in Arthur M. Ross, ed., *Unemployment and the American Economy* (New York: John Wiley & Sons, Inc., 1964), pp. 93–115.

increase in the importance of structural unemployment. It does not provide conclusive confirmation of the hypothesis, however.[15]

Still another factor which contributed to the belief that the high unemployment rates of the late 1950's and early 1960's may have been due to a major change in the importance of structural unemployment in the

Table 15-8

AVERAGE ANNUAL CHANGES IN EMPLOYMENT—GOODS PRODUCING
AND RELATED INDUSTRIES: 1948–1966 (THOUSANDS)

Industry	(1) 1948–53	(2) 1953–57	(3) 1957–62	(4) 1965–66
Manufacturing	339	−94	−85	1,052
Mining	−26	−10	−36	−4
Contract Construction	91	75	−45	100
Transportation and Public Utilities	20	−12	−63	103

Sources: Columns (1)–(3) Walter W. Heller, "The Administration's Fiscal Policy," in Arthur Ross, ed., *Unemployment and the American Economy* (New York: John Wiley & Sons, Inc., 1964), p. 98.
Column (4) U.S. Department of Labor, *Manpower Report of the President,* 1967, p. 20.

United States economy was the rise in the proportion of long-term unemployment in total unemployment. This is shown in Table 15-10. However, the data for the entire period 1947–66 also show quite clearly that there seems always to be an increase in the proportion of long-term unemployment when total unemployment rises. This took place in 1949–50 and 1954–55, as well as in 1958 and after. Therefore, in the light of the other evidence we have discussed, it seems reasonable to attribute the high long-term unemployment that took place to the general set of conditions induced by sluggish aggregate demand.

The relationship between long-term and total unemployment serves to point out the shady line that divides structural and deficient-demand unemployment. By reducing the number of job vacancies, deficient aggregate demand raises the probability that anyone who wishes to find a job will have to spend a relatively long time looking before he is successful. Thus, tendencies toward structural unemployment are no doubt intensified by deficient aggregate demand. Thus, it is likely that proper aggregate monetary

---

[15] This is forcefully pointed out by R. G. Lipsey, in "Structural and Deficient-Demand Unemployment Reconsidered," in Arthur M. Ross, ed. *Employment Policy and the Labor Market* (Berkeley and Los Angeles: University of California Press, 1965), pp. 210–55.

Table 15-9

UNEMPLOYMENT RATES IN GOODS PRODUCING INDUSTRIES
AND MANUAL OCCUPATIONS, 1957–1962

Industry or Occupation (Experienced Workers)		1953	1957	1961	1962	1966
Craftsmen, Foremen and Kindred Workers		.026	.038	.063	.051	.028
Operatives and Kindred Workers		.032	.063	.096	.075	.043
Laborers, Except Farm and Mine		.061	.094	.145	.124	.073
Manufacturing	*wage and salary workers*	.025	.050	.077	.058	.032
Mining, Forestry, Fishery		.049	.063	.116	.086	.038
Transportation and Public Utilities		.018	.031	.051	.039	.020
Total Unemployment		.025	.043	.067	.056	.039

Source: U.S. Department of Labor, *Manpower Report of the President, 1967*, pp. 217–18.

and fiscal policies can help stabilize the growth in the number of job vacancies, in general, and thereby facilitate the economy's adjustment to continuing structural change.

There is no doubt an interaction between policy actions designed to reduce deficient-demand unemployment and actions designed to reduce structural unemployment; actions which increase the level of aggregate demand are likely to be more effective when the labor force is adaptable and responsive to changing demand conditions; policies to reduce structural unemployment will be more effective when the overall level of demand for output and labor is strong. The appropriate mixture of aggregate and particular policy actions to reduce unemployment is a subject which could fruitfully use considerably more investigation and research than it has received.

the structure or composition of unemployment

In the immediately preceding section we found that it is often difficult to distinguish between structural and deficient-demand unemployment, partly because we have no measures of unemployment by *cause* and partly because structural and deficient-demand unemployment occur to some extent for similar reasons. In exploring the apparent similarities between structural and deficient-demand unemployment we noticed that the characteristics of the unemployed are more or less stable and change in a predictable way when the general level of unemployment changes. Thus, it is interesting and useful to consider the *structure* or composition of unemployment—the makeup of workers who are in particular occupations and industries, who differ in degree of skill, previous training, age, and so on. We have already considered the structure of unemployment to the extent that it changes when the level of aggregate demand changes; in doing this we had recourse to the theory of wage structure discussed in Chapter 13. Similarly, we shall consider the general structure of unemployment as it relates to the structure of wage rates because the structure of unemployment appears to be closely related to the wage structure. This relationship has been emphasized by M. W. Reder and

Table 15-10

FRACTION OF LONG-TERM
(11 WEEKS AND OVER)
UNEMPLOYMENT IN TOTAL
UNEMPLOYMENT,
UNEMPLOYED PERSONS
16 YEARS AND OVER:
1947–1966

Year	
1947	.256
1948	.208
1949	.279
1950	.330
1951	.221
1952	.190
1953	.183
1954	.316
1955	.322
1956	.271
1957	.280
1958	.411
1959	.368
1960	.340
1961	.412
1962	.369
1963	.354
1964	.341
1965	.306
1966	.258
1967	.224

Source: U.S. Department of Labor, *Manpower Report of the President, 1967*, p. 219; *1968*, p. 221.

is tied in with the theory of the short-run behavior of skill differentials, developed in Chapter 13.[16]

The relationship between the theory of the structure of unemployment and the theory of short-run behavior of the wage structure exists because of their common assumption of the social minimum wage (*SM*). The existence of a social minimum implies that excess supplies are more likely to exist in the markets for unskilled labor, new labor force entrants, young workers, etc., even in a situation where the markets for more skilled workers tend to be cleared, except for frictional unemployment. In Reder's words:

> The theory that is offered may be presented most simply in terms of two occupational classes: skilled and unskilled. The markets for skilled workers are, as a first approximation, assumed to adjust to excess supply or demand with sufficient rapidity as to leave relatively little evidence of unemployment. The markets for the unskilled bear the brunt of whatever unemployment there is in the community [because in response to a decline in demand, employers are assumed to move more skilled employees down the occupational ladder, finally laying off the least-skilled]. The two occupational classes, skilled and unskilled, are chosen as representative of the two extremes of the spectrum of manual jobs with all other jobs (e.g., semi-skilled) lying between them.

Reder recognizes that a similar structure of wages and unemployment may exist in white-collar occupations, although the chain of substitutes described may not exist between white- and blue-collar workers. The model implies that for persons on the fringe of the labor force unemployment rates are more likely to be the adjusting mechanism making for an equilibrium size of the labor force than are wage rates. That is, in response to a decline in the demand for labor (even one that tends to persist) unemployment rates of the least skilled rise, instead of wage rates declining, and the opposite occurs when demand rises. The increase in unemployment makes it less attractive for some of the marginal workers to remain in the labor force when demand declines and they leave; when demand rises, similar workers enter the labor force. This is probably an accurate description of the market for many women, youth, and older workers, especially those who are found among the lower-skilled occupations. A further implication is that at *any* time the unemployment rates of the less-skilled workers should be greater than that of the higher-skilled, at least within blue-collar occupations, and perhaps across both blue- and white-collar occupations. Tables 15-9 and 15-11 show that over the past twenty-five years, under conditions of reasonably full and of rather deficient employment, the unemployment rates of the less skilled were constantly higher than for workers of higher skills. This relationship exists within white- and blue-collar occupations and between the two occupation groups.

---

[16] M. W. Reder, "Wage Structure and Structural Unemployment," *The Review of Economic Studies*, October, 1964 XXXI, 4.

The theories of wage and unemployment structure predict the kind of rise in the unemployment rate differential between skilled and unskilled workers that took place during the depressed 1958–61 period. As the demand for labor falls relative to supply, employers try to hold on to their relatively skilled employees, in whom they have relatively greater investments in specific training, hiring costs, and so on, by moving them down the occupational ladder rather than laying them off. Thus, in the presence of a wage structure

Table 15-11

UNEMPLOYMENT RATES IN SELECTED OCCUPATIONS AND YEARS

Occupation	1940	1948	1956	1960	1963	1966
Managers, Officials, Proprietors, Except Farm	.27	.09	.008	.014	.015	.010
Clerical and Kindred Workers	.092	.023	.024	.038	.040	.028
Sales Workers	.089	.034	.027	.037	.042	.027
Craftsmen, Foremen, and Kindred Workers	.151	.029	.032	.053	.048	.028
Operatives and Kindred Workers	.129	.041	.054	.080	.074	.043
Laborers Except Farm and Mine	.336	.075	.082	.125	.121	.041

Sources: P. M. Hauser, "Differential Unemployment and Characteristics of the Unemployed in the United States," in National Bureau of Economic Research, *The Measurement and Behavior of Unemployment*, p. 263.

M. W. Reder, "Wage Structure and Structural Unemployment," *The Review of Economic Studies*, XXXI, p. 317.

U.S. Department of Labor, *Manpower Report of the President, 1967*, p. 217.

that does not adjust rapidly in the short run to changes in demand and supply conditions, and a social minimum wage that adjusts only under extreme conditions of excess demand or supply, the lowest-skilled workers not only have higher unemployment rates than others, on the average, but they also bear the brunt of increases in unemployment when demand is deficient. It is this underlying structure of unemployment that results in many of the common characteristics of structural and deficient-demand unemployment.

It is also clear from the analysis of the occupational structure of unemployment that worker characteristics related to occupation, such as age, sex, education, and race, will be related similarly to unemployment. Consequently, we find that unemployment is more common among nonwhites than among whites, among women than among men (although this relationship is

Table 15-12

UNEMPLOYMENT RATES BY AGE, SEX, AND COLOR, VARIOUS YEARS
(PERSONS AGED 16 YEARS AND OVER)

Year	White		Nonwhite		Males		
	Male	Female	Male	Female	18 and 19 years	35 to 44 years	55 to 64 years
1948	.034	.038	.058	.061	.096	.024	.031
1951	.026	.042	.049	.061	.070	.020	.028
1953	.025	.031	.048	.041	.072	.020	.028
1957	.036	.043	.083	.073	.123	.028	.035
1962	.046	.055	.109	.110	.138	.036	.046
1966	.028	.043	.063	.086	.102	.020	.026

Source: U.S. Department of Labor, Manpower Report of the President, 1967, pp. 214–215.

not as pronounced among nonwhites as among whites; this is probably due to the fact that while the median education of white females is slightly higher than that of white males, the median education of nonwhite females is over one year more than that of nonwhite males),[17] and that it is more common among young and older men than among "prime age" men. These relationships are shown in Table 15-12.

CONCLUSION

The preceding analysis of the varieties of unemployment and their causes suggests that a variety of economic policies is required to reduce unemployment, if reduction of the unemployment rate is thought to be desirable. Often, reduction of unemployment is desirable if only because unemployment affects disproportionately the poor, who we feel can ill afford the costs of being without work and who cannot in general be thought to have chosen their frequency of unemployment as a preferred long-run alternative. Of course, not all unemployment—even cases of frequent unemployment—is a phenomenon of the poor or lower-skill groups. Carpenters and other construction workers, for instance, experience frequent unemployment because of the temporary nature of each job and because of the vagaries of weather. However, they are rather highly paid workers, and we should no doubt find that part of their relatively high pay is remuneration for the casual nature of their employment.

If we consider the unemployment that exists when aggregate demand is high enough to reduce deficient-demand unemployment to near zero, it is

---

[17] U.S. Department of Labor, *Manpower Report of the President, 1967*, p. 241.

not clear that even the unemployment of the poor, the lower-skilled, the young, or the old should be considered undesired. As is well stated by M. W. Reder:

> In principal, unskilled workers who wish regular employment should be able to obtain analogous options [to salaried positions, at somewhat lower wages, of lawyers and other groups who normally experience many brief engagements of their services]. Indeed, much of what is termed disguised unemployment in underdeveloped economies (and domestic service everywhere) is essentially the acceptance of a low hourly rate of compensation and long (and indeterminate) hours in exchange for a steady real income. That unskilled workers regularly experience higher unemployment rates implies either that, given the terms of tradeoff (between higher hourly rates and steadier employment) that confront them, they prefer more unemployment than other labor grades or they have some special difficulty—not shared with the more skilled—in altering the terms of tradeoff [the social minimum would constitute such a difficulty].
>
> Considering the relative importance of intermittent job seekers among the unskilled (students, itinerants, partially retired persons, etc.) the role of worker preference in this matter should not be overlooked. Indeed, at very low levels of aggregate unemployment, differences of worker preference between higher hourly rates and steady employment, and employer adjustments thereto may well be the major factor in explaining the relatively high rate of unemployment among the unskilled. But at other times, it is almost surely the wage rigidity factor that predominates.[18]

There is almost no doubt, however, that when aggregate demand is deficient, the lost national income and reduced personal incomes of workers provide obvious justification for public policies to reduce unemployment. In addition, the structural unemployment which often goes with economic change and progress is difficult to construe as being desired by those who bear it, and one can make a good case that the structurally unemployed ought to be aided or compensated in some way by the rest of society, who in general benefit from economic change and progress.

The question remains, what kinds of policies will be most effective in combating the mix of unemployment that we experience? Let us first examine the probable impact of monetary and fiscal policies designed to stabilize the rate of economic growth. During the period 1947–66, the average monthly unemployment rate was .048 (based on the data in Table 15-7). If one examines years in which actual per capita gross national product was near its long-run average (years 1947, 1948, 1950, 1954, 1963, and 1964 in Figure 15-2), one observes an average unemployment rate during such years of also about .048. Thus, it would not seem unreasonable to set .048 as a level of unemployment which might well be achieved if monetary and fiscal policies were adopted that simply smoothed out the economy's occasional fluctuations in aggregate demand.

---

[18] Reder, "Wage Structure and Structural Unemployment," p. 318.

Although the negligible difference between the average unemployment rate during the twenty years 1947–66 and the average unemployment rate during years when gross national product per capita was near its long-run trend position seems to suggest that merely smoothing out the pattern of economic growth (so that per capita gross national product was near the trend line of Figure 15-2) would have had a negligible effect on average unemployment, it is not implausible that eliminating the troughs in business activity would not be completely offset by elimination of peaks. That is, improving the stability of business activity might well enable businessmen to invest more in physical capital and less in the acquisition of information and adjusting to it, and hence cause an upward shift in the position and slope of the trend of per capita gross national product. On the supply side, workers would be laid off less frequently and have a better idea of their long-run employment alternatives. Thus, workers, like business firms, could well experience an increase in the rate of return to investment if the amount of uncertainty was reduced via stabilization of the rate of economic growth. Increased investment in human capital would not only make it less costly for workers to adapt to structural changes in the economy, but increased certainty about the future would itself make adaptation more attractive, *given* prior investments in human capital. Thus, stabilizing the rate of economic growth could well lower average unemployment in the long run by increasing the average level of demand for labor and increasing the adaptability of workers to changes in the structure of the economy. The likely extent of such a reduction is impossible to estimate, and it is striking that one cannot easily put his finger on a plausible amount by which stabilization of the economy would reduce unemployment. This is an area which demands much more investigation by economists.

There still remains the question regarding the nature of subsequent unemployment reductions that would take place if anticyclical monetary and fiscal policies were permanently to shift the trend of economic activity. For once unemployment fell to its new "equilibrium" level, what scope would remain for further reduction? From Chapter 14, we feel that attempts to use monetary and/or fiscal policy other than to stabilize the rate of economic growth could reduce unemployment in the long run only at the expense of an accelerating inflation. Thus, the long-run effects of monetary and fiscal policy on the *average* level of unemployment must probably be confined to their impact via their effect on the growth of human and nonhuman capital and on facilitating adjustment to structural change. Thus, the long-run effects of monetary and fiscal policy on the *average* level of unemployment probably must operate through the effect of reduced uncertainty on the accumulation of human and nonhuman capital and on speeding labor force adjustments to changes in the structure of labor demand.

Needless to say, we are not constrained to rely exclusively on the aggregate stabilization policies to reduce unemployment over the long run. Measures are aimed directly at the social minimum wage (e.g., removing the pressure of minimum wage legislation, or curtailing industry-wide bargaining over the wages of lower-skilled workers); increasing the flexibility of the labor force through education, training, and retraining; providing more and better labor market information; and similar policies probably have a role to play in reducing the equilibrium levels of both structural and frictional unemployment. Such policies, in the opinion of the author, would almost certainly be necessary to reduce the unemployment rate permanently below .030 or so, and they probably are necessary to maintain unemployment below approximately .040, which is the author's guess about the level at which aggregate demand alone probably exhausts its long-run unemployment-reducing potential. However, even if such policies were effective in reducing the equilibrium level of unemployment below the level that could be obtained by using stabilizing monetary and fiscal policies alone, we should still ask whether the resources so used would produce a social value (including the value of the income redistribution concomitant with reducing unemployment) in excess of the value that would be produced by using them elsewhere, either in the public or private sector. For instance, it is at least questionable whether, in regard to the unemployment that occurs in a stable environment due to choice made by workers who are particular about the timing and nature of their jobs, the benefit of reducing the length and amount of such unemployment is worth the cost of resources in excess of the costs borne by workers and employers themselves; and certainly it would be foolish to think it obvious that *all* unemployment could or should be eliminated in a free labor market.

bibliography and suggested readings

INTRODUCTION AND APPENDIX TO CHAPTER I

BANCROFT, GERTRUDE, *The American Labor Force: Its Growth and Changing Composition.* New York: John Wiley & Sons, Inc., 1958.

DURAND, JOHN D., *The Labor Force in the United States, 1890–1960.* New York: Social Science Research Council, 1948.

FERGUSON, C. E., *Microeconomic Theory.* Homewood, Ill.: Richard D. Irwin, Inc., 1966.

FRIEDMAN, MILTON, *Price Theory: A Provisional Text.* Chicago: Aldine Publishing Company, 1962.

LEWIS, H. G., *Unionism and Relative Wages in the United States.* Chicago: University of Chicago Press, 1963.

LONG, CLARENCE D., *The Labor Force Under Changing Income and Employment.* Princeton, N.J.: Princeton University Press for the National Bureau of Economic Research, 1958.

SCHERER, JOSEPH, "Labor Force: Concepts, Measurements, and Use of Data," *The Journal of Business of the University of Chicago,* XXXI (January, 1958), 38–62.

STIGLER, GEORGE J., "Perfect Competition, Historically Contemplated," *Journal of Political Economy,* LXV (February, 1957), 1–17.

288

U.S. Bureau of the Census, *Historical Statistics of the United States, Colonial Times to 1957 and to 1962 and Revisions.*

U.S. *Census 1960 of Population*, Subject Reports: *Educational Attainment.*

U.S. Department of Labor, Bureau of Labor Statistics, *Employment and Earnings.* (published monthly)

PART I: THE SUPPLY OF LABOR—THEORY AND EVIDENCE

BARBASH, J., "Union Interests in Apprenticeship and Other Training Forms," *Journal of Human Resources*, III (Winter 1968), 63–85.

BECKER, GARY S., "A Theory of the Allocation of Time," *Economic Journal*, LXXV (September, 1965), 493–517.

————, "An Economic Analysis of Fertility," in *Demographic and Economic Change in Developed Countries*, A Conference of the Universities—National Bureau Committee of Economic Research. Princeton, N.J.: Princeton University Press, 1960.

————, *Human Capital.* New York: Columbia University Press, 1964.

BLANK, D. S. and G. J. STIGLER, *The Demand and Supply of Scientific Personnel.* New York: National Bureau of Economic Research, 1957.

BOWEN, William G., and T. A. FINEGAN, "Labor Force Participation and Unemployment," in *Employment Policy and the Labor Market*, ed. Arthur M. Ross, pp. 115–61. Berkeley and Los Angeles: University of California Press, 1965.

CAIN, GLEN G., *Married Women in the Labor Force.* Chicago: University of Chicago Press, 1966.

CARTTER, ALLAN M., "The Supply and Demand of College Teachers," *Journal of Human Resources*, I (Summer 1966), 22–38.

————, *Theory of Wages and Employment.* Homewood, Ill.: Richard D. Irwin, Inc., 1959.

COHEN, SANFORD, "The Supply Curve of Labor Re-examined," *Industrial and Labor Relations Review*, XIII (October, 1959), 64–71.

DANKERT, CLYDE E., "Shorter Hours in Theory and Practice," *Industrial and Labor Relations Review*, XVI (April, 1962), 307–22.

DOUGLAS, PAUL H., *The Theory of Wages.* New York: The Macmillan Company, 1934.

DOUGLAS, PAUL H., and ERIKA SCHOENBERG, "Studies in the Supply Curve of Labor," *Journal of Political Economy*, XLV (February, 1937), 45–79.

DUNCAN, BEVERLY, "Dropouts and the Unemployed," *Journal of Political Economy*, LXXIII (April, 1965), 121–34.

DURAND, JOHN D., *The Labor Force in the United States, 1890–1960.* New York: Social Science Research Council, 1948.

FEARN, ROBERT M., "Labor Force and School Participation of Teenagers." Unpublished Ph.D. dissertation, University of Chicago, 1968.

FERGUSON, C. E., *Microeconomic Theory*. Homewood, Ill.: Richard D. Irwin, Inc., 1966.

FINEGAN, T. ALDRICH, "Hours of Work in the United States: A Cross-Sectional Analysis," *Journal of Political Economy*, LXX (October, 1962), 452–70.

FRIEDMAN, MILTON, and SIMON KUZNETS, *Income from Independent Professional Practice*. New York: National Bureau of Economic Research, 1945.

HANOCH, G., "The 'Backward-Bending' Supply of Labor," *Journal of Political Economy*, LXXIII (December, 1965), 636–42.

HARBISON, F. H., and C. A. MYERS, *Education, Manpower and Economic Growth*. New York: McGraw-Hill Book Company, 1964.

KASPER, H., "Assets and the Supply of Labor," *The Southern Economic Journal*, XXXIII (October, 1966), 245–51.

———, "The Asking Price of Labor and the Duration of Unemployment," *Review of Economics and Statistics*, XLIX (May, 1967), 165–72.

KIKER, R. H., "The Historical Roots of the Concept of Human Capital," *Journal of Political Economy*, LXXIV (October, 1966), 481–99.

LEBERGOTT, STANLEY, *Manpower in Economic Growth*. New York: McGraw-Hill Book Company, 1964.

LESTER, RICHARD H., *Hiring Practices and Labor Competition*. Princeton, N.J.: Princeton University Industrial Relations Section, 1954.

LEWIS, H. G., "Hours of Work and Hours of Leisure," *Proceedings of the Industrial Relations Research Association* (December, 1956), pp. 196–206.

LIEBHAFSKY, E. E., "A 'New Concept in Wage Determination,' Disguised Productivity Analysis," *Southern Economic Journal*, XXVI, (October, 1959), 141–46.

MINCER, JACOB, "Labor Force Participation and Unemployment: A Review of Recent Evidence," in *Prosperity and Unemployment*, ed. R. A. and M. S. Gordon, pp. 73–112. New York: John Wiley & Sons, Inc., 1966.

———, "Labor Force Participation of Married Women," *Aspects of Labor Economics*. Princeton, N.J.: Princeton University Press, 1962.

PARNES, HERBERT S., *Research on Labor Mobility*. New York: Social Science Research Council, 1954.

STIGLER, GEORGE J., *The Theory of Price* (3rd ed.). New York: The Macmillan Company, 1966.

SCHULTZ, T. W., "Capital Formation by Education," *Journal of Political Economy*, LXVIII (December, 1960), 571–83.

———, ed., "Investment in Human Beings," *Journal of Political Economy*, LXX (October, 1962 Supplement). (See note 1, Chap. 4.)

WILKINSON, B. S., "Present Values of Lifetime Earnings for Different Occupations,"*Journal of Political Economy*, LXXIV, (December, 1966), 556–72.

PART 2: THE DEMAND FOR LABOR—THEORY AND EVIDENCE

BEAR, D. V. T., "Inferior Inputs and the Theory of the Firm," *Journal of Political Economy*, LXXIII (June, 1965), 297–99.

BISHOP, R. L., "A Firm's Short-Run and Long-Run Demands for a Factor," *Western Economic Journal*, V (March, 1967), 122–40.

BLANK, D. S., and G. J. STIGLER, *The Demand and Supply of Scientific Personnel*. New York: National Bureau of Economic Research, 1957.

CARTTER, ALLAN M., "The Supply and Demand of College Teachers," *Journal of Human Resources*, (Summer 1966), 22–38.

———, *Theory of Wages and Employment*. Homewood, Ill.: Richard D. Irwin, Inc., 1959.

DOUGLAS, PAUL H., *The Theory of Wages*. New York: The Macmillan Company, 1934.

DUNLOP, JOHN T., ed., *The Theory of Wage Determination*. New York: St. Martin's Press, 1957.

FERGUSON, C. E., *Microeconomic Theory*. Homewood, Ill.: Richard D. Irwin, Inc., 1966.

FRIEDMAN, MILTON, *Price Theory: A Provisional Text*. Chicago: Aldine Publishing Company, 1962.

HANSEN, B., "Marginal Productivity Wage Theory and Subsistence Wage Theory in Egyptian Agriculture," *Journal of Development Studies*, II (July, 1966), 367–408.

HICKS, J. R., *The Theory of Wages* (2nd ed.). London: Macmillan & Co., Ltd., 1964.

HILDERBRAND, GEORGE H., and TA-CHUNG, LUI, *Manufacturing Production Functions in the United States, 1957*. Ithaca: The New York State School of Industrial and Labor Relations, 1965.

LESTER, RICHARD H., "Results and Implications of Some Recent Wage Studies," in *Insights into Labor Issues*, ed. Richard H. Lester and Joseph Shister, pp. 197–237. New York: The Macmillan Company, 1948.

LEWIS, H. G., *Unionism and Relative Wages in the United States*. Chicago: University of Chicago Press, 1963.

LONG, CLARENCE, *The Labor Force Under Changing Income and Employment*. Princeton, N.J.: Princeton University Press for the National Bureau of Economic Research, 1958.

MANGUM, GARTH, *et al.*, "A Symposium: Manpower Projections," *Industrial Relations*, V (May, 1966), 1–71.

MARSHALL, RAY, "The Influence of Legislation on Hours," in *The Hours of Work*, ed. Clyde Dankert, Floyd C. Mann, and Herbert R. Northrup. New York: Harper & Row, Publishers, 1965.

MORGAN, JAMES N., *et al.*, *Income and Welfare in the United States*. New York: McGraw-Hill Book Company, 1962.

PARNES, HERBERT S., *Research on Labor Mobility*. New York: Social Science Research Council, 1954.

PETERSON, JOHN M., "Employment Effects of Minimum Wages, 1938–1950," *Journal of Political Economy*, LXV (October, 1957), 412–30.

REYNOLDS, LLOYD G., and PETER GREGORY, *Wages, Productivity, and Industrialization in Puerto Rico*, Homewood, Ill.: Richard D. Irwin, Inc., 1965.

ROBINSON, JOAN, *The Economics of Imperfect Competition*. London: Macmillan & Co., Ltd., 1965.

U.S. Bureau of the Census, *Statistical Abstract of the United States*. (issued annually)

U.S. Bureau of the Census, *Historical Statistics of the United States, Colonial Times to 1957 and Continuation to 1962*. (a statistical abstract supplement)

U.S. Department of Labor, Bureau of Labor Statistics, *Monthly Report on the Labor Force*. (issued monthly)

U.S. Social Security Board, *Social Security Bulletin*, (accompanied by annual statistical supplement 1965). Washington, Social Security Administration. (issued monthly)

PART 3: THE INTERACTION OF SUPPLY AND DEMAND—THEORY AND EVIDENCE

ALCHIAN, ARMEN A., and WILLIAM R. ALLEN, *University Economics* (2nd ed.). Belmont, Calif.: Wadsworth Publishing Company, Inc., 1967.

ARROW, K. J., "Towards a Theory of Price Adjustment," in *The Allocation of Economic Resources*, Moses Abramovitz, *et. al.*, pp. 41–51. Stanford, Calif.: Stanford University Press, 1959.

BECKER, GARY S., *Human Capital*. New York: Columbia University Press, 1964.

BECKER, JOSEPH M., ed., *In Aid of the Unemployed*. Baltimore: The Johns Hopkins Press, 1965.

BLANK, D. S., and G. J. STIGLER, *The Demand and Supply of Scientific Personnel*. New York: National Bureau of Economic Research, 1957.

CAGAN, PHILIP, "The Monetary Dynamics of Hyperinflation," in *Studies in the Quantity Theory of Money*, ed. Milton Friedman, pp. 25–117. Chicago: University of Chicago Press, 1956.

CARTTER, ALLAN M., "The Supply and Demand of College Teachers," *Journal of Human Resources*, I, (Summer 1966), 22–38.

————, *Theory of Wages and Employment*. Homewood, Ill.: Richard D. Irwin, Inc., 1959.

DENISON, EDWARD F., "Education, Economic Growth, and Gaps in Information," *Journal of Political Economy*, LXX (October, 1962), 124–28.

DOUTY, H. M., "Sources of Occupational Wage and Salary Rate Dispersion Within Labor Markets," *Industrial and Labor Relations Review*, XV (October, 1961), 67–74.

DUNLOP, JOHN T., "The Development of Labor Organization: A Theoretical Framework," in *Insights into Labor Issues*, ed. Richard A. Lester and Joseph Shister. New York: The Macmillan Company, 1948.

————, *Wage Determination Under Trade Unions*. New York: Augustus M. Kelly, Inc., 1950.

DUNLOP, JOHN T., ed., *The Theory of Wage Determination*. New York: St. Martin's Press, 1957.

ECKSTEIN, OTTO, and T. A. WILSON, "The Determination of Money Wages in American Industry," *Quarterly Journal of Economics*, LXXVI (August, 1962), 379–414.

FABRICANT, S., "Basic Facts on Productivity Change," National Bureau of Economic Research, *Occasional Paper No. 63*, New York, 1959.

FERGUSON, C. E., *Microeconomic Theory*. Homewood, Ill.: Richard D. Irwin, Inc., 1966.

FISHLOW, ALBERT, "American Investment in Education," *Journal of Economic History*, XXVI (December, 1966), 418–36.

FOGEL, WALTER A., "Job Rate Ranges: A Theoretical and Empirical Analysis," *Industrial and Labor Relations Review*, XVIII (July, 1964), 584–97.

FRIEDMAN, MILTON, *Price Theory: A Provisional Text*. Chicago: Aldine Publishing Company, 1962.

————, "What Price Guideposts," in *Guidelines, Informal Controls, and the Market Place*, ed. George P. Shultz and Robert Aliber, pp. 17–39. Chicago and London: University of Chicago Press, 1966.

GARBARINO, JOSEPH, "The Theory of Interindustry Wage Structure Variation," *Quarterly Journal of Economics*, LXIV (May, 1950), 281–305.

GORDON, MARGARET S., *The Economics of Welfare Policies*. New York: Columbia University Press, 1963.

HABER, WILLIAM, ed., *Labor in a Changing America*. New York and London: Basic Books, Inc., Publishers, 1966.

HANOCH, GIORA, "Personal Earnings and Investment in Schooling." Unpublished Ph.D. dissertation, University of Chicago, 1965.

HAUSER, P. M., "Differential Unemployment and Characteristics of the Unemployed in the United States," in *The Measurement and Behavior of Unemployment*, pp. 243–78. National Bureau of Economic Research. Princeton, N.J.: Princeton University Press, 1957.

HELLER, WALTER W., "The Administration's Fiscal Policy," in *Unemployment and the American Economy*, ed. Arthur M. Ross, pp. 93–115. New York: John Wiley & Sons, Inc., 1964.

HICKS, J. R., *The Theory of Wages* (2nd ed.). London: Macmillan & Co., Ltd., 1964.

HILTON, GEORGE W., "The Theory of Tax Incidence Applied to the Gains of Labor Unions," in *The Allocation of Economic Resources*, Moses Abramovitz, *et al.*, pp. 102–33. Stanford, Calif.: Stanford University Press, 1959.

JOHNSON, D. G., "The Functional Distribution of Income in the United States," *Review of Economics and Statistics*, XXXVI (May, 1954), 175–82.

JOHNSON, HARRY G., "Effects of Unionization: A Geometrical Analysis." unpublished paper.

KASPER, H., "The Asking Price of Labor and the Duration of Unemployment," *Review of Economics and Statistics*, XLIX (May, 1967), 165–72.

KEAT, PAUL G., "Long-Run Changes in Occupational Wage Structure 1900–56," *Journal of Political Economy*, LXVIII (December, 1960), 584–600.

KENDRICK, JOHN W., *Productivity Trends in the United States*. Princeton, N.J.: Princeton University Press, 1961.

KERR, CLARK, "The Impact of Unions on the Level of Wages," *Wages, Prices, Profits and Productivity*, Fifteenth American Assembly, Columbia University (June, 1959), pp. 91–108.

KRAVIS, I. B., "Relative Income Shares in Fact and Theory," *American Economic Review*, XLIX (December, 1959), 917–49.

LEBERGOTT, STANLEY, *Manpower in Economic Growth*. New York: McGraw-Hill Book Company, 1964.

LEE, EVERETT S., *et al.*, *Population, Redistribution and Economic Growth in the United States, 1870–1950*. Philadelphia: The American Philosophical Society, 1957.

LESTER, RICHARD H., "Results and Implications of Some Recent Wage Studies," in *Insights into Labor Issues*, Richard H. Lester and Joseph Shister, eds., pp. 197–237. New York: The Macmillan Company.

LEWIS, H. G., *Unionism and Relative Wages in the United States*. Chicago: University of Chicago Press, 1963.

LIPSEY, RICHARD G., "Structural and Deficient-Demand Unemployment Reconsidered," in *Employment Policy and the Labor Market*, ed. Arthur M. Ross, pp. 210–55. Berkeley and Los Angeles: University of California Press, 1965.

LIPSEY, R. G., and P. O. STEINER, *Economics* (2nd ed.). New York: Harper & Row, Publishers, 1969.

LONG, CLARENCE, *Wages and Earnings in the United States 1860–90*. Princeton, N.J.: Princeton University Press, 1960.

MACDONALD, R. M., "An Evaluation of the Economic Analysis of Unionism," *Industrial and Labor Relations Review*, XVIII (April, 1966), 335–47.

MAHER, JOHN E., "The Wage Pattern in the United States, 1946–1957," *Industrial and Labor Relations Review*, XV (October, 1961), 3–20.

———, "Union, Nonunion Wage Differentials," *American Economic Review*, XLVI (June, 1956), 336–52.

MARSHALL, F. RAY, *The Negro and Organized Labor*. New York: John Wiley & Sons, Inc., 1965.

MYERS, CHARLES A., and GEORGE P. SHULTZ, *The Dynamics of the Labor Market*. Englewood Cliffs, N.J.: Prentice-Hall, Inc., 1951.

OBER, HARRY, "Occupational Wage Differentials, 1907–47," *Monthly Labor Review*, LXVII (August, 1948), 127–34.

OI, WALTER, "Labor as a Quasi-Fixed Factor," *Journal of Political Economy*, LXX (December, 1962), 538–55.

PARNES, HERBERT S., *Research on Labor Mobility*. New York: Social Science Research Council, 1954.

PERLMAN, MARK, *Labor Union Theories in America*. Evanston, Ill.: Row, Peterson and Co., 1958.

PHELPS, EDMUND, H., "Money-Wage Dynamics and Labor-Market Equilibrium." *Journal of Political Economy*, LXXVI, 4, Part II, July/August 1968, pp. 678–711.

PHILLIPS, A. W., "The Relation Between Unemployment and the Role of Change of Money Wage Rates in the United Kingdom, 1861–1957," *Economica*, N.S. XXV (November, 1958), 283–99.

RAPPING, L. A., "Monopoly Rents, Wage Rates, and Union Wage Effectiveness," *Quarterly Review of Economics and Business*, VII (Spring, 1967), 31–47.

RAYACK, ELTON, "The Impact of Unionism on Wages in the Men's Clothing Industry, 1911–56," *Labor Law Journal*, IX (September, 1958), 351–61.

RAYBACK, JOSEPH G., *A History of American Labor*. New York: The Macmillan Company, 1966.

REDER, MELVIN, "The Theory of Occupational Wage Differentials," *American Economic Review*, XLV (December, 1955), 833–52.

———, "Wage Structure and Structural Unemployment," *Review of Economic Studies*, XXXI (October, 1964), pp. 309–21.

———, "Wage Differentials: Theory and Measurement," in *Aspects of Labor Economics*, pp. 257–317. Princeton, N.J.: Princeton University Press, 1962.

REES, ALBERT, "Postwar Wage Determination in the Basic Steel Industry," *American Economic Review*, XLI (June, 1951), 389–404.

———, "Wage Levels Under Conditions of Long-run Full Employment," *American Economic Review*, XLIII (May, 1953), 451–57.

———, "The Effects of Unions on Resource Allocation," *Journal of Law and Economics*, VI (October, 1963), 69–70.

———, "The Meaning and Measurement of Full Employment," in *The Measurement and Behavior of Unemployment*, pp. 13–60. National Bureau of Economic Research. Princeton, N.J.: Princeton University Press, 1957.

———, *The Economics of Trade Unionism*. Chicago: University of Chicago Press, 1962.

REES, ALBERT, and MARY HAMILTON, "The Wage-Price-Productivity Perplex," *Journal of Political Economy*, LXXV (February, 1967), 63–70.

REYNOLDS, LLOYD G., *The Structure of Labor Markets*. New York: Harper & Row, Publishers, 1951.

REYNOLDS, LLOYD G., and CYNTHIA H. TAFT, *The Evolution of Wage Structure*. New Haven: Yale University Press, 1956.

SCHULTZ, T. W., "Capital Formation by Education," *Journal of Political Economy*, LXVIII (December, 1960), 571–83.

SHULTZ, GEORGE P., IRWIN L. HERRNSTADT and ELDRIDGE S. PRICKETT, "Wage Determination in a Non-Union Labor Market," *Proceedings*, Tenth Annual Meeting of the Industrial Relations Research Association (September, 1957), pp. 1–13.

STIGLER, GEORGE J., "Perfect Competition, Historically Contemplated," *Journal of Political Economy*, LXV (February, 1957), 1–17.

———, "Information in the Labor Market," *Journal of Political Economy*, LXX (Supplement: October, 1962), 94–105.

TAFT, PHILIP, *Organized Labor in American History*. New York: Harper & Row, Publishers, 1964.

TAYLOR, GEORGE W., and FRANK C. PIERSON, eds., *New Concepts in Wage Determination*. New York: McGraw-Hill Book Company, 1957.

TROY, LEO, "Trade Union Membership, 1897–1962," National Bureau of Economic Research, *Occasional Paper No. 92*, New York, 1965.

ULMAN, LLOYD, "The Development of Trades and Labor Unions," in *American Economic History*, ed. Seymour E. Harris. New York: McGraw-Hill Book Company, 1961.

U.S. Bureau of the Census, *Historical Statistics of the United States, Colonial Times to 1957 and Continuation to 1962*.

U.S. Bureau of the Census, *Statistical Abstract of the United States.* (published annually)

U.S. Census of Population: 1960—Detailed Characteristics.

U.S. Census of Population: 1960, Vol. I.

U.S. Department of Commerce, *Survey of Current Business.* (issued monthly)

U.S. Department of Labor, *Manpower Report of the President, 1967.* Washington, D.C.: Government Printing Office. (issued annually)

U.S. Department of Labor, *Monthly Labor Review.* (published monthly)

U.S. Department of Labor, Bureau of Labor Statistics, "The Structure of Unemployment in Areas of Substantial Labor Surplus," *Study Paper No. 23*, Washington, D.C., 1960.

WEINTRAUB, SIDNEY, *Some Aspects of Wage Theory and Policy.* Philadelphia: Chilton Books, 1963.

WEISS, LEONARD, "Concentration and Labor Earnings," *American Economic Review*, LVI (March, 1966), 96–117.

WOLFBEIN, SEYMOUR L., *Employment, Unemployment, and Public Policy.* New York: Random House, Inc., 1965.

WRIGHT, D. M., ed., *The Impact of the Union.* New York: Kelley and Macmillan, 1956.

index